DATE DUE

			PRINTED IN U.S.A.

Introducing Canada

THE MAGILL BIBLIOGRAPHIES

The American Presidents, by Norman S. Cohen, 1989
Black American Women Novelists, by Craig Werner, 1989
Classical Greek and Roman Drama, by Robert J. Forman, 1989
Contemporary Latin American Fiction, by Keith H. Brower, 1989
Masters of Mystery and Detective Fiction, by J. Randolph Cox, 1989
Nineteenth Century American Poetry, by Philip K. Jason, 1989
Restoration Drama, by Thomas J. Taylor, 1989
Twentieth Century European Short Story, by Charles E. May, 1989
The Victorian Novel, by Laurence W. Mazzeno, 1989
Women's Issues, by Laura Stempel Mumford, 1989
America in Space, by Russell R. Tobias, 1991
The American Constitution, by Robert J. Janosik, 1991
The Classical Epic, by Thomas J. Sienkewicz, 1991
English Romantic Poetry, by Bryan Aubrey, 1991
Ethics, by John K. Roth, 1991
The Immigrant Experience, by Paul D. Mageli, 1991
The Modern American Novel, by Steven G. Kellman, 1991
Native Americans, by Frederick E. Hoxie and Harvey Markowitz, 1991
American Drama: 1918-1960, by R. Baird Shuman, 1992
American Ethnic Literatures, by David R. Peck, 1992
American Theatre History, by Thomas J. Taylor, 1992
The Atomic Bomb, by Hans G. Graetzer and Larry M. Browning, 1992
Biography, by Carl Rollyson, 1992
The History of Science, by Gordon L. Miller, 1992
The Origin and Evolution of Life on Earth, by David W. Hollar, 1992
Pan-Africanism, by Michael W. Williams, 1992
Resources for Writers, by R. Baird Shuman, 1992
Shakespeare, by Joseph Rosenblum, 1992
The Vietnam War in Literature, by Philip K. Jason, 1992
Contemporary Southern Women Fiction Writers, by Rosemary M.
    Canfield Reisman and Christopher J. Canfield, 1994
Cycles in Humans and Nature, by John T. Burns, 1994
Environmental Studies, by Diane M. Fortner, 1994
Poverty in America, by Steven Pressman, 1994
The Short Story in English: Britain and North America, by Dean
    Baldwin and Gregory L. Morris, 1994

Introducing Canada

An Annotated Bibliography of Canadian History in English

Brian Gobbett and Robert Irwin

Magill Bibliographies

The Scarecrow Press, Inc.
Lanham, Md., & London
and
Salem Press
Pasadena, Calif., & Englewood Cliffs, N.J.
1998

Lanham, Maryland 20706

4 Pleydell Gardens, Folkestone
Kent CT20 2DN, England

British Library Cataloguing in Publication Information Available

Library of Congress Cataloging-in-Publication Data

Gobbett, Brian. 1960–
    Introducing Canada : an annotated bibliography of Canadian history
in English / Brian Gobbett and Robert Irwin.
            p.   cm. — (Magill bibliographies)
    Includes indexes.
    ISBN 0-8108-3383-2 (alk. paper)
    1. Canada—History—Bibliography.   I. Irwin, Robert. 1961–   .
II. Title.   III. Series.
Z1382.G63   1998
[F1026]
016.971—dc21   98-3159
                                                CIP
ISBN 0-8108-3383-2 (cloth : alk. paper)

⊖™ The paper used in this publication meets the minimum requirements of
American National Standard for Information Sciences—Permanence of
Paper for Printed Library Materials, ANSI Z39.48–1984.
Manufactured in the United States of America.

TABLE OF CONTENTS

Acknowledgments

This work has benefited from the hand and insight of others. We are pleased to thank the following for perusing portions of this manuscript and offering suggestions: Ted Binnema, Robynne Healey, Bob Hesketh, Mark Levene, Heather Rollason, and David Mills. All errors of fact and interpretation remain our own. Our thanks to the Department of History and Classics at the University of Alberta for technical assistance. As well, our thanks to the following publishers for providing recent material: Addison-Wesley Publishers, broadview press, Fifth House Publishers, Harcourt Brace Canada, James Lorimer, Macfarlane Walter & Ross, McGill-Queen's University Press, Oxford University Press, Penn State Press, the University of British Columbia Press, the University of Manitoba Press, and the University of Toronto Press.

Introduction

An annotated bibliography of Canadian history, accessible to specialists and non-specialists alike, is long overdue. Canada is a remarkable country: it is the second largest country in the world by area; it shares the longest undefended political boundary in the world with the United States of America; a member of the Group of Seven, it is the largest trading partner of the United States; multi-racial, multi-ethnic, and multi-cultural, Canada prides itself on its tolerance and compassion; and it has been and remains a reliable western ally and firm supporter of international cooperation through the United Nations. Still, outside of Canada, few people have an approachable source which provides access to the history of this nation. This bibliography of works written in English helps to fill that void.

Canadian history is much more than a collection of stories about the past. Like national history in other countries, the events of Canada's past are part of its national identity and mythology. History helps define the country. As such, certain themes remain constant in the historical literature and continue to intrigue scholarly researchers. Throughout the pages which follow, readers will notice that the same questions recur. What is the relationship between aboriginal inhabitants and the settlement community? How does Quebec, with its French language and distinctive cultural traditions, fit into the Canadian national fabric? What is the role of the United States and Britain in Canada's past? How have ethnic and racial minorities been treated by the dominant Anglo-Celtic community? Why is Canada constantly challenged by regionalism and provincialism? What role has the environment played in Canadian development? What has been the experience of women, workers of both sexes, and the family? These questions have been answered numerous times, yet they continue to be asked as the answers seem insufficient to subsequent generations.

Interpretive traditions have similarly dominated Canadian historical writing. Staples history emerged as an interpretation in the 1920s and still resonates in the literature today. This interpretation focuses on economic considerations as the dominant aspect of Canadian life; Canada has always been a "hewer of wood and drawer of water" for international markets. Extractive industries such as pulp and paper, mining, oil and gas, agriculture, and fishing, therefore, play significant roles not only in economic terms, but also in the day-to-day lives and social organization of the population. Economically, horizontal and vertical linkages from these industries explain the development of Canada's industrial and service sectors as well. Geography, geology, and transportation routes between the resources and international markets thus play a preeminent role in Canada's past according to staples historians.

Donald Creighton, a dominant figure at the University of Toronto for forty years, incorporated political history and, to a lesser degree, social history into the staples approach. Because he focussed his attention on the competing commercial interests of the St. Lawrence River valley region, his interpretation is called laurentian history. Canada, according to this interpretation, was the political organization of St. Lawrence River valley merchants who found themselves in competition with American business interests for access to staples resources. The purpose of the country, therefore, was to ward off American aggrandizement and economic hegemony. Ironically, while Creighton is notorious for his conservative political philosophy, his interpretations still resonate in left-nationalist historical studies. The fulcrums for their work remain multinational corporations, American and (increasingly) global business interests and tactics, continued reliance upon extractive industries, and unduly harsh treatment of labour in order to meet American competition.

Some Canadian historians moved away from the laurentian and staples models in the 1950s, incorporating elements of American-style frontier history and metropolitan interpretations into their writing. These approaches, like the earlier staples and laurentian traditions, emphasised the role of capitalists, speculators, and farmers, but added sophistication to discussions of social and cultural tension. The new Canada was less a country in constant competition with the United States than a political reality to govern relations between metropolitan-based business interests and hinterland-based resource producers. This dynamic, along with elements of frontierism, explained the regional tension ever-present in Canada; the dominant demographic and political presence of Toronto, Montreal, and Vancouver; and the divergent social patterns of life in Canada.

Ramsay Cook's "Canadian Cerebations," in *International Journal* (1967), and J. M. S. Careless' "Limited Identities in Canada," in the *Canadian Historical Review* (1969), transformed the writing of Canadian history. Canadian historians, searching for a national history, had constantly encountered differentiation and conflict in their studies. Cook and Careless suggested that perhaps the national history could be found in these differences. Historians took the opportunity to study elements of Canada's past previously ignored and, like the new social history in the United States and Europe, created history based upon class, race, gender, and region. At the same time, Canadian universities experienced a period of explosive growth. As a result, the writing of Canadian history has grown exponentially since 1970. Still, the older themes of staples, laurentian, metropolitan, and frontier history act as interpretive devices and backdrops for much of this work.

This pattern of historical writing in Canada has influenced the way this bibliography is structured. First, the explosion of historical writing since 1970 and the new directions historians have taken make this year a watershed in historical writing. With few exceptions only books written between 1970 and 1996 are included in this bibliography. These works are the most easily accessible and most useful to the student and researcher. This bibliography is not, obviously, exhaustive, and we have sought only to introduce some of the major monographs and collections in each field. Annotations to the major journals in Canadian history are provided for those seeking article literature, and several collections of reprinted articles are cited because of their importance. Although many of the works are familiar to us, we have also relied upon the insights of academic reviews in some annotations. Second, this bibliography is organized into chapters around the traditional themes of Canadian history such as Native aspects of history, political history, economic history, intellectual history, and external affairs. In addition, however, this bibliography also reflects limited identities scholarship with chapters on gender, class, ethnicity, and region. Although much Canadian historiography since the 1970s is noted for its venture into the "new social history," many of these works still fit into traditional patterns and demonstrate the ongoing legacy of previous interpretations. Third, this bibliography emphasises the theoretical and interpretive perspectives of some books in the annotations. In this manner, readers will obtain an understanding of the material covered in the book as well as its importance to the historical traditions. For those searching for work by an individual author, an author index has been provided, and similarly, a general subject index is provided for those wishing to search for a particular topic. It is important to note that books are listed only once; our categories are, of course, artificial and manuscripts can easily cross over between, for example, working-class and family history. Joy Parr's *The Gender of Breadwinners* (1990), and Bettina Bradbury's *Working*

Families: Age, Gender and Daily Survival in Industrializing Montreal (1993),to cite two examples, are both important contributions to the study of gender, workers, region, and, particularly in Bradbury's volume, family. That they appear in different chapters reflects their different emphases and approaches.

We hope you enjoy this bibliography and find it useful as a research tool. Moreover, we hope it teaches the reader something about the writing of Canada's past. Should we fulfill these two goals, then we have made a useful contribution to the bibliographic literature and to the ongoing interpretation of Canada's past.

General Texts and Reference Materials

In the post-World War II era, it was common for prominent historians such as Donald Creighton, W. L. Morton, A. R. M. Lower, and J. M. S. Careless to attempt single-volume syntheses largely oriented toward political and constitutional history, and grounded in English-Canadian nationalism. These authors wrote these texts to communicate grand theories of Canadian development. With the emergence of the limited identities of region, class, ethnicity, and gender in the later 1960s, however, the publication of nation-building syntheses ceased and historical writing concentrated on topics of a more particular nature. Recent years have seen a revival of textbook writing, incorporating much of this new research, usually by teams of historians. This chapter examines some of these ventures, as well as readers of important articles, methodological works, journals, and reference materials that may be of use to the student or instructor.

General Works

Avery, Donald and Roger Hall, eds. *Coming of Age: Readings in Canadian History Since World War II*. Toronto: Harcourt Brace Canada, 1996.
While most historical surveys or collections tend to marginalise the recent past, *Coming of Age* examines some of the major political and social issues since World War II. The essays are often interdisciplinary in approach and the volume is divided into several thematic parts: Canadian identity, World War II, post-war national and regional trends, the turbulent 1960s and 1970s, foreign policy and national security, and contemporary debates involving Quebec, the constitution, health care, multiculturalism, and free trade. Most articles are of recent origin.

Bennett, Paul W. and Cornelius Jaenen, eds. *Emerging Identities: Selected Problems and Interpretations in Canadian History*. Scarborough, ON: Prentice-Hall, 1986.
Emerging Identities is an outstanding didactic text that explores twenty problems in Canadian history. Each chapter begins with a brief

introduction to the problem, then contains a review of selected primary sources, usually writings from the historical participants of the period, and concludes with excerpts from the interpretive work of historians. Through this construction, students obtain an understanding of historical interpretation and explore the nature of historical controversy. Students, consequently, are forced to treat historians in their proper context as interpreters rather than as chroniclers of the past. Although the text is now ten years old and a few topics seem to have passed from historical interest (and, in other cases, new interpretations have emerged), many of the themes discussed remain important in Canadian historical writing. The consequences of aboriginal-European contact, the Conquest of Quebec, the women's movement, Canadian-American relations, and the Quiet Revolution, for example, are still issues at the forefront of Canadian history. While the bibliography that follows each chapter is now dated, it still acts as a useful reference tool.

Bothwell, Robert, Ian Drummond, and John English. *Canada, 1900-1945*.
      Toronto: University of Toronto Press, 1987.
      _____. *Canada Since 1945: Power, Politics and Provincialism*.
      Toronto: University of Toronto Press, 1981; 2ⁿᵈ ed., 1989.
Written by specialists in external, economic, and political affairs, these volumes broach twentieth-century Canada in both an analytical and a narrative fashion. While, as the authors state, the "new social history and new economic history are not ignored," the focus of these works is on how "everyday life" is conditioned "by the state and concrete developments in state, economy and society." The result is that the authors draw attention to many of the issues that concern federally minded Canadians: the rise of the state, federal-provincial relations, the social and economic consequences of boom and bust, political developments within Quebec, and Canada's role within world affairs are constant themes. In the midst of demands for the decentralisation of constitutional powers, these works are worth reading.

Brown, Craig, ed. *The Illustrated History of Canada*. Toronto: Lester &
      Orpen Dennys Ltd., 1987; rev. ed., Lester Publishing, 1996.
This edited volume, with chronological chapters by six distinguished scholars, provides a comprehensive and aesthetically pleasing narrative of Canadian history. Robert Stacey, the picture editor, has lavishly illustrated the text with representations that will be familiar to many readers, as well as others that are rarely seen beyond archives or

museums; these function, as Stacey notes in his introduction, as a parallel commentary to the text rather than as a page-by-page representation. The text itself is arranged along a political chronology, though it strives to relate "how Canadians have lived and worked and seen themselves," and thus attempts to relate social history to political structures. Though depth of analysis and attention to regionalism are (perhaps necessarily) lacking, this work provides a successful single-volume synthesis of Canadian history and deserves to be widely used as an introductory text for the general reader.

Bumsted, J. M. *The Peoples of Canada: A Pre-Confederation History*. Toronto: Oxford University Press, 1992.
_____. *The Peoples of Canada: A Post-Confederation History*. Toronto: Oxford University Press, 1992.

Although most recent textbooks in Canadian history are prepared by teams of historians, Bumsted renews an older tradition of a single historian grafting together the multiple elements of Canadian history. As a result, *The Peoples of Canada* volumes reflect Bumsted's personal interests in the field and exhibit a unity sometimes lacking in other textbooks. In the preface to the first volume, Bumsted notes that his work "attempts to incorporate the new scholarship by embracing new perspectives and new emphases while by no means disregarding either key events in the traditional framework or values of the traditional historiography." To this end, these texts emphasise the social and cultural context of Canadian history and treat politics as an explanatory rather than unifying device. While maintaining a sense of chronology, the chapters focus on themes such as the resource economy, and rural and suburban society instead of more traditional nation-building themes. Its distinctive interpretive nature, detailed references, and superb bibliographic essay make Bumsted's texts most useful to those students already familiar with a general framework of Canadian history.

Bumsted, J. M., ed. *Interpreting Canada's Past*. 2 vols. Toronto: Oxford University Press, 1988; rev. ed., 1993.

Divided at Confederation, this two-volume essay collection is suitable as companion readers for any Canadian history survey course. The essays selected by Bumsted reflect his interest in cultural history and his background in research on the Atlantic provinces. Readers searching for a Prairie or especially British Columbia perspective will be disappointed with the coverage, but this is not unusual for Canadian history texts. What is different in this text is the emphasis on questions of identity. These books also offer students an opportunity to examine the creation of historical interpretation in Canadian history. Each section contains a good bibliographic selection of further readings.

The Canadian Centenary Series. 19 vols. Toronto: McClelland & Stewart, 1964-1988.

Inspired by a century of Confederation and much new scholarship, the nineteen volumes in the Centenary series — written by some of Canada's most distinguished historians — present a narrative history from pre-contact to the 1960s. Some of these volumes are spectacular works of synthesis and interpretation, particularly Dale Miquelon, *New France, 1702-1743* (1988), Fernand Ouellet, *Lower Canada, 1792-1841* (1980), Robert Craig Brown and Ramsey Cook, *Canada, 1896-1921* (1974), and John Herd Thompson with Allen Seager, *Canada, 1933-1939* (1985).

Careless, J. M. S. *Canada: A Story of Challenge.* Toronto: Macmillan, 1953; rev. ed., 1970.

Together with Donald Creighton and W. L. Morton, J. M. S. Careless is the foundation for many of the interpretations in Canadian history. This text, used for years in Canada's high schools, is a clear exposition of the metropolitan approach to Canadian history. Built on the foundations of staples history, which emphasised the importance of resource extraction, the metropolitan approach characterised Canadian history as directed and controlled through a hierarchy of metropolitan centres. London, Montreal, Toronto, regional cities, and the resource hinterland are seen as the binding elements of Canada's past. As a result, canoes, railways, and nation-building economic strategies have a prominent role in this text. Careless's approach is, however, more subtle than a strict staples interpretation. Values and cultural transference are included in his metropolitan-hinterland relationships. Readers should be aware, however, that the working class, ethnic minorities, and women play minor roles.

Conrad, Margaret, Alvin Finkel, and Cornelius Jaenen. *History of the Canadian Peoples: Beginnings to 1867.* Toronto: Copp Clark, 1993.

Finkel, Alvin and Margaret Conrad with Veronica Strong-Boag. *History of the Canadian Peoples: 1867 to the Present.* Toronto: Copp Clark, 1993.

These two volumes contribute significantly to the relatively recent attempts to provide a new synthesis to Canadian history. The authors are committed to the new social history as a vehicle for understanding Canada's past. Thus, these works react against a traditional political focus in which "women, people of colour, and issues relating to private life" are either ignored or treated unsympathetically. Instead, *History of the Canadian Peoples* seeks to resurrect the stories and significance of individuals such as Ezekiel Hart, a Jewish merchant who was elected to the Assembly of Lower Canada in 1807 but was declared ineligible to serve; Senefta Kizima, a fourteen-year-old girl who accompanied her parents from the Ukraine in 1912; and Tsudaike, a chief of the Nackwacto, who spoke in anger before a royal commission investigating land claims in 1914. Though these works divide themselves traditionally on either side of Confederation, the second volume contains a brief, but useful, transition chapter that introduces the reader to British North American society prior to 1867. In addition, each volume contains brief historiographic sections and a current bibliography.

Creighton, Donald. *Canada's First Century, 1867-1967*. Toronto: Macmillan, 1970.
This text is the last significant work by one of Canada's most respected and most controversial scholars. Creighton seized the opportunity of the Centennial to write a highly polemic text that clearly presents his laurentian interpretation of Canada's past. Creighton's finely crafted narrative is one of great political leaders carving out a place for the Canadian nation on the continent and of ignoble political leaders who failed to understand the threat of American manifest destiny. John A. Macdonald, Wilfrid Laurier, Robert Borden, and John Diefenbaker are fondly portrayed as unifying the nation economically along the natural geographic corridor of the St. Lawrence River valley while maintaining a connection with the British imperial system and its values to balance the American economic and political presence. William Lyon Mackenzie King, Louis St. Laurent, and Lester Pearson are disdainfully treated as obsequiously courting American favours while promoting a special place for French-Canadian values and customs. Creighton expresses a profound pessimism over the paths the nation has taken since 1945, and, in many ways, he sees Canada's first century as its last. Lacking references and a bibliography, *Canada's First Century* is limited in its usefulness as a text, but remains an important interpretive work.

Finlay, J. L. and D. N. Sprague. *The Structure of Canadian History*. Scarborough, ON: Prentice-Hall, 1979; 4th ed., 1993.

Finlay, J. L. *Pre-Confederation Canada: The Structure of Canadian History to 1867.* Scarborough, ON: Prentice-Hall, 1990.

Sprague, D. N. *Post-Confederation Canada: The Structure of Canadian History Since Confederation.* Scarborough, ON: Prentice-Hall, 1990.

First printed in 1979 and later divided into two texts, *The Structure of Canadian History* was revised substantially in the new fourth edition. Finlay and Sprague provide a thorough historical overview of the political, economic, and social development of Canada. While recent changes have added more social and cultural material to the text, their work remains an excellent example of the nation-building narrative tradition of Canadian survey textbooks; more than any other text currently available, *The Structure of Canadian History* uses an easy to follow political framework. In the pre-Confederation era, Finlay emphasises European colonial structures, the emergence of a distinctive French-Canadian community, the Conquest, British colonial rule, and the road to responsible government and Confederation. Similarly, Sprague leads students through the period of nation-building, the Laurier boom, the Mackenzie King era, the post-World War II transformation, and he emphasises the British and American influences on Canadian development. Like most texts on Canadian history, *The Structure of Canadian History* provides detailed suggested readings.

Francis, R. D., Richard Jones, and Donald B. Smith. *Origins: Canadian History to Confederation.* Toronto: Harcourt Brace, 1988; 3rd ed., 1996.

_____. *Destinies: Canadian History Since Confederation.* Toronto: Harcourt Brace, 1988; 3rd ed., 1996.

The third revised edition of this two-volume history of Canada continues to reflect both the strengths of the traditional nation-building narrative and the insights of limited identities history so prevalent in Canada in the 1970s and 1980s. The texts are organized around traditional political and economic themes but provide significantly more coverage of topics like aboriginal, gender, working-class, and regional history than older narrative texts. For example, *Origins* begins its sketch of Canadian history with the Blackfoot creation story about Napi or "The Old Man," and prominent women such as Emily Murphy and Dr. Emily Stowe receive treatment not only as suffragists but also as individual reformers in a broader context. The texts maintain an emphasis on traditional themes and chronology, nonetheless, and the chapters are organized in quick bites of information on various topics. These texts also contain important didactic tools: In each chapter, one topic is examined more thoroughly in a section titled "Where Historians Disagree." Each chapter is followed by a thorough bibliographic essay.

Francis, R. D. and D. B. Smith, eds. *Readings in Canadian History: Pre-Confederation*. Toronto: Harcourt Brace, 1984; 4th ed., 1995.
        . *Readings in Canadian History: Post-Confederation*. Toronto: Harcourt Brace, 1984; 4th ed., 1995.
This two-volume collection of readings is now a companion set for Francis, Jones, and Smith's *Origins* and *Destinies*. From the outset, these readers reflected the limited identities orientation in Canadian history, and the editors incorporate sections on aboriginal people, women, family, and labour. Still, the editors focus on traditional themes in Canadian history such as the Conquest, the National Policy, and the Depression. In early editions, each section incorporated two or three essays from conflicting viewpoints. Each revision, however, brings more emphasis on social and cultural history and less on the debates over interpretation. While the editors continue to keep abreast of new interpretations, older traditional approaches remain, thus striking a balance for readers.

Gaffield, Chad. *The Invention of Canada: Readings in Pre-Confederation History*. Toronto: Copp Clark, 1994.
        . *Constructing Modern Canada: Readings in Post-Confederation History*. Toronto: Copp Clark, 1994.
The companion volumes to Conrad and Finkel's *History of the Canadian Peoples*, these readers provide relatively contemporary examples of the use of social class, gender, ethnicity, religion, and region in elucidating the identities, relationships, and events that make up Canada's past. Utilising non-traditional sources and methodologies (often derived from the social sciences), the collective theme of these volumes emphasises that there is no single version of Canadian history; rather, these selections argue that there are "new ways to think about Canadian history, to understand the historical process, and to view the background of contemporary life." While other readers tend to organize the articles by theme, Gaffield chooses to organize them by time period and hence provides a distinctive approach to Canadian history.

Gilbert, A. D., C. M. Wallace, and R. M. Bray, eds. *Reappraisals in Canadian History: Post-Confederation*. Scarborough, ON: Prentice-Hall, 1992; 2nd ed., 1996.

_____. *Reappraisals in Canadian History: Pre-Confederation.* Scarborough, ON: Prentice-Hall, 1993; 2nd ed., 1996.

Reappraisals is one of the numerous collections of readings intended as a complementary text for the narrative surveys of Canadian history. What sets this reading text apart is the authors' effort to provide students with an appreciation of historical relativism and controversy. Gilbert, Wallace, and Bray have selected important themes in Canadian history and sought out the best complementary or often contradictory interpretations available. These collections bring together essays from an older generation of historians including W. J. Eccles, W. L. Morton, Donald Creighton, and P. B. Waite; from young scholars like Jan Noël, Glen Makahonuk, and Michèlle Martin; and from the leading historians of the era like Michael Bliss, Judith Fingard, Dale Miquelon, Gordon Stewart, Greg Kealey, and T. W. Acheson. The resulting mixture of interpretation and style provides for an interesting dynamic when reading the books. Students can also follow up each topic through the insightful introduction and the selection of further readings that the editors provide.

Granatstein, J. L., Irving Abella, T. W. Acheson, David Bercuson, Craig Brown, and H. Blair Neatby. *Nation: Canada Since Confederation.* 3rd ed. Toronto: McGraw-Hill Ryerson, 1990.

Bercuson, David, Kerry Abel, Donald Akenson, Peter Baskerville, J. M. Bumsted, and John G. Reid. *Colonies: Canada to 1867.* Toronto: McGraw-Hill Ryerson, 1992.

Originally published as *Twentieth Century Canada* (1983), *Nation* is now in its third edition and has been expanded and joined by a complementary text on the pre-Confederation era. While both texts bring together teams of prominent historians, the divergent dates for their original publication is reflected in the different orientations and philosophies of these two texts. While *Nation* is focussed on political and economic narrative and introduces students to some of the interpretive work on social history in the revised chapters, *Colonies* reflects the cultural and social orientation of more recent studies, downplaying, but not ignoring, the political context. Both texts, nonetheless, reflect the authors' keen interest in exploring the development of a social consciousness in the political, economic, and cultural realms of Canadian history. They attempt to provide the historical background necessary for students to understand issues such as contemporary Quebec nationalism, aboriginal rights, the social-welfare net, and the connection between business and politics so prominent in Canada today. Although the texts are well footnoted and contain references to much of the important literature, neither contains a bibliography or suggested readings section.

Granatstein, J. L., Irving M. Abella, David J. Bercuson, R. Craig Brown, and H. Blair Neatby. *Twentieth Century Canada*. Toronto: McGraw-Hill Ryerson, 1983; 2nd ed., 1986.
_____. *Twentieth Century Canada: A Reader*. Toronto: McGraw-Hill Ryerson, 1986.

These companion volumes focus on five major themes: the political process and political leadership, the rise of labour, immigration, the bureaucracy, and the new Quebec. The text provides a sound political narrative, interspersed with thematic chapters which examine particular subjects in greater detail; likewise, the collection of readings is organized around the principal themes identified in the text, though the selections tend to be complementary rather than argumentative. Both volumes contain introductory chapters and articles which introduce readers to late-nineteenth-century Canada and thus act as a transition to the main body of work. With the added influence of T. W. Acheson, the text has been revised and published in a third edition as *Nation: Canada Since Confederation* (1990).

Harris, R. C. and John Warkentin. *Canada Before Confederation: A Study in Historical Geography*. 2nd ed. Ottawa: Carleton University Press, 1991.

Originally published by Oxford University Press in 1974, this important volume explores the theme of humanity and land from modern European contact to Confederation. Geographers, Harris and Warkentin provide insights into settlement patterns, housing styles, agricultural development, and resource extraction, and emphasise the regional variations within Canada. This book contains numerous useful diagrams and maps, and readers will find it a good teaching resource.

MacKirdy, K. A., J. S. Moir, and Y. F. Zoltvany, eds. *Changing Perspectives in Canadian History: Selected Problems*. Toronto: J. M. Dent and Sons, 1967; rev. ed., 1971.

The first effort at teaching Canadian history through the problems approach, this book identifies twenty subjects of contention and importance in Canadian history and discusses each through primary documentation and excerpts from historical analysis. The problems covered in this approach reflect such traditional themes as the nature of

French-Canadian society, responsible government in the nineteenth century, the National Policy, and the Quiet Revolution. The strength of the book lies primarily in the period prior to 1900.

McNaught, Kenneth. *The Pelican History of Canada.* Toronto: Penguin
    Books, 1970; rev. ed., 1982.
This text is an excellent example of the left-nationalist approach to Canadian history. While his work should not be confused with the limited identities framework which emerged in the 1970s, McNaught's research interests lie in labour, immigration, and left-wing political groups, and these interests emerge in his interpretation. Unlike earlier texts written in the metropolitan or laurentian traditions, workers, immigrants, and their problems play a significant role in this work. Racism, nativism, capitalism, and American multinational corporations are treated critically, and the emergence of a social welfare state and the concept of a generous and sharing national framework are portrayed compassionately. His work retains a dominant narrative structure typical of this generation of texts. It lacks references and has a poor bibliography.

Morton, Desmond. *A Short History of Canada.* Edmonton: Hurtig, 1983.
This short and readable text provides a distinctive examination of Canadian history. It is divided into five parts: the first looks at the regional distinctiveness of Canada prior to Confederation; the second examines the Confederation era and nation-building efforts to unify the parts; the third covers the period of economic prosperity, pride, and optimism which preceded the Depression; the fourth develops the theme of Canada's growing international presence and its impact on the Canadian identity; and the last section proudly presents Canada's development as a leading international example of a generous welfare state. Holding the work together is a left-nationalist interpretation which looks towards the government as a benefactor and protector of the Canadian nation.

Silver, A. I., ed. *An Introduction to Canadian History.* Toronto: Canadian
    Scholars' Press, 1991.
This reader, unlike many of the others in Canadian history, is not designed as a companion volume to a narrative text. As such, it covers Canadian history from 1600 to 1970 and is organized around the major themes of Canada's past such as native-newcomer relations, the Conquest, the union of the Canadas, the 1885 rebellion, World War I, and modern Quebec.

Intended to stand alone as a source book, it brings together some of the seminal works in Canada and some of the most current scholarship in the field. Of the nineteen themes developed in the text, however, fourteen relate to the period before World War I. This focus limits the book's usefulness to any reader interested in the twentieth century.

Wilton, Carol, ed. *Change and Continuity: A Reader on Pre-Confederation Canada.* Toronto: McGraw-Hill Ryerson, 1992.

McKay, Ian, ed. *The Challenge of Modernity: A Reader on Post-Confederation Canada.* Toronto: McGraw-Hill Ryerson, 1992.

These two texts, which act as readers for *Colonies* (Bercuson, *et al.*), and *Nation* (Granatstein, *et al.*) take vastly different approaches to their topic matter. Wilton divides her book into 16 sections each containing three or more short excerpts from important interpretations; McKay uses only eight sections, each containing three important essays, often in excess of 25 pages. Wilton's approach focuses closely on key themes while providing samples of historical interpretation; McKay's approach results in students being forced to make linkages between detailed essays which at first appear unrelated. There are, however, some important similarities between the texts. Both are within the limited identities tradition and focus on cultural and social history. Aboriginal people, women, and workers are given priority. Ironically, given this emphasis, regional historians, especially those from British Columbia and the Prairies, will search largely in vain for an examination of this aspect of Canadian history. Students will also find the further readings sections that follow each section limited for research purposes.

The Writing of History

Berger, Carl. *The Writing of Canadian History: Aspects of English-Canadian Historical Writing Since 1900.* Toronto: University of Toronto Press, 1976; 2nd ed., 1986.

Scholarly examinations of Canadian historiography are, unfortunately, extremely limited. A rare exception, Berger's brilliant analysis seeks to explain attitudes which historians of Canada's past have brought to their studies and to relate their work to a broader intellectual and cultural milieu. Concentrating on historians born prior to World War I, Berger traces the professionalisation of history through the works of George Wrong and Adam Shortt; the themes of self-government and liberty in Wrong and Chester Martin; the maturation of economic history in the

1930s with particular regard to Harold Innis and his emphasis upon staple exports in moulding the Canadian economy and its institutions; the examination of metropolitan relationships by Arthur Lower (later developed more fully by J. M. S. Careless) and his attempts to apply a modified model of the Turner thesis to Canada's forest industry; Donald Creighton's expansion of Innis in the laurentian thesis; and the tension between region and nation most effectively illustrated by W. L. Morton. This sophisticated work concludes with a briefer discussion of the "new history" that has emerged since the 1960s.

Berger, Carl, ed. *Contemporary Approaches to Canadian History.* Toronto: Copp Clark, 1987.
Published as part of the New Canadian Readings Series, this collection of essays should not be confused with an earlier collection of seminal works also edited by Berger under the same title. In this book, Berger collects and reproduces historiographical articles which reflect trends in Canadian history following the 1969 publication of J. M. S. Careless's "Limited Identities in Canada" (reproduced in the collection). Four articles look at developments in regional history by focussing on the Maritimes, Quebec, the Prairies, and British Columbia, but ironically Berger does not include an essay on Ontario. These are followed by essays tracing developments in social history, women's history, working-class and labour history, native history, and ethnic history, and concludes with articles on the more traditional historical pursuits of biography and political history. Each essay is written by a noted expert in the field and is both thorough and authoritative. *Contemporary Approaches* introduces readers to some of the major trends in Canadian historical writing in the 1970s and 1980s.

Crowley, Terry, ed. *Clio's Craft: A Primer of Historical Methods.* Toronto: Copp Clark, 1988.
This collection is designed to make students aware of the general historiographical and theoretical approaches taken by Canadian historians. Divided into five sections around the themes of evidence, interpretation, methodology, paradigms, and pursuit, these essays lead students through the historical process. This collection, however, is extremely uneven in its presentation. Significant essays by Bruce Trigger on ethnohistory, John Fogarty on the staples approach in economic history, Ruth Pierson and Alison Prentice on feminism and history, and Bryan Palmer on Marxist and working-class history provide students with insight into these important fields and methods of study in Canadian history. Other essays

could just as easily have been left out of the book, and section five, "Doing History," is more confusing than instructive.

Gagnon, Serge. *Quebec and Its Historians: The Twentieth Century.* Trans. Jane Brierly. Montreal: Harvest House, 1985.
The study of the history of Quebec is, to the surprise of few, the site of considerable debate. The book is divided into two distinct sections. The initial portion examines the post-World War II demise of a "clerico-conservative" view of history and the emergence of secular, professional historical methods. In particular, Gagnon credits Guy Frégault, Marcel Trudel, and (a decade later) Louise Dechêne for ushering in a new era of historical investigation. Dechêne, with her commitment and contribution to the *Annales* tradition, reflected the belief more forcefully than the others that the study of history was a scientific activity. Much different in focus, the second section provides a vigorous analysis of the work of Fernand Ouellet. Highly critical, Gagnon argues that Ouellet's historical writings have many "unscientific traits," a propensity towards strong moral judgments, weak evidence, uncertain sources, and extreme bias.

_____. *Quebec and Its Historians: 1840 to 1920.* Montreal: Harvest House, 1982.
This work examines four French-Canadian historians who wrote in the nineteenth and early twentieth centuries: Francois-Xavier Garneau, Abbé Ferland, Benjamin Sulte, and Abbé Lionel Groulx. Through these historians, Gagnon traces the rise of a clerico-conservative tradition. This tradition found its greatest and longest-standing expression in the work of Abbé Groulx. Groulx saw the Conquest as a supreme tragedy, yet this event was not able to dent the integrity of the French Canadian race because of the protective and maternal role of the Roman Catholic clergy. His histories urged a return to pastoralism and that form of life embodied in the colonisation of the soil. The clerico-conservative tradition — which emphasised the role of the church and the peasant in the life of the French Canadian race — maintained a powerful influence on Quebec society until after World War II.

Schultz, John, ed. *Writing About Canada: A Handbook for Modern Canadian History.* Scarborough, ON: Prentice-Hall, 1990.
This collection contains ten essays by recognized authorities which examine the historiographic traditions of specific themes, including articles on politics, economics, ideas, regions, rural life and agriculture,

business, labour, women, ethnicity and war. Significant by its absence is a chapter on the writing of native history. Each chapter provides insight into the emergence and development of a particular area; in addition, the reference notes are a rich source in identifying seminal works and historiographical articles.

Taylor, M. Brook. *Promoters, Patriots, and Partisans: Historiography in Nineteenth-Century English Canada.* Toronto: University of Toronto Press, 1989.

Taylor provides an insightful study into the writing of history in nineteenth-century English Canada. The authors and histories discussed precede the appointment of G. M. Wrong at the University of Toronto in 1894 and C. W. Colby at McGill in 1895; thus, this work concerns itself primarily with the writing of history prior to its establishment as a professional discipline in Canada. Taylor identifies three traditions of history writers: the first, whom he identifies as "promoters" who often remained anonymous, sought their own material self-interest through the advocacy of their particular colony; with the rise of native-born historians, a second phase of patriot historians, particularly in Upper Canada, sought to assert a national interpretation in the years surrounding Confederation; and a final phase of partisanship emerged in the last decades of the nineteenth century, when visions of progress and the promise of peace, order, and good government proved to be illusory.

Journals and Reference Works

Acadiensis, 1971 — .

In 1969, in an influential article published in *Queen's Quarterly,* the late George Rawlyk predicted the study of Atlantic Canada was on the verge of a "research explosion" that would usher in a "New Golden Age of Maritime Historiography." In response to this increased research activity and the scarcity of academic journals specialising in (or even acknowledging) local or regional history, *Acadiensis* was established. It has become the most significant voice in promoting historical study of Canada's eastern seaboard. While strongly influenced by the limited identities of class, gender, ethnicity, and religion, the study of regionalism dominates. This emphasis is at times comparative, and some of the most insightful work appearing in this journal has, for example, sought to explain the affinities and contrasts between Atlantic Canada and the Prairies. Many of the best articles (with some external exceptions) are collected in *The Acadiensis Reader*, 2 vols. (1990) edited by Phillip Buckner and David Frank. The review essays are generally of superior quality.

Alberta History, 1953 — .
Formerly *Alberta Historical Review*, this quarterly is the official publication of the Historical Society of Alberta. Over the years it has been transformed from an important academic source into a magazine that emphasises popular writing and glossy presentation. References are kept to a minimum and photographs are emphasised; book reviews are a limited aspect of this journal, usually restricted to three or four per edition, and are often written by the editors.

BC Studies, 1968 — .
This distinctly interdisciplinary journal provides a sophisticated and academic forum for matters concerning British Columbia. Reflecting contemporary historical sensibilities, particular attention in recent years has been paid to aboriginal peoples, though articles often extend far beyond that subject area. Two recent, but intermittent, innovations to *BC Studies* include the reproduction of photographs accompanied by written commentaries, and *Forum* which brings together scholars for discussion and debate of controversial topics. This journal contains mature book reviews and a bibliography of published works relating to British Columbia.

British Journal of Canadian Studies, 1986 — .
The *BJCS* succeeded the *Bulletin of Canadian Studies* in 1986 as the twice-yearly publication of the British Association for Canadian Studies. Reflecting the increased interest in Canada abroad in recent years, the *BJCS* — published by the Centre of Canadian Studies in Edinburgh — provides an interdisciplinary forum for scholars living or researching in Britain or Ireland, though occasionally overseas scholars do contribute. The book reviews range across a variety of academic disciplines.

The Canadian Encyclopaedia. 4 vols. Edmonton: Hurtig, 1985; 2nd ed., 1988.
The definitive encyclopaedia of things Canadian, this work provides brief, but generally well-researched and insightful, articles on a large variety of topics. Richly illustrated and with a number of good maps, this is an excellent reference source. It is also available on CD-ROM.

Canadian Ethnic Studies, 1969 — .
Published by the University of Calgary, this interdisciplinary journal examines ethnic groups in Canada and abroad. Dealing with both historical and contemporary issues, *CES* explicitly seeks to make a contribution to the development of the multicultural nature of the Canadian identity. There is an excellent book review section and occasional review essays.

Canadian Historical Review, 1920 — .
The most prestigious journal in Canadian history, the *CHR* is a valuable source of information for popular historians, students, and academics. "Since its inception," editor Susan Houston noted in the seventy-fifth anniversary edition, the *Canadian Historical Review* "has been committed to making available to an interdisciplinary and international audience innovative and authoritative research in Canadian history." In its pages, the most successful and respected Canadian historians have published some of their most important work. In recent years, the journal has taken its role of promoting innovative work quite seriously, and young social historians concerned with gender, class, and race have dominated the articles. Besides its strength as a source of important essays, the *CHR* is also the most important source of book reviews in Canada and contains a lengthy bibliography of recently published manuscripts, articles, and unpublished theses on Canadian history.

Canadian Journal of History of Sport, 1970 — .
Originally published as the *Canadian Journal of History of Sport and Physical Education*, this journal's quality has parallelled the increasing sophistication of sport history. While some of Canada's most prominent sport historians make appearances, articles and book reviews are international in content.

Canadian Journal of Native History, 1982 — .
Published at the University of Regina, this journal explores historical and contemporary issues of native white relations. Many of the articles are written by native scholars and reflect native perspectives on the past.

Canadian Military History, 1992 — .
This well-illustrated biannual explores Canada's military history with particular emphasis upon the two world wars. Each issue contains scholarly articles, firsthand accounts, documents, and book reviews.

Canadian Papers in Rural History, 1978 — .
Published periodically, *CPRH* was founded and is edited by Queen's
University historian Donald Akenson. Intended as a forum for work in the
"new rural history," the journal has actually published a wide range of
work. Articles in the journal have focussed on traditional agricultural
history subjects like the adoption of tractors, gender perspectives on
nineteenth-century Ontario farm life, rural dialects in Ireland, and the
interpretation of rural life in New France and the Conquest. Recent
editions have included as many as nine essays on rural history, and
students may find the lack of focus or centralized theme in the individual
issues disconcerting.

Dictionary of Canadian Biography. 13 vols. Toronto: University of
    Toronto Press, 1966 — .
When James Nicholson died in 1952, his will left provision for the
establishment of a national biographical dictionary modelled on the
British *Dictionary of National Biography.* In fact, the structure of the
DCB is much different. The *DNB* was originally published arranged
alphabetically (though this failing is being corrected in the new *DNB*); in
contrast, the *DCB* (issued in French as the *Dictionnaire Biographique du
Canada*) has arranged its entries chronologically by date of death. The
initial volumes covered large spans of time (the first accounting for those
who died between 1000 and 1700), but beginning with volume VIII
(1851-1860) they progress a decade at a time. In addition to individual
biographies, some of the earlier volumes possess valuable introductory
essays such as Marcel Trudel's on New France and Naomi Griffiths's on
the Acadians. The *DCB* is extensively indexed and provides detailed
bibliographic material of both published and unpublished sources.

Histoire sociale/Social History, 1968 — .
This bilingual journal is representative of one of the major
historiographical trends in recent decades. Deeply committed, both in
methodology and in content, to the new social history, *Hs/SH* rejects the
traditional political and nation-building focus of Canadian history and
seeks to examine, as Eric Hobsbawm states, "the history of society."
While many articles are Canadian in focus, often topics range beyond the
Canadian experience. There is a lengthy and mature book review section
and, recently, a current annual bibliography on sources dealing with
Canadian population and historical demography.

Historical Atlas of Canada, I: From Beginnings to 1800. R. Cole Harris,
   ed. Toronto: University of Toronto Press, 1987.
Historical Atlas of Canada, II: The Land Transformed, 1800-1891. R. L.
   Gentilcore, ed. Toronto: University of Toronto Press, 1993.
*Historical Atlas of Canada, III: Addressing the Twentieth Century, 1891-
   1961.* Donald G. Kerr and Deryk Holdsworth, eds. Toronto:
   University of Toronto Press, 1990.
Eighteen years in the making, the *Historical Atlas of Canada* is as
important as it is beautiful. In a review essay in the *Canadian Historical
Review* (1995), Graeme Wynn noted "this massive project is audacious in
scope and of indubitable significance." The atlas begins with the Ice Age
and ends with the people of Canada in 1961. To accomplish their goal, the
editors organize material from the leading scholars in anthropology,
archaeology, geology, geography, sociology, economics, and history into
easy to read synopses and spectacular plates providing graphical
representation of the key issues. As a project of human geography, the
plates chart issues uncommon to atlases such as the style and structure of
an Iroquois longhouse and the freight tonnage hauled on Canada's major
railways. Probably because the demographic scope of Canadian life was
more limited, the atlas covering the period up to 1800 is the best of the
three. The other two atlases in the series make significant contributions,
nevertheless. Given the scope of the work, some critics have disputed the
choice of material included in the atlases and others have complained
about the complexity of the plates. Despite these criticisms, the atlases
remain one of the best sources in Canadian history and are an essential
component of any college library.

Hudson's Bay Company Record Society Publications. 33 vols. 1938-
   1981.
One of the most valuable sources of primary material in Canadian history,
this collection reproduces documents from the Hudson's Bay Company
archives. The HBC Record Society called upon the best scholars of the
day to edit and annotate individual traders' and post journals. The
documents selected span the period 1670 to 1870 and have become an
essential source for historians, anthropologists, and ethnologists. After
years of service in the Hudson's Bay Company library, the series editor
and the most prodigious fur trade scholar of his day, E. E. Rich, wrote *The
History of the Hudson's Bay Company*, 2 vol. (1958-59) which appear as
volumes 21 and 22 in the series. Researchers will usually find the books
catalogued by the name of the editor and the title.

Journal of Canadian Studies. Revue d'étude Canadiennes, 1966 — .
Published four times a year at Trent University, this multi-disciplinary journal has become one of the most respected publications in Canada. Its articles are of a particularly high quality yet are tooled for non-specialists because of its multi-disciplinary approach. The articles reflect broad themes in the study of Canadian literature, economics, politics, anthropology, sociology, and history rather than focussing on specialised and sometimes mundane topics. Thematic issues often appear with invited submissions from the leading scholars in the field. The themes covered in these special issues range from regionalism to political developments in Quebec to gender studies. Book reviews and review essays are written by senior and junior scholars alike and are generally of high quality.

Labour/Le Travail, 1976 — .
Originally published as *Labour/Le Travailleur* before being changed in 1984 to the more correct *Labour/Le Travail*, this journal is Canada's foremost forum dedicated to both the research and teaching of labour and working-class studies. Often revisionist and theoretical in nature, this journal quickly acquired a philosophy of labour studies that has gone beyond traditional modes of study and has incorporated issues such as gender, ethnicity, and culture. Book reviews and review essays are superb and extend beyond the confines of Canadian history; in addition, research and archival reports and documents relating to labour studies make frequent appearances and are of considerable use to researchers and instructors.

Manitoba History, 1926 — .
Originally published as the *Transactions of the Historical and Scientific Society of Manitoba*, this journal was completely restructured and renamed in 1980. Like its counterpart, *Alberta History*, this journal is now a glossy magazine and emphasises material of general public interest. It still maintains, however, a reputation for publishing high quality academic work alongside the more popular pieces. Each issue contains a report of the activities of the Historical Society of Manitoba, and many issues contain excerpted material from the archives in the province. The journal continues to publish quality book reviews and a yearly bibliography of publications relating to Manitoba's past.

National History: A Canadian Journal of Enquiry and Opinion, 1997 —.
In response to the dominance of limited identities scholarship, this new

journal seeks to analyse "in their broadest terms those Great National Matters which confront [Canadians]." Though the focus would seem to orientate naturally toward post-Confederation politics, *National History* seeks to be multi-disciplinary and welcomes articles pertaining to any era, so long as they relate to the evolution of the modern Canadian state. *National History* includes sections on recent archival acquisitions across Canada, notes and announcements pertaining to the profession, and, of course, book reviews.

Native Studies Review, 1984 — .
Published at the University of Saskatchewan, this journal provides an interdisciplinary forum for native studies within a western and northern Canadian context, though occasionally attention is drawn to indigenous peoples in other societies. In addition to articles dealing with both historical and contemporary themes, *NSR* contains a regular photographic feature titled "Native Images," collections of documents often introduced by scholars, and book reviews and review essays.

Ontario History, 1899 — .
Previously titled Ontario Historical Society *Papers & Records*, *OH* began publishing quarterly after World War II, an era that also saw the emergence of regional journals such as *Revue de l'histoire de l'Amerique française* (1947), *Saskatchewan History* (1948), and *Alberta Historical Review*, now *Alberta History* (1953). Though some may question the validity of Ontario as a region (or, as Arthur Lower asked in this journal in 1968, "Ontario — Does It Exist?"), this journal obviously does not. Like many regional journals, *OH* is popular with amateur historians, yet it also contains submissions by some of Canada's most prominent academics. There is a short book review section in recent issues.

Polyphony: The Bulletin of the Multicultural History Society of Ontario, 1977 — .
Established to celebrate and investigate the ethnic diversity of Ontario, *Polyphony* provides a forum for both popular and academic historians. Richly illustrated, this journal also reproduces relevant historical documents and utilizes oral history to record the diverse experience of individuals. Special issues — such as those on the Hungarian (1979-80) and Finnish (1981) populations, regional examinations such as those on Toronto (1984) and Thunder Bay (1987), and the issue on women and ethnicity (1986) — are worthy of note.

Prairie Forum, 1976 — .

Prairie Forum is an interdisciplinary journal published biannually by the Canadian Plains Research Centre (CPRC) and reflects the ongoing interest of Canadian history with regional issues. The journal's strength is found in its breadth. Each issue contains eight or more articles on topics ranging from current political trends to pre-contact archaeological studies of aboriginal hunting grounds to the role of the environment in prairie fiction to the nineteenth-century farmers' protest movement. In its issues, readers can follow debates regarding Canadian government policy towards the Métis or the classification of farmers as working class or petit-bourgeois. The journal also publishes book reviews on the Canadian prairies. A subscription brings membership in the CPRC and access to its newsletter and publication information.

Saskatchewan History, 1948 — .

Published twice a year by the Saskatchewan Archives Board, this journal is devoted to the history of the "Wheat Province." It is marked by academic essays, popular historical research, archival notes, and book reviews on material related to Saskatchewan. Unlike its counterparts in Manitoba and Alberta, *Saskatchewan History* has not changed to the more popular glossy magazine format or reduced its emphasis on high quality academic research. It has maintained its identity and format throughout its existence and remains an important source of prairie history.

Urban History Review. Revue d'histoire urbaine, 1972 — .

Like many academic journals in Canada, the *UHR* originated with the explosive growth of Canadian universities in the late 1960s and early 1970s. It remains the only journal devoted to urban studies in Canada and sometimes publishes articles on non-Canadian topics. The articles reflect the trends in North American urban history, ranging from studies of metropolitan systems to class and social stratification in the urban place to leisure and recreation patterns. The journal produces a lengthy bibliography of publications on urban history and high quality book reviews.

Native Aspects of History

Native history is one of the most exciting fields of scholarship in Canada. Two factors explain this interest in Native history. First, in a pattern quite different from the American context, large-scale European agricultural settlement was delayed in Canada. Instead, contact between Natives and European colonists occurred principally through a mutually beneficial trading system. The fur trade was one of the main economic and social spheres of activity in Canada from 1604 to 1870. Historians of this period, consequently, have considered the important role of Natives in the Canadian historical drama. Second, Native nationalism has emerged in Canada since the 1960s. The intense political debates over the status of Native peoples and the meaning of "aboriginal rights" have led Canadian historians to examine government policy toward Native people throughout the historical period. Combined, these two focuses have resulted in a plethora of new books, almost all of which emphasise Native agency in the historical process.

The emphasis upon Native agency has led to some interesting historiographical debates. In fur trade history, for example, conflicting views upon the rationale for Native participation in the fur trade divide scholars. On one side, a formalist interpretation has been built upon Harold Adams Innis' *The Fur Trade in Canada* (1930), A. S. Morton's *A History of the Canadian West to 1870-71* (1939), and E. E. Rich's *A History of the Hudson's Bay Company*, 2 vols. (1958-59). This interpretation assumes Native people to be rational economic individuals. Natives understood the advantages of European technology, traded furs to obtain it, and became dependent upon the trading companies. In contrast, substantivists assume Natives traded for non-economic reasons. Some ethnohistorians have associated Native trade with cultural dynamics. They argue that the creation of political alliances or the attainment of status were the primary reasons for Native participation in trade. The publication of Arthur Ray's *Indians and the Fur Trade* (1974) marked the emergence of a revisionist synthesis in Canadian scholarship. Although the terms "formalist" and "substantivist" are still used, many authors are revisionist and recognise that both rational economic and cultural perspectives are useful to understanding the fur trade.

Similarly, work on the Métis and government-aboriginal relations is divided by its emphasis upon Native agency. In *The Birth of Western Canada* (1936; rpt., 1961), George Stanley viewed the relationship as a contest between savagery and civilisation. Disconcerted by his characterisation of Native people, historians have re-interpreted this period. Some scholars argue Native people resisted government programs and policies, but ultimately lost their freedom. Building upon the fur trade literature and its emphasis upon Native efforts to moderate and control cultural changes, other scholars argue that Native and Métis people actively participated in the transitions of the modern era. Were Native and Métis peoples subjugated by a destructive colonial process engineered by government bureaucrats, or were these groups able to make choices which limited the impact of these policies?

General Works

Brown, Jennifer S. H. and Elizabeth Vibert. *Reading Beyond Words: Contexts for Native History*. Peterborough, ON: Broadview Press, 1996.
This collection of often innovative articles reflects a recent trend in Canadian historiography toward studies of an interdisciplinary nature. Recognising that both text and context are constructed, the contributors of this volume deconstruct language and action to provide insight into aboriginal voices. Articles are roughly ordered along chronological and topical lines, and explore themes such as contact, trade, disease and death, religion, women, Native authors, and oral tradition.

Coates, Kenneth S. and Robin Fisher, eds. *Out of the Background: Readings on Canadian Native History*. Toronto: Copp Clark, 1988; 2nd ed., 1995.
A collection of essays that demonstrates the breadth of research in Native history in Canada, this book is an excellent text and valuable addition to any library. The first and second editions of this book are dramatically different and reflect the changing pattern of research in this field. In the first edition, readers will find articles by the leading scholars of the 1970s and 1980s, including articles by Ken Coates, Robin Fisher, Cornelius Jaenen, Calvin Martin, A. J. Ray, and Bruce Trigger among others. The second edition not only reproduces a few of these essays and provides new work by some of these authors, but also includes articles by a number of new authors. The essays in the second edition, furthermore, represent

a much broader frame of reference and reflect the growing interest of scholars on post-fur trade Native-white relations.

Comeau, Pauline and Aldo Santin. *The First Canadians: A Profile of Canada's Native Peoples*. Toronto: James Lorimer, 1995.
Comeau and Santin examine issues of economic development, health and welfare, education, and law and justice. Although their focus is contemporary, they begin their argument with events surrounding the 1969 White Paper introduced by then Indian Affairs Minister Jean Chrétien. *The First Canadians* provides a critique of the attempt to revoke special status from Native Canadians, and traces the evolution of Federal-Native relations over the previous three decades. In addition to federal documents and a wide variety of secondary sources, this work is based upon the views and words of Natives themselves. For a selection of writing and speeches by Natives, see Penny Petrone, ed., *First People, First Voices* (1983).

Cox, Bruce Alden, ed. *Native People, Native Lands: Canadian Indians, Inuit and Métis*. Ottawa: Carleton University Press, 1987.
A collection of twenty original articles written primarily by anthropologists, *Native People, Native Lands* is a useful source for Canadian native history. The book is organized geographically into five parts: the Great Lakes-St. Lawrence region, the Boreal forest, the Prairies, the Pacific region, and the Yukon-Northwest Territories. The articles address significant issues of controversy in each region. In the Great Lakes-St. Lawrence section, for example, important articles by Brian Given and Susan Johnson examine the cause and nature of the seventeenth-century Iroquois wars. Their work rejects the conclusions of George Hunt and Bruce Trigger, and, instead, argues that the commercial fur trade played no role in this conflict.

Crowe, Keith J. *A History of the Original Peoples of Northern Canada*. Montreal: McGill-Queen's University Press, 1991.
Originally published in 1974, this updated version includes the significant changes that have occurred in northern Canada in the last twenty years. The book begins with the Ice Age and ends with the 1991 discussions for a Native homeland in the North, and covers both Arctic and sub-Arctic people. Crowe avoids theoretical discussions, keeps references to a minimum, and offers numerous maps, illustrations, and figures in this useful text.

Dickason, Olive Patricia. *Canada's First Nations: A History of Founding Peoples from Earliest Times.* Toronto: McClelland and Stewart, 1992. Winner of both the Governor General's award for non-fiction in Canada and the Macdonald Prize given by the Canadian Historical Association, *Canada's First Nations* is an excellent survey of Canada's original peoples. Dickason does an admirable job of compiling and disseminating the broad array of archaeological, anthropological, and historical research on Canada's Native peoples. The manuscript is particularly strong in the pre-contact and early contact period (Dickason's own research is concentrated in this period) but is weaker when describing Native-government issues in the modern era. The book provides the non-specialist with significant new information on the subjects of pre-contact Native communities, Native resistance to European colonisation, and the persistence of Native cultures. Readers will also become aware that Native people have been active agents in the Canadian past. Although the reader will be impressed by the significant role played by Native peoples in the development of the area now called Canada, they may become confused searching for linkages between chronology and theme in this text. Still, the book is a useful text, is thoroughly documented, and contains an extensive bibliography.

Dickason, Olive Patricia, ed. *The Native Imprint: The Contributions of First Peoples to Canada's Character.* Athabasca, AB: Athabasca University Educational Enterprises, 1995. An excellent collection of previously published articles, this volume concentrates on the pre-Contact experience. Essays focus upon themes such as the origins of aboriginal people in North America, how Native people view themselves, European perceptions, and the contact experience. Dickason includes excerpts from several pre-1815 primary sources.

Francis, Daniel. *The Imaginary Indian: The Image of the Indian in Canadian Culture.* Vancouver: Arsenal Pulp Press, 1992. This wide-ranging work examines the images of Natives that colonial and post-Confederation Canadians created in fiction, history texts, travel literature, advertisements, museums, and art. These images, of course, relate nothing about Natives; rather, Francis, in the tradition of Robert Berkhofer's *The White Man's Indian* (1979), argues that the "Indian" was a white invention that is most instructive in providing insight into non-Native cultural history. The common (and erroneous) stereotype of the vanishing Indian, for example, encouraged late-Victorian artists, photographers, and writers to attempt to capture often ironic images of Indians "as they really were" before they vanished.

Getty, A. L. and Antoine S. Lussier, eds. *As Long as the Sun Shines and Water Flows: A Reader in Canadian Native Studies*. Vancouver: Nakoda Institute and University of British Columbia Press, 1983.
This selection of essays focuses on Canadian Native history since the Royal Proclamation of 1763. The introductory essay by George Stanley explores Native-white relations through important events such as the 1763 proclamation, the treaties of the nineteenth century, and the 1969 White Paper; and James St. G. Walker's excellent concluding essay examines the image of the Native in Canadian historiography between 1971 and 1981. The two principal sections, in which a variety of authors participate (including older essays such as that by Diamond Jenness), examine, first, the evolution of Indian administration since 1763; and, second, Native responses to changing events and circumstances.

McMillan, Alan D. *Native Peoples and Cultures of Canada: An Anthropological Overview*. Vancouver: Douglas & McIntyre, 1988.
In 1932 the Canadian anthropologist Diamond Jenness published *The Indians of Canada*; this classic work gloomily predicted the disappearance of Natives, through either extinction or assimilation. Utilizing recent anthropological, archaeological, linguistic, and historical sources, McMillan provides a summary of Native ways of life and an obvious correction to Jenness' conclusions regarding the disappearance of Canada's aboriginal population. *Native Peoples and Cultures* is largely divided into geographical chapters, each dealing with events from prehistory to contemporary times. McMillan includes chapters on the Inuit and Métis and concludes by discussing some of the broader contemporary issues facing aboriginal groups.

Miller, David with Carl Beal, James Dempsey, and R. Wesley Heber, eds. *The First Ones: Readings on Indian/Native Studies*. Craven, SK: Saskatchewan Indian Federated College, 1992.
A collection of forty-eight articles, *The First Ones* is the most comprehensive survey of Native studies literature, and the most useful to historians. Articles address a broad range of subjects from historical, anthropological, and political perspectives, including Indian/Native studies in North America; origin paradigms and structures for history;

Indian/Native identities; Indian/Native world views; systemic approaches to life experience; Indian/Native relations to others; gradual recognition of inherent aboriginal rights; and Indian/Native political and economic expressions.

Miller, J. R. *Skyscrapers Hide the Heavens: A History of Indian-White Relations in Canada.* Toronto: University of Toronto Press, 1989; 2nd ed., 1991.

This survey of Native-white relations argues that aboriginal peoples were and continue to be active participants in this relationship. Miller believes that the relationship has evolved through four stages. In the first stage, the period from contact until the eighteenth century, Natives and newcomers cooperated commercially to exploit fish and fur resources. In the eighteenth century, Natives and newcomers joined in a necessary military alliance to defend the commercial system they had built. In the third stage, a period stretching from 1800 to 1945, both commercial systems and alliances became less relevant to the developing Canadian state and, as a result, coercive policies designed to encourage assimilation and cultural destruction. Native people developed networks of resistance to these policies and tried, successfully, to preserve their cultural identity. In the fourth and final stage, a resurgent Native nationalism emerged in Canada and aboriginals have joined once again with elements of the white community to redefine their relationship. While Miller makes significant effort to demonstrate Amerindian agency in this book, this text is about Native-white relations rather than aboriginal people. Students seeking knowledge about Native cultures and the changes that have occurred over time, will find little discussion of such issues. It is, nevertheless, the best survey of the issues, policies, and structures that underlay the relationships between Native and newcomer in Canada.

Miller, J. R., ed. *Sweet Promises: A Reader on Indian-White Relations in Canada.* Toronto: University of Toronto Press, 1991.

A companion reader to Miller's *Skyscrapers Hide the Heavens* (1991), this work contains twenty-five previously published essays emphasising historical perspectives. The essays are organized thematically and chronologically, and cover all aspects of the contact period from the fur trade to government policy. Unlike other readers in Native-white relations, Miller has not focussed the collection on recent publications, and has, instead, selected many essays published prior to 1970. The essays, therefore, reflect older traditional interpretations, modern ethnohistorical approaches, and interpretations emerging from Native scholars themselves. The reader, however, may be confused to find some of the older interpretations still given a position of prominence, especially since many have been discredited by recent scholarship.

Morrison, R. Bruce and C. Roderick Wilson, eds. *Native Peoples: The Canadian Experience.* Toronto: McClelland and Stewart, 1986; 2nd ed., 1995.
An excellent companion to Dickason's *Canada's First Nations* (1992), this volume presents essays on specific Native cultures across all regions of Canada. Essays generally seek to understand aboriginal culture in two ways: first, within its own framework, and not as an appendage to Euro-Canadian culture; and, second, essays often focus upon the relationship between individual groups and larger Canadian society.

Patterson, E. Palmer. *The Canadian Indian: A History Since 1500.* Don Mills: Collier-Macmillan, 1972.
This popular study represents some of the reaction against the Trudeau government's 1969 White Paper. Patterson rejects a bi-cultural view of Canada is rejected, and attempts "to see [Natives] as a people with a distinct past of their own" and to place them "at the centre of the narrative." While lucidly written, this work is based primarily on outdated secondary sources and treats Native peoples largely as monolithic entities.

Ray, Arthur, J. *I Have Lived Here Since The World Began: An Illustrated History of Canada's Native People.* Toronto: Lester, 1996.
Designed for the educated public, this volume provides a general introduction to both the aboriginal people of Canada and to some of the recent approaches to the study of Native history. Consistent with his previous work, Ray explores the economic history of Native people in a thorough and readable fashion; this volume also is replete with illustrations and maps that reflect the active roles that Natives occupied as economic agents. While more limited in cultural, ideological, and political analysis, Ray's study is the single best introduction available to the general reader.

Individual and Tribal Biography

Abel, Kerry. *Drum Songs: Glimpses of Dene History.* Montreal: McGill-Queen's University Press, 1993.

This finely crafted study of the Dene people of northern Canada is one of the best historical works written on Native peoples. *Drum Songs* begins with stories of Dene life prior to contact and proceeds chronologically through the fur trade period, the missionary period, the treaty period, and finally the period of modern economic development. Abel utilizes records of fur traders, missionaries, government representatives, and Dene oral tradition. *Drum Songs* clearly illustrates the Dene peoples' willingness and ability to adapt to changing circumstances.

Cruikshank, Julie. *Life Lived Like a Story: Life Stories of Three Yukon Native Elders*. Vancouver: University of British Columbia Press, 1990.

This life history presents the narratives of three Native women of Athapaskan and Tlingit heritage who were born in the years immediately before and after the Klondike gold rush. The three elders — Angela Sidney, Kitty Smith, and Annie Ned — provide narrative accounts of Native myths and origin stories, as well personal narratives that relate aspects of each woman's life history, including accounts of childhood, puberty, marriage, and contact with non-natives.

Dempsey, Hugh A. *Big Bear. The End of Freedom*. Lincoln: University of Nebraska Press, 1984.

Between 1870 and 1877, Canada signed treaties with the Native peoples of the Canadian prairies, offering reserves and annuities in return for a surrender of lands. Although Big Bear desired to establish a peaceful relationship with the government, he believed a better deal that preserved Cree autonomy could be obtained. He and his people continued to sustain a traditional way of life until starvation forced him to acquiesce in 1883. By that time, neither his people nor the government understood Big Bear's goals. His inability to control Cree violence at Frog Lake during the 1885 Rebellion provided the government with an opportunity to dispose of this troublesome chief. Convicted of treason for his role in the rebellion, Big Bear died in a penitentiary. This excellent biography blends Native-White relations with intra-band politics in Cree society.

_____. *Crowfoot, Chief of the Blackfeet*. Norman: University of Oklahoma Press, 1972.

Hugh Dempsey makes use of his family connections within the Blackfoot community, interviews conducted with Blackfoot elders in 1939 and 1940, and extensive archival resources to prepare this biography of

Crowfoot. Chief Crowfoot rose to power within Blackfoot society at a critical moment in the history of this tribal group: the bison were disappearing and American and Canadian settlers were encroaching upon Blackfoot territory. Crowfoot used his status and leadership abilities to convince his followers that peaceful adaptation was preferable to armed confrontation. As a result, the Blackfoot, unlike their Sioux and Cree neighbours, did not participate in armed conflict with government troops. Although dated, this biography remains an indispensable resource for students interested in the Blackfoot response to non-native expansion.

Flannery, Regina. *Ellen Smallboy: Glimpses of a Cree Woman's Life.* Montreal: McGill-Queen's University Press, 1995.
In a project which began as retrieval anthropology, Regina Flannery interviewed a number of Cree elders at Moose Factory on James Bay in the summers of 1933, 1935, and 1937. She was enthralled by the story told by Ellen Smallboy, a Cree woman in her eighties. Over the course of sixty years, Flannery consulted with many of the leading fur trade scholars and finally produced this biography. Flannery uses Smallboy's story to explore the challenges faced by the James Bay Cree in a period of dramatic change.

Hallowell, A. Irving, with Jennifer Brown. *The Ojibwa of Berens River, Manitoba: Ethnography into History.* Toronto: Harcourt Brace Jovanovich, 1992.
Irving Hallowell, an anthropologist, lived among the Berens River Ojibwa in the 1930s and wrote (but did not publish) this manuscript in the 1960s. Jennifer Brown discovered the manuscript in his papers, added a preface and afterword, and edited the text. The first three chapters of the book describe the process of cultural adaptation and readjustment in Ojibwa society brought on by participation in the fur trade, the actions of missionaries, and finally the advent of a government bureaucracy. The last three chapters describe the persistence of cultural characteristics in the Ojibwa community. This bi-focal approach helps the reader understand the duality of the contact experience. Although the text is old and some of the interpretations can be challenged, it remains an excellent study informed by an intimate link with the Elders of the Berens River community.

Heidenreich, Conrad. *Huronia: A History and Geography of the Huron Indians.* Toronto: McClelland and Stewart, 1971.

One of the pioneering works on the Huron, *Huronia* remains a useful resource and should be read along with the publications of Bruce Trigger. *Huronia* contains a wealth of quantitative information on Huron population, settlement patterns, economy, and trade networks. Furthermore, Heidenreich provides valuable maps and statistical tables to assist and enlighten even the experienced reader.

Marshall, Ingeborg. *A History and Ethnography of the Beothuk*. Montreal: McGill-Queen's University Press, 1996.

The first peoples of what is now Newfoundland, the Beothuk disappeared in the early nineteenth century. In the first section, Marshall presents a historical examination of the contact period. She argues that competition for resources in Newfoundland fostered a complex relationship between the Beothuk, the Europeans, the Mi'kmaq, and the Montagnais/Innu peoples. The Beothuk were eventually displaced as the strains in this relationship intensified. The second part of the book is a thorough ethnography of the Beothuk people and presents insight into the cultural traditions of this lost community.

Milloy, John S. *The Plains Cree: Trade, Diplomacy and War, 1790-1870*. Winnipeg: University of Manitoba Press, 1988.

Milloy provides a short readable account of Cree history from contact to the disappearance of the buffalo. Following the tradition established by David Mandelbaum's *The Plains Cree* (1936), Milloy argues the Cree expanded and moved westward during this period. He links this expansion with European contact in an interesting and intriguing study. He suggests that from 1670 to 1790, the Cree acted as middlemen in the fur trade and formed diplomatic, military, and trade alliances with the neighbouring Blackfoot and Mandan-Hidatsa tribes. Following the European penetration into the interior, the Cree moved into the role of provisioner and buffalo hunter, thereby spending greater time on the Plains. Horses were essential to this transition and Cree diplomacy took up the challenge. In the period 1850 to 1870 Cree military hegemony reached its zenith just as the buffalo, and a way of life, disappeared. Milloy's work is useful, if problematic. He has been challenged for accepting Mandelbaum's theory of a Cree migration and his reliance upon tribal structures in order to understand diplomacy, trade, and war.

Russell, Dale R. *The Eighteenth Century Western Cree and Their Neighbours*. Hull, PQ: Canadian Museum of Civilisation, 1991.

Russell re-examines and deconstructs the historical evidence and challenges David Mandelbaum's theories of Cree migration. Russell argues that the Cree were a parkland people exploiting the resources of this region as far west as the Rocky Mountains prior to the fur trade. The book has been critically reviewed by established fur trade researchers but is, nonetheless, a valuable contribution to the work on Native peoples' adaptation to the fur trade. Readers should use this book cautiously and compare the analysis with that of John Milloy and Arthur Ray.

Schmaltz, Peter S. *The Ojibwa of Southern Ontario*. Toronto: University of Toronto Press, 1991.

Schmaltz melds together Ojibwa oral tradition, archival records, and government publications to tell the story of the Ojibwa in southern Ontario. He begins with the Ojibwa migration into the region following European contact and ends with the Ojibwa political struggles of the 1980s. Schmaltz's work shares with other ethnohistorical texts a clear effort to understand the historical process from an Ojibwa point of view. Ojibwa perspectives on the fur trade, the Iroquois wars, and the nineteenth-century treaty process dominate this work. Indeed, there are occasions when the insights of fur trade revisionist history are ignored. This book is one of the key studies of Ojibwa, but should be used with the work of Charles Bishop and Laura Peers.

Smith, Donald B. *Sacred Feathers: The Reverend Peter Jones (Kahkewaquonaby) and the Mississauga Indians*. Toronto: University of Toronto Press, 1987.

Canadian historians have begun to understand that Native peoples often adopt aspects of Euro-Canadian culture, only to transform them to meet the realities of aboriginal life and community. In this important biography, Donald Smith examines this practice in some detail. Sacred Feathers emerged as an important Mississauga religious figure in the period of crisis following the War of 1812. Although the Mississauga had served as allies to the British in both the American Revolution and the War of 1812, they found themselves subjected to pressure to cede their lands, move onto reservations, and adopt Canadian cultural values. With delightful irony, readers learn that Sacred Feathers, a convert to Methodism, argued that acceptance of these conditions would lead to cultural survival for the Mississauga. Students interested in either assimilationist policies or the tactics of cultural survival employed by Native peoples will find this book useful.

Trigger, Bruce G. *The Children of Aataentsic: A History of the Huron People to 1660.* 2 vols. Montreal: McGill-Queen's University Press, 1976; 2nd ed., 1987.

This study is an important contribution to the history of non-literate people and challenges the work of an older school of historians such as C. H. McIlwain and George T. Hunt who assumed that native societies were static prior to the arrival of the Europeans. In writing the history of the Huron (the children of the creation figure Aataentsic), Trigger employs ethnohistorical methodologies which utilize anthropological, archaeological, and historical evidence, and emphasises the dynamic nature of Huron society prior to European penetration. These rich volumes illustrate the changing nature of Huron society from roughly 1550 to 1660 and present an analysis of the events which led to the Huron dispersal by the Iroquois in 1649.

_____. *Huron: Farmers of the North.* Toronto: Holt, Rinehart and Winston, 1969; rev. ed., 1990.

The revised edition of this classic book is the most approachable work on the Huron peoples. It draws on historical and archaeological literature to define and interpret Huron culture, economy, and settlement, with particular emphasis upon environmental aspects of Huron life.

Contact and the Fur Trade

Axtell, James. *The Invasion Within: The Contests of Cultures in Colonial North America.* Oxford: Oxford University Press, 1985.

In an internationally recognised work, James Axtell compares and contrasts Native contact experiences with the English colonies in New England and the French colony at Quebec. Familiar with the broad array of primary sources available in both French and English, Axtell brings life to all three cultural players in this historical drama. Believing that the missionaries served as the "shock troops" of the contact experience, Axtell concentrates his study on religious issues. Unlike many studies of contact, economic and political relationships are secondary. His book is sympathetic to Native culture and its spirituality, critical of the Puritan English and French Recollet missionaries, and equivocal toward the Jesuit missionaries. From a Canadianist perspective, Axtell's comparison of English and French missionary activity is a useful reminder that Jesuits tried to adapt their teachings to suit the environment and culture within which they operated. They did not believe that civilisation was a necessary precursor to conversion. Although it does not cover commercial and economic aspects of conflict effectively, this book, along with Cornelius Jaenen, *Friend and Foe* (1976), and Bruce Trigger, *Natives and Newcomers* (1985), is the foundation for any new studies on seventeenth-century French-Native contact.

Bishop, Charles A. *The Northern Ojibwa and the Fur Trade: An Historical and Ecological Study*. Toronto: Holt, Rinehart and Winston, 1974.
Although less recognised by historians, Bishop's *The Northern Ojibwa* is as important as A. J. Ray's *Indians in the Fur Trade* (1974). Like Ray, Bishop focuses on the fur trade and the process of change and adaptation among Native peoples. An anthropologist, Bishop is more concerned with Ojibwa adaptation strategies and acculturation than chronology. His conclusions, nevertheless, are similar to Ray's. He argues that prior to the 1821 merger of the North West Company and Hudson's Bay Company, the Ojibwa trappers and traders made successful adaptations to the fur trade and controlled the process of acculturation. Subsequent to the merger, however, a process of directed cultural change under the direction of missionaries and the government challenged the Ojibwa and threatened many of their cultural traditions.

Bolt, Clarence. *Thomas Crosby and Tsimshian: Small Shoes for Feet Too Large*. Vancouver: University of British Columbia Press, 1992.
In a refreshing analysis of the Methodist missionary activity amongst the Tsimshian, Clarence Bolt makes a strong case for Native agency. Unlike work on Anglican missionary William Duncan that emphasises the cultural breakdown in Tsimshian society, Bolt argues that the Tsimshian controlled the acculturation process. They invited Thomas Crosby to establish a Methodist mission in their territory and accepted those elements of Croby's teaching that suited the Tsimshian's own goals and aspirations. When the Methodist teachings and the growing paternalism interfered with the Tsimshian lifestyle, they rejected Thomas Crosby and invited other missionaries into their territory. Thoroughly researched and documented, this book is an excellent addition to the literature on missionaries and Native acculturation.

Brown, Jennifer. *Strangers in Blood: Fur Trade Company Families in Indian Country*. Vancouver: University of British Columbia Press, 1980.

Along with Sylvia Van Kirk, *Many Tender Ties* (1980), *Strangers in Blood* has become a central work of the social history of the fur trade. Jennifer Brown understood that families played an important role in both European and aboriginal society. She took this knowledge and began to examine the role of the family in the fur trade. At the focus of this work is the role of the fur traders' Native and Métis wives. In an interesting transference of roles, Brown concludes that the "Country wives" were essential to the successful operation of the fur trade. The maintenance of the family, however, appeared linked to the attributes of the male trader. The Nor'westers based in Montreal and operating in a much tighter kinship based upon corporate environment cared little for their wives beyond the trade, and made no effort to accommodate their Métis children into the world they had left or created. The Hudson's Bay men, on the other hand, separated from family and kin, developed long-standing relationships, and attempted to incorporate their children into the European world. This book is essential for any student interested in Canadian fur trade history.

Burley, David V., S. Scott Hamilton, and Knut R. Fladmark. *Prophecy of the Swan: The Upper Peace River Fur Trade of 1794-1823.* Vancouver: University of British Columbia Press, 1996.
Fur trade historians often discover that traditional forms of historical evidence are limited. This problem is especially significant in districts exploited by the North West Company. The Upper Peace River Country is such a district. Only two post journals and log books from the district, each covering a single year, have survived. The work of archaeologists David Burley, Scott Hamilton, and Knut Fladmark on this district is thus a welcome addition to the fur trade literature. Based upon 20 years of archaeological investigation, the authors construct an important account of life in the fur trade. The focus upon the archaeological evidence from the posts limits the authors' ability to comment on issues of Native agency, but they examine the inter-dependency of traders and Natives in the region, and he ecological destruction which followed the trade. The authors, moreover, provide a useful discussion of the St. John's Massacre of 1823 that led the fur traders to abandon the district for forty years.

Cole, Douglas. *Captured Heritage: The Scramble for Northwest Coast Artifacts.* Vancouver: University of British Columbia Press, 1985; 2nd ed., 1995.
The rise of natural history and anthropological museums and the common

myth of the vanishing Indian spurred dozens of collectors to visit the Northwest coast in the last decades of the nineteenth century. Beginning in the 1870s, American, European, and, after the turn of the century, Canadian museums, in an enterprise commonly known as retrieval anthropology or archaeology, bartered, bought, and stole so great a number of totem poles, masks, boxes, and other artifacts that by 1930 Franz Boas heard a native chief exclaim in the midst of a potlatch that all the bowls were "in the museums of New York and Berlin." Cole approaches this topic judiciously, outlining the obvious damage done by collectors such as George Dorsey and C. F. Newcombe, while also recognizing the contribution of museums to preserving native culture for future generations.

Cooper, Barry. *Alexander Kennedy Isbister: A Respectable Critic of the Honourable Company*. Ottawa: Carleton University Press, 1988.
Country-born and educated, Alexander Kennedy Isbister found his opportunities for advancement in the Hudson's Bay Company (HBC) limited despite his grandfather's position as an HBC officer. He left Rupert's Land as a young man and, after receiving further education in Scotland, became a lawyer, publicist, and critic of the HBC. Cooper uses the correspondence between Isbister and the British colonial office as the foundation for this look at the Victorian reformist challenge to the HBC's charter rights in Rupert's Land. Cooper's interest is focussed on the politics of the reform campaign, and is a useful complement to the work of E. E. Rich and John S. Galbraith.

Delâge, Denys. *Bitter Feast: Amerindians and Europeans in Northeastern North America*. Trans. Jane Brierley. Vancouver: University of British Columbia Press, 1993.
The English translation of Denys Delâge's prize-winning *Le Pays renversé: amerinidiens et européens en Amérique du nord-est, 1600-64*, (1985), *Bitter Feast* uses world-systems analysis to examine the early contact period. It is therefore a unique study of the fur trade experience and not easily adapted to either formalist or substantivist interpretations. Delâge argues that by 1664, contact had ensured a capitalist hegemony and had reduced Iroquoian and Algonkian peoples and their landscapes to mere dependencies or peripheries of a European world economic system. Central to Delâge's analysis is the belief that French, Dutch, and English traders had a superior economic position in the fur trade. An economic system based upon the principles of unequal exchange, led the

Iroquoian and Algonkian peoples to impoverishment. While Delâge's argument is intriguing, readers should be wary of his sweeping Marxist analysis. It is true that Native people did not comprehend the value of furs to the European traders and thus operated at a disadvantage in the trading process. However, it is also true that Europeans did not understand the value of certain commodities in Native society or the value of furs within that community. Furthermore, it is not clear that Native cultural elements of the trading process disappeared and were replaced by market relations.

Dickason, Olive P. *The Myth of the Savage and the Beginnings of French Colonialism in the Americas*. Edmonton: University of Alberta Press, 1984.
The study of *l'homme sauvage* has been primarily the work of literary specialists; in this brilliant and well-illustrated work, Dickason places that myth within the domain of the historian and, significantly, within the trans-Atlantic world of ideas. The first of two sections deals with early European images of the Amerindian. While such images were often multivalent in nature, classifying Amerindians as "savages" provided the ideological justification "to launch one of the great movements in the history of western civilization: the colonization of overseas empires." Second, Dickason examines the contact era from New France south to Florida and Brazil and the varied experience within each area.

Elias, Peter Douglas. *The Dakota of the Canadian Northwest: Lessons for Survival*. Winnipeg: University of Manitoba Press, 1988.
Arriving in the Canadian west from Minnesota after 1862, the Dakota are often considered to be a non-Canadian immigrant tribe and therefore not a part of the Canadian experience. In this useful book, Elias corrects this perspective. Since the Dakota were considered a non-Canadian Native people by the government, they were left to their own devices in Canada. Elias provides a full account of Dakota adaptive strategies in the Canadian Northwest as they try to establish farms, generate a livelihood in hunting and fishing, and take up wage labour.

Fisher, Robin. *Contact and Conflict: Indian-European Relations in British Columbia*. Vancouver: University of British Columbia Press, 1977; 2nd ed., 1992.
Fisher's analysis of Native-white relations in British Columbia between 1774 and 1890 views the Caribou gold rush as a significant dividing point. Prior to 1858 the fur trade economy and society had the effect of

enriching Native society; Fisher, therefore, is a revisionist scholar who portrays Native people as active and equal agents during this early contact period. Following 1858 with the arrival of miners, colonial administrators, missionaries, and other settlers, this mutually beneficial relationship was lost. Instead, Natives became marginalised economically, were viewed as potential converts by missionaries, and were treated harshly by colonial and, after 1871, provincial Indian policy. The second edition contains a useful historiographic preface in which Fisher discusses the scholarship of the 1980s and defends his work against critics.

Francis, Daniel and Toby Morantz. *Partners in Furs: A History of the Fur Trade in Eastern James Bay, 1600-1870.* Montreal: McGill-Queen's University Press, 1985.

Daniel Francis, a popular historian, and Toby Morantz, an anthropologist, combine to produce a readable, enjoyable, well-documented, and important revisionist study of the fur trade system around James Bay. Francis and Morantz note that while the Cree accepted and adapted to the fur trade economic system, this did not result in abject dependence or cultural destruction in their community. Hunting remained an important element of their community throughout the period of study, and indeed, the Cree role as post provisioner became their most important contribution to the fur trade. The fur trade is best described as a mutually beneficial partnership in which both sides perceived and sought advantages. Francis and Morantz conclude that the activities of missionaries in the nineteenth century, rather than the fur trade, threatened Cree cultural autonomy. Together with the work of A. J. Ray, Robin Fisher, and Bruce Trigger, this work challenged the prevailing view that Native people were passive and dependent participants in the fur trade.

Galbraith, John S. *The Little Emperor: Governor Simpson of the Hudson's Bay Company.* Toronto: Macmillan, 1976.

Following the merger of the Hudson's Bay Company and North West Company in 1821, George Simpson became Governor of the Northern Department. From that time until his death in 1860, he was the dominant business figure in the Canadian fur trade. John Galbraith investigates the business and personal life of this intriguing man and in the process reveals the business and imperial side of the fur trade. By looking at the corporate aspect of the trade, Galbraith provides scholars with a useful balance to the array of studies that examine Native participation in the fur trade.

Given, Brian J. *A Most Pernicious Thing: Gun Trading and Native Warfare in the Early Contact Period.* Ottawa: Carleton University Press, 1994.

This important book looks at the significance of the gun trade in the early contact period. Unlike other fur trade scholars, Given argues that the primitive guns of the seventeenth century had a limited impact on Iroquoian and Algonkian society, culture, and warfare. He notes that matchlock guns were traded to Natives in limited quantities during this period, and were decidedly inferior to the bow and arrow for hunting and warfare. Iroquoian and Algonkian demand for guns was related instead to perceived psychological benefits a gun provided in inter-tribal and Native-European warfare. Since this benefit was limited, Native people did not become dependent upon guns, nor lose their ability to manufacture traditional weapons. Given's work therefore suggests that notions of acculturation by Native peoples may be exaggerated. Based upon significant primary research, this book challenges traditional historical viewpoints regarding the impact of the gun trade.

Gough, Barry. *The Northwest Coast: British Navigation, Trade, and Discoveries to 1812.* Vancouver: University of British Columbia Press, 1992.

_____. *Gunboat Frontier: British Maritime Authority and Northwest Coast Indians, 1846-1890.* Vancouver: University of British Columbia Press, 1984.

_____. *Distant Dominion: Britain and the Northwest Coast of North America, 1579-1809.* Vancouver: University of British Columbia Press, 1980.

_____. *The Royal Navy and the Northwest Coast of North America, 1810-1914: A Study of British Maritime Ascendancy.* Vancouver: University of British Columbia Press, 1971.

One of the foremost authorities on British imperial policy in the Pacific northwest, Gough examines the role of British explorers and the Royal Navy in extending and maintaining the Empire from the earliest voyages to World War I. There are excellent discussions on various explorers, the British use of gunboats to real and perceived crises of law and order, and the nature of colonial and provincial Indian policy.

Grant, John Webster. *Moon of Wintertime: Missionaries and the Indians of Canada in Encounter Since 1534.* Toronto: University of Toronto Press, 1984.

Grant's survey of Native-missionary relations is broad in terms of both geography and chronology, although little mention is made of the Inuit and Métis. Grant perceptively notes the varied responses across time and space of Natives to Christian influence; as well, he reflects on the varying psychological motivations and historical patterns of different missionary groups. One of Canada's most prominent church historians, Grant is well-grounded in primary sources and secondary reading, and his approach is sensitive and generally balanced. For an account of the Oblates mission activities see, Raymond Huel, *Proclaiming the Gospel to the Indians and the Métis* (1996); for a useful and more eclectic collection, see John S. Moir and C. Thomas McIntire, eds., *Canadian Protestant and Catholic Missions, 1820s-1920s: Historical Essays in Honour of John Webster Grant* (1988).

Jaenen, Cornelius, J. *Friend and Foe: Aspects of French-Amerindian Cultural Contact in the Sixteenth and Seventeenth Centuries*. Toronto: McClelland and Stewart, 1976.
Through an examination based largely upon the writings of seventeenth-century Jesuit missionaries and informed by anthropological and archaeological insights, Jaenen has produced a valuable study of aboriginal-white relations in New France. In particular, he examines the attitudes toward and the effects upon each other by these two cultures. The Old World perceptions of the Native as either the noble or ignoble savage both demanded attempts at conversion. While the French were ethnocentric in their views, Natives likewise regarded the French as weak and disorganized, and had contempt for their perceived lack of control. Ultimately, the demographic and materialistic weakness of the French were key factors in their failed attempts to assimilate Natives.

Karamanski, Theodore J. *Fur Trade and Exploration: Opening the Far Northwest, 1821-1852*. Norman: University of Oklahoma Press, 1983.
Karamanski writes a heroic narrative of fur trade exploration in British Columbia and the Yukon. He focuses upon the personalities of the fur traders and the hardships they endured while exploring mountain rivers. Karamanski concludes that the failure of the fur trade to establish a prosperous inland trade network prior to 1852 is attributed to HBC governor George Simpson's failure to support the exploration with a coherent strategy for economic development. The conclusion is weakened, however, by Karamanski's failure to draw upon the ethnohistorical scholarship about Native-white relations. Native people do not appear as

active agents in this book, and their role in limiting the trading possibilities is entirely ignored.

Krech, Shepard, III, ed. *The Subarctic Fur Trade: Native Social and Economic Adaptations.* Vancouver: University of British Columbia Press, 1984.

A collection of articles on the fur trade in the Canadian north by leading ethnohistorians, *The Subarctic Fur Trade* is an important source of revisionist articles. The contributors include Arthur Ray, Charles Bishop, Toby Morantz, Shepard Krech III, Carol Judd, Hetty Brumbach, and Robert Jarvenpa. They all address the issue of change within Native communities in the subarctic. All authors argue that economic and social changes occurred as a result of the fur trade. Yet all also agree that the economic and social transitions could be accommodated within Native culture. Ray, for example, argues that rather than the fur trade exchange process, Hudson's Bay Company generosity led to the emergence of Native welfare dependency. In another case, Krech argues that one of the most problematic adaptations made amongst Athapaskan peoples was their continued treks to the fur trade posts, treks that took time away from traditional subsistence activities.

_____. *Indians, Animals and the Fur Trade: A Critique of Keepers of the Game.* Athens: University of Georgia Press, 1981.

The American Society of Ethnohistorians organized a discussion of arguments found in Calvin Martin's controversial *Keepers of the Game* (1978). This collection of essays represents the collective response from ethnohistorians such as Shepard Krech, Bruce Trigger, Charles Bishop, Dean Snow, Lydia Black, and William Sturtevant. Each of these writers notes that Martin's argument was based upon fallacies and inconsistencies, methodological flaws, and significant gaps in the evidence. Anyone interested in the ideas contained in *Keepers of the Game* would be advised to treat this book as a companion volume.

Mackie, Richard Somerset. *Trading Beyond the Mountains: The British Fur Trade on the Pacific, 1973-1843.* Vancouver: University of British Columbia Press, 1997.

Meticulously researched and well-argued, *Trading Beyond the Mountains* examines the fur trade in the Columbia District, a long-neglected topic. Mackie argues that the Hudson's Bay Company (HBC) was successful in gaining a monopoly over the fur trade in this area, even though American traders had equal rights of access. In addition, he argues that the HBC diversified its economy as early as the 1820s and developed a provisional and export in salmon, lumber, wheat, flour, and potatoes.

Martin, Calvin. *Keepers of the Game: Indian-Animal Relationships and the Fur Trade*. Berkeley: University of California Press, 1978.
Calvin Martin may be one of the last pure substantivist fur trade scholars. In this book, he argues that pre-contact eastern Algonkian society lived in a harmonious and spiritual relationship with the animals they hunted. The Native peoples were conservationists and had no commercial economic rationale for exploiting the natural resources. European contact destroyed this community. The spiritual connection with animals could not be sustained in the face of an onslaught of European diseases. The eastern Algonkians blamed the animals for their problems and made war against them. The European fur trade exploited this cultural disintegration and Algonkians used European technology to wage the war more effectively. This argument has been criticised from all directions. Students should read Shepard Krech III, ed., *Indians, Animals and the Fur Trade* (1981) as a companion volume, as well as the revisionist work of Arthur Ray or Richard White.

Murray, Peter. *The Devil and Mr. Duncan: A History of the Two Metlakatlas*. Vancouver: Sono Nis Press, 1988.
Journalist Peter Murray explores the motivation and activities of William Duncan in the creation of the model village of Metlakatla. Drawing primarily upon Duncan's own record of his achievements, Murray deals sympathetically with the missionary's activities. While readers will find this work approachable, scholars should still consult Jean Usher's *William Duncan of Metlakatla* (1974).

Newman, Peter. *Company of Adventurers*. Markham, ON: Viking/Penguin Books Canada Ltd., 1985.
_____. *Caesars of the Wilderness*. Markham, ON: Viking/Penguin Books Canada Ltd., 1987.
_____. *Merchant Princes*. Markham, ON: Viking/Penguin Books Canada Ltd., 1991.
This three-volume history of the Hudson's Bay Company traces the organization's commercial empire from its original charter in 1670 to contemporary times. The central theme of these works revolves around the role of the Hudson's Bay Company as a formative influence in

Canada's history and its resonance within the nation's collective memory. Newman's approach is popular in style, and his narrative concentrates on lively anecdotes, particularly if they involve Native sexual mores or racy relationships between white traders and aboriginal women. Unfortunately, Native people are often seen as passive and unsophisticated participants. These volumes have been heavily criticised by historians as lacking in analysis and originality, and for questionable use of source material.

Parker, James. *Emporium of the North: Fort Chipewyan and the Fur Trade to 1835*. Regina: Canadian Plains Research Centre, 1987.
Based on research conducted in the 1960s, Parker's book, despite the 1987 publication date, shows signs of age. *Emporium of the North* is an early representation of the revisionist trend in fur trade history. Chipewyan and Cree traders are separated from the larger context of the narrative, and Parker downplays their role in the fur trade. Because Fort Chipewyan was the principal inland trading post and supply depot for the North West Company from 1790 to 1820, and because most fur trade studies look at the Hudson's Bay Company posts, Parker's work remains an important study.

Payne, Michael. *The Most Respectable Place in the Territory: Everyday Life in Hudson's Bay Company Service — York Factory, 1788 to 1870*. Ottawa: National Historical Parks and Sites, 1989.
Unlike most recent work on the fur trade, this work examines the European experience rather than Native-white relations. Payne places life in the Hudson's Bay Company's most important administrative centre within the context of European social history. He examines issues such as the social structure, status, mortality, and occupations in this pre-industrial commercial establishment, and argues that life at York Factory compared favourably with that in Britain or Canada in the nineteenth century.

Peers, Laura. *The Ojibwa of Western Canada, 1780 to 1870*. Winnipeg: University of Manitoba Press, 1994.
The Ojibwa migrated to the western Canadian parkland and plains from the forested region around the Great Lakes, principally as fur traders and trappers. Anthropologists have concluded that this movement constituted a significant shift in lifestyle and culture. Laura Peers uses historical research tools to look at the western Ojibwa and discovers that many elements of Ojibwa forest culture were retained on the plains. Indeed, Peers calls into question the concept of "cultural area" and points out that

many Ojibwa moved back and forth between the two cultural zones. The portrait of the Ojibwa painted by Peers is one of determination and controlled adaptation. By emphasising cultural continuity rather than change, Peers' valuable revisionist work emphasises Ojibwa agency in moderating and managing cultural change.

Peyser, Joseph L., ed. *Letters from New France: The Upper Country, 1686-1783*. Champaign: University of Illinois Press, 1992.
Peyser provides a cumbersome, but informative, collection of documents and historical research on the French fur trade in the Great Lakes region. *Letters from New France* is divided into chronological chapters, with each chapter composed of both historical essays written by Peyser and previously untranslated archival documents. Although the value of the essays is limited by their eclectic nature, the documents and editorial notes provide a wealth of information.

Ray, Arthur J. *The Canadian Fur Trade and the Industrial Age*. Toronto: University of Toronto Press, 1990.
Ray discusses the transformation of the fur trade in northern Canada after 1870, and argues that contrary to popular perception, the fur trade continued as a vibrant economic pursuit in the Industrial era. Indeed, as living standards improved in the western world, the demand for furs and the prices paid for these commodities increased rather than decreased. These changes affected both the Hudson's Bay Company (HBC) and Native and Métis trappers. Rather than entering a period of decline, the fur trade shifted from a primarily barter trade system to a merchant capital system. Both the Hudson's Bay Company and Native trappers found their position in the fur trade threatened by this transition as independent fur buyers and independent white trappers entered the fur trade. The HBC in particular could not adapt to the changing circumstances. As a result, the "Honourable Company" slowly changed from fur buyer to wholesale and retail trade. In this thoroughly documented study, Ray offers readers a glimpse at the fundamental transitions that occurred in post-1870 Native-white relations.

_____. *Indians in the Fur Trade: Their Role as Trappers, Hunters, and Middlemen in the Lands Southwest of Hudson Bay 1660-1870*. Toronto: University of Toronto Press, 1974.
The first of his important studies of the fur trade, *Indians in the Fur Trade* remains a critical book for any student or scholar interested in this subject.

Prior to Ray's work, fur trade scholars often considered Natives passive participants in a European commercial system and their role was given only cursory acknowledgment. A ground-breaking work, *Indians in the Fur Trade* demonstrates that Native people had a long tradition of making adaptive responses to environmental, cultural, and political changes prior to the fur trade, and made adjustments to the presence of European traders and trade goods. Ray notes that Natives, by virtue of their monopoly on transportation and resource production in the Hudson's Bay Company trade system, were equal partners with the European traders. In this discussion, Ray emphasises the rational economic skills of Native middlemen, a subject he expands upon with Donald Freeman in *"Give Us Good Measure"* (1978). The process of adaptation continued as British traders moved into the western Canadian interior after 1763. The Cree moved into the provisioning trade and moved out onto the plains to hunt bison; the superior trapping skills of the Ojibwa led them to occupy the forests thus vacated. Only the denouement of the fur trade in 1870 led Native peoples toward dependence and subjugation.

Ray, Arthur J. and Donald Freeman. *"Give Us Good Measure": An Economic Analysis of Relations Between the Indians and the Hudson's Bay Company Before 1763*. Toronto: University of Toronto Press, 1978.

This exciting revisionist study of the fur trade argues that the system of exchange in the Hudson's Bay Company fur trade reflected both European economic rationales and Native customs and traditions. In what could be called a modified formalist approach, Ray and Freeman conclude that the fur trade was a commercial trade constrained by certain cultural practices. Traders had to learn and use Native cultural and political trade ceremonies in the barter exchange process, and Natives were forced to understand and exploit new economic opportunities and practices of the European commercial system.

Sioui, Georges E. *For an Amerindian Autohistory: An Essay on the Foundations of a Social Ethic*. Trans. Sheila Fischman. Montreal: McGill-Queen's University Press, 1992.

A post-modernist interpretation of Algonkian-Iroquoian and European relations, this book is an important addition to Canadian Native history. Sioui is extremely critical of the interpretations of both George T. Hunt and Bruce Trigger. He claims the Native peoples were waging a "desperate cultural war on an invader whose pathogenic allies made his presence a disaster." He, like Calvin Martin, thus places emphasis on the cultural attributes of Algonkian and Iroquoian peoples and European diseases as an explanation for the nature of Native-white relations.

Smith, Donald B. *Le Sauvage: The Native People in Quebec Historical Writing on the Heroic Period (1534-1663) of New France.* Ottawa: National Museums of Canada, 1974.

This short monograph examines the image of the Indian in French Canadian historical writing. Smith provides an analysis of the ambiguous image of Indians in the early Jesuit *Relations*, the enlightenment ideal of the "heroic Indian," the emergence of "Le Sauvage" in nineteenth-century historians such as Benjamin Sulte and François-Xavier Garneau, and finally, the discrediting of racial theories by Jacques Rousseau in the post-World War II era.

Thistle, Paul C. *Indian-European Trade Relations in the Lower Saskatchewan River Region to 1840.* Winnipeg: University of Manitoba Press, 1986.

Thistle's revisionist fur trade study reflects a modified substantivist perspective and emphasises cultural trade dynamics within native society over economic aspects of the fur trade. He argues that Native people in the Saskatchewan River valley did not feel culturally inferior to European traders or become dependent upon European trade goods for their subsistence. The basic parameters of their culture survived intact. Thistle points out that when Europeans violated Native cultural traditions such as the obligation to share food in times of scarcity, the traders often paid for this transgression with their lives. Thistle notes, furthermore, that European trade posts depended upon "home guard" Native hunters until at least 1840. Under these conditions, the fur trade became an amalgam of Native and European traditions and customs. Natives participated in the trade voluntarily and, more important, seasonally.

Trigger, Bruce G. *Natives and Newcomers: Canada's "Heroic Age" Reconsidered.* Montreal: McGill-Queen's University Press, 1985.

In a work broader in scope than *Children of Aataentsic* (1987), Trigger continues to correct the Eurocentric bias of much of Canadian historiography. Distinctly interdisciplinary in nature, this volume explores the "heroic age" from the earliest European explorers to 1663, when a royal government was established in New France. Trigger argues that traditional interpretations have paid too much attention to the activities of priests and government officials (who left most of the written records); instead, it was traders and their employees who were most significant in forging alliances and providing material goods that inevitably changed Native societies. Moreover, Trigger corrects the position of an earlier generation of economic historians such as Donald Creighton (who virtually ignored Natives) and Harold Innis for whom "native peoples remained economic stereotypes only minimally disguised in feathers." Instead, Natives had an economic and cultural vibrancy and were active agents in the trading process. This work remains one of the most forceful attempts to place Natives within the mainstream of Canadian history.

Upton, Leslie F. S. *Micmacs and Colonists. Indian-White Relations in the Maritimes, 1713-1867.* Vancouver: University of British Columbia Press, 1979.
Immigrants from New England began arriving in the Maritimes following the English acquisition of this territory in 1713; they were followed by large numbers of Loyalists after 1783. These immigrants encountered and slowly subjugated the indigenous Micmac population. In this book, Leslie Upton, one of the foremost historians of Loyalist migrations to Nova Scotia, describes this process in detail. Upton argues that the Micmac, who had controlled aspects of acculturation throughout the French colonial period (1604-1713) and consequently supported the French through guerilla warfare until 1759, were exhausted and unable to effectively resist British policies of subjugation and dispossession. Yet they survived. The Micmac lost their lands and their independence, but not their identity. Upton's well-researched story is a thought provoking contribution to the history of Native-white relations in eastern Canada.

Usher, Jean. *William Duncan of Metlakatla.* Ottawa: National Museums of Canada, 1974.
Frank Peake writes in *The Anglican Church in British Columbia* (1959) that "[our] initial response is surely one of admiration for the pioneer missionaries." Usher rejects the theme of the hero missionary. The megalomanic William Duncan, although strongly influenced by Victorian morales, achieved initial success among the Tsimshian at Metlakatla because of his willingness to incorporate aboriginal culture into his Victorian Christianity.

Van Kirk, Sylvia. *Many Tender Ties: Women in Fur Trade Society 1670-1870.* Winnipeg: Watson and Dyer, 1980.

This work, together with Jennifer Brown's *Strangers in Blood* (1980), transformed fur trade history. Brown examines the role of families in the fur trade, while Van Kirk concentrates primarily upon the role of women. Van Kirk divides the fur trade into three eras. In the first phase, fur traders married Native women not only to provide sexual comfort but also to facilitate trading relationships. These women were essential for both the commercial success of the trade and the survival of the traders themselves. These women, furthermore, sought marriage to a fur trader as a status vehicle. In the second phase, the female children of these early marriages became the preferred marital partners. Like their Native mothers, these women could act as intermediaries between the cultures and had the basic survival skills necessary for life in the interior. As children of the fur trade, however, Métis women had less autonomy than their mothers. In the third phase, missionaries challenged the nature of the fur trade marriage and obtaining a white wife became a status symbol for officers in the Hudson's Bay Company. Racism and the degradation of the fur trade family resulted.

White, Richard. *The Middle Ground: Indians, Empires and Republics in the Great Lakes Region, 1650-1815.* Cambridge: Cambridge University Press, 1991.
Richard White draws upon the significant array of fur trade scholarship to illustrate a new and important theoretical perspective for American history. He carefully notes that a new cultural system forged from both Algonkian and French cultural traditions emerged in order to facilitate trading relationships in the Great Lakes Basin. He calls this trading world "the middle ground." White then continues his analysis into the government era, when the American government replaced French traders as the partners in the middle ground world, to show how this system responded to outsiders and non-participants. Although White provides a useful phrase, "the middle ground," for understanding French-Algonkian relationships, his work is derivative of much recent Canadian scholarship. Readers of Jennifer Brown, W. J. Eccles, Cornelius Jaenen, Jacqueline Peterson, Arthur Ray, and Bruce Trigger will find many parallels. Canadian readers will find his brief coverage of the American government's role far more challenging and intriguing.

Yerbury, J. C. *The Subarctic Indians and the Fur Trade, 1680-1860.* Vancouver: University of British Columbia Press, 1986.
Unlike most ethnohistorians, Yerbury argues that the fur trade inspired

dramatic cultural change in the Athapaskan population near Hudson's Bay. The book has been sharply criticised. Although trained in anthropology, Yerbury makes little use of archaeological evidence or anthropological methodology; instead he tends to make inferences based upon the archival record. Nevertheless, *The Subarctic Indians* is a useful catalogue of historical events in the area west of Hudson's Bay and a good reminder that not all scholars agree that the fur trade allowed N ative people a degree of cultural autonomy.

The Métis Nation

Beal, Bob and Rod Macleod. *Prairie Fire: The 1885 North-West Rebellion*. rev. ed. Toronto: McClelland & Stewart, 1995.
Originally published by the now-defunct Hurtig Press in 1984, this balanced and readable introduction to the Northwest Rebellion integrates the personalities of Louis Riel and Gabriel Dumont into the larger conflict. Though the Native population was initially divided, *Prairie Fire* illustrates the sense of grievance that the aboriginal and Métis populations felt, provides a detailed examination of the largely inconclusive battles prior to Batoche, and discusses the long-term consequences of the Rebellion. The conflict solved little; instead this work argues that the most profound and far-reaching result was the divergent approaches to Riel that French- and English-Canadians took, and the political downfall of the Conservatives in Quebec following Riel's hanging in 1885.

Bumsted, J. M. *The Red River Rebellion*. Winnipeg: Watson & Dwyer, 1996.
A survey designed for the general reader Bumsted presents a balanced approach to the Red River Rebellion: for example, the Canadian government is portrayed as insensitive — but not conspiratorial — toward Native and Métis issues; similarly, Louis Riel is portrayed to be a tough-minded but flawed leader, rather than a heroic figure. This work lacks footnotes but includes a short historiographical essay and a lengthy appendix that provides biographies of some of the principal individuals involved in the Rebellion.

Ens, Gerhard J. *Homeland to Hinterland: The Changing Worlds of the Red River Metis in the Nineteenth Century*. Toronto: University of Toronto Press, 1996.
The first work to trace the Red River Métis throughout the nineteenth

century, Ens depicts these individuals as sophisticated economic actors and defines the Métis according to their economic and social position between the Native and their pre-capitalist world and the Euro-american capitalist world. Thus, he rejects attempts to define them according to biology or religion. Ens explains that the Red River emerged as a homeland of the Métis because, during the early nineteenth century, it was there that they could occupy their economic niche with confidence. By the late 1860s, however, this niche was disappearing as the importance of the fur trade declined, and the Métis began drifting away from Red River. In this context, Ens examines the Métis resistence of 1869-1870 as an unsuccessful effort by Riel to transform the Métis identity on political or constitutional terms. This work refutes the earlier notion by George Stanley that saw the Métis as a primitive people who were unable to adjust to a capitalist society. Moreover, it refutes the notion that the Métis did not adapt well to economic opportunities and challenges. Ens argues that the Métis depended on the buffalo robe trade rather than agriculture for sound economic reasons. Finally, this work takes issue with Fritz Pannekoek's *A Snug Little Flock* (1991), and argues that divisions within the Métis community were not primarily racial, linguistic, or religious, but were principally based upon economic and class lines.

Flanagan, Thomas. *Métis Lands in Manitoba*. Calgary: University of
    Calgary Press, 1991.
Written partly as a consultative report for the Canadian Department of Justice, *Métis Lands* argues that the administrative procedures of the Manitoba Act in the 1870s were fair and just and, indeed, produced a "cascade of benefits" to the Métis. The Manitoba Act of 1870, which brought Manitoba into Confederation and conferred language and school rights on Protestants and Catholics, also distributed over 1.4 million acres of land and title to Métis families. Much of the land given, to child and adult alike, was quickly sold to speculators; Flanagan argues that the prices received were fair and that the Canadian government justly fulfilled its obligations. This argument is, of course, controversial, and readers should also consult the work of Douglas Sprague; the debate between these two can also be followed in the *Journal of Canadian Studies* (1980), *Canadian Ethnic Studies* (1985), and *Prairie Forum* (1989). The debate on Riel is also present in Hartwell Bowsfield, ed., *Louis Riel: Selected Readings* (1988). For Riel's own writings, see G. F. G. Stanley, *et al.*, eds., *The Collected Writings of Louis Riel* 5 vols. (1985).

_____. *Riel and the Rebellion: 1885 Reconsidered.* Saskatoon:
   Western Producer Prairie Books, 1983.
In *Louis "David" Riel* Flanagan saw the Métis leader as a millenarian
prophet; in contrast, this revisionist and controversial work sees Riel as
a failed and flawed leader who, unhappy with land grievances, confused
over his prophetic role, and angry that the federal government would not
concede to his demands for a bribe, led the Métis people into rebellion.
Unlike Sprague and McLean, Flanagan argues that the Federal
government's bureaucratic inefficiencies prevented expeditious settlement
of land grievances with the Métis; however, this was not sufficient reason
to cause or justify open rebellion. This work also addresses the trial of
Louis Riel and concludes that it was conducted fairly, and that a
posthumous pardon is not justified.

_____. *Louis "David" Riel: "Prophet of the New World."* Toronto:
   University of Toronto Press, 1979; 2nd ed., 1996.
The debate over Louis Riel's mental state and motivation was a point of
controversy at his 1885 trial: supporters (though not Riel himself) argued
that he was insane and called for mercy; others simply saw him as a rebel
and demanded his execution. Flanagan treats seriously Riel's religious
ideas and argues that, in the tradition of Norman Cohn's *The Pursuit of
the Millennium* (1957), that Riel saw himself as a prophet and that his
religious beliefs should be interpreted as a form of millenarianism. The
Northwest Rebellion was, therefore, as much a religious movement as a
political one, though Flanagan fails to illustrate how fully this vision
influenced the beliefs and actions of Riel's followers.

McLean, Don. *1885: Métis Rebellion or Government Conspiracy?*
   Winnipeg: Pemmican Publications, 1985.
Combining advocacy history with conspiracy theory, McLean argues that
Chief Factor Lawrence Clarke, thought to be a friend of the Métis, and
Prime Minister John A. Macdonald acted to incite the Métis toward
rebellion in order to bring much-needed hard currency into the North-
West Territories and to build the Canadian Pacific Railway. This thesis
is, however, poorly supported and relies upon much speculation.

Pannekoek, Fritz. *A Snug Little Flock: The Social Origins of the Riel
   Resistance of 1869-70.* Winnipeg: Watson & Dwyer, 1991.
In a controversial work, Pannekoek notes that the Protestant clergy
contributed significantly to the social fabric of Red River society. One

significant legacy of the clergy, Pannekoek argues, was to create a sense of hostility between English and French mixed-blood peoples. As a result, the country-born were neither sympathetic nor indifferent to the Métis' cause during the first resistance as has previously been argued; instead, they were opposed to armed resistance to the Crown and chose careful neutrality after a recognition of their own weakness. Pannekoek is particularly critical of the failure of the Anglican clergy to provide appropriate leadership throughout the crises which the settlement faced. This portrayal may be somewhat harsh: William Cockran is portrayed as an irascible, senile individual who was incapable of providing leadership. In contrast, others have noted his noteworthy contributions to the Anglican mission and to the country-born in particular.

Peterson, Jacqueline and Jennifer Brown, eds. *The New Peoples: Being and Becoming Métis in North America.* Winnipeg: University of Manitoba Press, 1985.

This collection of conference papers broadly discusses the process of ethnogenesis, or the creation of a new cultural group, in this case the Métis people of North America. Whereas Marcel Giraud's classic *Le Métis canadien* (1945) attributed Métis's behaviour to, as the late John Foster argues in a contribution to this collection, their biological-cum-cultural antecedents, the authors of *The New Peoples* engage in a more scholarly quest for Métis cultural origins. On a historiographic note, Irene Spry takes issue with Fritz Pannekoek's thesis that the first Riel resistance was due, in part, to sectarian and racial conflict. Although most of the emphasis of this collection is on the Métis of the Great Plains, this volume remains the best single introduction to the Métis people.

Purich, Donald, J. *The Métis.* Toronto: Lorimer, 1988.

This survey of the Métis is a prime example of advocacy history. Purich, a lawyer and former director of the Native Law Centre at the University of Saskatchewan, traces the Métis struggle for constitutional protection, self-government, and land settlements from the nineteenth century to the 1960s. While Purich's analysis of events such as why some Métis did not support Riel in 1885 is weak, this volume enters into the Sprague-Flanagan debate on the side of the former and provides some useful background to the rise of the Métis rights movement.

Siggins, Maggie. *Riel: A Life of Revolution.* Toronto: HarperCollins, 1994.

This popular and sympathetic biography contributes to the ongoing discussion of the life and influence of Louis Riel. Siggins' sees Riel largely as a political leader struggling for aboriginal and Métis rights against the assembled forces of the Canadian government, the Hudson's Bay Company, and individuals such as the Anglican church leader Archbishop Machray. In emphasising the political role of Riel from the creation of Manitoba in 1870 to the 1885 Rebellion, Siggins contradicts interpretations that emphasise Riel's role as a millenarian prophet, or argue for his mental instability.

Sprague, D. N. *Canada and the Métis, 1869-1885*. Waterloo: Wilfrid Laurier University Press, 1988.

This provocative work examines the displacement of the Red River Métis and their failure to find a new home in the Saskatchewan valley. This displacement was allowed to occur, Sprague argues, because of duplicitous government policies, particularly in areas such as settling and honouring land claims. Indeed, *Canada and the Métis* argues that Prime Minister John A. Macdonald inflamed with a desire for a trans-continental railway, saw the 1885 rebellion as an opportunity to justify the existence of the Canadian Pacific Railway and gain support for additional financial subsidy for this nearly bankrupt organization.

Woodcock, George. *Gabriel Dumont*. Edmonton: Hurtig, 1975.

An influential and widely read popular historian, Woodcock has re-created Gabriel Dumont, a prominent Métis leader in the 1885 Rebellion, as a romantic hero. Woodcock emphasises the Métis perspective of the events of 1885; although they experienced some initial success at Duck Lake and Fish Creek under Dumont's leadership, their resistance ultimately ended with the tragedy at Batoche under Riel's guidance.

The State and the Economy

Abel, Kerry and Jean Friesen, eds. *Aboriginal Resource Use in Canada: Historical and Legal Aspects*. Winnipeg: University of Manitoba Press, 1991.

Land and resources are one of the most controversial aspects of Native-government relations in Canada. An issue with spiritual, moral, economic, and legal overtones, the question of land ownership and access has resonated throughout Canadian history. The papers in this collection were presented at a 1988 Conference on Aboriginal Land and Resources. They cover the range of issues including, pre-contact resource use, the fur trade, government regulation of resources, and court decisions and their impact on aboriginal claims.

Asch, Michael. *Home and Native Land: Aboriginal Rights and the Canadian Constitution.* Toronto: Methuen, 1984.
The patriation of Canada's Constitution in 1982 opened a debate regarding the status of aboriginal people in the Country. Section 35 of the Canada Act contains a recognition of aboriginal and treaty rights. These rights, however, remain undefined. *Home and Native Land* is a scholarly attempt to define aboriginal rights from an Native and Métis perspective. Asch carefully describes the various definitions of "self-determination" and "inherent rights" found within the aboriginal community. He draws upon his anthropological training to demonstrate how such conceptions have emerged within the various aboriginal cultural groups. Further, the book carefully documents the legal challenges that stand in the way of the various definitions.

Barman, Jean, Yvonne Herbert, and Don McCaskill. *Indian Education in Canada: Vol. 1. The Legacy.* Vancouver: University of British Columbia Press, 1986.
_____. *Indian Education in Canada: Vol. 2. The Challenge.* Vancouver: University of British Columbia Press, 1987.
Wide-ranging in terms of time and space, these volumes examine aspects of Native education over more than three centuries. Though the authors differ greatly in approach and style, the collective theme is the failure of Euro-Canadians to recognise the validity and utility of Native forms of education, and the often harsh implications of assimilationist philosophies and policies. The second volume, in particular, emphasises some of the most promising attempts by Natives to claim control over their own educational structures.

Brody, Hugh. *The People's Land: Eskimos and Whites in the Arctic.* Vancouver: Douglas and McIntyre, 1991.
Originally published by Penguin Books in 1975, this book remains a useful and readable account of Inuit-white relations in the eastern Arctic. Brody describes Canadian government policy toward the Inuit as a destructive colonial process similar to policies adopted toward Canadian Native peoples. In the Arctic, however, Brody notes that the policy has been implemented in a compressed forty-year time period following

World War II. The activities of missionaries, fur traders, and government administrators, consequently, have had a greater destructive impact than that experienced in southern Canada. Lacking references and spiced with dialogue, the book's academic usefulness is limited. Nevertheless, this work complements R. Quinn Duffy, *The Road to Nunavut* (1988) and Richard Diubaldo, *The Government of Canada and the Inuit* (1985). For an interesting examination of the "middle north" and differing perceptions of landscape and geography, see Hugh Brody, *Maps and Dreams: Indians and the British Columbia Frontier.* (1981).

Buckley, Helen. *From Wooden Ploughs to Welfare: Why Canadian Indian Policy Failed in the Prairie Provinces.* Montreal: McGill-Queen's University Press, 1992.
Buckley attempts to discredit the perception that the Native peoples of the prairie provinces were responsible for the emergence of a welfare culture on Canada's reserves. She argues that ill-advised government policy regarding reserve management, the inflexibility of the government policy structure, and local racism led to the failure of aboriginal efforts to create a new reserve-based economy. She suggests that only Native self-government and a just settlement of land claims will solve the problems created by the government policy.

Carter, Sarah A. *Lost Harvests: Prairie Indian Reserve Farmers and Government Policy.* Montreal: McGill-Queen's University Press, 1990.
Until recently, the history of Native peoples in the prairie provinces has focussed upon the fur trade or treaty-making period. Sarah Carter breaks from this tradition and produces an important and intriguing analysis of Native communities in the immediate post-treaty period. She attempts to dispel popular myths regarding the failure of Native agriculture in the Prairies. She notes that Native people made significant efforts to adapt agriculture but were blocked and thwarted by the Department of Indian Affairs. Carter argues that an incompetent federal bureaucracy promoted an agricultural policy built around the concepts of "peasant farming" and rejected Native efforts to establish commercially viable farms. Carter's analysis of government policy is based upon substantial archival records and government records. Her analysis is weakened, however, by her limited research into the nature of prairie agriculture in the late nineteenth century and her desire to cast government bureaucrats as villains.

56

Coates, Kenneth S. *Best Left as Indians: Native-White Relations in the Yukon Territory, 1870-1970.* Montreal: McGill-Queen's University Press, 1991.
Canadian Indian policy has vacillated between aggressive assimilation and benign neglect. In this book, Ken Coates carefully describes how this policy affected Natives in Canada's northern Yukon territory with special emphasis upon the role played by residential schools. Coates argues that the government at first attempted to educate and assimilate Native children by withdrawing them from their traditional communities and isolating them in residential schools. It quickly became apparent, however, that the process was expensive and less than effective. The government, consequently, decided that it was easier and cheaper to force Natives in the north to follow traditional lifestyle patterns. Natives, robbed of the traditional skills they would have learned as children and removed from the modern industrial world they learned in residential school, suffered rather than prospered.

Coates, Kenneth S., ed. *Aboriginal Land Claims in Canada: A Regional Perspective.* Toronto: Copp Clark, 1992.
One of the most important political issues in Canada today, aboriginal land claims are on the whole poorly understood. In this book, scholars familiar with the issues in each of Canada's six regions — British Columbia, the Prairies, Ontario, Quebec, Atlantic Canada, and the North — provide analytical introductory essays and a selection of documents that illustrate the issues involved in the land claims process. Together with the essays and documents on the Métis land claims and the Oka land claim crisis of 1990, this collection is a highly readable and informative introduction to this complex issue.

Cole, Douglas and Ira Chaikin. *An Iron Hand Upon the People: The Law Against the Potlatch on the Northwest Coast.* Vancouver: Douglas and McIntyre, 1990.
Cole and Chaikin explore the effort to eliminate the potlatch which acted, as one non-native contemporary noted, as "a huge incubus upon all the philanthropic, administrative or missionary effort for the improvement of the Indians." First introduced in 1884 (with subsequent amendments) the Potlatch law was only moderately "successful" in achieving its oppressive aims. Some tribes, such as the Kwakiutl and Gitksan, actively resisted the law (and, thus, exhibited some ability to control cultural change), judges and justices of the peace often were reluctant to prosecute offenders, and

merchants and the general public offered up little support for this measure. The potlatch festival flourished in the 1930s and the ban was eventually dropped in 1951.

Dickason, Olive P. and L. C. Green. *The Law of Nations and the New World*. Edmonton: University of Alberta Press, 1989.
A collaborative work by a historian and a lawyer, *Law of Nations* is a comparative analysis of the nature of aboriginal rights. Dickason relies upon theology, philosophy, and ancient Roman law to argue that Native self-government and title to the land exists in both a natural and divine sense. She points out that this perspective from ancient philosophy was slowly eroded by Christian imperative in order to justify imperial conquests. Green relies upon common law traditions to demonstrate that aboriginal rights only existed in so far as the Crown acknowledged these rights. Building his case upon enlightenment philosophy and legal precedent, Green argues that no sovereign right of governance exists in Native communities.

Diubaldo, Richard J. *The Government of Canada and the Inuit, 1900-1967*. Ottawa: Indian and Northern Affairs, 1985.
Prepared for the Department of Indian and Northern Affairs, this study examines the pattern of Inuit-government relations in Canada's Arctic. An experienced researcher and scholar of Canada's north, Diubaldo demonstrates his expertise throughout this publication. Although under contract to the government, Diubaldo does not hesitate to criticise government policy or the activities of missionaries and fur traders. He demonstrates an ongoing pattern of reaction to problems rather than planning on the part of the government.

Duffy, R. Quinn. *The Road to Nunavut: The Progress of the Arctic Inuit Since the Second World War*. Montreal: McGill-Queen's University Press, 1988.
Duffy tells the story of the 7,000 Inuit living in the eastern Arctic archipelago. He notes that the Inuit inhabit a region best described as a "lunar" landscape, and yet they have survived. More important, they have come to cherish their land. The book, however, is less the story of the Inuit than of government policy. Duffy notes that the federal and territorial governments played the role of parental guardian following World War II. They guided and instructed their Inuit children in the life skills necessary in the modern, technological world. As the Inuit matured,

they set out to control their own lives. Thus Nunavut, a new northern territory in which Inuit self-government appears to have been achieved, is the natural outcome of government policy over the last forty years.

Fumoleau, René. *As Long As This Land Shall Last: A History of Treaty 8 and 11 (1870-1939)*. Toronto: McClelland and Stewart, 1973.
Based upon both extensive archival and oral evidence, Fumoleau examines the context and content of Treaties 8 and 11. Although Treaty 11 was signed in 1921 (after years of discussion), Fumoleau discusses at length the years up to World War II, a period replete with discontent, broken government promises, and deceptions. Also see Richard Price, ed., *The Spirit of the Alberta Indian Treaties* (1979); and Treaty 7 Elders and Tribal Council with Walter Hildebrandt, Sarah Carter, and Dorothy First Rider, *The True Spirit and Original Intent of Treaty 7* (1996).

Getty, A. L. and Donald B. Smith, eds. *One Century Later: Western Canadian Reserve Indians Since Treaty 7*. Vancouver: University of British Columbia Press, 1978.
These essays from the Western Canadian Studies Conference all demonstrate the growing importance of understanding Native peoples as active historical agents. The collection begins with an excellent essay by A. J. Ray, "Fur Trade History as an Agent of Native History," and all the other essays concentrate on the actions of aboriginal people after 1870. Native control of art and education and Native understanding of the political process are at the centre of the most interesting pieces.

Hodgins, Bruce W. and Jamie Benidickson. *The Temagami Experience: Recreation, Resources, and Aboriginal Rights in the Northern Ontario Wilderness*. Toronto: University of Toronto Press, 1989.
In light of an important decision in Ontario courts regarding aboriginal rights to land and resources, Hodgins and Benidickson examine the issue of sustainable development in the Temagami region of northern Ontario. Their work illustrates the complexity of resource development in an important wilderness preserve, and examines connections and tensions between traditional aboriginal resource usage, concepts of scientific forest management, the logging industry, and modern environmental concerns.

Knight, Rolf. *Indians at Work: An Informal History of Native Indian Labour in British Columbia 1858-1930*. Vancouver: New Star Books, 1978; 2nd ed., 1996.

This work offers an important corrective to the myth that Natives participated minimally in British Columbia's developing resource economy following the demise of the dominant position they held in the fur trade. Instead Knight, in challenging Robin Fisher's *Contact and Conflict* (1977), argues that during the period from the onset of the gold rush to the Great Depression, Natives were employed in both domestic subsistence production and commercial or industrial activities. While Knight argues that the economic life of Natives was constantly under attack from non-native inhabitants and provincial authorities, he concludes that the Great Depression was fatal, particularly in jobs involving wage labour and in entrepreneurial activities.

Miller, Christine and Patricia Churchryk, with Marie Smallface Marule, Brenda Manyfingers, and Cheryl Deering, eds. *Women of the First Nations: Power, Wisdom, and Strength*. Winnipeg: University of Manitoba Press, 1996.
This collection of essays addresses the multiple roles and identities of Native women. *Women of the First Nations* is marked by the diversity of material it contains. Four of the thirteen essays are prepared by First Nations women, and other contributors include academics from history, anthropology, women's studies, and Native studies, as well as community workers. There is an excellent bibliography.

Miller, J. R. *Shingwauk's Vision: A History of Native Residential Schools*. Toronto: University of Toronto Press, 1996.
Chief Shingwauk hoped that missionary education and skills would bring great benefit to the Ojibwa. Such was not the case. Recent years have seen accounts and recollections of horrific abuse at Native residential schools. Miller's comprehensive account of these institutions ranges from their beginnings in New France until their demise in the 1960s, and is divided into three general sections. First, Miller examines early ventures in New France and British North America, and the extension of schools into western Canada in the late nineteenth and early twentieth centuries. Second, Miller looks at the experience within the residential school, primarily in the twentieth century. Finally, utilising some Native accounts, he provides a historical and contemporary assessment of the schools.

Pettipas, Katherine. *Severing the Ties that Bind: Government Repression of Indigenous Religious Ceremonies on the Prairies*. Winnipeg: University of Manitoba Press, 1994.

Pettipas writes about the government's assimilationist policies and the response of the Plains Cree. Beginning in the treaty-making period, the Canadian government embarked upon a policy of repression. Clear expressions of this policy came laws banning the Potlatch and the Sun Dance, but Pettipas argues that such laws had much deeper roots. Pettipas demonstrates that government repression of Cree spirituality was an effort to destroy Cree culture; ironically, however, the policy had the long-term effect of strengthening the culture.

Tennant, Paul. *Aboriginal Peoples and Politics: The Indian Land Question in British Columbia, 1849-1989*. Vancouver: University of British Columbia Press, 1990.
Few Native peoples in British Columbia have signed treaties relinquishing aboriginal title to the land. As a result, British Columbia's courts and political process are dominated by aboriginal land claims. In this important book, Paul Tennant skilfully, if not always impartially, documents the issues involved and illustrates the political processes at work in British Columbia. He finds the origins of the land question in the policies of Governor James Douglas and demonstrates how these early policies placed Native people at the mercy of provincial authorities. The attitudes and fears behind the British Columbia government's refusal to acknowledge an aboriginal claim and its concurrent, yet contradictory belief, that law and practice have extinguished any aboriginal claims are placed front and centre in the text. Tennant, meanwhile, portrays demands for Native self-government as a historically justified position.

Titley, Brian. *A Narrow Vision: Duncan Campbell Scott and the Administration of Indian Affairs in Canada*. Vancouver: University of British Columbia Press, 1986.
Duncan Campbell Scott advanced through the bureaucracy of Indian Affairs to the post of Deputy-Superintendent General and helped to shape the administration of Canadian Indian policy for over thirty years. In this study of Scott and the Department of Indian Affairs, Titley ably demonstrates how Scott and government policy advocated both the need for economic development and an assimilationist philosophy.

Tough, Frank. *As Their Resources Fail: Native Peoples and the Economic History of Northern Manitoba, 1870-1930*. Vancouver: University of Vancouver Press, 1996.
Frank Tough provides a thorough and detailed study of Native and Métis

contributions to the economy of northern Manitoba between 1870 and the Depression. Building upon the tremendous volume of fur trade literature that discusses the adaptability of Native communities, Tough argues that Native and Métis people continued to adapt to new economic opportunities in the modern era. They moved into commercial fishing, transportation, and forestry and, consequently, played an important role in the economic transition of the region from fur trade hinterland to industrial hinterland. His neo-Marxist analysis suggests that the inherent nature of industrial capitalism provides an explanation for hinterland dependency. Tough carefully documents his work and illustrates his argument with numerous maps, figures, and tables.

Waldram, James B. *As Long as the River Run: Hydroelectric Development and Native Communities in Western Canada*. Winnipeg: University of Manitoba Press, 1988.
Hydroelectric development in northern Alberta and Saskatchewan during the 1970s altered stream flow and damaged the livelihoods of local native communities. Beginning with a brief review of the treaty making process, Waldram argues that the same intransigence shown by government toward unwilling Native participants in the treaty process appeared in the context of hydro development. Despite protests by Native communities and demands for compensation, politicians and public utility executives dammed the rivers and transformed the local environment.

Weaver, Sally. *Making Canadian Indian Policy: The Hidden Agenda 1968-1970*. Toronto: University of Toronto Press, 1981.
Anthropologist Sally Weaver skilfully documents the emergence of the federal government White Paper on Indian policy in 1969. This document, one of the most important policy initiatives attempted by the Liberal government of Pierre Trudeau during his first year in office, reflects the American Indian policy known as termination. Trudeau sought to close the Department of Indian Affairs, transfer responsibility for Native issues to the provincial governments, declare Native peoples citizens, and terminate special status for Native people. Native peoples, frustrated by the lack of consultation and furious at the decision to terminate special status, produced the Red Paper response and forced the government to back away from its policy. The White Paper became the inspiration for the Native nationalist movement in Canada, and, ironically, resulted in a "reaffirmation of a unique cultural heritage and identity."

Political History

The study of political history dominated Canadian scholarship for much of the first century following Confederation. Important historians such as Donald Creighton, W. L. Morton, J. M. S. Careless, and A. R. M. Lower all wrote national histories, largely based upon a political narrative. The writing of biography also reflected this approach. Roger Graham's *Arthur Meighen* (3 vols.,1960-1965) and especially Donald Creighton's *John A. Macdonald* (2 vols., 1951, 1955) were sympathetic and exhaustive studies of important political figures. Creighton's volumes, in particular, represented a nation-building approach to political biography and became the standard to which all biographies were compared. The emergence of limited identities scholarship has influenced the domination and writing of political history. Emphasis upon regionalism, for example, has led to a renewed interest in provincial politics: David Smith's *Prairie Liberalism* (1975), to cite one example, argues persuasively that Saskatchewan's provincial Liberals were not the same as their federal counterparts. Likewise, the emergence of the new social history and more sophisticated methodological approaches have made their mark: John English's superb biography of Lester Pearson ventures beyond the political narrative into Pearson's relationship with his wife and the influence of his Methodist faith; similarly, important contributions by Tina Loo, Allan Greer, Ian Radforth, and others have cast a more critical and theoretical eye upon the traditional subject matter of state formation.

General Works

Bothwell, Robert. *Canada and Quebec: One Country, Two Histories.*
  Vancouver: University of British Columbia, 1995.
Originally a series of radio broadcasts, *Canada and Quebec* has been reformatted into readable prose. Bothwell has interviewed a wide range of academics, journalists, and politicians and solicited opinions about relations between French- and English-speakers from the Conquest to the 1990s and the prelude to the second referendum. The views expressed are diverse, and provide a sense of the differing interpretations surrounding events such as the Conquest, the Quiet Revolution, and the Meech Lake

Accord. A 12-hour audio series entitled "The History of Canada and Quebec" is also available.

Brennan, J. William. *"Building the Co-operative Commonwealth":
    Essays on the Democratic Socialist Tradition in Canada*. Regina:
    Canadian Plains Research Centre, 1984.
A collection of essays to celebrate the fiftieth anniversary of the founding of the Co-operative Commonwealth Federation (CCF), *"Building the Co-operative Commonwealth"* is a useful addition to books on the left tradition in Canada. The essays reflect the variety of themes and issues addressed by the CCF including pacifism, women's rights, social welfare, co-operatives, and private versus public ownership of industrial production. Together the essays challenge the "protest movement becalmed" theory that suggests that the CCF shed its ideological perspectives in a pragmatic search for political power.

Buckner, Phillip A. *The Transition to Responsible Government: British
    Policy in British North America, 1815-1850*. Westport, CT:
    Greenwood Press, 1985.
Between 1846 and 1850, the British North American colonies instituted responsible (or cabinet) government. In this system, the executive council, with the support of the legislative branch, formulated policy, the legislature voiced its approval or disapproval, and the governor enacted those policies approved. It was a transition from an older government system in which the governor took advice from an executive council dominated by local elites, and used the legislative branch to raise money. The first monograph study of the subject in nearly 50 years, *The Transition to Responsible Government* examines the initiatives leading to this transition. He argues that the transition was neither inevitable nor inconceivable in 1815. The transition to responsible government came about because of the increasing complexity of governing the colonies as populations increased and local elites became more difficult to manage.

Careless, Anthony G. S. *Initiative and Response: The Adaptation of
    Canadian Federalism to Regional Economic Development*. Montreal:
    McGill-Queen's University Press, 1977.
Anthony Careless examines the federal government's efforts to inspire regional economic development through programs like the Agricultural and Rural Development Act. Careless relies upon extensive interviews with ex-officials to explain the failure of this program to alleviate rural

poverty and regional inequities in Canada. This book has been harshly criticised.

Cook, Ramsay. *Canada, Quebec, and the Uses of Nationalism.* Toronto: McClelland and Stewart, 1986.
The ruminations of one of Canada's most important historians, this collection of essays explores — with a critical eye — various aspects of nationalism. Although Cook begins with the nationalism of the Europeans who "discovered" North America, most essays focus on the uses of nationalism over the last few decades in Quebec and Canada.

Dyck, Rand. *Provincial Politics in Canada.* Scarborough, ON: Prentice-Hall, 1986.
This work is a useful survey of provincial politics, and, while recognizing regional uniqueness, offers an explicitly comparative perspective. Much of the material presented is contemporary in nature, but there is substantial emphasis on the political history of each province.

Ferguson, Barry. *Remaking Liberalism: The Intellectual Legacy of Adam Shortt, O. D. Skelton, W. C. Clark, and W. A. Mackintosh, 1890-1925.* Montreal: McGill-Queen's University Press, 1993.
Ferguson examines the ideas of four Queen's political economists and their place in the intellectual and political climate of early twentieth-century Canada. *Remaking Liberalism* challenges the notion that social and political reform drew primarily from the idealist creed and the social gospel, and that Canadian liberalism lacked intellectual rigour and did not influence the evolution of social democracy. Ferguson traces the influence of the British and American debate of political economy on the "Queensians," and the evolution of their ideas toward the leading issues of their times — industrialism, agrarian expansion, the imperial question, wartime crises, constitutional status, and political and administrative reform.

Forbes, H. D., ed. *Canadian Political Thought.* Toronto: Oxford University Press, 1985.
This anthology of primary material provides an introduction to Canadian political thought. Chronologically, the selections range from 1799 to 1979, and Forbes emphasises the themes of nationalism and authority in both French- and English-Canada. This volume informally acts as a companion to Ramsay Cook's *French-Canadian Nationalism* (1969).

Kent, Tom. *A Public Purpose: An Experience of Liberal Opposition and Canadian Government*. Montreal: McGill-Queen's University Press, 1988.

A Liberal party insider during the Pearson era, Tom Kent has written a critical, left-nationalist critique of Pearson's political strategies. Kent argues that Pearson's government had the opportunity to reshape Canadian politics and society following the 1963 election but failed to accept or promote the budget and policies of Guy Favreau, Walter Gordon, Tom Kent, and Judy LeMarsh. Economic policy, notes Kent, should have been social policy. Pearson, however, lacked the moral courage to pursue this policy and, as a result, the opportunity was lost.

Miller, J. R. *Equal Rights: The Jesuits' Estates Act Controversy*. Montreal: McGill-Queen's University Press, 1979.

Passed by the Quebec legislature in 1888, the Jesuits' Estates Settlement Act compensated the Jesuit order for confiscation of property by Britain following the Conquest. The passage of the act spurred the rise of the Equal Rights Association, an organization dedicated to defending Canada from supposed Catholic aggression, and to opposing French and Catholic school rights outside of Quebec. *Equal Rights* examines the origins and nature of this particular piece of legislation, and places it within the larger context of English-French relations.

Robin, Martin, ed. *Canadian Provincial Politics: The Party Systems of the Ten Provinces*. Scarborough, ON: Prentice-Hall, 1972; 2nd ed., 1978.

With the exception of the chapter on Ontario, all essays in this volume have been extensively revised. *Canadian Provincial Politics* provides a brief survey of the political history and structure of each province.

Stevenson, Garth. *Ex Uno Plures: Federal-Provincial Relations in Canada, 1867-1896*. Montreal: McGill-Queen's University Press, 1994.

Strongly grounded in primary source material, *Ex Uno Plures* examines Canadian federalism during its formative years. Avoiding political theory and concentrating upon "political practices and especially on political disputes," Stevenson examines the balancing act between federal and provincial spheres of influence that was enshrined in the British North American Act, and the institutions and issues between the federal government and each province. Stevenson revises earlier interpretations that claim provincial rights emerged from the decisions of the courts.

Stewart, Gordon T. *The Origins of Canadian Politics: A Comparative*
    Approach. Vancouver: University of British Columbia Press, 1986.
Drawing upon the work of Bernard Bailyn and others, this skilfully crafted
volume argues for the lasting importance of the Constitutional Act of 1791
and the political developments that followed up to the 1850s. The
Constitutional Act established a strong executive that had broad patronage
powers; this contrasted to the independent legislature of the United States,
and to both the United States and Britain, where patronage was less
systematic. Stewart explores the crucial role of patronage in John A.
Macdonald's government and argues that it was an important factor in
creating an stable political system in a young country.

Verney, Douglas. *Three Civilizations, Two Cultures, One State.* Durham,
    NC: Duke University Press, 1986.
Upon reading George Grant's *Lament for a Nation* (1965), the historian
Charles Stacey reportedly concluded that it was full of "pure hate" against
the Americans. Grant, of course, feared the Americanization of Canada,
and — at different points in his life — saw it as inevitable. Verney tends
to disagree with the Canadian philosopher. Instead, he argues that French,
British, and American civilizations have each left a different residue in
both Canada's cultural identity and its constitutional evolution. Canadian
federalism emerged out of the needs of the French and British, and sought
stability in its imperial ties. With independence from the British Empire,
Verney argues that Canada needs to establish a purer constitutional
federalism.

State Formation and Confederation

Ajzenstat, Janet. *The Politics of Lord Durham.* Montreal: McGill-Queen's
    University Press, 1988.
Canadian historians often divide on Lord Durham and his (in)famous
Report (1839): French-Canadian historians sometimes see him as an
oppressor who urged assimilation for the greater happiness of
francophones; in contrast, some English-Canadian historians such as J. M.
S. Careless emphasise the notion of responsible government that emerged
out of Durham's recommendations. Ajzenstat places Durham in the
context of nineteenth-century liberal thought — particularly alongside
Alex de Tocqueville — and thoroughly examines his political philosophy.
Durham's advocacy of anglification for Lower Canada is not seen as
racist, but essential so that francophones could enjoy the rights and

freedoms that a liberal society held. Ajzenstat's intelligent analysis provides a unique perspective and helps to resurrect the reputation of both Durham and his *Report.*

Greer, Allan and Ian Radforth, eds. *Colonial Leviathan: State Formation in Mid-Nineteenth-Century Canada.* Toronto: University of Toronto Press, 1992.

Traditionally, Canadian historians have viewed the birth of responsible government and, later, the national vision of Confederation as, in some way, a process in which government was becoming responsible to the people. However, instead of celebrating the emergence of state apparatus and a hegemonic authority, the contributors to this volume — generally drawing from the theoretical work of P. Corrigan and D. Sayer's *The Great Arch: English State Formation as Cultural Revolution* (1985) — critically examine the process of state formation or, in other words, that process by which authority became pervasive and efficacious in society. Focusing upon British North America, individual essays examine state responses to insurrection, the role of the state in education, law, and economic matters, and the process of gender formation. Graeme Wynn concludes this exploratory volume with a more general examination of the role of the state and ideology in the three Maritime colonies. Wynn concludes that while the state grew more powerful in the nineteenth century, there were finite limits to its ability to organize the colonial landscape. Readers interested in a more extended argument of the role of the state in education should consult the insightful work of Bruce Curtis.

Loo, Tina. *Making Law, Order, and Authority in British Columbia, 1821- 1871.* Toronto: University of Toronto Press, 1994.

Drawing extensively upon legal history and post-structuralist theory, Loo analyses the process of state formation in nineteenth-century British Columbia. Through a select series of episodes, *Making Law* argues that during the gold rush and post-gold rush eras the monopolistic tendencies of the Hudson's Bay Company were replaced by classical or laissez-faire liberalism that emphasised free trade and individualism. The discourse between the state and its enfranchised citizens emphasised liberal notions about the individual, the economy, the law, and the state. Such developments, of course, had severe implications for British Columbia's Native population and Loo draws upon several incidents directly involving these groups to illustrate her thesis.

Martin, Ged. *Britain and the Origins of Confederation.* Vancouver:
University of British Columbia Press, 1995.
More than any other active historian, Ged Martin has sought to
reinvigorate and re-examine the issue of Confederation. *Britain and the
Origins of Confederation* places this central Canadian political event in an
Imperial context. Martin argues that in the three decades prior to
Confederation, "the British came to favour the eventual creation of a union
of British North America." In developing this thesis, Martin challenges
several common historical assumptions: that the union of 1841 was an
abject failure that had to be recast in the 1860s; that Confederation
inevitably occurred because it was the "right answer" for the economic,
political, and military challenges of the day; and that British economic
pressure and the threat of removing Imperial defenses were the trump card
against Maritime resistence. Instead Martin argues that Confederation was
an idea that had its pre-history and found its support in a British context.

Martin, Ged, ed. *The Causes of Canadian Confederation.* Fredericton:
Acadiensis Press, 1990.
Based upon a seminar organized by the Centre of Canadian Studies at
Edinburgh University, this collection of essays aims to reinvigorate
academic debate regarding Confederation. Traditional interpretations,
especially those by Donald Creighton, W. L. Morton, and P. B. Waite,
established a consensus in which Confederation "neatly solved all the
problems confronting British North America." Most of the papers in this
collection argue that Confederation was not an inevitable response and—
in contrast to laurentian history which emphasise Central Canada — they
explore the responses of the Atlantic region to political union. Several
authors also argue for the distinction between ideas of a union and the
actual terms of the union that emerged out of Charlottetown and Quebec
in 1864. Phillip Buckner's excellent essay provides a re-evaluation of the
historiography of Confederation; this essay also appeared in the *Canadian
Historical Review* (1990) where P. B. Waite and William M. Baker
provide a critique of his assessment. For older accounts of Confederation,
see W. L. Morton, *The Critical Years: The Union of British North
America, 1857-1873* (1964); Frank Underhill, *The Image of
Confederation* (1964); and P. B. Waite, *The Life and Times of
Confederation, 1864-1867* (1962). The classic study of one of the fathers
of Confederation and Canada's first prime minister remains Donald
Creighton, *John A. Macdonald* (2 vols.,1951, 1955).

Silver, A. I. *The French-Canadian Idea of Confederation, 1864-1900.*
   Toronto: University of Toronto Press, 1982.
At the time of Confederation, there were about a million people of French
origin in British North America, 85 per cent of whom lived in what is now
Quebec. At that time Quebeckers supported Confederation because it
separated Quebec from Ontario, and were concerned primarily with the
establishment of their culture and nationality only within their province.
In the last quarter of the nineteenth century, however, events such as the
hanging of Louis Riel, the Manitoba schools question, and the demand for
minority rights within Quebec when they did not seem to be respected in
the rest of Canada, fueled French-Canadian nationalism and a new concern
for francophones in other provinces. By 1900 Silver argues that
Quebeckers were committed to French-Canadian rights both inside and
outside of Quebec, and saw the maintenance of such rights as an essential
component of Confederation.

Post-Confederation National Politics

Avakumovic, Ivan. *The Communist Party in Canada: A History.* Toronto:
   McClelland and Stewart, 1975.
This work examines the Communist Party of Canada (CPC) from its
origins in the post-World War I era to the 1970s. Avakumovic provides an
intelligent narrative of the rise of the CPC to relative popularity in the
1930s, the relationship of the CPC to labour organizations and ethnic
groups, the interference by Russian and American officials in the Canadian
organ, and the crisis caused by Krushchev's de-Stalinization policy. This
work also provides some insight into Tim Buck's leadership of the CPC,
and in the persistent failure of the CPC to attract more support from
mainstream parties such as the CCF or, later, the NDP.

Bliss, Michael. *Right Honourable Men: The Descent of Canadian Politics
   from Macdonald to Mulroney.* Toronto: HarperCollins, 1994.
This collective biography examines ten prime ministers from John A.
Macdonald to Brian Mulroney. Well-written and brimming with anecdotes
and analysis, *Right Honourable Men* examines the descent of Canadian
politics from its focus on parliament and the leader, to its contemporary
form in which the masses exercise profound political power. Significantly,
Bliss argues that as this process has evolved, the public has raised its
expectations of its leaders. When leaders fail — as Brian Mulroney was
seen to have done in 1993 — their political party is dealt with harshly.

Right Honourable Men is a significant improvement upon similar — but more narrative — works such as Christopher Ondaatje and Donald Swainson's *The Prime Ministers of Canada* (1975) and Gordon Donaldson's *The Prime Ministers of Canada* (1994). Bliss concludes with a useful summary of (largely) secondary sources for each of the prime ministers he examines.

Brown, Robert Craig. *Robert Laird Borden: A Biography. Volume I: 1854-1914*. Toronto: Macmillan, 1975.
_____. *Robert Laird Borden: A Biography. Volume II: 1914-1937*. Toronto: Macmillan, 1980.
The principal study of Canada's eighth prime minister, these volumes provide an effective summary of Borden's public policies and attitudes, particularly over the first two decades of the twentieth century when he was leader of the Conservative party and prime minister (1911-1919). Brown is a recognized authority on this period and he provides an insightful analysis of events and issues such as railway policy, the Autonomy bills, reciprocity, the naval question, imperial relations, conscription, and the Unionist coalition. Brown also explores the links between Borden's nationalism and imperialism.

Clarkson, Stephen and Christina McCall. *Trudeau and Our Times. Volume I: The Magnificent Obsession*. Toronto: McClelland and Stewart, 1990.
_____. *Trudeau and Our Times. Volume II: The Heroic Delusion*. Toronto: McClelland and Stewart, 1994.
Pierre Trudeau occupies a central place in the national consciousness of contemporary Canada. These well-written volumes were published to popular acclaim and aim to provide a socio-cultural and intellectual history of both Trudeau and the country he was prime minister of for almost two decades. Though sometimes pre-occupied with a flimsy application of Jungian theory, the initial volume concentrates upon Trudeau's early life and career, and the emergence of his constitutional philosophy and polity; the second volume focuses upon his dramatic return to power in 1981 and his advocacy of modern liberalism. The authors have researched widely, interviewed hundreds of relevant individuals, and produced a highly readable — although too sympathetic some might argue — biography. For the Trudeau government's own vision of a just society, see Thomas S. Axworthy and Pierre Elliot Trudeau, eds. *Towards a Just Society: The Trudeau Years* (1990), especially Trudeau's concluding

essay. Some of Trudeau's own writings include his disappointing *Memoirs* (1993), and *Against the Current: Selected Writings, 1939-1996* (1996).

Cook, Ramsay. *The Maple Leaf Forever: Essays on Nationalism and Politics in Canada.* Toronto: Macmillan, 1971; 2nd ed., 1977.
These important essays explore various currents of nationalism. Informed by European historiography, Cook argues for a distinction between the nation-state and the nationalist-state, and — contrary to popular opinion — maintains that both English and French-speaking Canada have been victims of too much nationalism, rather than too little. The second edition includes an appraisal of the election of the Parti Québécois in 1976.

Cornellier, Manon. *The Bloc.* Trans. Robert Chodos, Simon Horn, and Wanda Taylor. Toronto: James Lorimer, 1995.
While this study of the Bloc Québécois — Canada's official opposition between 1993 and 1996 — logically emphasises the personality of Lucien Bouchard, it also sees the Bloc as a culmination of the past decades of the sovereignty movement. For a fuller study of Bouchard see, Lawrence Martin, *The Antagonist: Lucien Bouchard and the Politics of Delusion.* (1997)

Dawson, R. MacGregor. *William Lyon Mackenzie King. Volume I: A Political Biography, 1874-1923.* London: University of Toronto Press, 1958.
Neatby, H. Blair. *William Lyon Mackenzie King. Volume II: The Lonely Heights, 1924-1932.* London: University of Toronto Press, 1963.
_____. *William Lyon Mackenzie King. Volume III: The Prism of Unity, 1932-1939.* Toronto: University of Toronto Press, 1976.
These volumes form the official, although not comprehensive, biography of William Lyon Mackenzie King. The two volumes by Neatby, in particular, are effective surveys of King's political career, and provide insight into King's sometimes vague and imprecise political philosophy. Neatby's volumes also provide a valuable introduction to the policies of R. B. Bennett's government. See C.P. Stacey's *A Very Double Life: The Private World of Mackenzie King* (1976) for a sensational examination. Joy Esberey's *Knight of the Holy Spirit: A Study of W.L. Mackenzie King* (1980), is a poor attempt at psychohistory. Portions of King's famous diary are found in J. W. Pickersgill and Donald Forster, eds., *The Mackenzie King Record* (4 vols.).

English, John. *Shadow of Heaven: The Life of Lester Pearson, I*. Toronto:
     Lester & Orpen Dennys, 1989.
_____. *The Worldly Years: The Life of Lester Pearson, II*. Toronto:
     Alfred Knopf, 1992.
Well-written and intelligently argued, these two volumes exemplify
political biography at its best. The first volume covers Pearson's early life
and his emergence as a key member of the Department of External Affairs
and as a top diplomat, while the second volume is more concerned with his
political career. These volumes are not, however, only political in their
orientation; rather, English aims to place Pearson within broader social,
intellectual, and political contexts. For example, at a time when Canadian
society was becoming more secular, English traces Pearson from his strict
Methodist upbringing to someone who did not attend church, but denied
that he was an agnostic. In addition, English pays attention to Pearson's
family life, both as a young boy and as a married man. English does not
ignore the politician's spouse; instead, English details Maryon Pearson's
experience as one of the few university educated women of her era, and
how she was faced with the challenge of reconciling her education with
her role as wife and mother.

_____. *The Decline of Politics: The Conservatives and the Party
     System, 1901-20*. Toronto: University of Toronto Press, 1977.
Focusing on the first two decades of the twentieth century, English argues
the Canadian political system experienced a profound change during this
period: its nineteenth-century version was principally concerned with the
survival of the nation, had few other national goals, and found its "locus
of energy" primarily at the local level; this party system crumbled amid the
forces of industrialization, urbanization, and the corruption of patronage.
In contrast, by 1920 a more national party system had emerged. As leader
of an uncertain and transitional opposition in the early 1900s, Borden had
the opportunity to reconstruct the Conservative party in his own image.
The Halifax Platform (1907) — though it ultimately unraveled —
represented a vision of cleaner elections, progressive civil service reform,
and a broader national alliance of Quebec nationalists, imperialists,
progressives, and Conservative provincial premiers. English argues that
after Borden became prime minister he held to the ideals of a truly
national government. While World War I and, in 1917, the Union
government helped him to realize his aim, his coalition fell apart in the
post-World War I era.

Francis, R. Douglas. *Frank H. Underhill: Intellectual Provocateur.* Toronto: University of Toronto Press, 1986.
Frank Underhill was a central figure in the creation of the Co-operative Commonwealth Federation and the League for Social Reconstruction, a resident commentator for the *Canadian Forum*, and a prominent teacher and intellectual critic. Francis's biography provides a highly readable account of Underhill's life and career as an intellectual provocateur, and an insightful analysis of his commitment to liberal democracy.

Glassford, Larry A. *Reaction and Reform: The Politics of the Conservative Party under R. B. Bennett, 1927-1938.* Toronto: University of Toronto Press, 1992.
This work systematically explores the Conservative party under R. B. Bennett and provides an effective narrative of Bennett's leadership and government, and his attempts to adapt the party's "program, organization and image" to the needs of a modernizing Canada. In particular, Glassford provides an insightful account of Bennett's leadership victory in 1927, the electoral victory of the Conservatives in 1930, Bennett's "New Deal," and the internal factionalism that contributed to defeat in 1935. This work argues that under Bennett the Conservatives moved toward a more active, reform-minded government, a conclusion that is bound to be disputed by historians who see Bennett as the epitome of the sins of capitalism. For a sampling of the emotional outpouring of desperate Canadians to Bennett during the 1930s, see L. M. Grayson and Michael Bliss, eds., *The Wretched of Canada: Letters to R. B. Bennett, 1930-1935* (1973).

Granatstein, J. L. *The Ottawa Men: The Civil Service Mandarins, 1935-1957.* Toronto: Oxford University Press, 1982.
An excellent introduction to the personalities and policies of almost two dozen leading civil servants, *The Ottawa Men* argues that these men wielded enormous influence in federal government affairs from the Depression to the late 1950s. Granatstein's collective biography examines, among others, the careers of individuals such as O. D. Skelton, Loring Christie, and Lester Pearson in External Affairs, Mitchell Sharp in Finance, Gordon Towers at the Bank of Canada, and Jack Pickersgill at the Prime Minister's Office. The influence of the mandarins had waned by the late 1950s due to the retirement or death of several key individuals, the changing nature of government, and the election of a Conservative government after three decades of Liberal rule.

Gray, James H. *R. B. Bennett: The Calgary Years*. Toronto: University of
Toronto Press, 1991.
The first half of a projected two-volume biography of R. B. Bennett (there
is some hope that P. B. Waite will complete the project), *The Calgary
Years* provides a sympathetic account of Bennett's life and career up until
the time he became prime minister in 1930. Because some of Bennett's
correspondence was purged by himself and his secretary, there sometimes
are sketchy details regarding his familial relations. Gray emphasises
Bennett's lifelong attachment to his mother, his successful career as a
businessman and a lawyer, his strong imperialistic patriotism, and his early
career as a member of parliament and leader of the opposition.

Hall, D. J. *Clifford Sifton. Volume I: The Young Napoleon, 1861-1900*.
Vancouver: University of British Columbia Press, 1981.
_____. *Clifford Sifton. Volume II: A Lonely Eminence, 1901-1929*.
Vancouver: University of British Columbia Press, 1985.
Superior examples of traditional political biography, these meticulously
researched volumes provide enormous insight into the public life of
Clifford Sifton, perhaps the principal figure in shaping the modern prairie
landscape. Unfortunately, the papers of Sifton had been culled for personal
and business references by his family; thus, Hall focuses upon Sifton's
involvement in issues such as immigration, resource development, the
Manitoba School Question, the Crow's Nest Rate, the Alaska boundary
dispute, and extra-parliamentary efforts such as those involving reciprocity
and conscription.

Horn, Michiel. *The League for Social Reconstruction: Intellectual Origins
of the Democratic Left in Canada, 1930-1942*. Toronto: University of
Toronto Press, 1980.
The Depression of the 1930s produced a vigorous examination of the
existing capitalist system and the role of the state within it. Foremost
among the critics were a small group — including Frank Underhill, Frank
Scott, Eugene Forsey, Irene Bliss and Graham Spry — who established the
League for Social Reconstruction (LSR) in 1931-1932 and, for the next
decade, conducted an ill-defined and ultimately unsuccessful campaign to
encourage socialist ideals and practices. Though officially non-partisan,
members of the LSR were involved heavily with the CCF and instrumental
in writing the Regina Manifesto; in addition, they published critiques such
as *Social Planning for Canada* (1935) and *Democracy Needs Socialism*
(1938), and were instrumental in saving *The Canadian Forum*.

Mills, Allen. *Fool for Christ: The Political Thought of J. S. Woodsworth.* Toronto: University of Toronto Press, 1991.
J. S. Woodsworth has been perhaps the most common political choice for canonization within Canadian history: Grace MacInnes' *J. S. Woodsworth: A Man to Remember* (1953) was an extremely sympathetic portrayal of her father; and while Kenneth McNaught's *A Prophet in Politics* (1959) did not paint Woodsworth as a saint, it did emphasise his profound moralism. Mills seeks a more balanced account that explores the intellectual life of Woodsworth. For example, in his early career as a Methodist minister, Woodsworth's theological liberalism led him — in seeking to make the sacred relevant to a secular world — away from his faith. Thus, Mills tends to agree with the thesis that theological liberalism inevitably led toward secularization that has been put forth by the British historian Owen Chadwick and in Ramsay Cook's *The Regenerators* (1985). *Fool for Christ* draws attention to the inconsistencies of Woodsworth's life and provides insight into the intellectual formation of his views on economic and political issues, social reform, pacifism, and international affairs. For a full picture of Woodsworth's life, *Fool for Christ* should be read in conjunction with McNaught's earlier work.

Neatby, H. Blair. *Laurier and a Liberal Quebec: A Study in Political Management.* Toronto: McClelland and Stewart, 1973.
Henri Bourassa once stated that when Wilfrid Laurier arrived at the gates of heaven, the first thing he would do would be to propose an honourable compromise between God and Satan. Originally a 1950s doctoral dissertation, this well-argued study of Canada's first French-Canadian prime minister emphasises Laurier as a politician and the struggles he faced in the transition of his home province from a Conservative stronghold to a bastion of Liberal support. Thus, Neatby examines Laurier's delicate positioning on issues such as the hanging of Louis Riel, reciprocity, Manitoba Schools, and imperial concerns. Ultimately, Neatby argues that Bourassa's rigid position on Imperial relations, and issues such as minority school and language rights outside Quebec, helped to erode Laurier's political base and contributed to his defeat in 1911.

_____. *The Politics of Chaos: Canada in the Thirties.* Toronto: Macmillan, 1972.
Biographical in approach, *The Politics of Chaos* examines various responses to the Depression through the personalities of R. B. Bennett, William Lyon Mackenzie King, J. S. Woodsworth, Maurice Duplessis,

Mitch Hepburn, and William "Bible Bill" Aberhart. In addition, Neatby's extremely readable volume argues that the 1930s were particularly important in forging a national identity, promoting a new understanding of industrial society, and stimulating a more radical critique of the Canadian political system. Neatby also pays some attention to the personal impact of the Depression, and how the difficulties of the 1930s revealed splits between English- and French-Canada. For a readable and anecdotal survey of the 1930s, see Pierre Berton's *The Great Depression, 1929-1939* (1990). For a collection of primary material and brief portions of academic essays, see Michiel Horn, ed., *The Dirty Thirties: Canadians in the Great Depression* (1972).

Smith, David E. and Norman Ward. *Jimmy Gardiner: Relentless Liberal.*
   Toronto: University of Toronto Press, 1990.
Jimmy Gardiner was Premier of Saskatchewan from 1926 to 1929 and 1934 to 1935 before becoming one of the most powerful members of Mackenzie King's federal cabinet. Gardiner believed in free enterprise, small business, and made his primary objective the election of the Liberal party. Smith and Ward, while clearly impressed by Gardiner's political skills and his use of patronage, found little evidence of corruption.

Smith, Denis. *Rogue Tory: The Life and Legend of John G. Diefenbaker.*
   Toronto: Macfarlane Walter & Ross, 1995.
Well-written, *Rogue Tory* is the most comprehensive examination of Canada's 13th prime minister. Smith provides an extensive discussion of Diefenbaker's childhood, early career, and failed attempts to advance himself up the political ladder. The bulk of the work concerns his emergence as leader of the Conservative party, and his three terms as prime minister. Smith's account is more balanced than the harsh treatment Diefenbaker received in Peter C. Newman's important *Renegade in Power: The Diefenbaker Years* (1963; rpt., 1989): for example, Smith provides a favourable account of Diefenbaker's political philosophy of "One Canada," his success at broadening the base of the Conservative party, his attempts to ensure individual liberties, and his promotion of regional economic development. Smith is justifiably critical of the erratic leadership that Diefenbaker provided in his last years as leader and prime minister. *Rogue Tory* ends with an examination of Diefenbaker's presidential-like funeral in 1979, an event that revealed much of the personality of the Chief. For the usual self-serving memoir, see John Diefenbaker, *One Canada: Memoirs of the Right Honourable John G.*

Diefenbaker (3 vols., 1975). Also worth consulting is Basil Robinson, *Diefenbaker's World: A Populist in Foreign Affairs* (1989).

Trofimenkoff, Susan Mann. *Stanley Knowles: The Man from Winnipeg North Centre*. Saskatoon: Western Producer Prairie Books, 1982.
Based primarily on interviews with Stanley Knowles, this book is a sympathetic portrait of one of Canada's longest serving and most respected parliamentarians. Stanley Knowles was first elected to the House of Commons as the Cooperative Commonwealth Federation member from Winnipeg North Centre in 1944. He served the country from this post for nearly thirty-five years. Well informed and a relentless debater, Knowles promoted the concerns of the downtrodden, poor, unemployed, and elderly.

Wagner, Jonathan F. *Brothers Beyond the Sea: National Socialism in Canada*. Waterloo: Wilfrid Laurier University Press, 1981.
Brothers Beyond the Sea examines the relationship between the Nazi movement in Germany and the small number of German-Canadians who held similar views, most of whom resided in western Canada. Nazi sympathizers in Canada had little affinity with other fascist organizations, such as Adrien Arcand's National Socialist Christian Movement in Quebec; rather, they emphasised a racist and genetic definition of Germanness. Wagner examines the membership, organization, methods of propaganda, and eventual internment of over 800 Nazi sympathizers, most of whom were released prior to the end of the war.

Waite, P.B. *The Loner: Three Sketches of the Personal Life and Ideas of R. B. Bennett, 1870-1947*. Toronto: University of Toronto Press, 1992.
R. B. Bennett had the misfortune to govern Canada during some of the worst years of the Depression and, perhaps save for Brian Mulroney, has the worst reputation of any prime minister. Originally delivered as the 1991 Goodman Lectures, this slim volume examines three stages in Bennett's life: the influence of school, church, and family in his early years; his period as a Calgary businessman and Ottawa member of parliament during which he formulated his political beliefs; and, finally, his years as leader of the Conservative party and the important relationships with the women in his life. The focus is upon Bennett's personality rather than politics, and Waite creates a more sympathetic and human character than much of the mythology that has previously surrounded this man.

_____. *The Man from Halifax: Sir John Thompson, Prime Minister.*
Toronto: University of Toronto Press, 1985.
This is a comprehensive biography of Canada's fourth prime minister, who
enjoyed a rapid rise to political power but died in 1894 after only two
years in office. Waite provides significant insight into John Thompson's
personal life and strives to place this man within the context of his times.
Thompson emerges as an extraordinarily capable individual who was
confronted with difficult issues: upon entering cabinet in 1885 as minister
of justice, he was immediately faced with defending the Riel hanging;
likewise, the Manitoba School Question dogged the Conservatives in the
early 1890s. In spite of such difficult situations, Thompson established
Canada's criminal code in 1892, and his death deprived the Conservative
party of its most capable leader and set the stage for the Laurier victory in
1896. Waite also paints a compelling portrait of Thompson's wife, Annie
Affleck, who emerges as a key supporter and advisor.

Whitaker, Reginald. *The Government Party: Organizing and Financing
the Liberal Party of Canada, 1930-58.* Toronto: University of Toronto
Press, 1977.
Based upon an impressive array of primary source material, *The
Government Party* examines how the Liberal party raised money and
organized itself from 1930 when it was out of office, through to a period
of extended political success under Mackenzie King and Louis St.
Laurent. Whitaker examines the formation of the National Liberal
Federation in 1932 — an organization devoted to raising funds and
providing a national organizational structure — and its linkages to Liberal
governments. This work argues that these linkages varied enormously
from King to St. Laurent, and provides an important analysis of the rise of
a political bureaucracy, the close relationship between civil servants and
Liberal politicians, and the importance of external bodies in fundraising
and political advertising.

Young, Walter. *Democracy and Discontent: Progressivism, Socialism and
Social Credit in the Canadian West.* Toronto: McGraw-Hill Ryerson
Limited, 1969; 2nd ed., 1978.
A brief but useful survey of protest movements and parties in the Canadian
West, *Democracy and Discontent* naturally focuses upon the conditions
that led to the rise of the National Progressive Party, the Cooperative
Commonwealth Federation (CCF), and the Social Credit, and provides a
summary of the personalities and platforms of each party. The focus is on

the prairie provinces, though there are brief, and largely undeveloped, sections dealing with British Columbia. Young clearly empathizes with the plight of the ordinary citizen and the rise of the CCF; for example, the caption accompanying a photograph of R. B. Bennett proclaims that he was "too rich to understand the poor and too proud to admit it." Also see, Walter Young, *The Anatomy of a Party: The National CCF, 1932-61* (1969); and Ivan Avakumovic, *Socialism in Canada: A Study of the CCF-NDP in Federal and Provincial Politics* (1978).

The Welfare State

Banting, Keith G. *The Welfare State and Canadian Federalism*. Montreal: McGill-Queen's University Press, 1982.
In this well-researched and documented examination of the Canadian welfare state, Keith Banting argues that federalism and regional disparity have not affected the development of income security and redistribution in Canada. Programs designed to assist individuals such as family allowance, pensions, unemployment insurance, and welfare were far more important than regional assistance programs. Instead, Banting turns the relationship upside down and makes the case that the welfare state has changed the federal system and produced a more centralized bureaucracy and power structure.

Guest, Dennis. *The Emergence of Social Security in Canada*. Vancouver: University of British Columbia Press, 1980; rpt., 1995.
A useful survey of social security from colonial times to contemporary Canada, this volume explores the changing nature of the "welfare state." In particular, Guest examines the tension between the residual concept — which emphasised the Protestant work ethic and private relief — and the institutional concept, which has been increasingly influential since World War II.

Moscovitch, Allan and Jim Albert, eds. *The Benevolent State: The Growth of Welfare in Canada*. Toronto: Garamond Press, 1987.
The fifteen essays in this collection are sympathetic to the concept of a welfare state, and yet critical of the Canadian experience. Together they suggest that the Canadian welfare state is a haphazard creation unable to fulfill the idealistic goals of welfare proponents. This collection examines themes such as the conservative goals of social reformers, corporate welfare strategies, the role of women in welfare reform, and the

emergence of health insurance. Also see Raymond B. Blake and Jeff
Keshen eds., *Social Welfare Policy in Canada: Historical Readings*
(1995).

Naylor, C. David. *Private Practice, Public Payment: Canadian Medicine
    and the Politics of Health Insurance, 1911-1966.* Montreal: McGill-
    Queen's University Press, 1986.
This comprehensive survey argues that doctors viewed the issue of health
insurance through the lens of the professional, and consistently defended
their status as independent entrepreneurial providers of medical care. As
a result, doctors fought to control the publicly funded system, and their
ability to organize effective lobby groups defined the political debates
surrounding health insurance. Naylor's emphasis on the role of the
Canadian Medical Association and other professional associations, is a
useful complement to the bureaucratic and political emphasis found in
Malcolm Taylor's *Health Insurance and Canadian Public Policy* (1978).

Owram, Doug. *The Government Generation: Canadian Intellectuals and
    the State, 1900-1945.* Toronto: University of Toronto Press, 1986.
This important analysis — described by Owram as a mid-range synthesis,
that is, somewhere between a general overview and a specialized
monograph — discusses Canadian intellectuals and the growth of an
activist state in the first half of the twentieth century. Based upon a
prodigious amount of secondary and primary research, Owram defines
three general stages in the relationship between the intellectual and state
reform. Between the turn of the century and the onset of World War I, he
argues that the problems associated with urbanization and industrialization
spurred efforts at moral reform, principally through movements such as the
social gospel movement; in addition, this period saw the introduction of
the university community as a participant in the reform cause. The 1920s
saw the rise of the professional expert, most often in the form of social
scientists such as R. M. MacIver, O. D. Skelton, Norman Robertson, F. R.
Scott, and a host of others of almost all political persuasions, who rejected
the imperative of moral reform and, instead, were committed to the
governmental process in social reconstruction. This group matured in the
1930s and during World War II there emerged an intellectual elite
committed to Keynesian economics and an active interventionist state. By
1945 the wages of the civil service sector alone were five time as great as
the total Dominion budget in 1896. *The Government Generation* is a
valuable volume for intellectual historians and those interested in the

development of public policy. For a view that challenges Owram's claim that social reform disintegrated in the 1920s, see Nancy Christie and Michael Gauvreau's *A Full-Orbed Christianity: The Protestant Churches and Social Welfare in Canada, 1900-1940* (1996).

Snell, James G. *The Citizen's Wage: The State and the Elderly in Canada, 1900-1951*. Toronto: University of Toronto Press, 1996.

The current attack on entitlement clearly and rightly troubles those on old age pensions, who often present themselves (and are seen by others) as the pioneers of contemporary society. Snell examines the first half of the twentieth century — the period during which a "citizen's wage" in the form of an old age pension was established — and "discusses the ways in which old people's and society's appraisal of aging and the aged changed." He argues that perceptions of the elderly were fundamental to state assistance programs for that segment of the population: under Victorian poor laws, for example, old age was not automatically a criterion for receiving assistance, because "old age was not yet socially constructed in such a way that it was automatically associated with dependency." In addition, changing perceptions of the state were crucial in developing formal support for the elderly. Snell examines the emergence of state-sponsored residential institutions, formal and informal sources of support, and the way the elderly and other interests were able to shape entitlements. Snell concludes that the 1951 Old Age Security Act was the logical result of a long-term process.

_____. *In the Shadow of the Law: Divorce in Canada, 1900-1939*. Toronto: University of Toronto Press, 1991.

E. P. Thompson's study of the Black Act in eighteenth-century Britain argued that the law was not an impartial process, but rather an area in which contending social forces struggled for power. Similarly, Snell's study argues that the political, intellectual, and social climate in Canada inhibited divorce reform, as well as more liberal changes involving abortion, homosexual activities, and the dissemination of birth control. In general, divorce laws in Canada changed little from 1857 to 1968; formal divorce was relatively uncommon at the beginning of the twentieth century with only 11 recorded in 1900, while over 2300 were granted by 1939. Snell argues this increase in people turning to the state for divorce reflects the greater pressures and expectations on marriage,a diminution of the legitimacy of informal divorce, and a rise in perceived authority of the state. While state control may well have been weakening, the role of the state in familial matters was rising. In Quebec the response was much different from that of English Canada, and the number of judicial separations declined between 1900 and 1939.

Struthers, James. *No Fault of Their Own: Unemployment and the Canadian Welfare State, 1914-1941.* Toronto: University of Toronto Press, 1983.
Canadians who take pride in the state's altruistic support for the unemployed would do well to read this impressive study. Federal authorities used constitutional arguments and drew upon a nineteenth-century *laissez-faire* ideology in arguing that care for the unemployed was either the responsibility of municipalities and provinces, or the responsibility of the individual alone. Added to those beliefs was the perception that Canada was a rural, agrarian nation, and that the unemployed could easily seek work on farms. Struthers traces the causes and levels of unemployment, and the government's response over the course of almost three decades. He concludes that it was the exigencies of the Depression and, especially, World War II that moved the federal government to enact the Unemployment Insurance Act of 1941. Also see Struthers' *The Limits of Affluence: Welfare in Ontario, 1920-1970* (1994).

Taylor, Malcolm G. *Health Insurance and Canadian Public Policy: The Seven Decisions That Created the Canadian Health Insurance System.* Montreal: McGill-Queen's University Press, 1978.
This book remains the most thoroughly researched and documented study of the Canadian system of health insurance. The focus of the book is on the politics and administrative decisions since World War II that led to the creation of a publically funded system of medical and hospital care. Taylor discusses Saskatchewan's innovative decision to create a provincial hospital insurance scheme in 1947, the expansion of public funding to medical care in 1961, and also explores the policy decisions made by Ontario in the mid-1950s that forced the federal government to become involved in health insurance and to accept the recommendations of the Hall Commission in the 1960s.

Wills, Gale. *A Marriage of Convenience: Business and Social Work in Toronto, 1918-1957.* Toronto: University of Toronto Press, 1995.
In 1918 the Federation for Community Service (FCS) was established in Toronto by social workers and their financial supporters in the business community in order to breathe efficiency and standards of professional

practise into local charities. These two bodies often had vastly different interests and conflict emerged quickly and often. Social workers were rarely entirely free from the desires of big business; in 1957 the Social Planning Council was established by social workers to be separate from the FCS, but was quickly co-opted by business interests. Wills examines the ideological roots of social work in Christian moral reform and nineteenth-century utilitarian thought, the contradictions between those who practiced social work and those who administrated its finances, and the gendered nature of the social work community. Wills argues that as social work shifted from a volunteer activity to a paid position, the profession moved from one controlled by the female workers themselves to a male-dominated, hierarchical, and paternalistic structure. The professionalization of social workers, therefore, did not bring greater legitimacy and influence to the vast majority of its workers.

State Security and Law

Brown, Desmond H. *The Canadian Criminal Code of 1892*. Toronto: Osgoode Society and University of Toronto Press, 1989.
Canada was the first Dominion in the British Empire to codify its criminal law. Desmond Brown effectively and methodically examines the genesis of the criminal code. The book outlines British legal theory, early development of the British North American legal system, and changes in the British legal system in the late nineteenth century. Brown concludes that the most significant aspect of the criminal code was that Parliament, rather than the courts, became central to the development of law.

Carrigan, Owen. *Crime and Punishment in Canada: A History*. Toronto: McClelland & Stewart, 1991.
The first general history of crime and punishment, this volume explores specific themes — white-collar crime, juvenile delinquency, and the treatment of female offenders, for example — from the colonial era to contemporary Canada. This volume has been sharply criticized for its factual errors and unsupported interpretations.

Flaherty, David H., ed. *Essays in the History of Canadian Law. Volume I*. Toronto: University of Toronto Press, 1981.
_____, ed. *Essays in the History of Canadian Law. Volume II*. Toronto: University of Toronto Press, 1983.
Girard, Philip and Jim Phillips, eds. *Essays in the History of Canadian*

Law. Volume III: Nova Scotia. Toronto: University of Toronto Press, 1990.

Wilton, Carol, ed. *Essays in the History of Canadian Law. Volume IV: Beyond the Law, Lawyers and Business in Canada, 1830-1930.* Toronto: University of Toronto Press, 1990.

Phillips, Jim, Tina Loo and Susan Lewthwaite, eds. *Essays in the History of Canadian Law. Volume V: Crime and Criminal Justice.* Toronto: University of Toronto Press, 1994.

Foster, Hamar and John McLaren, eds. *Essays in the History of Canadian Law. Volume VI: British Columbia and the Yukon.* Toronto: University of Toronto Press, 1995.

Published with the support of The Osgoode Society and other legal organizations, these volumes contain some of the most current and innovative articles on Canadian legal history. Reflecting the new legal history, most articles are distinctly interdisciplinary and integrate legal matters within larger political and social contexts.

Friedland, Martin L. *A Century of Criminal Justice: Perspectives on the Development of Canadian Law.* Toronto: Carswell, 1984.

Martin Friedland is a lawyer and an important legal scholar; this book brings together eight essays in which he emphasises the development of Canadian law. The essays examine the creation of a criminal code, the impact of key cases upon the interpretation of the criminal code, the origins and implementation of the Official Secrets Act and the War Measures Act, the role of pressure groups in drafting the criminal code, and the constitutional dimensions of criminal law.

Gibson, Dale and W. Wesley Pue, eds. *Glimpses of Canadian Legal History.* Winnipeg: Legal Research Institute of Manitoba, 1991.

This eclectic collection focuses on the period to 1930 and illustrates how British legal traditions had difficulty adapting to the peculiar circumstances of Canadian culture and society; in addition, several essays focus on the relationship between social structures and the law.

Hannant, Larry. *The Infernal Machine: Investigating the Loyalty of Canada's Citizens.* Toronto: University of Toronto Press, 1995.

The prevailing view by scholars as ideologically diverse as Reg Whitaker and Larry Aronson argues that the Canadian state introduced security screening in 1946, and only then under enormous duress. Hannant pushes that date back to the 1920s and the investigation of naturalization applicants, and to 1931 when the systematic screening of civil servants began. Hannant discusses the motives and methods for investigating citizens, the creation of a state security-screening system, intelligence connections between Canada, Britain, and the USA, technical innovations, and the reaction of Canadians to security screening.

Kealey, Gregory and Reg Whitaker, eds. *RCMP Security Bulletins: The Early Years*. 7 vols. St. John's: Canadian Committee on Labour History, 1989— .
In the early 1980s, shortly after the passage of the Access to Information Act, Greg Kealey submitted an access request for Royal Canadian Mounted Police *Security Bulletins* that had been removed from public scrutiny. This ongoing project reproduces these bulletins — although the Canadian Security Intelligence Service has deleted some material — and provides insight into the RCMP's suspicions of supposedly subversive individuals, organizations, and groups for most years between the Winnipeg Strike and the end of World War II.

Keshen, Jeffrey A. *Propaganda and Censorship During Canada's Great War*. Edmonton: University of Alberta Press, 1996.
During World War I, the Canadian government armed itself with new regulatory and taxing powers, including vastly expanded authority in the area of official news management. Keshen explores the powerful nature of pre-war propaganda, the ardent and continuing patriotism of the press, and the legislative and *de facto* control of information by the government, both during and immediately after the war. Keshen provides an analysis of letters and diaries of soldiers, and briefly places the Canadian experience within an international context.

Knafla, Louis, ed. *Law and Justice in a New Land: Essays in Western Canadian Legal History*. Toronto: Carswell, 1986.
One of the few books devoted the legal history of western Canada, this collection of essays reflects the distinct concerns of legal historians in the West, particularly, disputes between the government and western Canadian Native peoples. Two essays are especially important: Thomas Flanagan's "From Indian Title to Aboriginal Rights" looks at the courts and Native land claims; and Douglas Sanders's "The Queen's Promises" examines the court interpretation of treaty rights. Other topics covered in this collection include the legal system of the Hudson's Bay Company, disputes over jurisdiction between the provincial and federal court

systems in British Columbia, and overviews of legal culture in the Canadian West.

Macleod, R. C. *The North-West Mounted Police and Law Enforcement, 1873-1905*. Toronto: University of Toronto Press, 1976.
Founded in 1873 and sent west to establish Canadian sovereignty and enforce Canadian law, the North-West Mounted Police hold an important place in Canada's cultural mythology. Macleod examines the "heroic era" of the police and concludes the Mounties were a fair and effective police force. He explores not only the role of the police in law enforcement and Indian administration, but also the important role of the police in social welfare, veterinary and medical service, administration of government programs, and in the accommodation of immigrants.

Macleod, R. C., ed. *Lawful Authority: Readings in the History of Criminal Justice in Canada*. Toronto: Copp Clark, 1988.
This collection of previously published essays is an excellent introduction to Canadian legal history, and examines topics examining the police, the courts, and the social history of the law in Canada. The book contains a good select bibliography. Also see Tina Loo and Lorna R. Mclean, eds., *Historical Perspectives on Law and Society in Canada* (1994).

McLaren, J., Hamar Foster, and Chet Orloff, eds. *Law for the Elephant, Law for the Beaver: Essays in the Legal History of the North American West*. Regina: Canadian Plains Research Centre, 1992.
The proceedings of a conference on Canadian and American legal history, this collection includes both comparative essays and essays examining a particular issue within either Canada or the United States. These essays examine topics such as the treatment of Chinese workers, the development of water law, and violence.

Scott, Frank R. *Essays on the Constitution: Aspects of Canadian Law and Politics*. Toronto: University of Toronto Press, 1977.
Frank Scott was both an academic and political activist. A leading scholar on constitutional history, he also wrote the Regina Manifesto, supported the CBC, advised the United Nations, and participated in the Royal Commission on Bilingualism and Biculturalism. This collection of 29 essays neatly summarizes his ideas regarding the Canadian constitution and the law. He argues in favour of a centralized, federal structure that recognizes the distinct position of French Canadians living in Quebec.

Snell, James G. and Frederick Vaughan. *The Supreme Court of Canada: History of the Institution*. Toronto: University of Toronto Press, 1985. Snell and Vaughan provide a critical institutional history of the Supreme Court's role in Canada prior to the implementation of the Charter of Rights. They argue that the Court pursued a conservative philosophy and lacked the activism of its counterpart in the United States. This conservatism reflected the Supreme Court's subservience to Parliament and its unwillingness to break from British traditions of precedence.

Swinfen, David B. *Imperial Appeal: The Debate on the Appeal to the Privy Council, 1833 - 1986*. Manchester: Manchester University Press, 1987.
The scope of *Imperial Appeal* extends beyond Canada to include Australia, South Africa, India, and other parts of the British Empire; however, since the Judicial Council of the Privy Council was the highest court of appeal in Canada until 1949, this book is a valuable source for Canadian legal historians. The decisions of the Judicial Council of the Privy Council, for example, have led to an increase in provincial authority, and to the concept of co-sovereignty of provinces and the federal government.

Weaver, John C. *Crimes, Constables, and Courts: Order and Transgression in a Canadian City, 1816-1970*. Montreal: McGill-Queen's University Press, 1995.
This thorough study surveys 150 years of law and criminal justice in Hamilton. Weaver notes changing pattern of criminal behaviour, the influence of technology on law and order, and the gradual centralization of the judicial system.

Whitaker, Reg and Gary Marcuse. *Cold War Canada: The Making of a National Insecurity State, 1945-1957*. Toronto: University of Toronto Press, 1994.
A natural companion to Larry Hannant's *The Infernal Machine* (1995), *Cold War Canada* explores state security during the Canadian equivalent of the McCarthy era. Whitaker and Marcuse document the security measures of the RCMP and government, provide excellent discussions of the Gouzenko and Herbert Norman episodes, and examine the security measures of some provinces. The authors are, of course, extremely critical of what passed for a liberal democracy, and of the too easy importation of American ideology and paranoia to Canadian soil.

Willis, John. *A History of Dalhousie Law School*. Toronto: University of
    Toronto Press, 1979.
Most nineteenth-century Canadian lawyers apprenticed in the law office
before taking their place at the bar. Founded in 1883, Dalhousie Law
School, one of the first common-law training centres in the British Empire,
challenged this orthodoxy and began the process of educating students in
the University environment. Willis also discusses the issues of curriculum
development and the ongoing problem of brain-drain from the Maritime
region.

Young, Brian. *The Politics of Codification: The Lower Canadian Civic
    Code of 1866*. Montreal: McGill-Queen's University Press, 1994.
A theoretically-informed work spanning legal, political, and intellectual
history, this volume rejects suggestions that the civil law of Quebec is
somehow foreign to liberal democracy, explores the origins of the
codification movement, the politics of collaboration between anglophone
and francophone elites, and the conjuncture of codification with the
collapse of seigneurial relations in favour of a liberal ideology centred on
freedom of contract.

Regional Politics: British Columbia

Blake, Donald. *Two Political Worlds: Parties and Voting in British
    Columbia*. Vancouver: University of British Columbia Press, 1985.
With the aid of two colleagues, Blake provides an analysis of BC voters
using material taken from a 1979 survey and attempts to place it in a
historical context. The authors present a "two worlds" thesis: that BC
voters often vote one way provincially and another federally. Thus, the
provincial Social Credit party spent decades in power, but there was no
comparable federal movement. In addition, they argue — among other
themes — that a strict class bias does not separate NDP and Social Credit
voters, and that British Columbia is not a stronghold of western alienation.

Carty, R. K., ed. *Politics, Policy, and Government in British Columbia*.
    Vancouver: University of British Columbia Press, 1996.
A useful introduction to British Columbian politics, policies, and
government, this volume is divided into four sections: Modern British
Columbia, The Political Stage, Governing the Province, and Patterns of
Public Policy. Though emphasis is upon contemporary politics and policy,
there is much of value to historians: for example, Michael Howlett and

Keith Brownsey explore the changing nature of the province's economic base, Paul Tennant examines the origin and evolution of aboriginal title, Donald Blake provides a historical overview of political themes and patterns, and Lynda Erickson analyses the political representation of women.

Fisher, Robin. *Duff Pattulo of British Columbia*. Toronto: University of
    Toronto Press, 1991.
While political biography is currently less important a genre than it was before the emergence of limited identities scholarship and the new social history, it still remains popular among general readers. Fisher's volume on Duff Pattulo — Liberal premier of British Columbia between 1933 and 1941 — re-asserts the importance of biography and argues that Pattulo, rather than W. A. C. Bennett, was the most influential leader of Canada's Pacific province. Fisher focuses upon the public individual more than the private, provides substantial insight and revision to Provincial-Federal relations of the 1930s and early 1940s, articulates Pattulo's northern vision, and chronicles the active interventionist nature of the BC government during the Depression.

Mitchell, David J. *Succession: The Political Reshaping of British
    Columbia*. Vancouver: Douglas & McIntyre, 1987.
Prior to her ascent up the political ladder, Kim Campbell ran for leader of the provincial Social Credit party in British Columbia. After finishing dead last, she shocked some political observers when she declared — in direct reference to the new leader, Bill Vander Zalm — that "charisma without substance is a dangerous thing." This volume examines Vander Zalm and the Social Credit party as the new premier attempted to return to a model of political success established by W. A. C. Bennett that emphasised a populist mixture of personality and economic growth. Mitchell also relates Vander Zalm's early efforts to inject his own moral beliefs into the party's political agenda.

_____.*W. A. C. Bennett and the Rise of British Columbia*. Vancouver:
    Douglas & McIntyre, 1983.
Based upon an extensive series of interviews with Bennett and others, this work provides a sympathetic view of "Wacky" Bennett and his two-decade reign as premier of British Columbia. Mitchell sees Bennett as an opportunist who jumped to the Social Credit in 1951, and led it to power the following year in wake of charges of corruption that plagued the

established provincial parties. *W. A. C. Bennett and the Rise of British Columbia* argues that the premier almost single-handedly molded the province until 1972, and pays substantial attention to Bennett's mega-projects and efforts at resource development.

Morley, J. Terrence, Norman J. Ruff, Neil A. Swanson, R. Jeremy Wilson, and Walter D. Young. *The Reins of Power: Governing British Columbia.* Vancouver: Douglas & McIntyre, 1983.
A collaborative effort, *The Reins of Power* contains chapters on the legislature, the premier and the cabinet, political parties, the public service, courts, provincial-municipal relationships, and British Columbia and Canadian federalism. While the emphasis is upon recent political history, the authors also discuss some historical themes such as the evolution of the party system and political parties, and some political personalities.

Regional Politics: The Prairies

Bell, Edward. *Social Classes and Social Credit in Alberta.* Montreal: McGill-Queen's University Press, 1994.
Political scientist Edward Bell takes an empirical approach to the 1935 and 1940 election victories of Social Credit in Alberta. Like Alvin Finkel and David Laycock, Bell notes that the Socreds were not a party of the agrarian petit-bourgeois. From his analysis of Bill Aberhart's writings, Bell concludes that Social Credit philosophy called for a radical reformation of capitalism. His analysis of voting results fits this perspective and demonstrates that the Social Credit party found its greatest support amongst the urban working class.

Caldarola, Carlo, ed. *Society and Politics in Alberta: Research Papers.* Toronto: Methuen, 1979.
Although stronger on theory than primary research, the papers in this volume are still a useful resource. *Society and Politics* is divided into five sections: party politics; political culture; class, status, and power; party support; and a statistical appendix.

Crunican, Paul. *Priests and Politicians: Manitoba Schools and the Election of 1896.* Toronto: University of Toronto Press, 1974.
Father Crunican examines the 1890 to 1896 Manitoba schools crisis from the perspective of church-state relations. His analysis suggests that

Premier Greenway's desire to deflect public attention from his failed railway policies led him to attack French language and denominational schools in Manitoba. Crunican provides a thorough narrative of events, and casts doubt on the abilities of church leaders to influence politicians as they sought a compromise position.

Eager, Evelyn. *Saskatchewan Government: Politics and Pragmatism*. Saskatoon: Western Producer Prairie Books, 1980.
Saskatchewan voters elected the first socialist government in North America in 1944 and consequently the province's political culture is often said to reflect radical tendencies. Eager argues that Saskatchewan voters were generally conservative and the governments they elected reflected a pragmatic approach to politics. She notes that the Commonwealth Cooperative Federation, New Democratic Party, and Liberal governments in Saskatchewan were less ideologically based than is generally perceived.

Elliot, David R. and Iris Miller. *Bible Bill: A Biography of William Aberhart*. Edmonton: Reidmore Books, 1987.
Bible Bill Aberhart created the Social Credit party, led it to victory in Alberta in 1935, and served as premier until his death in 1943. In this biography, Elliot and Miller link Aberhart's dispensational Christian theology with his political philosophy and success. Elliot and Miller note that Aberhart's strengths lay in his strong sense of conviction and organizational skills rather than his political ability. They characterize Aberhart as an anti-politician and authoritarian leader who failed to make a speech in the legislature until 1939, nearly four years after he became premier. Elliot and Miller conclude that the philosophy of Social Credit was secondary to Aberhart's pursuit of power.

Finkel, Alvin. *The Social Credit Phenomena*. Toronto: University of Toronto Press, 1989.
Alvin Finkel argues that the early Social Credit party was a populist party that critiqued the capitalist system from the left and thereby initially won support among a loose coalition of groups from farmers, labourers, and others in Alberta. During the later Aberhart years and especially under the stewartship of his successor, Ernest Manning, Finkel argues that the party shifted to the ideological right. The Social Credit party thus moved from a radical monetary-based reform party to a cadre party of right-wing paranoids. Finkel makes thorough use of the literature on populism to make his case, and has conducted significant primary research. For the

most recent — and contrasting — interpretation see Bob Hesketh, *Major Douglas and Social Credit* (1997).

Gibbins, Roger. *Regionalism: Territorial Politics in Canada and the United States.* Toronto: Butterworth, 1982.
Gibbins defines territorial politics as "the intrusion of territorial cleavages into national politics." He argues that the rise of a modern industrial and urban state was accompanied by the decline of territorial politics and the rise of class conflict, and compares and contrasts this phenomena in Canada and the United States. Gibbins notes that the important role of provinces — co-sovereign with the federal government — in enunciating Canadian regional interests has developed a distinctive regionalism in Canada. Unlike the United States where local governments, state governments, and regional interest groups participate in an effective lobby program, Canadian regionalism was characterized by inter-governmental diplomacy and negotiation.

Gibbins, Roger and Sonia Arrison. *Western Visions: Perspectives on the West in Canada.* Toronto: Broadview, 1995.
Gibbins and Arrison connect western Canadian discontent, protest, and regionalism to the federal political system and economic disparities. The writers assess the current political debates in Canada over constitutional change and provide a western Canadian perspective; there is also a useful discussion of western Canadian attitudes toward Quebec.

Gruending, Dennis. *Promises to Keep: A Political Biography of Allan Blakeney.* Saskatoon: Western Producer Prairie Books, 1990.
Dennis Gruending writes a laudatory biography of Allan Blakeney, Saskatchewan's NDP premier from 1971 to 1982. Gruending traces Blakeney's political philosophy to his youth in Nova Scotia, his experience as a Rhodes Scholar in Clement Attlee's Britain, and his role as a Saskatchewan civil servant in the government of Tommy Douglas. Gruending argues that Blakeney believed that democratic socialism required sound financial and business-like principles in order to succeed. Gruending also notes that Blakeney broadened the New Democratic Party platform away from agrarian socialism toward a labour party-based socialism more reflective of Saskatchewan's industrial and resource-based economy. The result of Blakeney's tenure as premier, consequently, was a shift in NDP party support from rural to urban constituencies.

Harrison, Trevor. *Of Passionate Intensity: Right-wing Populism and the Reform Party of Canada*. Toronto: University of Toronto Press, 1995.
The rise of the Reform Party as a neo-conservative western Canadian-based political movement has led to an outpouring of new research. In this critical book, Trevor Harrison places this party within the context of right-wing populism and traditional prairie protest movements. Also see Murray Dobbin's harsh assessment, *Preston Manning and the Reform Party* (1991); Sydney Sharpe's and Don Braid's critical account, *Storming Babylon: Preston Manning and the Reform Party (1992)*; and Thomas Flanagan's insider's perspective, *Waiting for the Wave* (1995).

Hesketh, Bob. *Major Douglas and Alberta Social Credit*. Toronto: University of Toronto Press, 1997.
More than any other work, this volume examines the impact of the ideas of Major C. H. Douglas on Social Credit in Alberta from 1932 to the late 1940s. Hesketh argues that William Aberhart understood Douglas' social credit theories better than many current scholars; indeed, the failure of the latter to do so, has led to important misunderstandings about Alberta Social Credit. Hesketh explores Douglas' conspiratorial world view, the relationship between Aberhart's religious beliefs and his understanding of Douglas social credit, and the nature of and support for Alberta Social Credit. Still worth consulting is C. B. Macpherson, *Democracy in Alberta: Social Credit and the Party System* (2nd. ed.,1962).

Kyba, Patrick. *Alvin: A Biography of the Honourable Alvin Hamilton*. Regina: Canadian Plains Research Centre, 1989.
One of the most influential ministers in the Diefenbaker governments from 1957-1963, Alvin Hamilton helped to rebuild the Conservative Party in Saskatchewan prior to his entry into federal politics. In the Diefenbaker government, he successfully implemented two important policy initiatives. As Minister of Northern Affairs and Natural Resources, Hamilton drafted the Roads to Resources program that inspired the development of infrastructure and electrical development in northern Canada; and, second, as Minister of Agriculture, Hamilton was instrumental in negotiating the first wheat sales to Communist China in 1960.

Laycock, David. *Populism and Democratic Thought in the Canadian Prairies, 1910-1945*. Toronto: University of Toronto Press, 1990.
David Laycock offers a sophisticated analysis of radical prairie politics built upon Ernesto Laclau's Marxist model and Lawrence Goodwyn's

cooperative model of populism. Laycock argues four variations of prairie populism existed in the period prior to World War II and each was associated with a different political party. These variations all shared a vision of popular democracy, but differed in their views of the capitalist system and the necessary response. He breaks the populist thought into the crypto-Liberal or Progressive group, the radical democratic or UFA group, the social democratic or CCF group, and the plebiscitarian or Social Credit group. All four variations struggled to modify and reform industrial capitalism to suit the peculiar interests of the prairie provinces.

Leeson, Howard. *Grant Notley: The Social Conscience of Alberta.* Edmonton: University of Alberta Press, 1992.
Grant Notley led the New Democratic Party in Alberta from 1968 until his tragic death in 1984, and was often a lonesome voice for democratic socialism in Alberta. Although the NDP never won more than a handful of seats under Notley's stewardship he is fondly remembered for his ability to reunify the socialist forces in Alberta following the demise of the Cooperative Commonwealth Federation.

Lupul, Manoly. *The Roman Catholic Church and the North-West School Question: A Study in Church-State Relations.* Toronto: University of Toronto Press, 1974.
Manoly Lupul uses the Roman Catholic ecclesiastical records extensively in this study of state support for denominational schools on the prairies and the political crisis it created during the creation of Saskatchewan and Alberta. Lupul notes that the attacks on denominational schools came from the political desire to achieve fiscal economy, a desire to enforce professional standards in teaching, and the desire of Ontario immigrants to replicate the Ontario school system.

Mardiros, Anthony. *William Irvine: The Life of a Prairie Radical.* Toronto: James Lorimer, 1979.
This sympathetic biography of William Irvine is the only work to address this remarkable man's public career. Irvine was a preacher, journalist, farm hand, carpenter, and socialist politician. Based in Calgary, he was active in the promotion of the social gospel, women's suffrage, the United Farmers of Alberta, social credit monetary theory, and the Cooperative Commonwealth Federation. His life is emblematic of the transition from religious idealism to secular reform in society. Mardiros provides ample details about Irvine's life, but is weaker on analysis.

McAllister, James A. *The Government of Edward Schreyer: Democratic Socialism in Manitoba*. Montreal: McGill-Queen's University Press, 1984.

The charismatic Edward Schreyer led the New Democratic Party to victory in Manitoba in 1969, the first time the province had elected a social democratic government. Like the NDP governments in Saskatchewan, McAllister argues that the Schreyer government was grounded in pragmatism rather than ideology. Schreyer reached out to diverse ethnic, religious, and occupational groups rather than implementing a socialist platform. Similarly, Schreyer made efforts to accommodate and cooperate with the federal Liberal party on issues of bilingualism and price and wage controls. Trudeau eventually rewarded this support with Schreyer's selection as governor-general in 1978.

McLeod, Thomas and Ian McLeod. *Tommy Douglas: The Road to Jerusalem*. Edmonton: Hurtig, 1987.

This biography traces the life of Saskatchewan's first social democratic premier, the "father" of medicare, and the first national leader of the New Democratic Party. Trained as a Baptist minister, Tommy Douglas witnessed tragic events during the Winnipeg General Strike of 1919 and the Estevan Coal Miners' Strike of 1931, when the Royal Canadian Mounted Police broke the strikes in violent confrontations. He went on to challenge established authority and became a spokesperson for the ordinary Canadian. His political career would be marked by pragmatism, Christian morality, socialism, and compassion. Although the book lacks a sophisticated analysis of Douglas's career, the prose helps give life to a man who was one of Canada's great political orators and premier of Saskatchewan from 1944 to 1960.

Melnyk, George. *Radical Regionalism*. Edmonton: NeWest Press, 1981.

Divided into sections on Culture, Mythology, and Ideology, the essays in this book are a classic statement of western Canadian regional protest in the 1970s. Melnyk's book, published in the aftermath of the National Energy Policy crisis of 1980, analyses western Canadian grievances and the need for regional coordination. Only through regional coordination, he argues, will the West's vision of Canada be fulfilled.

Pratt, Larry, ed. *Socialism and Democracy in Alberta: Essays in Honour of Grant Notley*. Edmonton: NeWest Press, 1986.

This collection of ten essays examines the problems of left-wing politics in Alberta and the strengths of Grant Notley's leadership within the New Democratic Party. The writers, all left-wing academics, lament the failures of the NDP in Alberta and try to explain it. In general the essays point to internal divisions between an urban-based labour/socialist wing and an agrarian-based populist wing within the Alberta NDP. While this dichotomy is useful, similar problems exist in British Columbia, Saskatchewan, and Manitoba where the NDP has had success.

Smith, David E. *The Regional Decline of a National Party: The Liberals on the Prairies*. Toronto: University of Toronto Press, 1981.
Under Prime Minister Mackenzie King, the prairie provinces were a bastion of Liberal support and one of the pillars of the party. By 1980, the Liberals received less than 25% of the popular vote in this region and could not win a single seat. Popular interpretations of this transformation often focus on the popularity of Saskatchewan-based Conservative Prime Minister John Diefenbaker; however, Smith argues that changes made within the Liberal party's organizational structure and a rising sense of self-confidence amongst prairie residents help to account for this change. For a more popular account see, Barry Wilson, *Politics of Defeat: the Decline of the Liberal Party in Saskatchewan* (1980).

_____. *Prairie Liberalism: The Liberal Party in Saskatchewan, 1905-1971*. Toronto: University of Toronto Press, 1975.
David Smith argues that the Saskatchewan Liberal Party, unlike its counterparts in Manitoba and Alberta, successfully co-opted the farmer populist vote in Saskatchewan through a party platform based on pragmatism rather than ideology. It lost this perspective to Tommy Douglas and the Co-operative Commonwealth Federation in 1944. Douglas, like his Liberal predecessors, governed Saskatchewan pragmatically, although more to the left of centre than previous Liberal governments, and won the accolades of Saskatchewan's primarily agrarian-based population. The Liberal Party, consequently, endorsed an ideological perspective — free enterprise capitalism — in order to combat the CCF and regain power. This shift, however, moved the Saskatchewan Liberals away from the centralist tendencies of the federal Liberals and opened the door to the rise of the Conservative party in Saskatchewan.

Thomas, Lewis H., ed. *William Aberhart and Social Credit in Alberta*. Toronto: Copp Clark, 1977.
This excellent collection presents a series of primary documents and

historical interpretations of both the Depression and the role of Social Credit in Alberta. Thomas's selections present a sympathetic portrayal of Aberhart as a reformer, and emphasise the radical elements of Social Credit policy such as debt moratoriums, marketing boards, and reforms in health and education.

Tupper, Allan and Roger Gibbins, eds. *Government and Politics in Alberta.* Edmonton: University of Alberta Press, 1992.
These essays by political scientists attempt to explain Albertans' tendency to support a "quasi-party" political system in which a single party dominates the political landscape for a generation at a time, a concept that has been at the focus of scholarly work since the publication of C. B. Macpherson's *Democracy in Alberta* (1953). *Government and Politics* examines themes such as the roles of the premier, federal-provincial relations, the media, and gender politics in defining Alberta's political culture past and future.

Regional Politics: Upper Canada and Ontario

Armstrong, Christopher. *The Politics of Federalism: Ontario's Relations with the Federal Government, 1867-1942.* Toronto: University of Toronto Press, 1981.
Issues of federal and provincial jurisdiction have been, and continue to be, a principal source of tension between these two levels of government. Armstrong examines the struggle of Canada's most politically and economically powerful province to assert its autonomy in the face of federal interference. Ontario, in a way that Albertans may find ironic, led the move toward greater provincial rights, particularly in issues involving natural resources. The federal government was most successful in expanding its jurisdiction and authority during the two world wars and the crisis of the 1930s.

Brode, Patrick. *John Beverley Robinson: The Bone and the Sinew of the Compact.* Toronto: University of Toronto Press, 1984.
A staunch advocate of things British, John Beverley Robinson was, in turn, Attorney-General; a member of the House of Assembly, Legislative Council, and Executive Council; and finally Chief Justice. *The Bone and the Sinew* is a sympathetic and well-researched biography of Robinson's public life that emphasises his British Tory and anti-American sentiments.

Careless, J. M. S., ed. *The Pre-Confederation Premiers: Ontario Government Leaders, 1841-1867*. Toronto: University of Toronto Press, 1980.

This work examines five men — William Draper, Robert Baldwin, Francis Hincks, John A. Macdonald, and John Sandfield Macdonald — who held the office of co-premier from the union of 1841 to Confederation. The authors collectively argue that this period saw the entrenchment of the concept of responsible government, the enlargement of self-government in Canada, and the rise of the premier as the political head of both the administration and the party.

Humphries, Charles W. *'Honest Enough to be Bold': The Life and Times of Sir James Pliny Whitney*. Toronto: University of Toronto Press, 1985.

Sir James Pliny Whitney was the Conservative premier of Ontario from 1905 until his death in 1914. Confronted with rapid urban and industrial changes and a corrupt political system, Humphries argues Whitney was a reformer in areas of health, education, and politics, and aggressively used the state to promote resource development. Though some will disagree that Whitney was as progressive a reformer as Humphries suggests — Whitney remained in favour of prohibition and opposed to female suffrage — this remains a fine political biography.

Johnson, J. K. *Becoming Prominent: Regional Leadership in Upper Canada, 1791-1841*. Montreal: McGill-Queen's University Press, 1989.

This collective biography of 283 men who sat in the Upper Canadian House of Assembly provides a mass of detail concerning these elites. While Johnson does not discuss the process of becoming prominent or explore notions of leadership, he has assembled data relating to five broad subjects: occupational choice, wealth and land, local office-holding, patronage and status, and the nature of parliamentary representation. A lengthy appendix provides specific biographical detail and sources for those individuals not included in the *Dictionary of Canadian Biography*.

McDougall, Allan K. *John P. Robarts: His Life and Government*. Toronto: University of Toronto Press, 1985.

The Conservative premier of Ontario from 1961 to 1971, John Robarts is given credit in this volume for presiding over the modernization of Ontario politics. During this period government bureaucracy and the premier's executive powers expanded, and regional government, budgets, and school boards were rationalized. Robarts thus represents a transition from the old rule of Leslie Frost in the 1950s to the more modern government and leadership of Bill Davis in the 1970s. For Frost see Roger Graham, *Old Man Ontario: Leslie M. Frost* (1990).

Morley, J. T. *Secular Socialists: The CCF/NDP in Ontario — A Biography*. Montreal: McGill-Queen's University Press, 1984.

Until 1990 the NDP had not enjoyed much electoral success in Ontario. In this biography of the New Democratic Party in Ontario, Morley traces the internal workings and personality of the party. Unlike the middle-aged baby boomer, the CCF/NDP in Ontario has not — contrary to some views — taken a lurch to the right in its development. Rather, Morley argues that the party's platform and structure resemble that originally conceived in the 1930s. Also see Dan Azoulay, *Keeping the Dream Alive: The Survival of the Ontario CCF/NDP, 1950-1963* (1997).

Noel, S. J. R. *Patrons, Clients, Brokers: Ontario Society and Politics, 1791-1896*. Toronto: University of Toronto Press, 1990.

This is a superb analysis of nineteenth-century political behaviour in Old Ontario. Noel sees three phases of patron-client relations. The first was a simple clientism in which individuals engendered loyalty through, for example, allotting large tracts of land or administrative appointment. Colonel Thomas Talbot, for example, had a half million acres settled through his agency, and William "Tiger" Dunlop was able to call out his clients — the "Huron Invincibles" or, as they were known by some, the "Bloody Useless" — in order to guard against a possible American attack in 1837-1838. By mid-century, important political brokers had emerged. These included individuals such as Charles Poulett Thomson (Lord Sydenham) who used extensive patronage to gain support for Union, or Francis Hincks, who played an essential part as a broker in bringing together the Baldwin-Lafontaine coalition. The post-Confederation era saw the emergence of party machine patronage, a strategy that was effectively appropriated by Oliver Mowatt. There was not, however, the widespread disappearance of earlier forms of patronage, and the simple clientism of an earlier era still remained common. More general is Donald C. Macdonald, *The Government and Politics of Ontario* (1985).

Oliver, Peter. *G. Howard Ferguson: Ontario Tory*. Toronto: University of Toronto Press, 1977.

First elected to the Ontario legislature in 1905, Howard Ferguson went on to become premier between 1923 and 1930. Unlike James Whitney, Ferguson embraced hostility with Ontario's francophones, practiced party politics and patronage, and encouraged the private exploitation of Ontario's resources over public involvement. Ferguson did have a reforming impulse, his principal contribution being to the schools and curriculum of the province. After helping R. B. Bennett defeat the King government in 1930, Ferguson was appointed Canadian high commissioner in London.

Prang, Margaret. *N. W. Rowell: Ontario Nationalist*. Toronto: University of Toronto Press, 1975.
Newton Rowell was involved in a wide range of public positions and issues: he was the Ontario Liberal leader between 1911 and 1917, jumped ship to become an Ottawa politician in Borden's Union government, was prominent in the first assembly of the League of Nations where he advocated a greater international role for Canada, and was a leader in the formation of the United Church in 1925. In 1937 he became chair of the Rowell-Sirois Royal Commission on Dominion-Provincial Relations, though a stroke deprived him of any real influence in the final result. Prang's lengthy biography provides insight into some of the important public issues that confronted Ontario and Canada in the first part of the twentieth century.

Read, Colin. *The Rising in Western Upper Canada, 1837-8: The Duncombe Revolt and After*. Toronto: University of Toronto Press, 1982.
Popular interpretations have often argued that the 1837-38 rebellion in Upper Canada was a broad-based expression by ordinary people who had legitimate grievances against an oppressive Tory oligarchy , and that William Lyon Mackenzie was the unequivocal leader. Read challenges this interpretation. In this account of the rebellion led by Dr. Charles Duncombe, Read draws attention to the little-discussed uprising in south-western Upper Canada and — in a careful analysis of the participants — argues that most were of American or Upper Canadian origins who sought narrow political reform. Also see Colin Read and Ronald J. Stagg, eds. *The Rebellion of 1837 in Upper Canada: A Collection of Documents* (1985), which contains a lengthy and excellent introduction to both the documents and the rebellion.

Saywell, John T. *"Just Call Me Mitch": The Life of Mitchell F. Hepburn*. Toronto: University of Toronto Press, 1991.

One of the most controversial and flamboyant figures ever to inhabit the premier's office, Mitch Hepburn became leader of the Ontario Liberal party in 1930 and premier in 1934. Saywell's comprehensive political biography explores the enigmatic nature of Hepburn's personality and his politics. Hepburn, for example, embraced a radical populist rhetoric, but was sometimes accused of acting like a demagogue; on other occasions he adopted a progressive stance toward unions, but still was able to repress them ruthlessly. When Hepburn walked into the political sunset in 1942 (save for a failed comeback in 1945), he left the provincial Liberals in such disarray that they did not return to power in Ontario for more than four decades.

Regional Politics: New France and Quebec

Behiels, Michael. *Prelude to Quebec's Quiet Revolution*. Montreal: McGill-Queen's University Press, 1985.

Maurice Duplessis dominated the political environment during the period under discussion. Behiels examines two ideological movements — liberalism and neo-nationalism — that helped to contribute to the demise of the Union Nationale and laid the foundations for the Quiet Revolution. Neo-nationalists such as André Laurendeau and Pierre Laporte who propagated their views in *Le Devoir* embraced the nationalism of abbé Groulx but also accepted the reality of an urban, industrial, secular society. In contrast to Groulx, they saw the state, rather than the church, as the vehicle to achieve their aims. A second group of intellectuals — which included Pierre Trudeau and other founders of the journal *Cité Libre* — embraced liberal and social democratic values as necessary corollaries of a modern Quebec. The neo-nationalists became the more influential group within Quebec provincial politics in the 1960s, while the *citélibrists* (as Behiels identifies them) directed their energies to the federal sphere. This superb intellectual history supports the "new middle-class" thesis that argues that it was this group that brought about the reforms within Quebec in the 1960s.

Bernier, Gérald and Daniel Salée. *The Shaping of Québec Politics and Society: Colonialism, Power, and the Transition to Capitalism in the 19ᵗʰ Century*. Washington: Crane Russak, 1992.

Neo-Marxist in orientation, this work attempts to trace the transition of an *ancien regime* colonial society to an industrial capitalist culture. Arguing that Lower Canada more resembled feudal Europe than any other part of North America, the authors interpret the English merchant elite as the key supporter of an inchoate regime that stifled land and industrial development for their own gain. Therefore, events such as the 1837-38 Rebellion, far more pronounced in Lower Canada than Upper Canada, can be seen as an effort to overthrow the merchant bourgeoisie.

Black, Conrad. *Duplessis.* Toronto: McClelland and Stewart, 1977.
Save for a five year period during World War II, Maurice Duplessis was *Le Chef* of Quebec politics from the mid-1930s until his death in 1959. Traditionally, English-language historians have emphasised his dictatorial style; the corruption of journalists, officials, and the ballot box; and his defense of rural, Catholic Quebec against the pernicious influences of unions, communists, and Liberals. In Black's view, Duplessis — who created the Union Nationale in 1936 — emerges as a more tolerant figure who supported workers (though not, of course, militant union leaders), and helped to modernize Quebec society. Abuses of civil liberties are lightly dealt with, and the strength of Duplessis's political character, and the obvious loyalty he engendered, is emphasised. While many have criticized this work as too sympathetic toward Duplessis, it nevertheless serves a useful purpose as the principal English-language source on him, and as a useful corrective to the dominant theme of corruption that has surrounded his administration.

Coleman, William. *The Independence Movement in Quebec, 1945-1980.* Toronto: University of Toronto Press, 1984.
In this important contribution to the origins of the Quiet Revolution, this volume challenges the middle-class thesis: that is, the emergence of a socio-economic and demographic revolution in the post-World War II era fomented the reforms and changes of the 1960s and 1970s. Coleman critiques variations of this thesis and explores the world of ideas and ideologies and how these help to form social classes. Those wishing to understand the sovereignty movement more fully should also consult two primary sources: René Lévesque, *An Option for Quebec* (1968); and Pierre Vallières, *White Niggers of America* (1971).

Cook, Ramsay, ed. *French-Canadian Nationalism: An Anthology.* Toronto: Macmillan of Canada, 1969.
Though now dated, this still useful collection introduces readers to the

history and interpretations of French-Canadian nationalism. The first section provides several interpretations of the rise and evolution of nationalism; while the second provides selections from French-Canadian intellectuals who promoted *la survivance* in various ways.

Dirks, Patricia. *The Failure of l'Action libérale nationale*. Montreal: McGill-Queen's University Press, 1991.

In the late nineteenth century, Honoré Mercier argued that French-speaking Canadians must unite above party lines in order to protect linguistic interests within Confederation. The Depression of the 1930s heightened the belief that *la survivance* could indeed be lost. In response, Paul Gouin, Mercier's grandson, became the leader of a new party, *l'Action libérale nationale* (ALN). While there was no unanimity as to the future course of the ALN, it generally opposed the dominance of big business, favoured rural reconstruction, and sought to implement a program to improve the economic and social well-being of the francophone while maintaining traditional values. Louis-Alexandre Taschereau and the Liberal party refused to abandon economic liberalism and embrace the platform of the ALN; in contrast, Maurice Duplessis promised to make the economy work for francophones without affecting "honest" capital, and he was able to win many ALN members to the Union Nationale. Dirks argues that the ALN was, therefore, influential in transferring power from Taschereau to Duplessis without drastic socio-economic changes, and helped to legitimize purely provincial parties within Quebec.

Gougeon, Gilles. *A History of Quebec Nationalism: Conversations with Seven Leading Quebec Historians*. Trans. Louisa Blair, Robert Chodos, and Jane Ubertino. Toronto: James Lorimer & Company, 1994.

Highly readable and entertaining, this volume was a best-seller when it was first published in French in the post-Meech Lake era. Gougeon has interviewed seven historians — each an expert in his field — who comment on various expressions of French-Canadian nationalism from New France to the 1990s. Although nationalism obviously took many forms, the general theme of this volume is that of *la survivance* in the face of perceived or real threats.

Greer, Allan. *The Patriots and the People: The Rebellion of 1837 in Rural Lower Canada*. Toronto: University of Toronto Press, 1993.

Interpretations of the Lower Canadian rebellions often emphasise material and economic conditions, the influence of the Patriote leaders, or, in the "perception" of Lord Durham, the influence of racial conflict. Grounded in a rich international historiography that suggests that agrarian uprisings were crucial to most revolutions in history, Greer's study argues that the rural peasant took a more activist role than has been previously acknowledged. Greer rejects Fernand Ouellet's argument that the rebellion was primarily a result of a long period of economic discontent; instead, while the peasantry did experience economic troubles, and did follow urban, bourgeois leaders, they did so because the rhetoric and agenda of the patriots was in harmony with their own experience. Indeed, as the "revolution" developed, the *patriote* leaders were influenced by the peasantry to adopt a more radical position toward issues such as feudal exactions and agrarian reform. *Patriots and the People* is divided into two main parts: the first provides an introduction to the peasant mentality, while the second elaborates upon the actual unfolding of the uprising, including an analysis of the role that ethnicity and gender played. For a more thorough discussion of troop movements and specific battles, see Elinor Senior, *Redcoats and Patriotes: The Rebellions of Lower Canada, 1837-38* (1985); and Mary Fryer, *Volunteers and Redcoats, Rebels and Raiders* (1987). For a popular introduction, see J. Schull, *Rebellion: The Rising in French Canada* (1971; rpt. 1996).

Horton, Donald J. *André Laurendeau: A French-Canadian Nationalist, 1912-1968*. Toronto: Oxford University Press, 1992.
For more than four decades André Laurendeau was at the centre of the Quebec nationalist movement. This superb biography traces both Laurendeau's life and the evolution of the nationalist movement. As a young man Laurendeau espoused the anti-Semitic rhetoric that was too common in both English- and French-speaking Canada. Laurendeau, unlike some others, later felt shame over these views and vehemently denounced them. In addition, as a young man, Laurendeau was also a separatist for a time; this was abandoned, however, after a stay in France where he came to see the clerico-conservative vision as too narrow and limited for his liking. Drawing upon the tradition of Henri Bourassa, Laurendeau became a leading proponent of a bi-cultural nation, and between 1963-1968 he co-chaired the Royal Commission on Bilingualism and Biculturalism. He died, unfortunately, before the Commission's recommendations could be implemented, and in the midst of a rising current of separatism. For a broad sampling of Laurendeau's writings see,

André Laurendeau: Witness for Quebec (1973), selected and translated by Philip Stratford.

Laforest, Guy. *Trudeau and the End of a Canadian Dream*. Montreal: McGill-Queen's University Press, 1995.
The dualist vision of federalism considers Confederation a compact between two founding nations or peoples and represented, as historian Réal Belanger has recently stated, "a pact between these two . . . who would respect each other in the future, and who together, would be able to achieve great economic ventures, and other great things." Laforest argues that duality, in its various guises, was central to the Canadian patriotism (or dream thereof) of important French-Canadian figures such as Louis-Hippolyte LaFontaine, George-Etienne Cartier, Henri Bourassa, André Laurendeau, Daniel Johnson Sr., and Claude Ryan. Recent political policies and developments — of which Pierre Trudeau was the principal architect — threaten this interpretation and promise to put an end to the "Canadian dream." Drawing upon the political and philosophical traditions of Aristotle, Machiavelli, John Locke, Johann Gottlieb Fichte, and others, Laforest produces a critical analysis of Trudeau's thought and actions since the 1980s referendum. In addition, this volume provides a provocative analysis of the development of Trudeau's political thought over several decades, the Allaire and Bélanger-Campeau reports, and the legacy of the conquest of 1759-1763. The more positive visions of André Laurendeau and F. R. Scott are also put forward.

Lawson, Philip. *The Imperial Challenge: Quebec and Britain in the Age of the American Revolution*. Montreal: McGill-Queen's University Press, 1989.
The conquest of New France by the British posed a problem that has been too often, Lawson argues, trivialized: How was Britain going to incorporate Quebec — mostly French and Catholic — into the Empire? Philip Lawson, until his recent death a prolific scholar of Hanoverian Britain, thus turns his attention to the social and political context of the Quebec Act of 1774. He argues that some political elites in England showed a willingness to allow religious freedom and the restoration of some aspects of French law in meeting the challenge of establishing a British colony comprised of over 70,000 French Catholics. In addition, the author seeks to examine how events in the Empire influenced Britain, and argues that the Quebec Act produced a thorough and sophisticated analysis of British assumptions and constitutional traditions. Although this

connection is only tenuously maintained, the foundations implicit in the Quebec Act helped to lead to Catholic emancipation in England a half century later. This excellent work places constitutional developments in an international context.

Levitt, Joseph. *Henri Bourassa and the Golden Calf: The Social Program of the Nationalists of Quebec (1900-1914)*. Ottawa: Éditions de l'Université d'Ottawa, 1969.
Grandson of Louis-Joseph Papineau, founder of *Le Devoir*, and an important federal and provincial politician, Henri Bourassa was a principal proponent that Canada should be an Anglo-French country. Levitt traces the response of Bourassa and his *nationaliste* colleagues to the rapid economic and social changes in the 15 years prior to World War I. The common perception that Bourassa rejected modern industrial society is not correct; rather, Levitt argues that Bourassa was a "utopia corporatist" who was optimistic that change could be effected and was committed to social action. While Bourassa believed that individual and class interests were subordinate to the common good, he opposed the suppression of individual liberties. This view contrasts enormously with Lita-Rose Betcherman's portrayal of Bourassa in *The Swastika and the Maple Leaf* (1975), which sees him as an admirer of the corporatist philosophies of Hitler and Mussolini. For Bourassa's own writings, see Joseph Levitt, ed., *Henri Bourassa on Imperialism and Biculturalism, 1900-1918* (1970).

McRoberts, Kenneth and Dale Posgate. *Quebec: Social Change and Political Crisis*. Toronto: McClelland & Stewart, 1976; 3rd ed., 1988.
Social Change and Political Crisis is broadly concerned with the modernization of the Quebec state and society; more specifically, it examines the relationship between politics and government and socio-economic development. The authors argue that from the 1920s to the 1950s "there was a 'lag' of political change behind social and economic change"; this was due, in part, to the influence of traditional ideologies, the conservative nature of Maurice Duplessis and his government, and the dominance of American economic elites. With the transition to a modern industrial economy and the rise of a distinct bureaucratic Francophone middle class, the new nationalism of the Quiet Revolution strongly advocated new functions for government in the 1960s. In addition, this transition saw the increased development of linguistic and class divisions, out of which the Parti Québécois also emerged.

Monet, Jacques. *The Last Cannon Shot: A Study of French-Canadian Nationalism, 1837-1850*. Toronto: University of Toronto Press, 1969; 2nded., 1976.

The Last Cannon Shot examines the decade following the "troubles"of 1837 — a period that Monet claims is French Canada's greatest decade. Monet explores the *Canadien* reaction to three issues — the union of Lower and Upper Canada, the campaign for responsible government, and the agitation for annexation to the United States — and concludes that by 1850 most French- and English-Canadians had accepted a bicultural point of view, and decided to live together within the bosom of a single state.

Monière, Denis. *Ideologies in Quebec: The Historical Development*. Trans. Richard Howard. Toronto: University of Toronto Press, 1981.

Originally published in French in 1977, this volume (updated to include the Parti Quebecois government and the referendum of 1980) provides a neo-marxist interpretation of the role of ideology in Quebec's historical evolution, and examines how the ruling elites utilized ideology to entrench their economic superiority. While Monière has been criticized for being excessively dogmatic in his analysis, historians have noted that this work serves a useful historiographic purpose by illustrating how the Quebec Left interprets its past.

Munro, Ken. *The Political Career of Sir Adolphe Chapleau, Premier of Quebec, 1879-1882*. Lewiston, NY: Edwin Mellen Press, 1992.

Although this critical portrait principally traces the career of Adolphe Chapleau as premier of Quebec between 1879 and 1882, it also broaches much broader themes. An influential statesman, Chapleau emphasised what French and English Canada had in common, had a vision of Confederation rooted in French-Canadian history, sought to encourage the francophone entrepreneur, and won a reputation as a defender of French-Canadian rights outside Quebec. Significantly, as a Conservative federal cabinet minister, Chapleau — after a long night of soul searching — agreed to the hanging of Louis Riel in 1885; this helped to prevent, Munro maintains, greater hostilities between French- and English-Canadians.

Oliver, Michael. *The Social and Political Ideas of Quebec Nationalism, 1920-1945*. Montreal: Véhicule Press, 1991.

Originally presented as a Ph.D. dissertation in 1956, this work has been published without any substantive revision. Oliver's study of the diverse nature of French-Canadian nationalism provides a sympathetic, yet insightful, analysis of the ideas of Henri Bourassa, and a more critical examination of those of abbé Groulx, *L'Action française*, and the nationalism that they inspired. Between these poles of nationalist thought, Oliver locates the ideas of André Laurendeau and traces his evolution toward a more progressive nationalism. Oliver's erudite analysis provides insight into how a left-leaning academic approached French-Canadian nationalism in the 1950s.

Quinn, Herbert F. *The Union Nationale: Quebec Nationalism from Duplessis to Lévesque.* 1963; 2nd ed., Toronto: University of Toronto Press, 1979.

Following a brief examination of the historical and cultural background to politics in Quebec, this study traces the rise to power of the Union Nationale in the 1930s to its apparent demise in the mid-1970s. Quinn examines the socio-economic and intellectual origins of the Union Nationale in workmanlike fashion and naturally emphasises the administrative, economic, and provincial-federal policies of Maurice Duplessis. He concludes with a brief examination of Antinio Barrettee, the Union Nationale leader in the 1960 election, the return to power under Daniel Johnson in 1966, and the party's struggle for existence in the 1970s. This study was first published in 1963 and has been updated, but not extensively revised. Quinn fails, therefore, to incorporate a prodigious amount of recent historiography into his analysis.

Thomson, Dale C. *Jean Lesage and the Quiet Revolution.* Toronto: Macmillan, 1984

Premier of Quebec between 1960 and 1966, Lesage is considered by some — and certainly by Thomson — to be the father of the Quiet Revolution. This work provides a detailed account of Lesage's life and of the administrative and governmental reforms that were part of the modernization of Quebec. While Lesage did not set out to initiate many of these changes, Thomson clearly sets the Quiet Revolution during Lesage's two terms in office and sees him as the key catalyst. While there is little discussion of some of the broader implications of the Quiet Revolution, Thomson does trace the early political career of René Levesque, who was a key figure in the Lesage administration.

Thomson, Dale, ed. *Quebec Society and Politics: Views from the Inside.* Toronto: McClelland and Stewart, 1973.

Though now dated, this collection had its origins at the Johns Hopkins

Centre of Canadian Studies in Washington, D.C. where ten French-speaking academics were invited to discuss Quebec's history, politics, and economics. The articles has been translated, and several chapters added. The authors examine Quebec nationalism, relationships with the Federal government, political institutions, economic developments, the Catholic Church, international relations, and the October Crisis of 1970.

Trofimenkoff, Susan Mann. *Action Française: French Canadian Nationalism in the Twenties*. Toronto: University of Toronto Press, 1975.

Concerned over linguistic threats to the French language and of the evils of modernity, abbé Groulx joined the *Action Française* (previously called the *Ligue des Droits du française*) in 1917. The *Action Française*— which took its name from the more famous French organization in order to enhance its own status — comprised a small number of men (of whom Groulx was the most prominent) who took up the campaign to purify the French language, and to bolster French-Canadian pride and strength of purpose. Divided from within, and under pressure from the papacy in Rome and politicians in Quebec, the *Action Française* ceased in 1928.

Vigod, Bernard L. *Quebec Before Duplessis: The Political Career of Louis-Alexandre Taschereau*. Montreal: McGill-Queen's University Press, 1986.

Even though Louis-Alexandre Taschereau was premier of Quebec between 1920 and 1936 and a member of the provincial legislature for well over three decades, his political career has received scant attention. Susan Mann Trofimenkoff's excellent survey *Dream of Nation* (1982), for example, pejoratively presents Taschereau as Duplessis's principal teacher regarding patronage and paternalism, and has little comment on the policies of his government. In contrast, Vigod examines in some detail the accomplishments of the Taschereau Liberals in education, welfare, and labour legislation, and its efforts — in the face of backward-looking nationalists — to modernize the economy. This work also provides substantial insight into the strained relationship between Taschereau, a devout Catholic, and the church.

Regional Politics: Atlantic Canada

Beck, J. Murray. *Joseph Howe. Volume 1: Conservative Reformer, 1804-1848*. Montreal: McGill-Queen's University Press, 1982.

_____. *Joseph Howe. Volume 2: The Briton Becomes Canadian,*
   1848-1873. Montreal: McGill-Queen's University Press, 1983.
In contrast to the harsher view presented in James A. Roy's *Joseph Howe:*
A Study in Achievement and Frustration (1935), Beck presents a more
favourable analysis of the individual who many believe was the most
important Nova Scotia politician of the nineteenth century. Although
Howe is presented as a complex and sometimes contradictory individual,
the emphasis is on his public life and his achievements as a writer,
reformer, and politician.

Blake, Raymond B. *Canadians at Last: Canada Integrates Newfoundland*
   as a Province. Toronto: University of Toronto Press, 1994.
Ray Blake examines the decade following Newfoundland's entry into
Canada in 1949 and concludes that the Liberal Party dominated
Newfoundland politics because the federal Liberals dispensed social
welfare to the people of Newfoundland, and because the Newfoundland
and federal Liberal party platforms were easyily integrated. Blake is
critical of Canada's unwillingness to offer assistance to Newfoundland's
nascent industrial sector, of Maritime complicity in this decision, and of
the Liberals' willingness to allow cheaper Canadian products to dominate
the marketplace. As a result, this excellent study concludes that
Newfoundland's economy failed to integrate into the larger Canadian
economy and remained dominated by the fishery and other resource
extraction industries.

Conrad, Margaret. *George Nowlan: Maritime Conservative in National*
   Politics. Toronto: University of Toronto Press, 1986.
Unlike in the prairies, regional-based political parties have found little
support in the Maritime provinces. Most Maritimers place their political
faith with the Liberal or Conservative parties. Maritime politicians,
however, do champion the causes of their region and George Nowlan is
an excellent example of a determined regional politician within a national
political party. He rose in the ranks of the provincial Conservative party
in Nova Scotia, served as president of the party until 1947, and thereafter
entered federal politics serving as Minster of Revenue in the Diefenbaker
government. Together with Robert Stanfield, Nowlan effectively
championed Maritime interests within the Conservative party. In her
biography of Nowlan, Margaret Conrad effectively places the politician
within the context of his era and explores these concerns in detail. It is an
excellent and throughly referenced addition to the field.

Doyle, Arthur T. *Front Benches and Back Rooms: A Story of Corruption, Muckraking, Raw Partisanship and Political Intrigue in New Brunswick.* Toronto: Green Tree, 1976.
In his critique of New Brunswick politics between 1912 and 1927, Doyle defines the era as one of naked Tory corruption, responsible Liberal muckraking, and extraordinary partisan politics. He notes that the Liberal defeat of the Tory government in 1917 following a series of scandals was accompanied by a radical dismantling of the Conservative political machine including the dismissal of nearly 80% of the provincial bureaucracy. In the era after 1925, both corruption and muckraking became less apparent in New Brunswick politics. Based on newspapers and Royal Commission manuscripts, this book is a useful examination of politics in an era of intense party partisanship.

Mackenzie, David. *Inside the Atlantic Triangle: Canada and the Entrance of Newfoundland into Confederation, 1939-1949.* Toronto: University of Toronto Press, 1986.
This work examines the evolution of Canadian policy toward Newfoundland (NFL) in the decade preceding its entrance into confederation. Mackenzie argues the World War II was crucial in stimulating Canadian interest in NFL, explores Canadian and British policy toward the "problem" of NFL, and discusses the post-war decision of Newfoundlanders to choose confederation.

Neary, Peter. *Newfoundland in the North Atlantic World, 1929-1949.* Montreal: McGill-Queen's University Press, 1988.
This work examines the 20 years prior to NFL entering confederation. To a greater extent than David Mackenzie's *Inside the Atlantic Triangle* (1986), Neary emphasises the role of the British government in the 1949 union. Neary provides a useful and detailed study of the political, diplomatic, and constitutional history of this period.

Pryke, K. G. *Nova Scotia and Confederation, 1864-1874.* Toronto: University of Toronto Press, 1979.
The decision to join Canada in 1867 provoked a stormy debate in Nova Scotia. Reform/Liberal politicians led by Joseph Howe campaigned against Confederation in 1867 and won a large victory in the provincial elections. Previous interpretations emphasised Nova Scotia's concerns regarding the tariff and connections to Britain, but in this study of Nova Scotia politics, Pryke suggests that the debate reflected ideological splits

amongst Nova Scotia politicians over the role of the electorate and executive in the political process. Following a detailed examination of two constituencies, Pryke argues that this split between decentralist Reformers and federalist Conservatives was eventually resolved in Nova Scotia by competition for the spoils of power. Contests for control of patronage quickly transformed the debate into a more traditional Canadian division of interests.

Rawlyk, G. A. *The Atlantic Provinces and the Problems of Confederation*. St. John's: Breakwater Books, 1979.
A collection of twelve essays prepared by Professor Rawlyk and eight other contributors for the Pepin-Robarts task force on Canadian federalism, this book is an insightful examination of the perceptions of Atlantic Canadians towards the Canadian state from 1967 to 1978. The portrait which emerges suggests that Atlantic Canadians are less parochial in their outlook than popular opinion would suggest and willing to make significant compromises within the Canadian federal structural.

Woodward, Calvin. *The History of New Brunswick Election Campaigns and Platforms*. Toronto: Micro Media, 1976.
A book and microfiche related to New Brunswick elections, *The History of New Brunswick Election Campaigns* is into three parts. First, a brief overview of elections in New Brunswick since 1866. Second, short descriptive accounts of each campaign. And third, a collection of party platforms and campaign literature from each election campaign. The last section of the book is available only on fiche and is an excellent research source for students and scholars.

Regional Politics: the North

Dacks, Gurston. *A Choice of Futures: Politics in the Canadian North*. Toronto: Methuen, 1981.
Published shortly after the Berger report on the Mackenzie Valley Pipeline, Dacks reflects the emphasis on the homeland/hinterland dichotomy of northern development. He examines northern economic development since World War II, the emergence of the resource-extraction economy, and the isolation of northern residents from the higher echelons of power. Well-researched and thoroughly referenced, this book is an excellent introduction to northern political economy.

Dickerson, Mark O. *Whose North? Political Change, Political Development, and Self-government in the Northwest Territories.* Vancouver: University of British Columbia Press, 1992.

Political Scientist Mark Dickerson explores the roots of the peculiar apolitical local government structure in the Northwest Territories. He notes that what appears a chaotic system to observers from the south, reflects the attitudes, beliefs, values, and expectations of northern residents, the majority of whom are Dene, Inuit, Inuvialuit, or Métis. This multicultural community, together with the generation of non-Native northerners who came to power in the 1970s, have created a local government structure that suits their particular needs and desires.

Grant, Shelagh D. *Sovereignty or Security? Government Policy in the Canadian North, 1936-1950.* Vancouver: University of British Columbia Press, 1988.

The Canadian government virtually ignored the Arctic in the period prior to World War II. The northern war projects of 1942 to 1944 and the beginning of the Cold War, however, led to increasing Canadian concerns about American military activity in the region. Shelagh Grant analyses the duality of the Canadian response. As she notes, the Canadian government wanted a secure North and wanted it free from American domination. But Canada would not pay the price of security, she concludes and the American presence in the Arctic grew unchecked. This book is very critical of the policy decisions of the Canadian government and sympathetic to the few figures who comprised the "northern nationalists."

Economic and Business History

This field of study is one of the oldest and most thoroughly developed in Canadian history. The staples interpretation of Canadian economic history, associated with the writings of Harold Adams Innis and W. A. Mackintosh, is the foundation for laurentian and metropolitan syntheses of Canadian history. The staples approach emphasised the exploitation of natural and renewable resources for external markets and associated economic linkages in Canadian economic development. The staples thesis continues to influence Canadian historians and helps to shape this bibliography. Because of the continued importance of resource production in Canada, this chapter contains a section devoted to staples exploitation, although not specifically to staples interpretations. More recently, Canadian economic and business history has been influenced by other interpretive models. Left-nationalist historians have seized upon the inherent dependency tenets of the staples interpretation and world systems analysis, and have produced accounts that emphasise the role of international capital and markets in Canadian development. Writers such as Kari Levitt, R. T. Naylor, Wallace Clement and others maintain that the combination of a staples economy with its emphasis on exports and entrepreneurial failure among Canada's business community have produced a weak national economic structure that allows exploitation by outside interests. Neo-classical interpretations have also emerged. Neo-classical economic history downplays the role of staples production and argues that the Canadian economy resembles other industrialized economies in the world. Two fields where the literature is most developed — Central Canada and the transformation of the Atlantic regional economy — have been isolated as separate sections in this chapter.

General Works

Baskerville, Peter, ed. *Canadian Papers in Business History*. Victoria: Public History Group, 1989— .
Intended to be a series similar to *Canadian Papers in Rural History*, this series has never duplicated the success of its rural counterpart. The two volumes published contain a wide variety of articles; although the title

suggests a focus on business history, the essays also reflect trends in social and economic history.

Bliss, Michael. *Northern Enterprise: Five Centuries of Canadian Business.* Toronto: McClelland and Stewart, 1987.

A chronicle of Canadian business drawn primarily from secondary literature, *Northern Enterprise* is an outstanding reference source for economic and business historians. One of Canada's best business historians, Michael Bliss looks not only at the business endeavours that have dominated the Canadian experience, but also at the entrepreneurs who ran them. Two implicit arguments hold the work together. First, business should be left to the private sector and government should play a minor enabling role at best. Second, Canada has a vibrant domestic business sector and the left-nationalist emphasis on foreign ownership is overstated and misguided. The annotated bibliography following each chapter is a useful tool for students and researchers alike.

Cameron, Duncan, ed. *Explorations in Canadian Economic History: Essays in Honour of Irene M. Spry.* Ottawa: University of Ottawa Press, 1985.

A collection of fifteen essays, *Explorations* is divided into sections on political economy, resource development, and the Canadian community. This work does not offer a new synthesis for Canadian economic history. Instead, the staples tradition of Harold Adams Innis is prominent throughout the work. The first section examines theoretical perspectives on the Canadian economy; the second section contains the histories of potash, asbestos, mining, and water development; and the final section brings together a series of specialised essays on government, welfare, community, and development. Although readers will find many interesting essays on specialised topics, the only theme linking the various essays is a general criticism of neo-classical economics.

Carroll, William K. *Corporate Power and Canadian Capitalism.* Vancouver: University of British Columbia Press, 1986.

Carroll attacks the work of proponents of the dependency school in this statistical study of Canadian capitalism. Carroll notes that concern over foreign ownership in the Canadian economy is misplaced. After cross-tabulating corporate growth and inter-locking directorates in top Canadian businesses, he argues that commercial, financial, and industrial capital were primarily in Canadian hands. Historians and economists will find several problems with the book, not the least of which is the sociological rather than historical methodology, but the general conclusions reflect the mainstream work in the field. *Corporate Power and Canadian Capitalism* is a useful work alongside the contrary findings of R. T. Naylor, Kari Levitt, and Gordon Laxer.

Easterbrook, W. T. *North American Patterns of Growth and Development*. Edited with an introduction by Ian Parker. Toronto: University of Toronto Press, 1990.
Published five years after Easterbrook's death in 1985, *North American Patterns* has been ably edited and introduced by Ian Parker. Easterbrook examines larger patterns of economic development from European settlement to the early twentieth century in Canada, Mexico, and the United States. Distinctly interdisciplinary, Easterbrook's complex historical narrative emphasises staples theory and the role of entrepreneurs in both centre and marginal economies.

Easterbrook, W. T. and Mel Watkins, eds. *Approaches to Canadian Economic History*. Toronto: McClelland and Stewart, 1967; rpt., 1978.
Although this collection of dated articles is organized around the themes of staples, land policy and agriculture, banking and capital formation, and the state, the staples thesis runs throughout all sections. The greatest value of this volume is its provision of short, readable excerpts of a previous generation of economic historians, along with its introduction to traditional theories of staple production. For a selection of Harold Innis' essays — Canada's most important staple historian — see Daniel Drache, ed., *Staples, Markets, and Cultural Change: Selected Essays by Harold A. Innis* (1995).

Laxer, Gordon. *Open for Business: The Roots of Foreign Ownership*. Toronto: Oxford University Press, 1989.
A work in the left-nationalist tradition of Canadian history, *Open for Business* reflects many of the dependency theory themes found in Kari Levitt, *Silent Surrender* (1974), R. T. Naylor, *The History of Canadian Business* (1975), and Wallace Clement, *Continental Corporate Power* (1977). Unlike these earlier authors, however, Laxer compares the Canadian policy decisions with those made in countries like Sweden, Japan, and Czechoslovakia. This comparative work leads to some interesting conclusions. Levitt, Naylor, and Clement conclude that a weak

Canadian business class allowed multinational corporations to dominate the economic landscape. Laxer points in a different direction. He argues that the weakness of Canada's agrarian and labour classes allowed businesses in Canada to pursue economic wealth outside of a nationalist framework. As a result, the state, a servant of business in Canada, did little to encourage an indigenous industrial system. Multinational branch plant industries, producing significant profits for Canadian businessmen with little associated risk, were the result.

Marr, William L. and D. G. Paterson. *Canada: An Economic History*. Toronto: Macmillan, 1980.
Marr and Paterson ask questions about economic growth and development within the framework of the new economic history. The authors do not attempt to link this information to the larger political and social contexts of Canadian history. This work is therefore, purely economic in its focus, a point emphasised by the book's use of themes rather than chronology as an organising device. The book contains numerous statistical indicators and is framed by neo-classical economic models.

McCalla, Douglas, ed. *The Development of Canadian Capitalism: Essays in Business History*. Toronto: Copp Clark, 1990.
Reflecting the growth of innovative work in Canadian business history since 1970, this collection of seminal articles is organized around the themes of colonial business, railways and business, business and government, new technologies, organizational change and labour, and post-war capitalism. Each section begins with a short introductory essay outlining the major trends in the literature. The book also contains a short bibliographic essay of further readings.

_____, ed. *Perspectives on Canadian Economic History*. Toronto: Copp Clark, 1987.
The first edition of *Perspectives on Canadian Economic History* is a compilation of previously published essays using neo-classical economic theory to investigate traditional themes of Canadian economic history. Together they reflect how Canadian economic history has moved away from a traditional staples thesis interpretation. Readers will find valuable essays on topics such as nineteenth century agriculture in Quebec, transportation policy, and the wheat boom, all of which call older interpretations into question. McCalla provides a useful commentary before each section, and a short selection of further readings.

McCalla, Douglas and Michael Huberman, eds. *Perspectives on Canadian Economic History*. 2nd ed. Toronto: Copp Clark, 1994.
The second edition of *Perspectives on Canadian Economic History* contains a completely new selection of essays and topics. Like the earlier edition, however, this collection emphasises the emergence of "neo-classical" economic interpretations and downplays the importance of the staples thesis in Canadian economic history. The essays selected span from the fur trade to the post-war industrial economy, and the editors have provided useful introductions to each topic and a short selection of further readings.

Naylor, R. T. *Canada in the European Age, 1453-1919*. Vancouver: New Star Books, 1987.
Already dated even at the time of its publication, *Canada in the European Age* primarily examines the past five centuries (with a somewhat confusing retrospect on the Crusades) of colonial and national economic history. Ideologically at odds with Michael Bliss' *Northern Enterprise* (1987) (Bliss proclaimed it of no use in preparing his own volume), Naylor concerns himself with broad trends and forces such as the acquisitive and destructive nature of capitalism and capital formation.

_____. *The History of Canadian Business, 1867-1914*. 2 vols. Toronto: James Lorimer, 1975.
These volumes examine Canada's economic structure from the National Policy to World War I. Severely criticised for its errors of fact, and either highly praised or excoriated for its interpretation, *The History of Canadian Business* argues that Canada did not move beyond staple production and economic colonization in the period prior to the war. Instead, under the influence of foreign technology and investment, tariff policies, and the centralizing tendencies of Canadian banks, an earlier period of industrialization that was allied with British capital and substructures was merely replaced by an industrialization dependent upon the United States.

Neill, Robin. *A History of Canadian Economic Thought*. London: Routledge, 1991.
Well-researched, although sometimes burdened with fractured prose and vague arguments, this volume integrates Canadian economic theory and policy. While recognizing the international context in which economic theories develop and operate, Neill is sensitive to the unique nature of

Canadian geography, culture, and industrialization. Neill devotes a largely theoretical chapter to the Scottish-Canadian economist John Rae, a chapter on the Nationalist School of Canadian economic theory, and substantial attention to staples theory and French-Canadian economic thought. Neill's work is a significant improvement on C. D. Goodwin's *Canadian Economic Thought* (1961), although the latter still offers some valuable insights into the nineteenth century. Neill has provided a comprehensive and current bibliography.

Norrie, Ken and Doug Owram. *A History of the Canadian Economy.* Toronto: Harcourt Brace, 1987; rev. ed., 1996.
Written jointly by an economist and a historian (and thus collectively they return to an older tradition of political economy), this work constitutes the best available survey of Canadian economic history. In contrast to much Canadian economic history which tends to be eclectic and uneven, this work presents a readable and logical analysis. Strongly chronological in orientation, *A History of the Canadian Economy* emphasises the historical importance of staples production. Norrie and Owram pay attention to regional variation (though less attention is given to British Columbia and the North) and aim to integrate economic events into broader political, demographic, and social themes.

Pomfret, Richard. *The Economic Development of Canada.* Toronto: Methuen, 1981.
Together with Marr and Paterson's *Canada: An Economic History* (1980), this volume represented the first significant attempt to update W. T. Easterbrook and H. G. J. Aitken's *Canadian Economic History*, which was first published in 1956. While Marr and Paterson employ a modified staples thesis (though much more analytical and nuanced than in Easterbrook and Aitken), Pomfret sees little in Canadian economic history after 1850 that would require a specific theory; indeed, Pomfret rejects the dominance of the staples theory and argues that there is little in Canada's development that would distinguish it from other industrialized countries.

Rea, Kenneth J. *A Guide to Canadian Economic History.* Toronto: Canadian Scholars' Press, 1991.
Produced by one of Canada's senior economic historian, *A Guide to Canadian Economic History* is an excellent introduction to the literature in Canadian economic history. Rea divides the book into forty-two sections and provides a useful introduction to the approaches and

methodologies that have been utilized. Each introductory essay is followed by graphs and charts that highlight important statistical information relevant to the topic. This book is an essential guide to any student or researcher unfamiliar with Canadian economic history.

Taylor, Graham D. and Peter Baskerville. *A Concise History of Business in Canada*. Toronto: Oxford University Press, 1994.

This survey of Canadian business history is thoroughly referenced and reflects the outstanding research skills of the authors and the developments within the field. The authors successfully break from the political-economy traditions of the staples thesis, and reveal a complex and multi-dimensional business community. Relying primarily on secondary sources the authors focus the work on three themes: changing patterns of business organization, the particular character of Canadian business, and the international setting of Canadian business. Although the book lacks the strong argumentative focus of Michael Bliss' *Northern Enterprise* (1987), the outstanding references and isolated vignettes discussing key figures and historical controversies make *A Concise History of Business in Canada* a superior text book.

Watkins, M. H. and H. M. Grant, eds. *Canadian Economic History*. Ottawa: Carleton University Press, 1993.

This collection continues to develop the staples thesis interpretation effectively illustrated in Easterbrook and Watkins, eds., *Approaches to Canadian Economic History* (1984). The papers reproduced in this book were primarily written in the 1970s and early 1980s and focus on the "staple trap," or foreign control and underdevelopment, which characterizes the Canadian economy.

Staples, Resource Management, and Transportation

Armstrong, Christopher and H. V. Nelles. *Monopoly's Moment: The Organization and Regulation of Canadian Utilities, 1830-1930*. Philadelphia: Temple University Press, 1986.

This wide-ranging and stimulating volume argues that with the creation of new technologies such as gas and electric power, street railways, and the telephone, there also emerged companies—or monopoly-makers—that sought to utilize and control these new technologies. While monopoly-makers for a time were unfettered by government or union control, there emerged a movement to regulate perceived excesses of corporate power through a vast array of means that involved both public and private agencies. Though not explicitly comparative, *Monopoly's Moment* notes that while the regulatory process was more often than not at the local or state level in the United States, in Canada the federal government more often assumed that role. In addition, for a variety of reasons (and not, therefore, purely ideological) Canadians relied more often than the United States upon public ownership as one means of controlling monopolies. In typical Canadian fashion, however, they were less reliant on this form of regulation than many European states.

Blanchard, J. *A History of the Canadian Grain Commission, 1912-87.* Winnipeg: Canadian Grain Commission, 1987.
In Canada, the federal government regulates the inspection, grading, storage, handling, and transportation of grain products. Its authority in this field is designated to the Canadian Grain Commission. Blanchard provides readers with a short administrative history of the Grain Commission that is long on details regarding statutory legislation and administrative structure and short on analysis.

Breen, David. *Alberta's Petroleum Industry and the Conservation Board.* Edmonton: University of Alberta Press, 1989.
A superb analysis of Alberta's oil and gas industry prior to 1960, this work traces the formation of the Turner Valley Gas Conservation Board and, especially, the Petroleum and Natural Gas Conservation Board. Breen argues that the province drew upon the American experience in establishing regulatory boards and that, in comparison to the experience to the south, these boards were remarkably effective. In addition, the Conservation Board was closely allied with Alberta's Social Credit government and was instrumental in influencing energy policies after the Leduc find in 1947. This work serves as a useful ideological counterweight to Larry Pratt and John Richard's *Prairie Capitalism* (1979).

Cruise, David and Alison Griffiths. *Lords of the Line: The Men Who Built the CPR.* Markham: Viking, 1988.
Well-researched but popular in orientation, *Lords of the Line* chronicles the machinations and more ordinary affairs of six corporate leaders of the Canadian Pacific Railway (CPR). Though they represent fewer than one half of the CPR's presidents, George Stephen, William Van Horne, Thomas Shaughnessy, Edward Betty, D. C. Coleman, and Ian Sinclair

dominated the high politics of the company for much of its first century
of existence. This collective biography uses anecdotal evidence to argue
for the importance of these men, at the expense of hundreds of thousands
of employees who actually "built the CPR."

Darling, Howard J. *The Politics of Freight Rates: The Railway Freight
      Rate Issue in Canada.* Toronto: McClelland and Stewart, 1980.
This manuscript was edited and completed following the death of Howard
Darling in 1977. Darling examines both the economic and political
explanations in freight rate issues over the previous century, and logically
emphasises the importance of rate issues in Atlantic Canada and the West.

Doern, G. Bruce and Glen Toner. *The Politics of Energy: The
      Development and Implementation of the National Energy Policy.*
      Toronto: Methuen, 1985.
Doern and Toner attempt to provide a neutral interpretation of one of the
most controversial policy decisions made by the government of Pierre
Trudeau. The National Energy Policy (NEP) of 1980 was designed to
limit the role of the multinational oil companies in Canada's oil and gas
industry and bring a larger share of the revenue from oil and gas to the
federal treasury. The policy, however, pitted the interests of the western
producing provinces and the oil companies against the national agenda of
the federal government. It inspired western Canadian regional angst,
produced a recession in Alberta, and spawned the separatist Western
Canada Concept party. Two themes emerge in their work. First, they
sympathise with the position of Pierre Trudeau and demonstrate quite
capably that federal-provincial financial arrangements placed an
unwarranted financial strain on the federal treasury. Second, they argue
that the NEP was poorly conceived and implemented.

Eagle, John. *The Canadian Pacific Railway and the Development of
      Western Canada, 1896-1914.* Montreal: McGill-Queen's University
      Press, 1988.
John Eagle provides a detailed account of the business history of the
Canadian Pacific Railway (CPR) in western Canada. During the period
1896 to 1914, western Canada's network of branch lines and spur lines
was built, and Eagle successfully chronicles each move by the CPR. The
ability of CPR managers to align their corporate interests with national
interests expressed by the federal government was clearly instrumental to
the company's success.

Fairbairn, Garry. *From Prairie Roots: The Remarkable Story of the Saskatchewan Wheat Pool*. Saskatoon: Western Producer Prairie Books, 1984.

A cooperative grain handling and marketing company, the Saskatchewan Wheat Pool is the largest agricultural company in Canada. As editor of the *Western Producer*, a weekly newspaper published by the Pool, Fairbairn had access to all the internal documents of the company and interviewed several of the key individuals. He uses this information to write a balanced account of the evolution of the pool from a cooperative wheat marketing agency into a fully integrated agricultural conglomerate. He ties the transitions in the company with changes in Canada's cereal grain economy and international marketing commitments. While Fairbairn does not engage scholarly debates over the relationship of cooperatives to the capitalist business community, he provides a wealth of information about the most successful cooperative enterprises.

Ferguson, Barry Glen. *Athabasca Oil Sands: Northern Resource Exploration, 1875-1951*. Regina: Canadian Great Plains Research Centre, 1986.

Ferguson examines the numerous efforts by entrepreneurs, scientists, and politicians to access the 800 billion barrels of oil trapped in the oil sands around Fort McMurray, Alberta. Ferguson demonstrates that technology advanced incrementally and that no single technological breakthrough occurred. Further, Ferguson argues that both government and business were involved in the process. The book is both chronological and thematic, with useful chapters on the role of the Geological Survey of Canada, the Research Council of Alberta, and the early business-government exploitation ventures such as the Abasand and Bitumont projects.

Fleming, Keith B. *Power at Cost: Ontario Hydro and Rural Electrification, 1911-58*. Montreal: McGill-Queen's University Press, 1992.

Established in 1906, Ontario Hydro became the largest utility in North America. As a public utility, it began as early as 1911 to plan and provide service to rural customers and became the North American leader in this field. Still it took over forty-five years for Ontario Hydro to reach 95% of Ontario's rural households. In this well researched book, Fleming describes this lengthy process in detail. He emphasises the cooperation between the utility and government to extend rural electricity delivery and the limitations of the system. By making this story available to scholars and students, Fleming has opened the door to research on topics such as changing agricultural patterns, rural industrialization, and the increasing urbanization of rural communities.

Foster, Peter. *The Sorcerer's Apprentices: Canada's Super-Bureaucrats and the Energy Mess.* Toronto: Collins, 1982.

The best of the books written by popular historian Peter Foster, *The Sorcerer's Apprentices* is a critical indictment of the Canadian government's National Energy Policy (NEP) written at the height of the crisis. Although Foster acknowledges the problems created by falling oil prices, he portrays the NEP as a disaster caused by fraud and incompetence in the federal bureaucracy.

Gillis, R. Peter and Thomas Roach. *Lost Initiatives: Canada's Forest Industries, Forest Policy and Forest Conservation.* New York: Greenwood, 1986.

A highly polemical work broaching the fields of economic, environmental, and political history, *Lost Initiatives* is a survey of Canadian forest policy with particular emphasis on the period 1882 to 1939. It contains chapters on New Brunswick, Quebec, Ontario, and British Columbia, and an innovative section on federal government policy based on comprehensive archival research. The authors argue that forest policy developed primarily through business-government cooperation and emphasised exploitation rather than conservation. The authors are particularly critical of the failure of both business and government to take advice from the emerging professional foresters. Although the authors make an excellent case for the unsustainability of Canadian forest exploitation, they are weaker when analysing the role of economic factors in policy formation. Like agriculture, mining, and oil and gas, forestry depended upon international markets and was forever at the mercy of the vagaries of international commodity price fluctuations.

Gould, Ed. *Oil: The History of Canada's Oil and Gas Industry.* Vancouver: Hancock House, 1976.

This survey presents a narrative history of Canada's oil and gas industries over the past century. Well-illustrated, this volume presents a sanitized version of the personalities and history of the oil patch with little discussion of American interests and dominance, environmental policies, or Native issues.

Gray, Earle. *Wildcatters: The Story of Pacific Petroleum and Westcoast Transmission*. Toronto: McClelland and Stewart, 1982.
_____. *The Great Canadian Oil Patch*. Toronto: Maclean-Hunter, 1970.

Earle Gray is an excellent popular historian whose books are well-researched introductory narratives to the Canadian oil industry. *The Great Canadian Oil Patch* is an illustrated account of the development of the oil industry from the earliest discoveries in 1858 to the achievement of self-sufficiency in 1970. *Wildcatters* is the story of one of Canada's successful independent oil companies, the first independent gas transmission company, and the grandiose visions that inspired the companies' founder, Frank MacMahon.

House, J. D. *The Last of the Free Enterprisers: The Oilmen of Calgary*. Toronto: Macmillan, 1980.

Written for scholars and general readers interested in resource economics, this work examines the personalities and structures of Alberta's oil and gas industry. To no one's surprise, House's quantified account reveals the overwhelming male dominance of Calgary's "oil men"; other aspects of the study focus on the structure of the industry, the decision-making process, and the interrelation between governments and business. House presents a strong critique of government monopolies in the oil and gas business but calls for a social contract between public and private interests.

Kilbourn, William. *Pipeline: Trans-Canada and the Great Debate; A History of Business and Politics*. Toronto: Clarke, Irwin, 1970.

In 1956 Canadian politics was shaken by the Trans-Canada pipeline debate. The government of Louis St. Laurent proposed to have an American company build Canada's first transcontinental natural gas pipeline with financial assistance from the federal government. John Diefenbaker led a nationalistic attack on the project in the House of Commons. Kilbourn's book is a narrative of the events surrounding this debate, but offers little analysis or insight. Readers interested in this topic will, however, find it a useful and accurate introduction.

Lamb, W. Kaye. *History of the Canadian Pacific Railway*. New York: Macmillan, 1977.

Like Pierre Berton's *The National Dream* and *The Last Spike* (1970-71), this book on the Canadian Pacific Railway (CPR) considers it the string that held the country together. Unlike Berton's work, however, nationalism and personality are not the dominant themes. This volume tells the story of the CPR from its nineteenth-century origins to 1970, provides an excellent narrative of the political and corporate machinations that dominate this story, examines changing technology, the problems of construction, and contains an excellent collection of photographs.

Laxer, James. *Oil and Gas: Ottawa, the Provinces, and the Oil Industry.* Toronto: Lorimer, 1983.
Oil and Gas is a left-nationalist interpretation that is extremely critical of multinational oil companies. Laxer examines the transformation of the Canadian government's policies toward oil and gas following the 1973 OPEC crisis and follows the events through to the failure of the 1980 National Energy Policy. Laxer notes that oil and gas finally entered into the realm of national policy in Canada, but that the government had retreated from its more strident nationalist policies by 1982. The book is thoroughly referenced and should be used with G. Bruce Doern and Glen Toner, *The Politics of Energy* (1985), in order to gain a more complete picture of Canada's energy policy.

Leonard, Frank. *A Thousand Blunders: The Grand Trunk Pacific Railway Company and Northern British Columbia.* Vancouver: University of British Columbia Press, 1995.
This award-winning book examines the building of Canada's second transcontinental railway in northern BC. Leonard not only examines the political, financial, and business transactions of the construction process but also looks at the role of labour and local communities in building the Grand Trunk Pacific. His discussion of the impact of the railway on aboriginal populations in northern British Columbia is especially thoughtful. For a superb study of a smaller BC railway, see Barrie Sanford, *McCulloch's Wonder: The Story of the Kettle Valley Railway* (1978).

Mackay, Donald. *Empire of Wood: The MacMillan-Bloedel Story.* Vancouver: Douglas and McIntyre, 1982.
This popular history traces H. R. MacMillan's arrival in British Columbia, his co-founding of a lumber brokerage firm in 1919, and, after successive mergers and expansions (including one with his American partner J. H. Bloedel, the establishment of the forest product conglomerate MacMillan-Bloedel. Lacking in analysis, but replete with anecdotes, this work

concentrates primarily upon personalities (especially MacMillan's) and
the decision-making process at the boardroom level. For another comment
see Mackay's, *Heritage Lost: The Crisis in Canada's Forests* (1985). For
a biography of MacMillan, see Ken Drushka, *HR: A Biography of H. R.
MacMillan* (1995).

_____. *The People's Railway: A History of Canadian National*.
     Vancouver: Douglas and McIntyre, 1992.
During and following World War I, the financial difficulties of numerous
railways reached critical proportions; in response, the federal government
moved toward public ownership and the Canadian National Railways
(CNR) system was established. Designed for the general reader, Mackay's
history argues, in teleological fashion, for the importance of railways —
and, in particular, of the CNR — for the national unity of Canada.
Unfortunately, *The People's Railway* contains little information on the
thousands of working individuals who made up the railway.

Marchak, Patricia. *Green Gold: The Forest Industry in British Columbia*.
     Vancouver: University of British Columbia Press, 1983.
Green Gold is a polemical attack on British Columbia forest policies that
draws upon historical research to make its case that forestry in British
Columbia could not be sustained under 1980 policies. Drawing upon
Harold Adams Innis and dependency theorists, Marchak begins by
asserting that little of the surplus value of the forest industry accumulates
to the people of British Columbia. She then argues that seasonal work
patterns, the transient nature of the workforce, and high unemployment
are all the result of corporate policy in the British Columbia forest
industry. Finally Marchak makes a compelling argument that the residents
of lumber towns have little power in determining the nature of resource
exploitation.

Marchak, Patricia, Neil Guppy, and John McMullan, eds. *Uncommon
     Property: The Fishing and Fish Processing Industries in British
     Columbia*. Toronto: Methuen, 1987.
This edited collection is broadly concerned with the political economy of
fishing, and the anthropological, historical, and sociological aspects that
emerge out of such an enterprise. *Uncommon Property* is divided into
three sections: the first section examines the historical context of British
Columbia's fisheries, the role of capital, governments, and markets, and
attempts to place the fishery in an international context; second, several

articles examine the labour process, the organization of workers, and the role of Native people in the fishery; and finally, there is a brief consideration of regions dependent on the fishery and an analysis of efforts to overcome extreme over dependance and regional subordination. For a feminist and neo-Marxist account of labour in the BC fisheries, see Alicja Muszynski, *Cheap Wage Labour: Race and Gender in the Fisheries of British Columbia* (1996).

McCullough, A. B. *The Commercial Fishery of the Canadian Great Lakes*. Ottawa: Parks Canada, 1989.
This brief survey provides a historical overview of one of the world's largest fresh-water fisheries. In particular, McCullough examines government regulation and intervention, jurisdictional issues, the changing nature of the fishery, the processing and marketing of fish, labour conditions, and the economic impact of the Great Lakes fishery.

Mouat, Jeremy. *Roaring Days: Rossland's Mines and the History of British Columbia*. Vancouver: University of British Columbia, 1995.
Even though the Fraser and Caribou gold rushes inspired much excitement and myth, the history of mining in British Columbia — and in particular hard rock mining — has received little attention. This excellent study traces mining in Rossland from its dramatic boom in 1890 to its post-World War I decline. Mouat discusses the role of technology, railways, labour relations and conditions, and the growth of Cominco in Rossland, and argues that the history of mining in this city reflects the history of British Columbia as a whole.

Nelles, H. V. *The Politics of Development: Forests, Mines and Hydro-Electric Power in Ontario, 1849-1941*. Toronto: Macmillan, 1974.
One of the best books written in Canadian history, *The Politics of Development* traces the political ramifications of the emergence of the twentieth-century staple products in Ontario. Nelles argues that the development of these new staples, and their overall importance to the economy, reduced the role of the Canadian state to that of "a client of the business community." The book not only brings breadth to the development of business enterprises surrounding these resources but also makes significant commentary on Canadian-American trade relations and Canadian federal-provincial economic relations. Furthermore, Nelles provides pioneering research on environmental history and the role of public enterprise in the Canadian economy.

Newell, Dianne. *Technology on the Frontier: Mining in Old Ontario.*
    Vancouver: University of British Columbia Press, 1986.
Focussing on three large geographic areas, Dianne Newell provides a
readable and thoroughly researched account of the role of technology in
Ontario mining from 1840 to 1890. Newell demonstrates that Canada
borrowed most of its mining technology from Europe, Britain, and the
United States and then adapted it to meet the peculiar conditions of
Ontario's mining operations.

Newell, Dianne, ed. *The Development of the Pacific Salmon-Canning
    Industry.* Montreal: McGill-Queen's University Press, 1989.
Henry Doyle was a key promoter of the British Columbia Packers'
Association during the boom years of the salmon canning industry at the
onset of the twentieth century. Though he left the Packers' Association in
1904 after only two years as its leader, he left behind meticulous and
thoughtful papers regarding the salmon industry during the first 30 years
of the twentieth century. Newell has selected portions from Doyle's
diaries, letters, and account books and has effectively introduced and
annotated them.

Paterson, Donald G. *British Direct Investment in Canada, 1890-1914:
    Estimates and Determinants.* Toronto: University of Toronto Press,
    1976.
Paterson investigates the role of British capital during the dynamic "wheat
boom" era of Canadian history and tries to explain the eventual decline of
the British role in the Canadian economy. Using a variety of evidence and
a large statistical data base, Paterson notes that British capitalists invested
primarily in staple-based resource industries and avoided establishing the
industrial branch plants favoured by American investors. British firms,
moreover, insisted on British control and British managers, often to the
detriment of financial success. The combination of a resource-based
investment strategy and large capital losses during a period of economic
expansion eventually led to a withdrawal of British capital from Canada.

Pratt, Larry. *The Tar Sands: Syncrude and the Politics of Oil.* Edmonton:
    Hurtig, 1976.
While the technology, politics, and potential of the tar sands has evolved
considerably since 1976, this work still provides useful background to
policies regarding that resource. Pratt documents the efforts of Ottawa
and Alberta to regulate the multinationals such as Syncrude who were

involved in the northern fields; he ultimately concludes, however, that government efforts were half-hearted and did not reflect the common interests of Canadians. Pratt's critique is severe, and he concludes by arguing for a publicly-owned presence in the oil and gas industry.

Proulx, Jean-Pierre. *Basque Whaling in Labrador in the Sixteenth Century*. Ottawa: Parks Canada, 1993.
Arguing that Canadian historians have too often overlooked the exploitation of the East coast fishery in the second half of the sixteenth century, this work examines the individual whalers and fishermen who came from the Basque region. Relying on English, French, and Spanish sources, *Basque Whaling* examines the origins of the whale hunt, methods and technology employed, and the importance of whaling in the Basque economy. For a broader perspective, readers may wish to consult Proulx's *Whaling in the North Atlantic from Earliest Times to the Mid-19th Century* (1986).

Regehr, T. D. *The Canadian Northern Railway: Pioneer Road of the Northern Prairies, 1895-1918*. Toronto: Macmillan, 1976.
In the tradition of laurentian history, the Canadian Pacific Railway, Canada's first transcontinental line, holds the status of cultural icon. Its builders are looked upon as late nineteenth century nation builders. William Mackenzie and Donald Mann, the promoters of the Canadian Northern Railway, have not been treated as kindly. Regehr argues that their contribution to nation building is equal to that of the CPR promoters. His sympathetic account is filled with details regarding the innovative business practices and the risky, perhaps even corrupt, financial arrangements of the Canadian Northern Railway. The promoters' visions of grandeur and the unforeseen consequences of depression and war led to the failure of this railway company and its eventual inclusion in the Canadian National Railways.

Richards, John and Larry Pratt. *Prairie Capitalism: Power and Influence in the New West*. Toronto: McClelland and Stewart, 1979.
Well-researched and insightful, *Prairie Capitalism* explores resource policies and politics concerning the new staples of oil, gas, and potash in Saskatchewan and Alberta. This work argues that the state developed from passive rentier policies in the 1940s and 1950s to a more entrepreneurial stance by the 1970s. In adopting such a stance, provincial governments often allied with multinational corporations in fighting

against the policies of central Canada. Ironically, although Saskatchewan and Alberta have very different political and ideological histories, their resource management and policies were often quite similar.

Skogstad, Grace. *The Politics of Agricultural Policy-Making in Canada.* Toronto: University of Toronto Press, 1987.
This book is a valuable addition to Vernon Fowke's now-dated *Canadian Agricultural Policy: The Historical Pattern* (1946), and an excellent companion to C. F. Wilson, *A Century of Canadian Grain* (1978). Skogstad looks at the role of both political and economic factors in the development of agricultural policy. Her study is also concerned with the role of federal-provincial relations in policy formation. Skogstad focuses upon issues of grain transportation, supply management in dairy and poultry production, and agricultural commodity price stabilisation programs. She argues that farm income stability was the primary concern for policy-makers and that federal government action occurred primarily during periods of crisis when political rewards would be greatest.

Spector, David. *Agriculture on the Prairies, 1870-1940.* Ottawa: Parks Canada, 1983.
Spector provides an excellent summary of agricultural development on the Canadian prairies. Spector demonstrates that cereal grain production remained the dominant agricultural practice in the southern prairies because it proved to be the most profitable commodity in the rich black and dark brown soils of the region. Livestock, consequently, always played a supportive rather than dominant role on the Canadian prairies.

Stevens, G. R. *History of the Canadian National Railways.* New York: Macmillan, 1973.
A contribution to the "Railroads of America" series, this volume traces the development of the Grand Trunk, Intercolonial, and Canadian Northern, all of which were precursors of the Canadian National. By 1922 these, and a menagerie of other lines, had been amalgamated and the Canadian National Railways (CNR) was born. The emphasis is on the political and entrepreneurial personalities, and the text is rich with anecdotes. This work argues that far from being a fiscal burden, the CNR was a servant in promoting Canadian nationalism.

Swift, Jamie. *Cut and Run: The Assault on Canada's Forests.* Toronto: Between the Lines, 1983.

Guided by a need to develop a new social vision to combat the effects of
poor resource management, *Cut and Run* explores forestry policy from the
pre-Confederation period onward. Swift also examines the impact of new
technology on labour and the environment, and a series of political
scandals revolving around the forest industry. Swift has conducted a
series of interviews with those involved in the industry in an effort to
provide some analysis into the difficulties and problems faced.

White, Clinton O. *Power for a Province: A History of Saskatchewan
Power*. Regina: Canadian Plains Research Centre, 1976.
Although Saskatchewan first considered the idea of an integrated,
provincially controlled power generation and distribution system in 1912,
the Saskatchewan Power Corporation system was not completed until
1964. In this detailed, and thoroughly referenced study, White argues that
political disputes between the provincial government and municipal
authorities, rather than economic conditions, were responsible for the
slow process of development.

Wilson, C. F. *A Century of Canadian Grain: Government Policy to 1951*.
Saskatoon: Western Producer Prairie Books, 1978.
A Century of Canadian Grain is a lengthy and turgid study of policy
formation in the Canadian grain business. Wilson divides the book into
four sections. The first deals with the era to 1930, and examines the
establishment of a temporary Canadian Wheat Board in World War I and
the formation of the wheat pools. The second section deals with the Great
Depression until the creation of the permanent Canadian Wheat Board in
1935. The third section reviews the operations of the Wheat Board
through World War II and charts the government's efforts to reestablish
a private marketing system. The final section examines the post-war
government wheat marketing initiatives. The book is descriptive rather
than analytical and offers an impressive overview of policy formation.

Business, Entrepreneurs, and Professionals

Armstrong, Christopher and H. V. Nelles. *Southern Exposure: Canadian
Promoters in Latin America and the Caribbean, 1896-1930*. Toronto:
University of Toronto Press, 1988.
Most work in Canadian economic and business history has focussed upon
the role of foreign capital in Canada. In this book, Armstrong and Nelles
instead examine Canadian investment and investors abroad. Beginning at

the turn of the century, Canadian banks began to loan money to Canadian businessmen active in Latin America and the Caribbean. By 1930, consolidated corporate entities such as Brazillian Traction had emerged. Throughout the book, the personalities of the investors and their activities in the London-based world capital market are emphasised.

Ball, Norman R. and John N. Vardalas. *Ferranti-Packard: Pioneers in Canadian Electrical Manufacturing.* Montreal: McGill-Queen's University Press, 1994.

Well-illustrated and readable, *Ferranti-Packard* is an insightful corporate history placed within the context of Canadian political and business history. The authors explore the origins of electrical technology in Canada in the last decades of the nineteenth century, and the major technological innovations of Ferranti Canada and Packard Electric in the twentieth. As well, since Ferranti was a branch of a British firm and Packard a United States subsidiary prior to their merger in 1958, this work offers insights into two different corporate cultures and traditions.

Baskerville, Peter, ed. *The Bank of Upper Canada: Documents.* Toronto: Champlain Society, 1987.

Established in 1822, the Bank of Upper Canada was, until its liquidation in 1866, one of the largest and most important financial institutions of its era and locale. Baskerville's lengthy introduction provides a narrative of the Bank's history and analyses its role in the colony's economic development and its linkages to government and other financial institutions, both in Canada and abroad. Though many of the Bank's records were destroyed in the 1870s, Baskerville has been able to reproduce an impressive collection of letters, financial statements, and reports. A series of appendixes includes a listing of the bank's directors, statutes relating to the bank, and assorted financial data.

Bliss, Michael. *A Canadian Millionaire: The Life and Business Times of Sir Joseph Flavelle.* Toronto: Macmillan, 1978.

Based on an insightful reading of Joseph Flavelle's voluminous personal papers, Bliss traces this entrepreneur from his small-town Methodist roots to his position as a successful businessman and pork-king of the British empire. During World War I, Flavelle served as chairman of the Imperial Munition Board; as well, this period saw his pork company make enormous profits, and rumours of profiteering emerged, a charge from which Bliss absolves him. Flavelle was a strict Methodist, and Bliss illustrates how this entrepreneur's religious faith contributed to and influenced his business and philanthropic activities.

_____. *A Living Profit: Studies in the Social History of Canadian Business*. Toronto: McClelland and Stewart, 1974.
Industry, integrity and thrift were the values of the Canadian businessman during the Laurier era and they shaped the responses of Canadian businessmen to a host of economic and social problems. In this thoroughly documented work, Bliss examines the thoughts and attitudes of Canadian entrepreneurs. Unlike their American counterparts, Canadian businessmen were not individualistic robber barons. They fought for the right to make money but believed all should share in that right. Michael Bliss eloquently demonstrates that these values led Canadian businessmen to become cautious supporters of state regulation and political interference in the economy.

Brym, Robert J., ed. *The Structure of the Canadian Capitalist Class*. Toronto: Garamond, 1985.
Based upon a series of conference papers, this highly theoretical work examines the nature of the capitalist class and its impact on economic development. While essays such as that by Jorge Niosi focus on contemporary issues such as the bourgeoisie advocacy for free trade, other essays are historical in nature: Karen Anderson, for example, examines the organization of capital for financing the Canadian Pacific Railway, and Gordon Laxer, largely focussing on the late nineteenth and early twentieth centuries, explores the industrial weakness of Canada.

Clement, Wallace. *Continental Corporate Power: Economic Elite Linkages Between Canada and the United States*. Toronto: McClelland and Stewart, 1977.
A classic work in the left-nationalist tradition, *Continental Corporate Power* is a study of the role of multinational corporations in Canada. Clement argues that in Canada both capital and power are concentrated in the hands of a small elite network comprising both Canadians and Americans. This elite, Clement critically concludes, have opened the Canadian economy to domination by American capital and American corporations. For other works that reach similar conclusions, readers should consult Kari Levitt, *Silent Surrender* (1970), and R. T. Naylor, *History of Canadian Business* (1975).

Cook, Peter. *Massey at the Brink: The Story of Canada's Greatest Multinational and Its Struggle to Survive.* Toronto: Collins, 1981.
Journalistic in style and content, *Massey at the Brink* explores the formation of the Massey empire from Daniel Massey's purchase of a foundry in the mid-nineteenth century to its fiscal crisis of the 1970s. Cook emphasises the managerial elite, corporate chiefs, and board members in influencing the direction of the company, as well as the cyclical nature of markets for farm machinery around the world. Cook devotes substantial space and provides particular insight in analysing the events that led up to the company's fiscal crisis.

DeMont, John. *Citizens Irving: K. C. Irving and His Legacy.* Toronto: McClelland and Stewart, 1991.
Based on numerous interviews (though not, of course, with K. C. Irving who had not granted an interview in the three decades prior to this book), *Citizens Irving* explores one of the largest corporate family enterprises in North America. This work explores Irving's business origins, the emergence of the family empire, and the rivalry with the McCain family, the other dominant family business in New Brunswick. For an account that concentrates on selected themes of the Irving empire, see Russell Hunt and Robert Campbell, *K. C. Irving: The Art of the Industrialist* (1973).

den Otter, Andrew A. *Civilizing the West: The Galts and the Development of Western Canada.* Edmonton: University of Alberta Press, 1982; rpt., 1986.
Largely concerned with the expansion of industrial capitalism into southern Alberta, *Civilizing the West* details the story of Sir Alexander Galt and his son Elliot in utilizing the area's industrial and commercial opportunities to the family's own best advantage. The elder Galt made huge returns as a land speculator in eastern Canada, and when the CPR choose a southern route through Alberta, his good fortune was repeated. In addition, the Galts were extensively involved in mining, timber, irrigation projects, and land colonization. The Galts apparently "civilized" this region by helping to introduce immigrants, industrial capitalism, and Western culture and practices; den Otter, unfortunately, has little insightful to say on how "civilization" influenced the Native people.

Finkel, Alvin. *Business and Social Reform in the Thirties.* Toronto: James Lorimer, 1979.

This neo-Marxist study explores business-government relations during the Depression and argues that traditional explanations have ignored the role of business in influencing important government reforms in areas such as marketing boards, unemployment insurance, subsidized housing, and banking regulation that emerged in this era. Worried that capitalism was being seriously eroded, business interests looked to stabilize the system and limit competition by, for example, the creation of state-regulated marketing boards and the Bank of Canada. Likewise, the business community sought to promote stability through strategic involvement in social welfare policies. This work has been criticized, at times, for its oversimplified view of both business interests and the legislative process.

Fleming, R. B. *The Railway King of Canada: Sir William Mackenzie, 1849-1923*. Vancouver: University of British Columbia Press, 1991.
Sir William Mackenzie was a leading railroad baron and businessman, with wide access to the political elite of his day. In particular, Mackenzie was known for his entrepreneurial activities involving street railways, resource sector development, utilities in Canada and overseas, and (together with Donald Mann) the Canadian Northern Railway. This financial empire declined precipitously with World War I. Fleming's account is largely sympathetic and, perhaps due to a lack of primary source material left by Mackenzie, concentrates on his public image more than his private persona.

Frost, Stanley Brice. *James McGill of Montreal*. Montreal: McGill-Queen's University Press, 1995.
James McGill immigrated to Canada in 1766 and became a successful trader and businessman. Frost presents an uncritical interpretation of McGill's public and private roles as a leading Montreal figure. Most substantially, upon his death in 1813, McGill left an estate that helped endow the university that bears his name.

George, Roy E. *A Leader and a Laggard: Manufacturing Industry in Nova Scotia, Quebec and Ontario*. Toronto: University of Toronto Press, 1970.
This study compares two regions — central Canada and Nova Scotia — and their very different rates of growth in manufacturing from World War II to the early 1960s. Lumping Quebec in with Ontario, *A Leader and a Laggard* briefly introduces the historical differences of these two regions, provides an analysis of cost comparisons, and introduces the reader to

some of the efforts that have been made to stimulate manufacturing in Nova Scotia.

Gidney, R. D. and W. P. J. Miller. *Professional Gentlemen: The Professions in Nineteenth-Century Ontario.* Toronto: University of Toronto Press, 1994.

An outstanding work of synthesis, *Professional Gentlemen* deals with a topic that has attracted a large international audience but has received little attention from Canadian scholars. Gidney and Miller argue that the idea of a profession is historically grounded and should be examined in light of how people understood this concept in the past. This work is divided into two main parts. First, Gidney and Miller examine the Georgian concept of the professional, principally through the work of lawyers, doctors, and clerics. This concept emphasised the importance of a liberal arts education and the notion of "the gentleman" to the professional ideal. Second, the authors explore how the concept of the Georgian professional was modified within the ideology of modern professionalism, with its emphasis upon scientific education and technical expertise. In tracing this transition in the last part of the nineteenth century, the authors broaden their discussion to include other professions, including surveyors, engineers, teachers, dentists, pharmacists, and architects.

Gilmour, J. M. *Spatial Evolution of Manufacturing: Southern Ontario, 1851-91.* Toronto: University of Toronto Press, 1972.

Rich in maps and tables, this work concentrates on the changing patterns of manufacturing in Southern Ontario, and, more specifically, the creation of highly industrialized areas. Gilmour argues that an export-based model of economic development has particular validity for this region. He also explores the role of staple production and the relationship between staples and other products in promoting economic growth; as well, Gilmour argues that political independence from the United States is a theme that economic models must consider.

MacPherson, Ian. *Building and Protecting the Co-operative Movement: A Brief History of the Co-operative Union of Canada, 1909-1984.* Ottawa: The Co-operative Union of Canada, 1984.

Although this book is neither as analytical nor as sophisticated as MacPherson's *Each for All*, it is an important institutional history of the umbrella organization for co-operatives in Canada. Based upon the minutes and publications of the Co-operative Union of Canada, the book is best used as an introduction to the key individuals in the co-operative movement and the problems they faced in formulating and implementing a co-operative philosophy.

_____. *Each for All: A History of the Co-operative Movement in English Canada, 1900-1945*. Toronto: Macmillan, 1979.
Canadians are active participants in cooperative business enterprises. These cooperatives are engaged in retail and wholesale trade; grain, dairy, fruit, and livestock marketing; oil refining; and banking. In this ground-breaking study, MacPherson traces the cooperative movement through its formative years. The narrative is interspersed with theoretical chapters outlining the changing philosophy of cooperation. Two general arguments emerge. First, cooperation, following along the lines of Lawrence Goodwyn's work on Texas populism, is an anti-capitalist philosophy that sought to replace competition with cooperation. Second, cooperatives succeeded when they offered effective management, received government support, and addressed commonly held grievances, but failed when disrupted by factionalism and confronted by organized opposition.

McDowall, Duncan. *The Light: Brazilian Traction, Light and Power Company Limited, 1899-1945*. Toronto: University of Toronto Press, 1988.
The Light was one of Canada's most successful international business ventures. Controlled by Canadians, financed by international capital, based upon American and British technology, and operated by Canadian and Brazilian managers, this company provides a much needed perspective on Canadian business history. Canada's business community, like those in other industrialized countries, was international in its scope. McDowall's story demonstrates quite clearly the adaptability of Canada's entrepreneurs and the important links between government and business in promoting Canadian economic activity.

_____. *Steel at the Sault: Francis Clergue, Sir James Dunn and the Algoma Steel Corporation, 1901-56*. Toronto: University of Toronto Press, 1984.
This work traces the careers of two entrepreneurs, Francis Clergue and James Dunn, the Algoma Steel Corporation, and the interactions between personality, business, and government. Largely narrative in structure, *Steel at the Sault* argues that Algoma was a tenuous operation from the

start and survived only with continuous government support. Only during the 1930s, under the leadership of Sir James Dunn, did Algoma become more self-reliant, though contacts and contracts with governments continued to be important. McDowall emphasises corporate and political personalities, and, unlike Craig Heron's *Working in Steel* (1988), there is little in this work relating to the working-class experience.

Miquelon, Dale. *Dugard of Rouen: French Trade to Canada and the West Indies, 1729-1770*. Montreal: McGill-Queen's University Press, 1978.
Primary documents surviving from the French trade to Canada in the eighteenth century are rare, and so are monographs dealing with this topic. Miquelon's excellent study examines one surviving collection — the papers of Robert Dugard, a French merchant who arranged for at least 75 voyages between France and the French colonies. This highly readable book surveys the formation and financing of Dugard's company, the context in which he traded, and the transition toward increased government monopolies. Although Miquelon makes little of the merchant's religion, Dugard and several of his partners were Huguenot; this hints toward the thesis developed by J. F. Bosher in *The Canada Merchants* (1987) that the French Protestants were increasingly an important element in the French trade in Canada.

Niosi, Jorge. *Canadian Capitalism: A Study of Power in the Canadian Business Establishment*. Toronto: Lorimer, 1981.
_____. *The Economy of Canada: A Study of Ownership and Control*. Montreal: Black Rose, 1981.
Niosi is a critic of Canadian capitalism but is equally critical of left-nationalist historical interpretations that emphasise foreign capital and foreign control of Canadian businesses. In these two books, Niosi demonstrates that Canada's middle-class entrepreneurs exert a dominant influence in Canadian corporations and the formation of Canadian economic policy.

Ommer, Rosemary E., ed. *Merchant Credit and Labour Strategies in Historical Perspective*. Fredericton: Acadiensis Press, 1990.
Emerging out of a conference held at Memorial University, these papers broadly address merchant credit systems and labour practices in staple economies from the Atlantic coast to British Columbia. While merchant credit afforded the opportunity to exploit resources, it has also been seen

by individuals such as Rosemary Ommer in "The Truck System in the Gaspé" as regressive and exploitive of labour. Several authors, however, take a much different view of the creditor-debtor relationship: the essays by David MacDonald, Douglas McCalla, and Alan Taylor argue, in varying degrees, for more reciprocal relations between these parties.

Santink, Joy. *Timothy Eaton and the Rise of His Department Store.* Toronto: University of Toronto Press, 1990.
In spite of its recent fiscal difficulties, Eaton's — which opened in 1869 — has been Canada's largest and most important department store for much of the past century. Santink finds that the emergence of Eaton's shared much with similar stores in the United States, France, and Britain. On a more personal and local level, Santink explores the interrelation between Eaton's Methodist faith and his business, and between Toronto's industrial working-class and an emerging consumer culture.

Smith, Philip. *Treasure Seekers: The Men Who Built Home Oil.* Toronto: Macmillan, 1978.
————. *Harvest from the Rock: A History of Mining in Ontario.* Toronto: Macmillan, 1986.
————. *It Seems Like Only Yesterday: Air Canada, the First 50 Years.* Toronto: McClelland and Stewart, 1986.
Smith's books serve as popular, useful, and well researched introductions to students interested in these topics in Canadian business history. A business journalist and historian, Smith focuses primarily on the role of entrepreneurs and managers within these business ventures but is aware of major issues of concern within the historical community such as monopoly versus competition, east versus west regionalism, and the role of international markets. Unfortunately, the books' use to students is limited by a lack of bibliographic references.

Surtees, Lawrence. *Pa Bell: A. Jean de Grandepré and the Rise of Bell Canada Enterprises.* Toronto: Random House, 1992.
Based on extensive interviews and primary research, Surtees traces the career of A. Jean de Grandepré and the transformation of Bell Canada from a domestic utility into an aggressive global corporation. While de Grandepré presided over expansive efforts such as a multi-billion dollar telecommunications project in Saudi Arabia, he was also a key and influential figure in urging regulatory activity to keep foreign competitors away from internal monopolies. This work unfortunately lacks an index.

Wetherell, Donald, with Elise A. Corbet. *Breaking New Ground: A Century of Farm Equipment Manufacturing on the Canadian Prairies.* Saskatoon: Fifth House Publishers, 1993.

Except for an obvious market, the manufacturing of farm equipment on the Prairies had few natural or acquired advantages, particularly prior to World War II. As a result, manufacturers from Eastern Canada and the United States supplied most large equipment. After World War II prairie manufacturers achieved some modest success, particularly after component manufacturing became more common. This success, Wetherell and Corbet argue, was heightened by the formation of the Prairie Implement Manufacturers Association in 1970 which provided a forum for information and concerns to be shared.

Wilson, Bruce G. *The Enterprises of Robert Hamilton: A Study of Wealth and Influence in Early Upper Canada, 1776-1812.* Ottawa: Carleton University Press, 1983.

An important work that deserves wide consideration, *The Enterprises of Robert Hamilton* explores the activities of one entrepreneur between the American Revolution and his death in 1809. Hamilton did not come north to Upper Canada after the revolution as a wealthy man; rather, he succeeded where many others failed through land speculation, by integrating himself into the laurentian economy, and by receiving and forwarding goods from Montreal and (through kinship connections) the United States. Even though Hamilton deviated from the Upper Canadian Tory norm in his pro-Americanism, he received wide patronage powers (and large land grants) through his appointment as a judge and a justice of the peace. His financial empire faded away following his death, and Wilson argues that the new elite after 1815 were not merchants but, rather, emerged more frequently from the political and administrative strata.

Young, Brian. *In Its Corporate Capacity: The Seminary of Montreal as a Business Institution, 1816-76.* Montreal: McGill-Queen's University Press, 1986.

The Sulpician order in New France and Quebec was the seigneur of large tracts of land, including in the case of the seminary of Montreal, the entire island of Montreal. Framed by Marxist and European models, Young traces the seminary from its role as a feudal landlord to one that had, particularly after the 1840s, embraced a capitalist approach to land and labour. Though Young ignores religious factors that may have impinged upon the seminary's development and actions, this innovative and well-researched study carefully considers notions of class, power relations, and the evolution of institutions as industrial capitalism emerged in the nineteenth century.

_____. *George-Etienne Cartier: Montreal Bourgeois*. Montreal: McGill-Queen's University Press, 1981.

George-Etienne Cartier has most often been portrayed by historians as a father of Confederation and an advocate of a bi-cultural nation. In this work, Cartier's contributions to Confederation are dealt with briefly; instead, Young argues that Cartier is best understood as a "Montreal bourgeois" and explores how being a member of this class influenced Cartier's attitudes and action as a politician and businessman. As a member of the entrepreneurial elite, Cartier disavowed American democracy, sought British definitions of appearance and status, and advocated banking and educational reforms that would help control and socialize the lower orders.

_____. *Promoters and Politicians: The North Shore Railways in Quebec*. Toronto: University of Toronto Press, 1978.

The North-Shore railway project was perceived as a French-Canadian project to open the North-Shore of the St. Lawrence River valley for colonisation and development. Local municipalities, the provincial government, and the Roman Catholic clergy were all involved in the project. When a line from Quebec City to Montreal and to Ottawa was eventually completed, it nearly bankrupted the provincial government. The railway was eventually incorporated into the Canadian Pacific Railway (CPR) system. The book is more than simply the history of a government sponsored railway project. Brian Young forces the reader to deal with inter-urban rivalry in Quebec, the role of the Roman Catholic church in promoting industrial rather than just agrarian growth in Quebec, and the role of French Canadians in the construction of the CPR.

Banking and Finance

Dick, Trevor J. O. and John E. Floyd. *Canada and the Gold Standard: Balance-of-Payments Adjustment Under Fixed Exchange Rates, 1871-1913*. Cambridge: Cambridge University Press, 1992.

In a book useful to specialists in monetary policy and economic history, Dick and Floyd argue that Canadian monetary policy did not conform to price-specie-flow analysis during the classical gold standard period. They posit instead a portfolio theory in which gold inflows occur through reallocation of assets rather than improvements in the trade balance. This work should be compared with Georg Rich, *The Cross of Gold* (1988). Economists and historians trained in economic theory will find the book engaging and provocative.

Nagy, Pancrace. *The International Business of Canadian Banks.* Montreal: Centre for International Business Studies, 1983.
Although this book is not a historical study, it is a valuable resource for students interested in the history of Canadian banking. Canadian banks play a large role in the world of international finance and by 1982 nearly forty percent of their assets were in international finance. Nagy explains why Canadian banks have been more active in international finance than the banks from other industrial countries and discusses the implications this activity might have for Canadian banking.

Neufeld, E. P. *The Financial System of Canada: Its Growth and Development.* Toronto: Macmillan, 1972.
This book is the most thorough survey of the development of the Canadian financial system available to students and researchers. Neufeld's *Bank of Canada Operations, 1935-54* (1955) established his reputation as a premier scholar of Canadian finance. In this book, Neufeld expands his subject area to include all aspects of Canada's banking and financial system or, broadly defined, the Canadian capital market. This book contains numerous references, tables, and charts and is essential reading for those interested in this subject.

Piva, Michael. *The Borrowing Process: Public Finance in the Province of Canada, 1840-1867.* Ottawa: University of Ottawa Press, 1992.
Piva provides the first comprehensive examination of Canadian finance for the pre-Confederation era. He argues that during the Union period, Canadian finance was focussed upon transportation issues, specifically railways and canals, and that political differences had little impact on this aspect of public policy. He also notes that the state, through its financial policies, was the engine for the Canadian economy during this period. Canada's export-based staple economy actually imported more than it exported and the capital needed to finance these imports was generated by the state and the railways that relied upon the state. This book is thoroughly referenced and a useful resource.

Rich, Georg. *The Cross of Gold: Money and the Canadian Business Cycle, 1867-1913*. Ottawa: Carleton University Press, 1988.
Rich examines the role of money supply and the banking system with regard to Canada's business cycle during the classical gold standard period. Although Canada lacked a central bank during this period — and consequently has been perceived as an outstanding example of an unmanaged monetary system operating on the gold standard — Rich argues that Canada's chartered banks engaged in active reserve management, smoothing interest rate fluctuations, and violated the rules of the gold standard in a pattern similar to a powerful central bank. Even more important, Rich argues that the policies adopted by the chartered banks amplified the reaction of Canada's business cycle to external market shocks. This book is a provocative addition to Canadian economic history, but, like Trevor Dick and John Floyd, *Canada and the Gold Standard* (1992), is unapproachable for those lacking a basic training in economics.

Rudin, Ronald. *In Whose Interest? Quebec's Caisse Populaires, 1900-45*. Montreal: McGill-Queen's University Press, 1990.
The *Caisses Populaires* — a type of cooperative credit union — emerged through the influence of Alphonse Desjardins in order to pool the resources of poor French-Canadians against the challenges and intrusions of industrialization, trade unionism, banks, and the English. Rudin argues that despite good intentions to aid poorer classes and nationalistic causes, the *Caisses Populaires* were dominated administratively by the petite-bourgeoisie and tended to provide services primarily to that group. World War II increased savings for workers and challenged the traditions of the *Caisse Populaires* and a new middle class that was not as tied to the clerico-conservative tradition of the institution emerged.

_____. *Banking en français: The French Banks of Québec, 1835-1925*. Toronto: University of Toronto Press, 1985.
This book is both a traditional business history of nine Quebec banks and a study of finance in Quebec. Rudin challenges traditional interpretations that suggest French-Canadians failed to participate effectively in the world of Canadian business. He argues persuasively that unwillingness of English banks to finance French-Canadian business enterprises opened a niche market for French-Canadian bankers. He thus suggests that cultural barriers not only kept historians from discovering the entrepreneurial nature of French-Canadians, but ironically also ensured the success of

French-Canadian financial institutions. Rudin's well referenced book is a significant contribution to historical debates about the business acumen of French-Canadians in Quebec.

Watts, George S. *The Bank of Canada: Origins and Early History.* Compiled and edited by Thomas Rymes. Ottawa: Carleton University Press, 1993.
George Watts, a long-time employee of the Bank of Canada, wrote the articles compiled here between 1972 and 1976 and represent an insider's view of the history of Canada's central bank. Watts discusses themes such as the original purpose of the Bank of Canada during the Great Depression, and how the Bank addressed events emerging from war, the establishment of the International Monetary Fund, and increasing international trade.

The Economy of Central Canada

Armstrong, Robert. *Structure and Change: An Economic History of Quebec.* Toronto: Gage, 1984.
Divided into four broad chronological sections — New France, post-Conquest, Confederation, and the twentieth century — this work seeks to place the Quebec economy in a national and international context. Armstrong's work is strongly informed by a neo-liberal perspective, and labourers, workers, and entrepreneurs merely exist as economic beings; thus, there is little discussion of religion, education, demographic, or other factors which might influence economic development. *Structure and Change* does, however, provide a good overview and analysis of the historiographic debates that surround Quebec economic history.

Bosher, J. F. *The Canada Merchants, 1713-1763.* New York: Oxford University Press, 1987.
This examination of French merchants examines the changing nature of trade in the half century between the Treaty of Utrecht and the end of the Seven Years War, and strives to set the colony of New France within the larger context of the French empire. Bosher argues that the earlier period saw the dominance of Roman Catholic merchants who did business largely within their kinship networks. By the 1740s, due to French fiscal ineptitude and structural weakness, overseas trade became more open to Huguenot and Jewish merchants who had more extensive international ties. With the end of the Seven Years War, many merchants, both Roman

Catholic and Huguenot, experienced bankruptcy. Along with Dale Miquelon's *Dugard of Rouen* (1978), *The Canada Merchants* serves as a sound introduction to the French trade with New France in the eighteenth century. Also see Bosher's recent collection of essays, *Business and Religion in the Age of New France, 1600-1760* (1994).

Darroch, Gordon and Lee Soltow. *Property and Inequality in Victorian Ontario: Structural Patterns and Cultural Communities in the 1871 Census*. Toronto: University of Toronto Press, 1994.
A quantitative and statistical analysis based upon a random sample of 5699 individuals from the 1871 census of Canada, this book considers the relationship of age, occupation, location, birthplace, religion, and ethnic origin to land ownership, home ownership, and literacy. The work highlights the primacy of private property during this era.

Drummond, Ian. *Progress Without Planning: The Economic History of Ontario from Confederation to the Second World War*. Toronto: University of Toronto Press, 1987.
The second of a three volume economic history of Ontario, *Progress Without Planning* is a valuable reference tool for historians and economists. It is filled with detailed information and 150 pages of statistical appendices and references. Drummond argues that both traditional staples interpretations and Marxist dependency theory fail to explain the growth and development of Ontario's economy. Instead, he suggests that the invisible hand of the market, especially the international market, was a far more important factor. Although the book has been commended for the detail it makes available to researchers, it has been sharply criticised for relying upon older literature and failing to engage the major historical debates. Also see Douglas McCalla, *Planting the Province: The Economic History of Upper Canada, 1784-1870* (1993); and Kenneth J. Rea, *The Prosperous Years: The Economic History of Ontario, 1939-75* (1985).

Fisher, Sidney Thomson. *The Merchant-Millers of the Humber Valley: A Study of the Early Economy of Canada*. Toronto: NC Press, 1985.
Fisher utilizes a biographical approach to describe the important role of various grist, saw, and woollen mills in the area around Toronto. Fisher demonstrates that prior to the utilization of steam and industrial technology in the milling industry, the merchant-millers capably managed a diversity of economic activity from milling to shopkeeping to

tavernkeeping and acted as important catalysts of local growth. The book is a useful introduction to some of the important figures of Upper Canadian society.

McCalla, Douglas. *Planting the Province: The Economic History of Upper Canada, 1784-1870*. Toronto: University of Toronto Press, 1993.

This important work argues that the traditional focus on staple production by economic historians like Harold Innis and William MacIntosh has produced an unequal, inaccurate, and oversimplified view of (in this case) Upper Canadian economic development. Instead, McCalla argues for a much more complex view of economic development based upon mixed farming, government expenditures, manufacturing, and other value-added industries. This book is one of the best examples of the neo-classical approach to Canadian economic history and an important addition to Canadian historiography.

_____. *The Upper Canada Trade: A Study of the Buchanans' Business, 1834-72*. Toronto: University of Toronto Press, 1979.

Something of a rarity in Canadian historiography, this important work examines the business activities of a single family firm. Immigrants from Scotland, Peter and Isaac Buchanan established a wholesaling firm in the 1830s that became, by the 1850s, one of Upper Canada's largest. This family-dominated firm owed much to Glaswegian customs and personal connection, and besides its main operation in Hamilton, it had branches in Toronto, Montreal, New York, and Liverpool. The Buchanans' diverse operations thus illustrate something of the international context and metropolitan rivalries that were a part of Upper Canadian trade. Personal tragedy, economic depression, and the changing nature of the retail business ultimately brought about the failure of the Buchanan enterprise by the 1870s. Together with McCalla's *Planting the Province* (1993), this volume serves to challenge the dominance of the staples interpretation in colonial Canadian society.

McCallum, John. *Unequal Beginnings: Agriculture and Economic Development in Quebec and Ontario Until 1870*. Toronto: University of Toronto Press, 1980.

McCallum argues that prior to 1870, Ontario's economy developed more rapidly than Quebec's primarily because of the higher productivity of Ontario farms. Following a staples model, McCallum concludes that the larger agricultural land base and superior climate of Ontario led to surplus wheat production for external markets, and that the resulting linkages to the domestic economy fostered economic growth. Two debates can be explored through this book. First, McCallum disputes Fernand Ouellet's sociological and psychological interpretations as an explanation for the failure of Quebec agriculture and, instead, sees economic and environmental considerations as predominant. Second, McCallum is at odds with the conclusions of Doug McCalla who has cast doubt about the validity and domination of a staples interpretation of Ontario history.

McCullough, A. B. *The Primary Textile Industry in Canada: History and Heritage*. Ottawa: National Historic Sites, 1992.
Emphasising the period prior to World War II, McCullough traces the history of Canada's textile industry through the themes of technology, tariffs, finance and ownership, labour, and architecture. Well-illustrated, this volume is a valuable introduction to one of Canada's largest (in the period considered) employers. The emphasis is descriptive and narrative, rather than analytical, and the book concludes with a section on early textile mills that are still standing.

McInnis, Marvin. *Perspectives on Ontario Agriculture, 1815-1930*. Gananoque, ON: Langdale Press, 1992.
A short and readable compilation of four recently published essays by one of Canada's foremost historians of agriculture. The essays reflect McInnis's belief that the emphasis placed on wheat exports by the staples interpretation is unwarranted. In the first essay, McInnis carefully illustrates that only a small sector of Ontario agriculture relied upon wheat production and that the primary market for its produce was Quebec rather than Britain. In the second essay, he notes that on the whole agriculture in Quebec and Ontario reflected similar patterns. The third essay suggests that by 1870, Ontario agriculture had shifted from wheat production to mixed agriculture. The final essay examines productivity rates in Ontario agriculture from 1870 to 1926, and questions the importance of agriculture to Canada's economic growth during this period.

Rea, Kenneth J. *The Prosperous Years: The Economic History of Ontario, 1939-75*. Toronto: University of Toronto Press, 1985.
The first volume published in the three-volume economic history of Ontario, Rea examines the post-Great Depression period. *The Prosperous Years* is organized thematically with chapters on the labour force, land

resources, transportation and communication, services, education and health, primary industries, and manufacturing. Each chapter reviews the major economic developments of the period and relates them to the governmental policies of the era. *The Prosperous Years* is, therefore, more a study in political economy rather than in business history.

Tulchinsky, Gerry. *The River Barons: Montreal Businessmen and the Growth of Industry and Transportation.* Toronto: University of Toronto Press, 1977.

Montreal was Canada's most important city in the nineteenth century and *The River Barons* is the story of the city's transition from pre-industrial to industrial metropolis. Although Tulchinsky challenges Donald Creighton's *Commercial Empire* (1937), which depicts Montreal merchants as primary nation-builders, his thesis fits into the metropolitan framework of Canadian history. He is interested in the railroads that Montreal businessmen hoped would secure the western hinterland to Montreal, and the industries that used the water power of the Lachine canal. Tulchinsky looks specifically at the entrepreneurs who financed and controlled these enterprises. He concludes that the entrepreneurs of Montreal, sought only profits and economic growth for their city. Their activities were not founded in economic nationalism or "defensive expansionism." They offered allegiance to Canada and empire only so far as it benefited their own interests.

Wylie, William T. *The Blacksmith in Upper Canada: A Study of Technology, Culture and Power.* Gananoque, ON: Langdale Press, 1990.

The most important achievement of this book is the detailed reconstruction of the work and daily life of blacksmiths in the region from Windsor to Ottawa. Wylie draws on material artifacts, archival records, newspapers, and travel accounts to create an interesting account of small scale business enterprises firmly entrenched in the local market economy of Upper Canada. This work de-emphasises the importance of the staples trade.

The Atlantic Economy

Alexander, David. *Atlantic Canada and Confederation: Essays in Canadian Political Economy.* Compiled by Eric Sager, Lewis Fischer and Stuart Pierson. Toronto: University of Toronto Press, 1983.

This collection of nine essays by David Alexander, compiled and published after his death, is fitting tribute to one of Atlantic Canada's premier historians. The essays — primarily focussed on Newfoundland — provide a concise and effective introduction into the nature of regional entrepreneurial failure that was the subject of much of Alexander's work. The book contains a useful bibliography of Alexander's published material.

_____. *The Decay of Trade: An Economic History of the Newfoundland Saltfish Trade, 1935-65*. St. John's: Institute for Social and Economic Research, 1977.

During his too brief academic career, the late David Alexander established himself as an important contributor to the history of Atlantic Canada. Alexander chronicles the declining tonnage and value of the saltfish exported from Newfoundland. Although entry into Confederation theoretically improved the province's trading position, Alexander concludes, perhaps too harshly, that Canadian policies ignored the potential market development of the saltwater fishery in favour of the production of frozen fish, most of which was not manufactured in Newfoundland. Alexander further argues that in return for her entry into Confederation, Newfoundland had every right to expect the federal government to be cognizant of the economic and social realities of the province, and to protect and enhance the saltfish trade.

Balcom, B. A. *The Cod Fishery of Île Royale, 1713-58*. Ottawa: Parks Canada, 1984.

This slight volume surveys the cod fishery around Fort Louisbourg during the French regime. Balcom argues that in addition to the military presence at Louisbourg, the area also supported a vibrant (though declining after 1740) fishery. Balcom's treatment of the material conditions, technology, and social structure also briefly introduces the reader to the life of the eighteenth-century fisherman.

Burrill, Gary and Ian McKay, eds. *People, Resources, and Power: Critical Perspectives on Underdevelopment and Primary Industries in the Atlantic Region*. Fredericton: Acadiensis Press, 1987.

The seventeen papers in this book are divided into sections on agriculture, fishing, forestry, and mining and energy. The editors provide an excellent introduction that helps synthesise individual essays and provide brief overviews at the beginning of each section. Together the essays demonstrate the resource rich heritage of the Atlantic region, the impressive presence of local and international capital in the region, and the structural weaknesses in the economy that have led to regional underdevelopment.

Cadigan, Sean T. *Hope and Deception in Conception Bay: Merchant-Settler Relations in Newfoundland, 1785-1855*. Toronto: University of Toronto Press, 1995.
The Newfoundland merchant community has traditionally been blamed for the province's failure to develop a diversified economy. Merchants, it is claimed, stifled agriculture and used credit and wage and lien laws to prevent the usage of wage labour by planters. In this well researched and provocative study, Sean Cadigan demonstrates that it was Newfoundland environment — especially its poor agricultural prospects — rather than any merchant-based schemes that led to a failure to diversify. Further, he examines the emergence of the myth of a corrupt merchant class.

Fischer, L. R. and E. W. Sager, eds. *The Enterprising Canadians: Entrepreneurs and Economic Development in Eastern Canada*. St. John's: Maritime History Group, 1979.
Fourteen papers and six summaries of discussions from the second conference of the Atlantic Canada Shipping Project, this collection contains essays discussing the meaning of entrepreneurship and empirical case studies of families, merchants, traders, and towns in Atlantic Canada. Most authors conclude that the traditional Atlantic Canadian merchant community responded rationally to the changing economic climate in the nineteenth century, but failed to develop the managerial systems needed to succeed in the emerging industrial world.

Inwood, Kris, ed. *Farm, Factory and Fortune: New Studies in the Economic History of the Maritime Provinces*. Fredericton: Acadiensis Press, 1993.
This collection of eleven articles — many of which have been printed elsewhere — reflects most of the major themes of maritime economic history, including themes such as the structure of colonial agriculture, employment and welfare in the post-World War I era, and the changing nature of the Maritime economy. Although the Maritimes entered Confederation with a relatively healthy and vibrant economy, the region quickly became a have-not area in Canada. The authors in this collection avoid blaming Maritime entrepreneurs or metropolitan discrimination for

this regional disparity. Instead, several essays suggest that the strength of the Maritime economy in the Confederation era has been overstated and that the emphasis placed on forest and industrial production understates the overall importance of agriculture to the economy.

Ommer, Rosemary. *From Outpost to Outport: A Structural Analysis of the Jersey Gaspé Cod Fishery, 1767-1886*. Montreal: McGill-Queen's University Press, 1991.

J. M. S. Careless' "The Lowe Brothers, 1985-70" (*BC Studies*, 1969) examined the international linkages of colonial British Columbian business operations. Similarly, Rosemary Ommer looks at the triangular nature of cod fishing and markets through a study of Charles Robin & Company: capital, entrepreneurial spirit, and skilled labour originated from Jersey, a small British island off the coast of France; a production base was established in the Gaspé fishery; and markets were found in the Mediterranean, South Africa, the West Indies, and South America. Because of the nature of this relationship, few backward or forward economic linkages emerged in the Gaspé; rather, Ommer finds that it was in Jersey that ships were built and subsidiary industries emerged. Ommer argues that Charles Robin & Company utilized the "truck" system — and thus tied fishermen to the company through indebtedness — in order to prevent sufficient capital accumulation from emerging in the Gaspé.

Ryan, Shannon. *Fish Out of Water: The Newfoundland Salt Fish Trade, 1814-1914*. St. John's: Breakwater Books, 1986.

In the nineteenth century Newfoundland's economy was based upon the production of cod for an international market. Ryan describes how Newfoundland failed to maintain its position as the dominant supplier of salt-cod, failed to diversify beyond its staple base, and eventually regressed into economic and political dependency. Unlike other work which suggests that entrepreneurial failure and structural problems led Newfoundland to lose control of the international market, *Fish Out of Water* highlights the problems faced by Newfoundland business enterprises in accessing international markets. Filled with detailed statistical information and thoroughly referenced, this book is crucial for understanding staples-based export systems and the Atlantic fishery.

Sager, E. W. and G. E. Panting. *Maritime Capital: The Shipping Industry in Atlantic Canada, 1820-1914*. Montreal: McGill-Queen's University Press, 1990.

Emerging out of the Atlantic Canada Shipping Project at Memorial University, this work revisits the demise of the Maritime shipping industry by the end of the nineteenth century. In 1880 Canada had the world's fourth largest merchant marine; a generation later, this ranking had fallen dramatically. Traditional explanations, including that by Harold Innis, had emphasised the declining demand for sailing ships and the failure of the Maritime shipping industry to make the transfer to new technology and industrial capitalism. Instead, Sager and Panting argue that as the industry became concentrated in the hands of merchants, as opposed to specialized ship owners, ship ownership was merely one enterprise in a diversified portfolio; increasingly, as revenues declined, these merchants transferred capital to other industries such as railways, utilities, banking, and manufacturing. Comparisons with steam-powered steel ships and railways further heightened the (often inaccurate) pessimism associated with Maritime shipping and spurred investment elsewhere. Finally, central Canadian priorities and British interests did not always reflect the economic interests of the Maritime shipping industry. Sager and Panting have produced an important study of the Atlantic region's most important nineteenth-century industry.

Samson, Roch. *Fishermen and Merchants in 19th Century Gaspé: The Fishermen-Dealers of William Hyman and Sons*. Ottawa: Parks Canada, 1984.
This brief work concentrates on the cod fishery and dried cod industry in the nineteenth century, largely through the records of William Hyman, a Gaspé fish dealer. It provides a brief narrative of Hyman and Sons, technical and social aspects of exporting dried cod, and a brief analysis of the fiscal realities of this industry.

The State and the Economy

Baggaley, Carman. *The Emergence of the Regulatory State in Canada, 1867-1939*. Ottawa: Economic Council of Canada, 1981.
Following a brief introduction to theoretical issues concerning regulation, this study seeks to explain how and why government regulation is introduced. Particular attention is paid to regulatory activities involving staples production, marketing boards, transportation, health and safety, and the insurance industry. At times, *The Emergence of the Regulatory State* draws comparisons between the Canadian and American experiences.

Ball, Norman, ed. *Building Canada: A History of Public Works*. Toronto:
   University of Toronto Press, 1988.
Explaining the development of the infrastructure upon which the
Canadian economy operates is the theme of this collection. The thirteen
chapters in *Building Canada* range through subjects such as bridges,
roads, highways, urban transit, railways and canals, dams, electricity,
water and sewer, garbage, airports, and public buildings. The collection
serves as a valuable introduction to a relatively ignored subject.

Bickerton, James P. *Nova Scotia, Ottawa and the Politics of Regional
   Development*. Toronto: University of Toronto Press, 1990.
This detailed and well-researched study examines regional economic and
industrial development and its relationship to a centralized authority. In
this instance, the case study is Nova Scotia and its relationship to Ottawa,
but much of what the author argues may be extrapolated to Atlantic
Canada. Bickerton provides a historical overview of the political economy
of Nova Scotia and Atlantic Canada, particularly the economies of
agriculture, fishing, forestry, and industry. Intertwined is Bickerton's
analysis of provincial-federal relations and politics, and of the failure of
the central government to provide a coherent economic plan for Atlantic
Canada.

Bothwell, Robert. *Nucleus: The History of Atomic Energy of Canada*.
   Toronto: University of Toronto Press, 1988.
In this sequel to *Eldorado* (1984), Bothwell examines the Atomic Energy
of Canada Limited, a crown corporation responsible for research into
nuclear technology. Wartime exigencies and Canadian persuasion led to
British scientists undertaking atomic research in Canada; by the 1950s the
CANDU reactor produced at Chalk River, Ontario, was being marketed
worldwide. As in the nationalization of the uranium industry, C. D.
Howe's influence in establishing Atomic Energy was large, and Canada
was committed from the outset to selling its technology abroad, a position
that has, at times, produced controversial debate.

_____. *Eldorado: Canada's National Uranium Company*. Toronto:
   University of Toronto Press, 1984.
Rich in detail and analysis, *Eldorado* provides a technical and complex
history of the formative years of Canada's uranium industry. Eldorado
began mining uranium on the shores of Great Bear Lake in the 1930s;
with the onset of World War II, Eldorado was nationalized under the

supervision of C. D. Howe. Though other companies were allowed to mine, all uranium was marketed and sold through Eldorado, principally to the United States. This exclusive relationship meant that when the American demand for Canadian uranium disappeared in the late 1950s, the company was left in a precarious and uncompetitive situation.

Campbell, Robert M. *Grand Illusions: The Politics of the Keynesian Experience in Canada, 1945-75*. Peterborough, ON: Broadview Press, 1987.
Campbell argues that while Canadian politicians may have used the rhetoric of Keynesian economics after 1945, Canadian economic policy was never truly Keynesian in nature. Political, social, and economic interests could never be isolated and separated in the Canadian experience and, as a result, public policy was eclectic and ad hoc. This book is primarily a work of ideas and does not reflect significant archival research.

Clark-Jones, Melissa. *A Staple State: Canadian Industrial Resources in the Cold War*. Toronto: University of Toronto Press, 1987.
Following World War II, Clark-Jones argues that the Canadian government and multinational corporations conspired to make Canada a "hewer of wood and drawer of water" for the American military-industrial complex. Further, Canada's emphasis on resource mega-projects has tied the country firmly to the American orbit.

Crane, David. *Controlling Interest: The Canadian Gas and Oil Stakes*. Toronto: McClelland and Stewart, 1982.
Controlling Interest defends the Trudeau government's 1980 National Energy Policy. In a well referenced study, David Crane argues that Canadian oil and gas policy prior to 1980 led to American domination of Canada's oil and gas industry. Given the growing importance of the oil industry to Canada's economy, Crane attempts to justify the National Energy Policy's reforms to land leasing policy and its subsidisation of Canadian exploration firms and notes that the National Energy Policy's goal of fifty percent Canadian ownership was probably insufficient.

Cruikshank, Ken. *Close Ties: Railways, Governments and the Board of Railway Commissioners, 1851-1933*. Montreal: McGill-Queen's University Press, 1991.
In light of the recent disbanding of the Crow rate and the bitter legacy it

left, this study provides a valuable introduction to the history of railway regulation. Cruikshank examines the historical background to the creation of the Board of Railway Commissioners in 1904, and their belief in the value of scientific expertise in setting regulatory policy and rates. Cruikshank disagrees that regulatory agencies were creations of the industries regulated and argues for the notion of regulatory pluralism based upon interest group politics.

Doern, G. Bruce, ed. *The Regulatory Process in Canada*. Toronto: Macmillan, 1978.
An important analysis of regulatory agencies and the regulatory process, this collection of essays is divided into two main parts: first, Doern addresses broader concerns such as the impact of socioeconomic processes, provincial-federal relations, and consumer interest in influencing regulatory concerns; second, he presents case studies of regulatory activity, including essays on the National Energy Board and the Canadian Transport Commission, among others.

Forster, Ben. *A Conjunction of Interests: Business, Politics, and Tariffs, 1825-1879*. Toronto: University of Toronto Press, 1986.
Tariff policy has always been central to Canadian politics. Imperial preferences, reciprocity with the United States, and protective tariffs are prominent in Canadian electoral campaigns. In a clear and relatively concise account, Ben Forster reviews the numerous political decisions in the era leading to the 1879 protective tariff (often called the National Policy). Forster demonstrates that Canadians debated the tariff issue ferociously and that a variety of interests always existed. In one of his more important conclusions, he argues that the 1879 protective tariff was designed to satisfy revenue needs and political pressure groups. Despite being called the National Policy, it did not reflect a great national vision.

Gordon, Marsha. *Government in Business*. Toronto: C. D. Howe, 1981.
Prepared for the C. D. Howe Institute, *Government in Business* is a detailed assessment of the role of state enterprises in Canada. Gordon not only addresses the haphazard nature of these business adventures, but also critically assesses their economic performance. This work reflects the different dimensions of government enterprise and provides a justification for a government presence in the business. Gordon examines themes such as natural monopolies such as public utilities, nation-building corporations such as railways and airlines, regional development

enterprises, bailouts, high-risk and high-technology businesses, and resource companies. This book is well-researched, thoroughly referenced, and provocative.

Gorecki, Paul K. and W. T Stanbury. *The Objectives of Canadian Competition Policy, 1888-1983.* Montreal: Institute for Research on Public Policy, 1984.

A comprehensive and sympathetic account of Canadian competition policy, this book concludes that three objectives underlie the Canadian laws. Competition policy should, first, protect consumers and businessmen from the abuse of economic power; second, maintain and encourage free competition; and, third, encourage low cost production and distribution of goods. American style populism with its attack on trusts had little or no role in the formation of Canadian policy. Instead, Canadian competition policy tried to define proper and improper market behaviour and thus reflected the historical circumstances in which it was created. Although lacking in detailed archival research, this book is a useful reference tool.

Laxer, James. *Canada's Economic Strategy.* Toronto: McClelland and Stewart, 1981.

Laxer argues that the 1960s and 1970s saw a transformation in economic policy by both the Liberal and Conservative parties. The Liberals, traditionally a party of continentalism, regional interests, and limited central government, inverted their platform and promoted an increased role for the federal government at the expense of both multinationals and the regions. Conversely, the Conservatives repudiated the policies of John A. MacDonald and became champions of continentalism and regional interest. Laxer's study is, unfortunately, hindered by its lack of references and sources.

Owram, Doug. *Building for Canadians: A History of the Department of Public Works, 1840-1960.* Ottawa: Public Works Canada, 1979.

This volume traces one of the oldest departments in Canada's administrative history from the formation of the colonial Board of Works in 1840 to the Glassco Commission in 1960. The approach of *Building for Canadians* is chronological, and Owram emphasises issues of jurisdiction, structure, and authority, as well as important individuals and projects.

Phidd, Richard and G. Bruce Doern. *The Politics and Management of Canadian Economic Policy.* Toronto: Macmillan 1978.

This work explores the process of economic policy formation. The authors argue that policy formation emerges out of a dynamic of legislative, bureaucratic, and public interests and influences. Generally, they argue that since World War II policy has been transformed from a simpler, more concentrated structure that was dominated by the Department of Finance to a far more diffuse process by the 1960s and 1970s. This was so because of the decreased emphasis on Keynesian demand management and an increased emphasis on supply-oriented policies.

Rea, Kenneth J. and J. T. Macleod, eds. *Business and Government in Canada: Selected Readings.* Toronto: Methuen, 1976.
This collection is a synthesis of recent work that suggests that capitalist theory and political organization can not be separated. They argue that the state and business have always been linked in the Canadian experience and that to study either in isolation is to misunderstand the system. They organize the readings into four sections. Sections one and four offer theoretical insights into the state-business relationship. Sections two and three provide narrative analysis of the regulatory relationships that have emerged. The authors conclude that the alliance between business and government has significant repercussions for the political process and may pose a threat to liberty in Canada.

Regehr, T. D. *The Beauharnois Scandal: A Story of Canadian Entrepreneurship and Politics.* Toronto: University of Toronto Press, 1990.
In the early 1930s, a political scandal erupted around the building of a huge hydro-electric project on the St. Lawrence River. The Beauharnois scandal implicated Prime Minister Mackenzie King, Ontario premier Howard Ferguson, and numerous other politicians in a sordid tale of campaign contributions and political favours. The book's focus is exclusively on the scandal. Although Regehr highlights the intimate relationship between business and government in Canadian resource development projects, he does not draw out the relationship as maturely as H. V. Nelles' *The Politics of Development* (1974). Furthermore, Regehr fails to examine the economic or the technological ramifications of the hydro-electric project itself.

Schull, Joseph. *The Great Scot: A Biography of Donald Gordon.* Montreal: McGill-Queen's University Press, 1979.

Lacking much formal education, Donald Gordon still became, in succession, a leading figure in the newly established Bank of Canada, chairman of the Wartime Prices and Trade Board, president of the Canadian National Railways (CNR), and, at the age of 65, president of Brinko which ambitiously constructed a massive hydro-electric project in Newfoundland. Schull's biography is largely narrative, and, despite being commissioned by the CNR, presents both the genius and warts of Gordon.

Stevenson, Garth. *The Politics of Canada's Airlines: From Diefenbaker to Mulroney*. Toronto: University of Toronto Press, 1987.
Transportation policy is one area of Canadian economic history where the role of government has always been predominant. Historians, however, have always been overly pre-occupied with railways and canals. In this study, Garth Stevenson examines the changing government policies regarding the airline business. Prior to Diefenbaker, the Canadian government provided Trans-Canada airline, later Air Canada, with a virtual monopoly over transcontinental air traffic. Responding to consumers, the Diefenbaker government ended the monopoly and introduced a new policy founded in regulated competition. Stevenson argues this policy served Canadians well and expresses doubt that the Mulroney government policy of unrestricted competition will provide Canadians with equal benefits.

Traves, Tom. *The State and Enterprise: Canadian Manufacturers and the Federal Government, 1917-31*. Toronto: University of Toronto Press, 1979.
Tom Traves argues that until the end of World War I, Canadian manufacturers could rely upon the power of the state to protect them from the uncertainty of the business cycle. Following the war, however, they found their privileged position challenged by a changing economic environment and the increasing political agitation of labour and farm organizations. Traves examines the efforts of four industries to restore a predictable and secure business environment. Sugar and newsprint manufacturers called for state regulation of their industry; steel and automobile manufacturers relied on the passive intervention of the state through tariffs and taxation. In all four cases, Traves notes, the manufacturers were less than successful. The Canadian political community of the era was too divided and factional for the manufacturers to dominate and control the government. Traves concludes that the Canadian state in the post-World War I era responded to a variety of

group and class interests, and the compromises which emerged produced a balanced capitalist order in the country.

Tupper, Allan and G. Bruce Doern, eds. *Public Corporations and Public Policy in Canada.* Montreal: Institute for Research on Public Policy, 1981.

Recognizing the diverse nature of crown corporations, Tupper and Doern provide a series of case studies which examine the establishment and objectives of these provincial and federal enterprises. Collectively, *Public Corporations* examines Canada's largest and most important crown corporations, including transportation services such as the Canadian National Railway, hydro utilities, mining and energy operations, and Telesat, a satellite communications enterprise that was both a private and public venture. As well, these essays argue against monolithic interpretations of crown corporations and recognize the multiple factors in their origins and in the public policy goals they pursue.

Intellectual, Cultural, Educational, and Science History

In 1946, Frank Underhill's presidential address to the Canadian Historical Association called for "a new history writing which will attempt to explain the ideas in the heads of Canadians"; at that time Underhill — along with individuals such as W. L. Morton, John Irving and, in French Canada, abbé Groulx — represented a small number of intellectual historians whose vision went beyond staples, politics, and railways. It was not until the late 1960s and early 1970s, however, that intellectual history became commonplace within the profession: for example, S. F. Wise's important "Sermon Literature and Canadian Intellectual History" (1965) brought attention to religion as a source for understanding Canada's past, and Carl Berger's brilliant *Sense of Power* (1970) examined the intellectual content of Canadian imperialists. The emergence of intellectual history was influenced, as was the historiography of education, science, and medicine, by the new social history. Important intellectual historians such as A. B. McKillop and Doug Owram stressed the importance of developing affinities between ideas and broader society; C. E. Phillip's teleological *The Development of Education in Canada* was revised both in content and methodology by J. D. Wilson, R. M. Stamp, and L.-P. Audet in 1970; and the work of Geoffery Bilson, S. E. D. Shortt, and Michael Bliss in the recent field of medical history was informed strongly by these new currents of scholarship.

A Sense of Place

Armour, Leslie and Elizabeth Trott. *The Faces of Reason: An Essay on Philosophy and Culture in English Canada, 1850-1950*. Waterloo: Wilfrid Laurier University Press, 1981.

The only survey of English-Canadian philosophy, *The Faces of Reason* provides a sophisticated introduction to almost two dozen philosophers, from lesser known individuals such as John Clark Murray and Wilfred Currier Keirstead to the better known John Watson and Harold Innis. Given the vast spaces and enormous diversity of Canada, Armour and Trott argue that ideas capable of spanning vast spaces and linking subcultures — in a manner similar to J. A. Macdonald's railway — are vital in understanding and maintaining the political and intellectual scheme that is Canada. In particular, Armour and Trott adopt a definition of reason that seeks to establish an ordered world view out of the chaos of time and place. This theme, for example, is traced through the natural theology of James Beaven, the idealism of John Watson, and the values and communication theory of Harold Innis. For an anthology of writings by Canadian philosophers, see J. D. Rabb, ed., *Religion and Science in Early Canada* (1988). For a study of a more contemporary philosopher, see William Christian, *George Grant: A Biography* (1993).

Berger, Carl. *The Sense of Power: Studies in the Ideas of Canadian Imperialism, 1867-1914.* Toronto: University of Toronto Press, 1970. *The Sense of Power* is a landmark study in the relatively recent emergence of a mature intellectual history within Canada. Combining a traditional focus on biography with newer currents of intellectual history, Berger popularised a methodology that influenced a whole generation of graduate students. Moreover, while notables such as Chester Martin, A. R. M. Lower, and Donald Creighton have all explored various facets of imperialism, no one had attempted to explicate the intellectual origins of imperialists such as Colonel George Denison, George Munro, and Sir George Parkin. Berger challenges Lower's *Colony to Nation* (1946). Whereas Lower argued that "heroes" strove for Canada's independence and "enemies" for maintaining the British tie, Berger argues that imperialism was, in fact, a variety of Canadian nationalism. The influence of this work was profound: In 1978, George Rawlyk praised *The Sense of Power* for being the right kind of book — written at the right time — for a reading public searching for meaningful ideological constructs in an often confused nation.

Errington, Jane. *The Lion, the Eagle, and Upper Canada: A Developing Colonial Ideology.* Montreal: McGill-Queen's University Press, 1987. The history of Upper Canada has generally been told, in whiggish fashion, as the triumph of the Loyalists in their struggle against both the Canadian wilderness and the insidious nature of American republicanism. Errington challenges this view. She argues that the argument that S. F. Wise proposed in the nationalist 1960s, which advocated the strident anti-Americanism of the Loyalist mind, must be modified. Instead, while some British-born officials found it impossible to embrace anything American, Loyalists and the colonial elite found much among the Republican heritage that was agreeable. Thus, ideological, social and economic ties developed between Loyalist leaders and their southern counterparts, although in the face of American expansionism and the War of 1812 a strong critique of Republicanism did develop. Errington insightfully develops her thesis that Upper Canadian ideology cannot be viewed as a monolithic entity.

Francis, R. Douglas. *Images of the West: Changing Perceptions of the Prairies, 1690-1960*. Saskatoon: Western Producer Prairie Books, 1989.
Written by an Ontarian who first went to the Prairies as a young man, this book presents a series of changing images of the West over the past three centuries. The first image discussed, for example, presents the West as a Prairie wasteland, a view that was held from the days of the early fur traders and explorers until the mid-nineteenth century. Each chapter contains a short introduction in which the formation of the image within the historical imagination is discussed; thereafter, Francis presents an anthology of historical and contemporary material that traverses across a variety of genres and often beautifully illustrates his argument.

Jasen, Patricia. *Wild Things: Nature, Culture, and Tourism in Ontario, 1790-1914*. Toronto: University of Toronto Press, 1995.
Being a tourist, Patricia Jasen argues in this superb and innovative work, is predicated upon being in a state of mind in which the imagination plays a key role. Of course it is much more than just that, and Jasen explores how romantic notions about the wilderness and wild men were a prelude to, or accompanied by, the forces of colonization. The growth of tourism — largely an activity of the middle class who established their "right" to holidays and travel as a part of their collective identity — therefore parallelled immigration, the founding of a country, and the exploitation of natural resources. Natives were often sought as guides, and many preferred the better pay and easier work; close contact with the non-native, however, also sometimes had pejorative effects. Jasen also touches on notions of gender and its relationship to tourism. This work — which begins with Niagara Falls — and Ian McKay's examination of the invention of Peggy's Cove (*Journal of Canadian Studies*, 1988) critically introduce readers to two of Canada's more famous tourist destinations.

Litt, Paul. *The Muses, the Masses, and the Massey Commission*. Toronto: University of Toronto Press 1992.

The Massey Commission recommendations of 1951 have become entrenched in Canadian nationalist mythology: confident of its international status following the war, and wary of over-dependence upon American culture, the Commission endorsed broad cultural responsibilities for the federal government, including strengthening controls over radio, television, the creation of the Canada Council, and funding for universities. Litt examines the origins, activities, and influence of the Commission, and places it within its cultural, political, and social contexts. For an excellent analysis of the active cultural life of Canadians prior to the Massey Commission, see Maria Tippett, *Making Culture: English-Canadian Institutions and the Arts before the Massey Commission* (1990).

Marks, Lynne. *Revivals and Roller Rinks: Religion, Leisure, and Identity in Late-Nineteenth-Century Small-Town Ontario.* Toronto: University of Toronto Press, 1996.
This innovative and important work ranges well beyond religious history into studies of gender, labour, leisure, and the family. Utilizing both quantitative and qualitative sources, *Revivals and Roller Rinks* is an exploration into the social and cultural meanings of religion and leisure in three small Ontario towns, Thorold, Campbellford, and Ingersoll. This nuanced and complex work examines the links between religion and leisure. Protestant culture — with its class, gender, familial, and theological meanings embedded within it — both provided and rejected a range of leisure options. For example, the feminization of church congregations was reflected in, and helped to reinforce, the leisure options available to women, while men had much greater access to the leisure and associational world beyond the church. Marks also examines how the Knights of Labor and the Salvation Army in the 1880s served to reinforce class consciousness, while the Crossley-Hunter revival in Thorold temporarily overcame class and gender tensions. Much like Joy Parr's *The Gender of Breadwinners* (1990), *Revivals and Roller Rinks* promises to be both an important methodological study and a significant contribution to the history of small-town Ontario.

McKay, Ian. *The Quest of Folk: Antimodernism and Cultural Selection in Twentieth-Century Nova Scotia.* Montreal: McGill-Queen's, University Press, 1994.
This important and innovative work explores antimodernism in twentieth-century Nova Scotia. In particular, McKay examines the creation of the

idea of Folk in the work of folklorist Helen Creighton, handicraft revivalist Mary Black, and others. Their "quest of the Folk" involved the explicit rejection of modern urban life and of class and ethnic differences, and the construction of a Nova Scotian identity that harkened back to a Golden Age and glorified the idyllic fishing village and the masculine and feminine identities that supposedly accompanied it. McKay's brilliant study is grounded in the socio-economic context of Nova Scotia — the industrial base of the province had collapsed following World War II — and in a neo-Gramscian approach to notions of cultural hegemony.

McKillop, A. B. *Contours of Canadian Thought*. Toronto: University of
    Toronto Press, 1987.
This collection of eight articles by one of Canada's leading intellectual historians aims to shed light on the nineteenth-century Anglo-American intellectual world. Professor McKillop's general philosophy of intellectual history, expressed in the first two chapters, affirms his belief in the inherent value of ideas. However, unlike A. O. Lovejoy and Perry Miller, McKillop believes that such ideas cannot be viewed as autonomous entities; rather he argues, much like the American historian John Higham, for an intellectual history within a broadly contextual approach, thus developing affinities with social and cultural history. Subsequent essays examine the Victorian debate among science, humanism, and religion; the emergence of the research ideal at the University of Toronto; the philosophical idealism of Canada's foremost philosopher of the nineteenth century, John Watson of Queens; and postwar attitudes of the English-Canadian intelligentsia. Together these essays examine "the attempts of people who were moralists of different hues to come to grips with modernity as they understood it."

Mills, David. *The Idea of Loyalty in Upper Canada, 1784-1850.*
    Montreal: McGill-Queen's University Press, 1988.
This examination of the political rhetoric from the arrival of the Loyalists until the mid-nineteenth century concludes that the idea of loyalty was of primary concern, not only in gaining political legitimacy, but also in acceptance into provincial society. Initially, loyalty was defined as the rejection of republicanism and the embrace of the British monarch, empire, and constitution; after the political battles of the 1820s and 1830s, however, the concept became more assimilative. Loyalty thus became a concept to be embraced not only by the Loyalists and their immediate descendants, but also by moderate reformers, a fact which helped pave the

way for responsible government. While indebted to the work of S. F. Wise in the 1960s, this insightful volume documents the changing nature of conservatism in early Upper Canada.

Owram, Doug. *Born at the Right Time: A History of the Baby Boom Generation*. Toronto: University of Toronto Press, 1996.

Since 1970 historical writing in Canada has been increasingly studied through the limited identities of ethnicity, gender, and class; in contrast, Owram approaches the recent past through the idea of a generation, in this case the baby-boomers born between 1946 and 1962. As Owram notes, it is relatively rare in history that people think of themselves as a generational identity, but this group of 7.5 million Canadians have gained an identity due to their sheer numbers, their relative affluence, and their link to the turbulent 1960s. *Born at the Right Time* focuses upon the first 25 years of the boomers' history. Since Owram approaches his topic via the study of history as a life cycle, the emphasis is upon childhood, family, adolescence, and the university experience. In each of these areas, Owram analyses the dominant issues and events that defined the boomers. For example, informed by Benjamin Spock and his best-seller, *Common Sense Book of Baby and Child Care*, the family accepted the philosophy of "child-obsession" that demographics had begun. As would be expected, Owram devotes significant attention to the youth radicalism and sexual revolution of the 1960s. This well-written overview is the starting point for further studies on the baby-boom generation.

_____. *Promise of Eden: The Canadian Expansionist Movement and the Idea of the West, 1856-1900*. Toronto: University of Toronto Press, 1980; 2nd ed., 1991.

Influenced by the work of J. M. S. Careless, W. L. Morton, Henry Nash Smith, and Carl Berger's *The Sense of Power* (1970), this landmark study examines the expansionist movement that emerged in the 1850s in the Canadas and continued to the end of the century. During the first part of the nineteenth century, Canadians viewed the West as a "semi-arctic wilderness." The growing demand for new agricultural land in Canada West, however, led the expansionists to reconstruct the image of the West following the exploring expeditions sent out by both colonial Canada and Britain in the 1850s. The new image of the West as an Edenic garden proved to be illusory, and in the face of unfulfilled promises and expectations, Western alienation and a distinct view of history were born.

Rees, Ronald. *New and Naked Land: Making the Prairies Home.*
    Saskatoon: Western Producer Prairie Books, 1988.
One of the few Canadian works to incorporate some of the new
conceptual ideas found in modern landscape studies, this work examines
the variance between imagery, perceptions, and reality during the so-
called settlement era of the prairies. Rees takes the reader through the
experiences of settlement — the image of the prairies crafted by boosters
and propagandists, the dispersed settlement patterns and reduced
importance of village life, the creation of the homestead and gardens, and
the "cult of trees" — noting at each step the difficult adjustment of
immigrants to the broad, flat, treeless expanse of the prairie environment.
Most immigrants, he concludes, never completely accept the landscape,
choosing instead to modify it.

Shortt, S. E. D. *The Search for an Ideal: Six Intellectuals and Their
    Convictions in an Age of Transition.* Toronto: University of Toronto
    Press, 1976.
Like Carl Berger in his *Sense of Power* (1970), Shortt uses a biographical
analysis to explore the history of ideas between 1890 and 1930. Shortt's
study concentrates on the social and cultural context of the lives of six
intellectuals. From his study, he concludes that two intellectual currents
dominated their thoughts. The idealist perspective, based in the Victorian
quest for order and spiritual conception of life, waned, and those trained
in humanities based in this perspective failed to cope with the new world.
The empirical, based in the new material reality of modern science,
waxed, and those trained in social sciences found new opportunities to
use their skills.

Wise, S. F. *God's Peculiar Peoples: Essays on Political Culture in
    Nineteenth-Century Canada.* A. B. McKillop and Paul Romney, eds.
    Ottawa: Carleton University Press, 1993.
S. F. Wise is perhaps the foremost interpreter of Upper Canadian
conservatism. Rejecting Donald Creighton's claim that such a tradition
began with John A. Macdonald, Wise pushes the foundations of toryism
back to the experiences and anti-Americanism of the Loyalists and the
ideology of late eighteenth-century England. Wise argues that early
toryism helped produce a political culture that ultimately favoured
Confederation. These essays, written in the 1960s and 1970s, have had
enormous significance: David Mills, Paul Romney, and Curtis Fahey have
modified Wise's work, while Jane Errington has explicitly challenged it.

Moral Reform, Religion, and Secularization

Airhart, Phyllis, D. *Serving the Present Age: Revivalism, Progressivism, and the Methodist Tradition in Canada*. Montreal: McGill-Queen's University Press, 1992.
Airhart examines the transformation of Methodism from its nineteenth-century emphasis on revivalist meetings and the conversion of sinners to, by 1925 as part of the United Church, a religion that had become "frequently associated with a group accused of being unsympathetic to evangelical aims." Because of an emphasis on piety rather than theology, Methodists were less affected by intellectual currents such as Darwinism and higher criticism. Their revivalistic piety, however, failed to reach the increasingly urban masses; therefore, in the first decades of the twentieth century, Methodist leaders developed a progressive piety that emphasised social Christianity rather than individual conversion.

Allen, Richard. *The Social Passion: Religion and Social Reform in Canada, 1914-28*. Toronto: University of Toronto Press, 1971.
The first major work in religious history following S. F. Wise's "Sermon Literature and Canadian Intellectual History" (1965), *The Social Passion* established itself as a contemporary classic and brought religion into the mainstream of the new social history. Concentrating upon left-wing clerics and social reformers such as William Ivens, Charles Gordon, Salem Bland, and J. S. Woodsworth, Allen argues that the Social Gospel movement — composed mainly of Methodists and Presbyterians — reached its heights of influence in the decade following the outbreak of World War I. Finding its intellectual origins in the thought of Albrecht Ritschl, Walter Rauschenbusch, and the British preachers R. J. Campbell and Hugh Price Hughes, and inspired by concerns over social conditions resulting from massive immigration, urban growth, and the return of war veterans, the Social Gospel advocated a progressive theology that would lead to the new Jerusalem. This commitment to social reform waned in the 1920s, however, because Canadians were increasingly reluctant to accept the radical elements of the movement.

Berger, Carl. *Science, God, and Nature in Victorian Canada*. Toronto: University of Toronto Press, 1983.
This work discusses the rise, expression, and decline of natural science. Derived from the British tradition of popular science, natural history societies emerged in the nineteenth century, largely dominated by middle-

class English-Canadians who often had both imperial and, after mid-century, American connections. Until the late Victorian period, natural theology sought to express religious insights through the study of nature, a pursuit which found great resonance within nineteenth-century popular culture. The Darwinian revolution, however, helped to fragment the Victorian amalgam of science and religion; with this crisis of legitimacy and the relative decline of natural history, the rise of intensely specialised and more difficult sciences ensued.

Burkinshaw, Robert. *Pilgrims in Lotus Land: Conservative Protestantism in British Columbia, 1917-1981.* Montreal: McGill-Queen's University Press, 1995.
In 1921 Anglicans and Presbyterians were the dominant congregations in British Columbia, followed by relatively weak bodies of Methodists and Baptists. Burkinshaw's excellent study surveys the decline of the first two denominations and the emergence of conservative protestantism, a trend which accelerated even during the increasingly secular post-World War II period. This growth of conservative religious belief occurred because of the flexible nature of evangelical religion, which was able to cut across denominational lines while maintaining its crucicentrism and conversionism; its ability to effectively target immigrant groups (particularly Mennonite Bretherns); and, ironically, the secular nature of British Columbia which hastened — in the face of clearer choices — the development of pilgrims. Burkinshaw also discusses the socio-political impact of the rise of evangelicals; conservative Christians, for example, were more likely to support the provincial Social Credit government and helped to keep it in power for most of the post-World War II period.

Christie, Nancy and Michael Gauvreau. *A Full-Orbed Christianity: The Protestant Churches and Social Welfare in Canada, 1900-1940.* Montreal: McGill-Queen's University Press, 1996.
The first decades of the twentieth century are often seen as a period of religious decline and declension, accompanied by the emergence of a welfare state that took on much of the reforming impulse that churches had lost. An extremely well-researched and important work, *A Full-Orbed Christianity* challenges that interpretation. Christie and Gauvreau argue that evangelicalism was flexible and adaptable, and that the social evangelism that emerged in the twentieth century — in contrast to its nineteenth-century variety that emphasised inductive theology — helped Protestant churches to retain significant cultural and public authority.

Individuals such as Hugh Dobson, Charles Gordon, and others were able
to define social problems, and then respond to them with church
initiatives in areas such as child welfare, public health, pensions,
unemployment insurance, and rural life reforms. Christie and Gauvreau
explicitly challenge both the secularization thesis argued by Ramsay Cook
and David Marshall, and the origins of the welfare state put forth by Doug
Owram.

Clarke, Brian P. *Piety and Nationalism: Lay Voluntary Associations and
   the Creation of an Irish-Catholic Community in Toronto, 1850-1895.*
   Montreal: McGill-Queen's University Press, 1993.
The rise of the new religious history in English Canada has focussed upon
clerics and church elites, and has primarily sought to explicate the
Protestant experience. In the wake of mid-nineteenth century migrations
to Ontario and Toronto, Clarke examines the evolution of an Irish-
Catholic identity. His emphasis is principally upon the laity, and he argues
that in the wake of increased immigration Irish Catholics were attracted
to two different types of organizations: ones that were more under the
direct influence of the church, and others devoted to Irish nationalism. In
a superb gendered analysis, Clarke illustrates how women were
predominately drawn to organizations that emphasised piety, and men to
those that were more loosely-affiliated with the church and, instead,
emphasised Irish nationalism. The latter organizations were not ultimately
a threat to the Roman Catholic church, and the generation that followed
defined themselves on the basis of both ethnicity and religion.

Clifford, N. Keith. *The Resistance to Church Union in Canada, 1904-
   1939.* Vancouver: University of British Columbia Press, 1985.
Approximately one-third of the members of the Presbyterian church
refused to join Methodists and Congregationalists in forming the United
Church of Canada in 1925. As members of a voluntary association of
believers, these Presbyterians sought to preserve their denomination
despite the policies of the General Assembly of their church. *The
Resistance to Church Union* argues that those who opposed union
differed from the majority of Presbyterian members in their perceptions
of the correctness of the Social Gospel, and in their responses to the
secularization of Canadian society.

Cook, Ramsay. *The Regenerators: Social Criticism in Late Victorian
   English Canada.* Toronto: University of Toronto Press, 1985.

The late Victorian era has been viewed by historians as a time of great societal tension and challenge. Ramsay Cook, one of Canada's foremost contemporary historians, argues that the way in which Protestant churches responded to intellectual challenge, urban-industrial growth, immigration, and socio-economic cleavages within society functioned to make Christianity less relevant. Cook pursues two central themes: first, that Darwinian science and historical criticism provoked a religious crisis and led many to attempt to salvage Christianity by transforming it into a social religion; and, second, that the preoccupation with the individual's salvation was replaced by a concern for social salvation. The sacred — at least in the individuals whom Cook examines — thus merged with the secular, and this growth of theological liberalism provided the foundation for the Social Gospel movement which followed. Winner of a Macdonald Prize, this work has been extremely influential in defining the main currents of Canadian religious history.

Crerar, Duff. *Padres in No Man's Land: Canadian Chaplains and the Great War*. Montreal: McGill-Queen's University Press, 1995.
Padres in No Man's Land tells the story of over 500 Protestant and Roman Catholic chaplains during World War I, a previously neglected topic. Crerar discusses the role of patronage in selecting chaplains of military service, the jobs they were asked or forbidden to do, the message they preached, and what happened to some following the war. In particular, Crerar emphasises the message chaplains brought to the front: that the war had significance with God's larger plan, and that soldiers, via their physical sacrifice, could participate in the moral and spiritual regeneration of society.

Fahey, Curtis. *In His Name: The Anglican Experience in Upper Canada, 1791-1854*. Ottawa: Carleton University Press, 1991.
Fahey argues that aside from S. F. Wise, William Westfall and J. W. Grant, historians have shown little inclination to move beyond the study of particular individuals, denominations, and churches and into the intellectual content of Upper Canadian religion. Avoiding a narrow political study, Fahey seeks to place Anglican personalities and policies within a broader social and intellectual context from the formation of the province of Upper Canada until the mid-century secularization of the clergy reserves. This perspective helps to explain, for example, the Anglican commitment to a church-state relationship even when it became apparent that disestablishment was inevitable. Even while clinging to this

belief, however, political defeats in the 1840s and 1850s forced some Anglican clerics to retreat from this view of the Church of England as the guardian of social and political order, and instead concern themselves primarily with the spiritual welfare of their own members. For Anglicans in Nova Scotia, see J. Fingard, *The Anglican Design in Loyalist Nova Scotia, 1783-1816* (1972).

Gauvreau, Michael. *The Evangelical Century: College and Creed in English Canada from the Great Revival to the Great Depression.* Montreal: McGill-Queen's University Press, 1991.

Distinctly revisionist in nature, this work has made a significant contribution to Canadian religious and intellectual historiography. Gauvreau argues that the influence of Darwin and higher criticism was not a major factor in the post-Victorian secularization of society; rather, the Christian faith and science were complementary and the evangelical creed was flexible enough to accommodate the intellectual currents suggested by Darwin, natural science, and biblical criticism. This work thus explicitly challenges the secularization thesis put forth by individuals such as Ramsay Cook and David Marshall. Gauvreau does, however, argue that evangelical colleges and clerics did experience a crisis of biblical authority. This occurred in the decade preceding World War I with the advent of form criticism imported from German universities and with an emerging historicism which revealed the relativism of historical writing. This dense and original work is required reading for those wishing to understand current debates surrounding Canadian religious historiography.

Grant, John Webster. *A Profusion of Spires: Religion in Nineteenth-Century Ontario.* Toronto: University of Toronto Press, 1988.

Reflecting contemporary trends towards the writing of regional and religious history, Grant provides a readable survey of the nineteenth-century Ontario experience. Strongly narrative, this work treats seriously the religious practices of natives and examines both Protestant denominations and the Roman Catholic faith as channels of spiritual knowledge. Grant divides the nineteenth century into two main periods: the first, up until about Confederation, was marked by the establishment of religious structures and patterns; following Confederation, this work discusses the challenges and opportunities facing Christian churches, though little attention is given to the impact of Darwin, higher criticism, or the issue of secularization.

Marshall, David B. *Secularizing the Faith: Canadian Protestant Clergy and the Crisis of Belief, 1850-1940.* Toronto: University of Toronto Press, 1992.

Focussing upon Methodist, Presbyterian, and, after 1925, United Church clerics in the century prior to World War II, Marshall has made an important contribution to the secularization debate. Within the tradition established by Ramsay Cook, Marshall argues that Protestant culture sought accommodation with the forces of modernity in order to transform the nation into the kingdom of God; ironically, in seeking to make society more sacred, religion became more secular, a concern which clerics expressed even as early as the 1870s. Thus, influences and events such as voluntarism, theological liberalism, Darwinian thought, biblical criticism, urban revivalism, missionary work, and World War I inadvertently contributed to the secularization of society. This controversial and important work includes an excellent introduction that discusses the historiography of Canadian religion in an informed manner.

McGowan, Mark and David B. Marshall, eds. *Prophets, Priests, and Prodigals: Readings in Canadian Religious History, 1608 to Present.* Toronto: McGraw-Hill Ryerson Limited, 1992.

This collection of readings is organized around the themes of Christian missions and Native people, religion in the colonies, the construction of religious identity, missions at home and abroad, and faith and doubt. McGowan and Marshall provide a brief, but useful, historiographic essay, and there is a bibliography of important articles and monographs.

McKillop, A. Brian. *A Disciplined Intelligence: Critical Inquiry and Canadian Thought in the Victorian Era.* Montreal: McGill-Queen's University Press, 1979.

This important work seeks to explain the relationship between the rise of critical inquiry and moral affirmation or, more simply, the interplay between the desire to use the intellect and the desire to maintain conviction. This tension was alleviated, McKillop argues, through a "disciplined intelligence," and was expressed by moral philosophers in a variety of ways: Scottish common sense, Paleyite natural theology, and, after 1870, philosophical idealism all were means of reconciling Christian piety and philosophical inquiry. This book is significant in two ways: It affirms the value of ideas and moral issues in Victorian thought, and emphasises the influence that Darwin and the rise of critical inquiry had on the old orthodoxy of ideas.

Murphy, Terrence and Roberto Perin, eds. *A Concise History of Christianity in Canada*. Toronto: Oxford University Press, 1996.

It is a mark of the maturity of the writing of religious history that such a work as this could be written. *A Concise History of Christianity*, with chapters by five scholars, replaces the nationalistic and institutionally based three-volume *History of the Christian Church in Canada* by H. H. Walsh, John Moir, and J. W. Grant (1966-1972), and adds a Roman Catholic perspective that is obviously lacking in Rawlyk's *The Protestant Experience* (1990). Based on a wide variety of secondary and primary sources, this work pays significant attention to popular religion and the relationship between religion and social realities such as gender, ethnicity (including sustained treatment of natives), and class. Chapters are divided along linguistic lines; also, in seeking a more relevant periodization, chapters end and begin with events such as the ultramontane revival in French Canada (around 1840) and the disestablishment of the clergy reserves in English Canada (1854). For a more general and comparative survey, see Mark A. Noll, *A History of Christianity in the United States and Canada* (1992).

Noel, Jan. *Canada Dry: Temperance Crusades before Confederation*. Toronto: University of Toronto Press, 1995.

In 1822 the first known temperance society in British North America was established. Over the next three decades over a half million colonist took the total abstinence pledge and the 1850s saw the passage or near-passage of prohibition laws in New Brunswick, Nova Scotia, and the Province of Canada. Noel's rich and well-crafted study analyses the sudden growth of the temperance movement in British North America and Red River prior to Confederation. She argues that the temperance movement was multifaceted in composition, and not confined to the energies of middle-class reformers. The movement also changed over time: the first phase up to the 1850s was marked by an evangelical revivalism that emphasised personal, voluntary pledges; thereafter, the movement became more secularized and emphasised a legislative response. Throughout the pre-Confederation era, Noel argues that religious and material interests were inseparable in the growth of temperance. Noel also notes the regional differences, with temperance having less appeal west of Old Ontario. Finally, she argues that those committed to temperance reform were indeed successful in sobering up society, with less frequent drinking on the job being the most widespread change.

Perin, Roberto. *Rome in Canada: The Vatican and Canadian Affairs in the Late Victorian Age*. Toronto: University of Toronto Press, 1990.
Charles Lindsay's *Rome in Canada* (1877) argued that the Vatican was extending its dark domain over the free-born Britons of Canada. Lindsay's work represented an aggressive Anglo-Saxon nationalism that was — it was thought — countered by the Roman Catholic church. Perin discusses the historical development of the Catholic church in Canada, the position and role of the Vatican in a wide range of Canadian matters, and Catholic education and immigration. *Rome in Canada* includes an excellent analysis of the role of papal delegates in Canada and rehabilitates Archbishop Adélard Langevin of St. Boniface as a practical and balanced defender of Catholic minority rights. For an excellent collection of essays dealing with English-speaking Catholics, see Terrence Murphy and Gerald Stortz, eds., *Creed and Culture: The Place of English-Speaking Catholics in Canadian Society* (1993).

Phillips, Paul T. *A Kingdom on Earth: Anglo-American Social Christianity, 1880-1940*. University Park, PA: The Pennsylvania State University Press, 1996.
Grounded in the relevant secondary literature, this transatlantic synthesis examines social Christianity during a crucial and unique era. Underlying the interdominational commitment to social Christianity was a concern for the socio-economic and political environments, and a belief that where the secular and the sacred mixed, the latter would prevail in the regeneration of society. *A Kingdom on Earth* discusses the rise of social Christianity as a major force in public life in North America and Britain, its religious and societal beliefs, and its changing nature and influence. This is an excellent comparative work, although things Canadian are less fully dealt with than those of Britain or the United States. Two collections that examine aspects of Christianity in an international context are George Rawlyk and Mark A. Noll, eds., *Amazing Grace: Evangelicalism in Australia, Britain, Canada, and the United States* (1993); and Mark A. Noll, David W. Bebbington, and George A. Rawlyk, eds., *Evangelicalism: Comparative Studies of Popular Protestantism in North America, the British Isles, and Beyond, 1770-1990* (1993).

Rawlyk, George A. *The Canada Fire: Radical Evangelicalism in British North America, 1775-1812*. Montreal: McGill-Queen's University Press, 1994.
Although recent polls and popular perceptions indicate that Canada

currently has less reverence for religious matters than its neighbours to the south, George Rawlyk and other church historians have asserted the centrality of Christianity to Canada's colonial past. Drawing upon his previous work on Henry Alline and the New Light revival — as well as more recent examinations of revivalistic preachers such as William Black, David George, Freeborn Garrettson, Henris Harding, and others — Rawlyk explores the nature of evangelicalism in British North America. While evangelicalism was a complex kaleidoscope that embraced various traditions and fundamentals, *The Canada Fire* argues that radicals were marked by their heavy stress on the New Birth experience and activist witnessing. Rawlyk concludes that radical evangelicalism in British North America was more populist, democratic, and anti-authoritarian than its American counterpart. This work also provides a valuable and forceful introduction to evangelical rituals such as the camp meeting, believer's baptism, and the long communion. Two edited collections that provide access to relevant primary source material are G. Rawlyk, ed., *New Light Letters and Spiritual Songs, 1778-1793* (1983); and David Bell, ed., *Newlight Baptist Journals of James Manning and James Innis* (1984).

_____. *Champions of the Truth: Fundamentalism, Modernism and the Maritime Baptists*. Montreal: McGill-Queen's University Press, 1990. These three lectures from the Winthrop Pickard Bell lecture series represent Rawlyk's "preliminary probes" into the experiences of the Maritime Baptist Convention in the 1920s and 1930s. Rawlyk builds on his earlier work on Henry Alline and the New Lights and creates linkages into the evangelical and revivalist traditions of the religious past in the Maritimes. In the process, he provides an intriguing and challenging analysis of the conflicts between modernists and fundamentalists within the Maritime Baptist congregations.

_____. *Ravished by the Spirit: Religious Revivals, Baptists, and Henry Alline*. Montreal: McGill-Queen's University Press, 1984. In *A People Highly Favoured of God* (1972) and *Nova Scotia's Massachusetts: A Study of Massachusetts-Nova Scotia Relations 1630 to 1784* (1973), Rawlyk identified the important role played by itinerant preacher Henry Alline and religious revivalism in Nova Scotia. These four essays, delivered as the 1983 Hayward Lectures at Acadia University, analyse the ongoing effects of these revivalist, evangelical traditions in the Atlantic region. Rawlyk traces the impact of Henry Alline and the New Lights on Baptist traditions and discovers that the shadow from this movement continued to influence the Baptist church well into the mid-nineteenth century. For a brief, but still useful, biography of Alline, see J. M. Bumsted, *Henry Alline, 1748-1784* (1971).

Rawlyk, George A., ed. *The Canadian Protestant Experience 1760 to 1990*. Burlington, ON: Welch Publishing Company Inc., 1990.
A chronological account by five well-known historians of religion, this survey provides a readable account to the Protestant faith in Canada. This work is as much analysis as narrative, and seeks to discuss issues such as the liberal and (especially) evangelical traditions, the role of ethnicity and immigration, the interaction between international, national and regional religious experiences, popular and elite religion, issues of secularization, and the changing nature of Protestantism. While little emphasis is placed on the Protestant churches and their relationship with Native population, this volume is particularly valuable in examining some of the intellectual currents and individuals active in affecting the Protestant faith.

Semple, Neil. *The Lord's Dominion: The History of Canadian Methodism*. Montreal: McGill-Queen's University Press, 1996.
Comprehensive and meticulously researched, this survey explores Methodism — English Canada's principal denomination in the nineteenth century — from its earliest days in Canada until the formation of the United Church in 1925. The book is divided into two broad sections. The first chronicles the transatlantic nature of early Methodism, early ventures to evangelize Natives and to influence the moral and social nature of society, and the enthusiastic nature of the revival meeting. Second, Semple discusses the growth and consolidation of Canadian Methodism beginning in the second half of the nineteenth century, education efforts and reforms, the church's response to intellectual and demographic challenges, and mission work in western Canada and overseas. The maturation of Methodism was accompanied by increased emphasis upon middle-class values designed to promote the church's vision of God's kingdom on earth. Semple concludes with the forces within Methodism that led to the formation of the United Church. For a regional and more eclectic treatment, see Charles H. H. Scobie and John Webster Grant, eds., *The Contribution of Methodism to Atlantic Canada* (1992).

Stackhouse, John, Jr. *Canadian Evangelicalism in the Twentieth Century: An Introduction to Its Character*. Toronto: University of Toronto Press, 1993.

While historians have devoted considerable attention to the study of religion over the past decade, much of this work has focussed on the Victorian era and the first decades of the twentieth century. Stackhouse extends the study of religion well into the current century and provides a preliminary analysis of the character of Canadian evangelicalism. This work is composed of two principal parts. The first examines the evangelicalism of two prominent figures, T. T. Shields and Premier William Aberhart, both of whom are dismissed as eccentrics and not typical of the mainstream movement. More substantively, Stackhouse examines a number of evangelical colleges and institutions that constitute the mainstream and argues that they reflected either a "sectish" mindset that separated itself from modern culture, or "churchish" evangelicalism that embraced a wider variety of Christians and exhibited little hostility toward contemporary culture. For a broad-ranging collection, see G. A. Rawlyk, ed., *Aspects of the Canadian Evangelical Experience* (1997).

Stouffer, Allen P. *The Light of Nature and the Law of God: Antislavery in Ontario, 1838-1877*. Montreal: McGill-Queen's University Press, 1992.
While regional in nature and lacking in a national and (more importantly) an international perspective, this work explores antislavery sentiments in Ontario. Stouffer identifies 132 antislavery leaders and concludes that British immigrants largely led the charge against slavery.

Valverde, Mariana. *The Age of Light, Soap, and Water: Moral Reform in English Canada, 1885-1925*. Toronto: McClelland and Stewart, 1991.
While organizations and individual reformers such as the Women's Christian Temperance Union, the Salvation Army, and J. S. Woodsworth have all received some attention, the language used by moral reformers has scarcely been examined. Claiming that "history [is] a discipline . . . in a methodological crisis," Valverde examines the issue of social purity through the vehicle of discourse analysis. This interdisciplinary approach argues that the symbols and rhetoric surrounding issues such as immigration, racial purity, prostitution, and urban decay were framed to transcend gender, race, and class divisions within society; the aim, she argues, was not so much to suppress vice but to re-create and re-moralise deviants and Canada as a whole. For a study of Sabbatarian campaigns, see C. Armstrong and H. V. Nelles, *The Revenge of the Methodist Bicycle Company: Sunday Streetcars and Municipal Reform in Toronto, 1888-1897* (1977).

Van Die, Marguerite. *An Evangelical Mind: Nathanael Burwash and the Methodist Tradition in Canada, 1839-1918.* Montreal: McGill-Queen's University Press, 1989.

Biographies of non-political Victorian personalities are severely lacking. Van Die's study of Nathanael Burwash, the most significant Methodist theologian of the nineteenth century, helps to correct this deficiency. More important, Van Die reacts against the work of Ramsay Cook and Brian McKillop, who argue that the rise of critical thought, Darwinian science, and historical criticism all conspired to encourage many religious individuals to salvage Christianity by transforming it into a social religion. Instead, *An Evangelical Mind* argues that biblical fundamentalism and religious scepticism were not the only two responses to modernity available to Victorian Christians. Nathanael Burwash, a theologian and educator of note, maintained a flexible evangelicalism which met the challenge of science and higher criticism. For more than thirty years Burwash worked to develop a systematic theology that was receptive "to the rising scientific ethos" while also conserving "the central ligaments of the Wesleyan tradition." Theology was not, therefore, replaced with sociology as some have argued; rather, it continued to be flexible and adaptive in order to remain prophetic within a new environment. *An Evangelical Mind* provides insight into an important Victorian figure, and contributes to a significant historiographic debate.

Vaudry, Richard W. *The Free Church in Victorian Canada, 1844-1861.* Waterloo: Wilfrid Laurier University Press, 1989.

In 1843 Thomas Chalmers led almost 40 percent of the membership out of the Established Church of Scotland and formed the Free Church of Scotland. The Great Disruption had important consequences outside of Scottish borders, and Vaudry traces the establishment and rise of the Free Church in Canada. By 1861 it was the fourth largest church in Canada West, comprising over 10 percent of the population. Vaudry examines the ideological principles, organizational structure and finances, and educational and reform-minded activities that characterized the Free Church in the mid-nineteenth century. In 1861 the Free Church joined with the United Presbyterians to form the Canadian Presbyterian Church; in 1875 the latter joined the national Presbyterian Church in Canada. Two other regional studies are Eldon Hay, *The Chignecto Covenanters: A Regional History of Reformed Presbyterianism in New Brunswick and Nova Scotia, 1827-1905* (1996); and Laurie Stanley, *The Well-Watered Garden: The Presbyterian Church in Cape Breton, 1798-1860* (1983).

Warsh, Cheryl Krasnick, ed. *Drink in Canada: Historical Essays.*
   Montreal: McGill-Queen's University Press, 1993.
The historiography of drink in Canada has often focussed upon issues
such as temperance and prohibition. While not ignoring these issues, the
essays collected in *Drink in Canada* introduce readers to economic,
social, and medical aspects of liquor consumption. Of particular interest
is Warsh's introductory essay that places the contents of *Drink in Canada*
within the Canadian and international historiography. For local studies
that emphasise the political or state aspects of liquor control, see Gerald
A. Hallowell, *Prohibition in Ontario, 1919-1923* (1972); and especially
Robert A. Cambell, *Demon Rum or Easy Money: Government Control of
Liquor in British Columbia from Prohibition to Privatization* (1991).
James H. Gray, *Booze: The Impact of Whiskey on the Prairie West* (1972;
rpt.: 1995) is anecdotal and entertaining. Reginald G. Smart and Alan C.
Ogborne, *Northern Spirits: A Social History of Alcohol in Canada* (1996),
is wide-ranging, but lacks analysis and historical context.

Westfall, William. *Two Worlds: The Protestant Culture of Nineteenth-
   Century Ontario.* Montreal: McGill-Queen's University Press, 1989.
This imaginative work examines the centrality of religion in nineteenth-
century Old Ontario. In particular, it discusses the Churches of England
and Scotland, built upon the "virtue of order," and the Methodist faith,
which was largely a "religion of experience." In the early part of the
century, these two approaches — manifested primarily through the
personalities of John Strachan and Egerton Ryerson — clashed, resulting
in religious and political conflict. By mid-century, however, animosity
between the two faiths began to dissipate and there followed a relatively
unified intellectual and institutional Protestant culture that fused order and
experience. Though Westfall is guilty of presenting Anglicanism and
especially Methodism as monolithic faiths, he provides an insightful
analysis into the religious world of nineteenth-century Old Ontario.

Wright, Robert. *A World Mission: Canadian Protestantism and the Quest
   for a New International Order, 1918-1939.* Montreal: McGill-Queen's
   University Press, 1991.
The post-World War I Protestant church faced a world replete with
potential obstacles, both within Canada and the international community.
This work examines how these churches reacted to international
challenges, including the rise of communism in Russia, fascism in Europe,
and militant forms of nationalism in Asia. Through an examination of

clerics, church leaders, and official church organs, Wright concludes that the "Christian internationalism" that emerged following World War I was not liberal in content, but rather emerged from a tradition of late nineteenth-century evangelicalism. While belief in the moral superiority of the West had been shaken by the war, the evangelical consensus of most mainline missions still emphasised the centrality of Christ and the necessity of conversion. While this consensus did not survive the next war, Wright concludes that missions did play an important role in cultivating goodwill between developed and undeveloped countries.

Education and the University

Axelrod, Paul. *Making a Middle Class: Student Life in English Canada During the Thirties*. Montreal: McGill-Queen's University Press, 1990.
The first comprehensive survey of student life in Canadian universities, this work reflects the growing interest in the social history of higher education. While Axelrod provides an insightful discussion on the social composition of those who went to university and what they were taught, his primary focus lies in examining the role of the university in socializing young people into the values of the middle class. This work also provides insight into the socio-political environment of the 1930s: Save for a minority who were attracted to the Canadian Student Assembly or the CCF youth movement, universities had the effect of entrenching conservative values.

Axelrod, Paul and John G. Reid, eds. *Youth, University, and Canadian Society: Essays in the Social History of Higher Education*. Montreal: McGill-Queen's University Press, 1989.
The fourteen essays in this collection are an illustration of the breadth of scholarship examining the development and role of universities in Canada, and provide a good introduction to the numerous histories of individual universities. The essays are prepared by some of Canada's most prominent social historians, and examine aspects of the university experience organized around sections entitled region, gender, and social class, student life and culture, the campus at war, student movements and social change, and the learning environment.

Barman, Jean. *Growing Up British in British Columbia: Boys in Private School*. Vancouver: University of British Columbia Press, 1984.

The large numbers of British who immigrated to British Columbia in the late nineteenth and first half of the twentieth centuries sought to re-invent their Britishness by establishing private schools for boys, especially on Vancouver Island, the lower mainland, and in the Okanagan Valley. In addition to describing the character and agenda of these schools, Barman argues that graduates assumed important socio-economic and leadership positions, and therefore wielded influence disproportionate to their numbers. Two collections that examine education in the West include, J. Donald Wilson and David C. Jones, eds. *Schooling and Society in Twentieth Century British Columbia* (1980); and Nancy M. Sheehan, J. Donald Wilson, and David C. Jones, eds. *Schools in the West: Essays in Canadian Educational History* (1986).

Berger, Carl. *Honour and the Search for Influence: A History of the Royal Society of Canada.* Toronto: University of Toronto Press, 1996.
In 1881 the Marquess of Lorne, Governor General of Canada from 1878 to 1883, proposed the creation of a literary and scientific society; the following year, the Royal Society of Canada was formed. Berger surveys the Society's role in publishing and transmitting knowledge, and its interaction with some of the predominant themes in Canada's intellectual development. Ultimately, however, the Society was less successful as an institution, and most of its influence was derived from the individual efforts of its members.

Cameron, James D. *For The People: A History of St Francis Xavier University.* Montreal: McGill-Queen's University Press, 1996.
For The People traces the nineteenth-century migration of Highland Catholic Scots, the establishment of St Francis Xavier as an agent of religious, economic, and social advancement, and significant developments and personalities in the institution's history to the 1960s. There are numerous comparisons with other colleges: for example, unlike some protestant colleges like Victoria College (Methodist) and McMaster (Baptist), students at Xavier were not split over the challenges of higher criticism and theological modernism.

Curtis, Bruce. *True Government by Choice Men? Inspection, Education, and State Formation in Canada West.* Toronto: University of Toronto Press, 1992.
The legislation of the 1840s has been seen as particularly significant in the establishment of Ontario's school system. One aspect of this reform

was the establishment of district school inspectors who acted as conduits of information between schools and the state. In this study Curtis examines 37 men who acted as district school inspectors between 1843 and 1850. This function emerged largely out of the political instability of the late 1830s and, Curtis argues, the duty of the inspector was to help ensure political legitimacy in the face of radical agrarian and republican agitation. This prosopographic study is richly informative; indeed, it is fortunate for both Curtis and the reader — although not nineteenth-century pupils — that men such as Dexter D'Everardo, who found it necessary to monitor the time he spent chewing each mouthful of food, became school inspectors. Despite his own denials, this well-argued study does in fact advocate some variation of social control theory.

_____. *Building the Educational State: Canada West, 1836-1871.* London, ON: Althouse Press, 1988.

Curtis traces the emergence of a highly centralised school system in the three decades after the education reforms of the 1840s. Informed by a neo-Marxist theory of state formation and drawing primarily upon a reading of education reports, school acts, and department correspondence, this work argues that within the parameters of an industrializing society, state authorities utilized the school system to establish the norms and values of this new society. This systematization involved issues such as the enforcement of attendance, the increasing establishment of a common curriculum, and the standardization of teacher training.

Fraser, Brian J. *Church, College, and Clergy: A History of Theological Education at Knox College, Toronto, 1844-1994.* Montreal: McGill-Queen's University Press, 1995.

Established in 1844, Knox College was arguably the first such establishment in Canada; that this would be so is not unexpected: While Presbyterians have debated whether the emphasis in church colleges should be on piety or learning, the concern for profession training has always been present. Fraser's survey of Knox College argues that the intellectual environment was dynamic. The confessional orthodoxy of the founders of the college, for example, did not survive the nineteenth century unscathed; instead, Knox scholars adopted new methods of study, particularly in biblical interpretation and history. Likewise, neo-orthodoxy replaced progressive orthodoxy following church union in 1925, and more divergent versions of orthodoxy were expressed in the decades that followed. The primary concern of *Church, College, and Clergy* is with the

Knox faculty and its attitude and relationship toward the church and its clergy. For other studies of theological colleges, see George Rawlyk and Kevin Quinn, *The Redeemed of the Lord Say So: A History of Queen's Theological College, 1912-1972* (1980); and D. C. Master's older work, *Protestant Church Colleges in Canada: A History* (1966).

Gaffield, Chad. *Language, Schooling, and Cultural Conflict: The Origins of the French-Language Controversy in Ontario*. Montreal: McGill-Queen's University Press, 1987.

Chad Gaffield addresses a well-worn topic in a distinctively revisionist fashion. While previous works on this subject have tended to place language debates within a national political perspective, Gaffield traces the controversy surrounding French language schooling in Prescott County to local social and economic concerns in the Ottawa valley and as such reflects the social historical perspective which has come to dominate the history of education in Canada. Using both quantitative and qualitative evidence, Gaffield argues that Quebec migration into the valley in the 1850s, and a continued economic malaise during the 1873-1878 recession were important factors leading to disputes between local French and English elites over school policies. The refusal of Franco-Ontarians to accept "voluntary assimilation" eventually led to a crisis and, after 1889, a migration of French Catholic students from public to separate schools.

Gidney, R. D. and W. P. J. Millar. *Inventing Secondary Education: The Rise of the High School in Nineteenth-Century Ontario*. Montreal: McGill-Queen's University Press, 1990.

This book traces the development of the grammar school from its sectarian and upper-class origins to the modern ideal of the high school. Gidney and Millar acknowledge the role played by Egerton Ryerson, the Chief Superintendent of Schools for three decades, but argue that he did not always get what he desired. Instead of a separate curriculum for men and women, and a distinction between grammar and common schools, with the former emphasising the classics (all of which Ryerson desired), what emerged by the 1880s was a coeducational institution where science, English, and "useful learning" dominated the curriculum with little distinction between common and grammar schools. Significantly, the rise of the high school was not orchestrated by central authorities; rather, middle-class parental influences ensured that there would be strong elements of local control. The element of social control that education exerted is, therefore, downplayed.

Hiller, Harry H. *Society and Change: S. D. Clark and the Development of Canadian Sociology*. Toronto: University of Toronto Press, 1982.
In this provocative study, Harry Hiller examines the emergence of sociology through the lens of its most influential Canadian practitioner, S. D. Clark. Clark's experimentation with the frontier thesis and Chicago sociology intellectually challenged a generation of Canadian scholars. Hiller blends a history of sociology in Canada with Clark's evolution as a scholar, and illustrates the linkages between larger societal issues and the scholarly pursuits of an individual academic.

Houston, Susan E. and Alison Prentice. *Schooling and Scholars in Nineteenth-Century Ontario*. Toronto: University of Toronto Press, 1988.
Wider ranging and more nuanced than Allison Prentice's *The School Promoters* (1977), *Schooling and Scholars* traces the emergence of a public school system and the schooling experience of teachers and their pupils. There are three parts to this study: the first examines pioneer schooling; the second explores mid-nineteenth-century school reforms; and finally the reader is introduced to the school system that existed for both the majority and minorities by the 1870s. While Houston and Prentice argue that few jurisdictions outstripped Ontario's efforts to create a centrally administered system of education, they also downplay the element of social control somewhat by noting the wide diversity of education and the influence of local factors. Following the current trend, this work also lessens the dominant role of Egerton Ryerson; in revising this argument further, the Anglican bishop John Strachan is not portrayed as a reactionary villain of progressive education, but as one who might have been more progressive than many contemporaries.

Johnston, Charles M. *McMaster University. Volume I: The Toronto Years*. Toronto: University of Toronto Press, 1976.
_____. *McMaster University. Volume II: The Early Years in Hamilton, 1930-57*. Toronto: University of Toronto Press, 1981.
Founded by Baptists to produce "a Christian school of learning," McMaster University is well served by this two-volume history. Johnston effectively links institutional, curricular, ideological and societal issues in his thematic approach and discusses both the triumphs of higher education and the anti-intellectual currents of a church-sponsored institution. His focus in the first volume is on the relationship between the Baptists, the university, and the secular University of Toronto; in the second volume,

he explores issues of state intervention, the rise of professional faculties, and the conflict between research and teaching. Also see Hilda Neatby, *Queen's University: And Not to Yield, 1841-1917* (1978), and F. W. Gibson, *Queen's University: To Serve and Yet be Free, 1917-1961* (1983).

Macleod, Malcom. *A Bridge Built Halfway: A History of Memorial University College, 1925-1950*. Montreal: McGill-Queen's University Press, 1990.

A Bridge Built Halfway examines Newfoundland's two year junior college which later became Memorial University. Both an institutional history and a social history of higher education in Newfoundland, *A Bridge Built Halfway* links the college to the rise of a middle class and the modernisation of Newfoundland in the twentieth century.

Magnuson, Roger. *A Brief History of Quebec Education: From New France to the Parti Quebecois*. Montreal: Harvest House, 1980.

A preliminary survey of Quebec education, this work focuses upon the institutional development of Quebec education with little reference to the social context so apparent in many contemporary works. In particular, Magnuson emphasises issues of church-state and French-English relations that have dominated the Quebec school system. Based largely upon secondary sources, this book provides a short, readable summary of Quebec education for the non-expert. Also see Stanley B. Frost, *McGill University: For the Advancement of Learning* (1980).

McKillop, A. B. *Matters of Mind: The University in Ontario, 1791-1951*. Toronto: University of Toronto Press, 1994.

Traditionally, university histories concentrate upon institution-building and the public lives of their administrators. McKillop's brilliant work, in contrast, reflects the current trend to emphasise the social role of education and, especially in this case, to place higher education into a broader intellectual context. *Matters of Mind* provides an insightful analysis of issues such as the denominational origins and secularization of Ontario's universities, the influence of Darwinian thought, the shaping of character through the liberal arts curriculum, the entrance of women, the emergence of the research ideal, the increasing emphasis on public utility following World War I, and the increasing role of state-sponsored higher education. The study concludes in 1951, by which time most World War II veterans had graduated, and when Ontario and its universities were on the verge of a demographic, social, economic, and intellectual "revolution in matters of mind." This work is perhaps overly concerned with the University of Toronto; since Toronto currently lacks a mature, academic history, *Matters of Mind* serves as a useful introduction to that institution. For a useful and wide-ranging study of an important president of the University of Toronto, see James Greenlee, *Sir Robert Falconer: A Biography* (1988); also, see Paul Axelrod, *Scholars and Dollars: Politics, Economics, and the Universities of Ontario, 1945-1980.* (1982).

Prentice, Alison. *The School Promoters: Education and Social Class in Mid-Nineteenth-Century Upper Canada.* Toronto: McClelland and Stewart, 1977.

The School Promoters represents one of the first sustained efforts of the new social history to examine the history of education in Canada. This is an important work, both for its place within Canadian historiography and its content. Rejecting the traditional view of Egerton Ryerson as a type of prelapsarian hero — a view propagated most forcefully by C. B. Sissions's work on Ryerson in the 1930s and 1940s — Prentice examines the "school promoters" in mid-century Upper Canada (principally Ryerson) and attempts to elucidate the prevailing ideology of the times, and to assess educational attitudes toward the question of class. Although her conclusions and methodology have been, at times, criticised as overly simplistic, Prentice concludes that universal education operated as a means by which the state exerted social control over an expanding and increasingly industrializing nation.

Reid, John G. *Mount Allison University: A History to 1963.* 2 vols. Toronto: University of Toronto Press, 1984.

Founded in Sackville, New Brunswick, by the Methodist church, Mount Allison is one of Canada's foremost liberal arts universities. While the institutional development of Mount Allison is at the centre of his work, Reid's analysis focuses on the intervention of the state, the tension between academic freedom, and social purpose endemic to a church-sponsored institution, the role of power in the diffusion of knowledge, and the relationship between the university and the surrounding community.

Selles, Johanna M. *Methodists and Women's Education in Ontario, 1836-1925.* Montreal: McGill-Queen's University Press, 1996.

The emergence in the nineteenth century of a movement favouring women's education has only recently been of interest to Canadian historians. Selles explores women's education under Methodist auspices and examines the religious and gender ideology that informed this education. *Methodists and Women's Education* discusses the establishment of ladies' colleges, the admission of women to early seminaries, colleges and university, and reconstructs what life was like for female students within the context of changing ideologies, curricula, and views on women's education. Selles concludes by examining some influential personalities, including a chapter on Margaret Addison, dean of Annesley Hall and of women students at Victoria College.

Shore, Marlene. *The Science of Social Redemption: McGill, the Chicago School, and the Origins of Social Research in Canada.* Toronto: University of Toronto Press, 1987.
This dense and thoroughly researched book has a great deal to say about the history of sociology in Canada and, in particular, in one sociology department. In the 1920s McGill University in Montreal was the first Canadian school to establish a department of sociology. Carl Dawson, the protagonist in establishing this department, was under two direct influences: his Baptist heritage from which he drifted while at Chicago, and Robert Park's human ecology, characteristic of the Chicago School, which emphasised empirical knowledge and (real or imagined) scientific objectivity. Sociology was thus established through a compromise between social workers (who wished to reform society) and academic inquiry, which in the nationalistic 1920s pursued an active research program into immigration, rural life, western settlement, and urbanization. This compromise was ultimately shattered in the 1930s. *The Science of Social Redemption* is an important work; it emphasises the role of Carl Dawson and the Chicago School in the development of sociology in Canada, as well as the previously neglected role of Baptists in the social reform movement.

Waite, P. B. *The Lives of Dalhousie University. Volume I: 1818-1925.* Montreal: McGill-Queen's University Press 1994.
_____.*The Lives of Dalhousie University. Volume II: 1925-1980.* Montreal: McGill-Queen's University Press, 1997.
While university histories sometimes focus upon administrative detail and curriculum, these volumes explore the lives of Dalhousie from its origins as a small privately-funded college to a major Canadian university. The

emphasis is upon students and professors, male and female students, the interaction of the university with the Halifax community, as well major trends and developments within the university itself.

Wilson, J. Don, Robert M. Stamp, and Louis-Philippe Audet, eds. *Canadian Education: A History*. Scarborough, ON: Prentice-Hall, 1970.
Strongly informed by the work of English and American historians such as Brian Simon and Bernard Bailyn, articles in this collection go beyond narrow and often whiggish biographical and institutional studies. The initial Canadian venture into the new educational history, *Canadian Education* argues that "educational history should be regarded as social history" and that education is "a reflection of the social order." While the content of this work sometimes falls short in articulating the experience of students, teachers, women, and minority groups, this failing was without doubt a reflection of the state of Canadian social history in 1970. While some new themes were developed — such as Wilson's reappraisal of Egerton Ryerson as an administrator rather than a hero — the legacy of this collection lies in its promotion of social history into the confines of educational foundations.

Science, Technology, and Medicine

Ainley, Marianne Gosztonyi, ed. *Despite the Odds: Essays on Canadian Women and Science*. Montreal: Véhicule Press, 1990.
This welcome addition to the history of science in Canada attempts to account for why women have been only minimally presented as participants in the scientific community, and to provide a corrective to the obvious masculine imbalance that exists. In her introduction, Ainley explains why women's contribution to Canadian science (broadly defined in this volume) have been ignored; subsequent sections explore the contribution of women scientists to their fields, provide more detailed biographical sketches of some individuals, and discuss contemporary concerns affecting Canadian women and science.

Ball, Norman R. *Mind, Heart and Vision: Professional Engineering in Canada, 1887-1987*. Ottawa: National Museums of Canada, 1987.
Published in cooperation with the Engineering Centennial Board, *Mind, Heart and Vision* is overtly nationalistic and celebratory. Rather than a history of professional engineering, this work provides a summary of the

accomplishments of Canadian engineers and is profusely illustrated with photographs and diagrams. While a useful introduction to the innovations of Canadian engineers, this volume is ultimately lacking in analysis.

Bilson, Geoffery. *A Darkened House: Cholera in Nineteenth-Century Canada.* Toronto: University of Toronto Press, 1980.
A Darkened House examines the spread of cholera, the efforts by medical and public health officials to control the disease, and the intellectual, cultural, and social effects of the disease in Canada. Cholera devastated Canada between 1832 and 1871: Doctors and medical practitioners did not understand the disease, sanitation and housing conditions were deplorable, immigration facilities were poorly managed, and public health organisations and hospitals were non-existent. The epidemics that resulted created significant changes in Canadian society: Communities considered spiritual solutions to the crisis since science offered little assistance; doctors took the first steps toward professionalisation; widespread intolerance and distrust of immigrants emerged in Canada; French-English relations deteriorated; and public health and community management entered the sphere of politics.

Bliss, Michael. *Plague: A Story of Smallpox in Montreal.* Toronto: HarperCollins, 1991.
A self-described "non-fiction novel," *Plague* presents the story of the 1885 smallpox epidemic in Montreal, the last such incidence in any urban centre in the western world. Rich in anecdotes, personalities, and drama, *Plague* is an insightful and readable work. Also, see Allan Everett Marble, *Surgeons, Smallpox, and the Poor: A History of Medicine and Social Conditions in Nova Scotia, 1749-1799* (1993).

_____. *Banting: A Biography.* Toronto: McClelland and Stewart, 1984.
Based on the voluminous Banting Papers, this is an excellent biography of one of Canada's most prestigious scientists. Bliss demonstrates the centrality of science to Banting's life; however, outside of the great moment early in his career, his work produced nothing of importance. Tormented by his failures, Banting became an embittered and unhappy individual.

_____. *The Discovery of Insulin.* Toronto: McClelland and Stewart, 1982.

The Discovery of Insulin is the "day by day and dog by dog" story of the quest for a treatment of diabetes in the 1920s. Bliss plays the role of detective throughout the book as he searches for the individual to whom credit should be given for the discovery of insulin. He deftly demonstrates that the sloppy experimental practices and faulty premises upon which the search was undertaken produced the discovery and mass production of insulin through the combined contributions of Frederick Banting, Charles Best, J. B. Collip, J. R. Macleod, and Eli Lilly pharmaceuticals.

Bogaard, Paul A, ed. *Profiles of Science and Society in the Maritimes Prior to 1914.* Fredericton: Acadiensis Press and Centre for Canadian Studies, Mount Allison University, 1990.

Robert Bruce's Pulitzer Prize-winning *The Launching of Modern American Science, 1846-76* (1987) provided a comprehensive treatment of the complex interaction between science and American society. *Profiles of Science and Society,* to which Bruce contributes the foreword, attempts a similar approach within a Maritime context. Concentrating on the nineteenth century, the dozen essays in this volume examine "the practise of science and how it was woven into the fabric of [this region's] social community — its public policy and its individual life." *Profiles of Science and Society* is divided into three sections: the first briefly provides an overview of the quantity and categories represented by scientific publications in the Maritimes; the second focuses upon individuals such as George Lawson and William Dawson; and finally, public perceptions and support for petroleum exploration, astronomical enterprises, and applied science are explored.

Dodd, Dianne and Deborah Gorham, eds. *Caring and Curing: Historical Perspectives on Women and Healing in Canada.* Ottawa: University of Ottawa Press, 1994.

This collection of essays emphasises the role and agency of women health care providers from the 1880s to the present, a role that was much different from that performed by men. Essays explore the complex and sometimes contradictory role that nurses negotiated in a changing medical establishment, the evolution of midwifery and the medicalization of childbirth, the influence of lay reformers, the response of working-class women to health services, and the emergence of female physicians.

Eggleston, Wilfrid. *National Research in Canada: The NRC 1916-1966.* Toronto: Clarke, Irwin, 1978.

The Department of Scientific and Industrial Research was established in 1916 and renamed the National Research Council (NRC) in 1925. The NRC maintained an arms-length relationship with the federal government, conducted independent research, coordinating research projects, and sponsored university-based research and study. Eggleston provides a detailed institutional history of the NRC, with particular attention to personalities.

Foster, Janet. *Working for Wildlife: The Beginning of Preservation in Canada.* Toronto: University of Toronto Press, 1978.
Working for Wildlife is one of the first books published on Canadian history in the field of environmental history. Foster looks at the wildlife conservation movement in the period 1885 to 1925 and concludes that a small group of devoted civil servants convinced politicians to make wildlife conservation a government policy. During this period significant changes in attitudes occurred, and many Canadian measures were a response to the popular conservation measures adopted in the United States. Unlike the American literature on the conservation movement, however, Foster never links the changing attitudes in Canada with Progressive era reforms, or increasing support for scientific analysis.

Gridgeman, N. T. *Biological Sciences at the National Research Council of Canada: The Early Years to 1950.* Waterloo: Wilfrid Laurier University Press, 1979.
Middleton, W. E. K. *Physics at the National Research Council of Canada, 1929-52.* Waterloo: Wilfrid Laurier University Press, 1979.
The government of Canada created the National Research Council (NRC) during World War I in order to coordinate scientific research for war-related industrial production. Like its earth science counterpart, the Geological Survey of Canada, the NRC therefore serves industry, government, and science. These two volumes trace the activities of two important divisions in the NRC. Readers will find interesting commentaries on the research projects undertaken by the NRC and a good discussion of the problems a centralised research institution faces when dealing with regional diversity.

Inglis, Alex. *Northern Vagabond: The Life and Career of J. B. Tyrrell — The Man Who Conquered the Canadian North.* Toronto: McClelland and Stewart, 1978.
J. B. Tyrrell was an explorer, geologist, surveyor, and historian who

worked in the Geological Survey of Canada (GSC) in the 1880s and 1890s, before pursuing a career as a prospector, entrepreneur, and writer. Tyrrell's most important work as a scientist came in the Canadian north (the Athabasca Tar Sands and Keewatin Barren Lands were but two the areas he studied), and Inglis ties this work into a general overview of the GSC and the political climate of the period.

Jarrell, Richard A. *The Cold Light of Dawn: A History of Canadian Astronomy*. Toronto: University of Toronto Press, 1988.
This well-illustrated volume chronicles the history of astronomy in Canada from the arrival of the first Europeans to the present. The early period of astronomy was largely utilitarian and concerned with surveying or determining longitude or latitude. While state support for a more "pure" scientific approach can be seen in the nineteenth century, Jarrell traces the rise of Canadian astronomy to the establishment of the Dominion Observatory in Ottawa in 1905. In the post-World War II era, astronomy was decentralized from the three major observatories in Ottawa, Toronto, and Victoria as universities became more active.

Killan, Gerald. *David Boyle: From Artisan to Archaeologist*. Toronto: University of Toronto Press, 1983.
David Boyle was one of the important self-taught naturalists who transformed Canadian science in the late nineteenth century. Killan skilfully illustrates Boyle's important role in the development of archaeology in Canada. As curator of the museum of the Canadian Institute and superintendent of the Ontario Provincial Museum, Boyle excavated many of Ontario's important Iroquoian archaeological sites, and urged both international scholars and the general public to turn their attention to this subject.

Levere, Trevor H. *Science and the Canadian Arctic: A Century of Exploration, 1818-1918*. Cambridge: Cambridge University Press, 1993.
During the nineteenth century there was considerable interest in the Canadian arctic by outside interests, and approximately 200 voyages were commissioned to this seemingly bleak land. The initial ventures were often politically motivated: With the end of the Napoleonic Wars, the idle British navy renewed its search for the Northwest Passage and sought to establish sovereignty over the artic. Most science, therefore, concerned geographic and navigational discoveries. However, the search for Sir John

Franklin beginning in 1845 — he eventually died west of King William Island in 1847 — spurred a new era of scientific activity in a variety of disciplines. Levere's model study concludes with the first Canadian-sponsored expedition (1913-1918) that sought to establish Canadian sovereignty in the northern reaches of the continent.

Levere, Trevor H. and Richard A. Jarrell, eds. *A Curious Fieldbook: Science and Society in Canadian History*. Toronto: Oxford University Press, 1974.

The editors have gathered almost 80 selections from wide-ranging primary sources relating to science and Canadian society between 1616 and 1919, with particular attention paid to Victorian Canada and the period prior to World War I. Incorporating both French- and English-Canadian material, sources emphasises the utilitarian and social roles of science, although interest in pure science became more common by the twentieth century. Levere and Jarrell contribute an excellent general introduction and briefer comments at the beginning of each chapter.

McLaren, Angus. *Our Own Master Race: Eugenics in Canada, 1885-1945*. Toronto: McClelland and Stewart, 1990.

Between 1929 and 1972, the Alberta Eugenics Board authorized over 2000 sterilizations. Grounded in wide-ranging international literature, *Our Own Master Race* explores the eugenics movement in Canada, particularly efforts to sterilize those who were deemed "unsuitable" by society. McLaren provides portraits of prominent eugenicists such as Madge Thurlow Macklin, Helen MacMurchy, and William Hutton, and provides an intellectual history of how the movement became prominent among some middle-class professionals. The eugenics movement had regional, age, class, and gender biases: sterilization mostly occurred in British Columbia and Alberta, and most "patients" were young women and of working-class origin. McLaren pays little attention to the social and political context in which the eugenics movement emerged.

McLaren, Angus and Arlene Tigar McLaren. *The Bedroom and the State: The Changing Practices and Politics of Contraception and Abortion in Canada, 1880-1980*. Toronto: McClelland and Stewart, 1986; rpt., 1990.

The historical literature on contraception and abortion in Canada is sketchy and inchoate. A rare exception, *The Bedroom and the State* surveys issues of birth control and abortion between 1880 and 1980, though the focus is largely on the period between 1920 and 1980; in addition, with the exception of a single chapter on Quebec, the emphasis is squarely upon English Canada. The authors argue that fertility control was an important issue in both the private and public domains. At the turn of the century, for example, some commentators felt that falling birth rates reflected the declining vitality of the Canadian nation and, therefore, opposed limiting the size of families. In addition, while some early socialists encouraged the use of contraception, others opposed it, arguing that the problems of society were largely economic and not related to family size; in a socialist society there would be sufficient means to support larger families and birth control would be unnecessary. The authors argue that the politics of contraception have undergone dramatic transformation in the twentieth century: birth control, once taboo, became more respectable in the 1930s; and with the population explosion in the Third World, Canadian advocates now incorporate family planning into their aid programs. In general, Canadian laws relating to birth control and abortion have been more restrictive than those in England or the USA.

Millard, J. Rodney. *The Master Spirit of the Age: Canadian Engineers and the Politics of Professionalism*. Toronto: University of Toronto Press, 1988.
In contrast to Ball's *Mind, Heart and Vision* (1987), this work examines the engineer's struggle to achieve professional status, and it successfully charts the engineers' campaign to monopolize numerous occupations in Canada. A product of industrialization, engineers wrestled with the need for examinations and standards, and a desire to protect and educate older self-trained practitioners. This dual purpose caused serious conflict between 1887 and 1927 as the newly-formed Society of Civil Engineers sought to define its mission. Slowly, the society convinced governments throughout the country to legislate controls on the engineering profession.

Mitchinson, Wendy. *The Nature of Their Bodies: Women and Their Doctors in Victorian Canada*. Toronto: University of Toronto Press, 1991.
This work makes an important contribution to both the social history of medicine and the role of gender in the Victorian world. Drawing upon an international body of secondary literature, Mitchinson argues that culture and medicine are intricately related; a study of the history of medicine thus reveals both medicinal and social attitudes toward women. Male bodies were viewed as the norm and any deviation from that standard was

seen as abnormal. This helps to account for the perceived mental and physical frailty of women, the fact that gender expectations for women were more explicit than for men, and the emergence of obstetrics and gynaecology in the late nineteenth century while similar specialities did not emerge for men. Mitchinson concludes by arguing that women were not merely victims of gender domination by the medical profession; rather, the examination of medical records leads her to argue that women exercised choice in their treatment (particularly if they were of a higher socio-economic status), and that Victorian women showed strength in carrying out daily tasks even in spite of illnesses.

Mitchinson, Wendy and Janice McGinnis, eds. *Essays in the History of Canadian Medicine.* Toronto: McClelland and Stewart, 1988.
The seven essays in this collection all reflect the relationship between social conditions and medicine that now dominates the field of medical history in Canada. Four of the essays examine public health reform in the nineteenth century. Together they demonstrate the important role of public opinion in the development of public health institutions and the limitations faced by medical professionals. The collection also includes an excellent historiographical introduction and bibliography.

Rayner-Canham, Marelene F. and Geoffrey W. Rayner-Canham. *Harriet Brooks: Pioneer Nuclear Scientist.* Montreal: McGill-Queen's University Press, 1992.
There has been very little discussion of early Canadian women scientists. This brief volume examines the life and career of Harriet Brooks, a pioneer women physicist who worked with notables such as Ernest Rutherford, J. J. Thomson, and Marie Curie, and who made considerable contributions to the early study of the phenomenon of radioactivity. Born in Exeter, Ontario, in 1876, and educated at McGill, Brooks taught and researched at Bryn Mawr and Barnard College, and continued her work at McGill, the Cavendish laboratory, Cambridge, and the Curie Institute in Paris. Like many other female scientists of her era, Brooks saw her scientific career end with her marriage.

Sheets-Pyenson, Susan. *John William Dawson: Faith: Hope, and Science.* Montreal: McGill-Queen's University Press, 1996.
This biography helps fill a significant void: J. W. Dawson was an internationally known geologist and paleontologist, principal of McGill for almost four decades, a founder of the Royal Society of Canada, the

only individual to hold the presidency of both the American and British associations for the advancement of science, and one of the foremost critics of the theories of Charles Darwin. Sheets-Pyenson explores Dawson's rational activism and "scientific" approach to all he pursued, including his evangelical faith. Relying upon Dawson's extensive published material and private correspondence, Sheets-Pyenson examines Dawson's life and career, his institution-building and educational work at and beyond McGill, his views on science and religion, and his inter-familial relationships.

Shortt, S. E. D. *Victorian Lunacy: Richard M. Bucke and the Practice of Late Nineteenth-Century Psychiatry.* Cambridge, MA: Cambridge University Press, 1986.

This book is less a study of Richard Bucke than an examination of Victorian psychiatry through the perspective of one of its most important Canadian practitioners. Shortt provides a compelling tale of life at the "typical" asylum which Bucke ran in London, Ontario. Although psychiatrists of this period offered little help for their patients, Bucke, like other practitioners, had endless optimism and slowly moved toward more aggressive, if not more useful, treatments of mental illness. Psychiatry, Shortt concludes, was influenced and changed by its social context. This book is thoroughly referenced and, because it places Canadian psychiatry in an international perspective, is one of the most useful books in Canadian medical history.

Shortt, S. E. D., ed. *Medicine in Canadian Society: Historical Perspectives.* Montreal: McGill-Queen's University Press, 1981.

This collection of essays provides a good starting point for any study of the history of medicine in Canada. While the literature in 1981 had severe limitations, Shortt has collected nineteen essays that primarily focus upon important medical practitioners, their careers, and activities over a broad chronological time period. For a study of medical licenses, laws, and legislation, see Ron Hamowy, *Canadian Medicine: A Study in Restricted Entry* (1984).

Sinclair, Bruce, N. R. Ball, and James O. Petersen, eds. *Let Us Be Honest and Modest: Technology and Society in Canadian History.* Toronto: Oxford University Press, 1974.

A companion volume to Levere and Jarrell's *A Curious Fieldbook* (1974), this collection of primary documents explores aspects of technology from early contact to the Great Depression. The emphasis is upon the social history of technology: that is, that technology reflects something of the texture and nature of Canadian society.

Waiser, W. A. *The Field Naturalist: John Macoun, the Geological Survey, and Natural Science*. Toronto: University of Toronto Press, 1989.

This book is a study of one of Canada's most interesting naturalists, and pursues two primary themes: first, *The Field Naturalist* is both a biography and an analysis of an important scientific career; second, it demonstrates the close relationship between politics and science in nineteenth-century Canada. Waiser demonstrates that Macoun consciously assumed the mantle of both scientist and promoter, and as such filled the role required of a government-sponsored surveyor, explorer, and botanist. As a result, despite his lack of formal training and his sloppiness as a botanical collector and field naturalist, Macoun advanced quickly in the ranks of the Geological Survey of Canada.

Warsh, Cheryl Krasnick. *Moments of Unreason: The Practice of Canadian Psychiatry and the Homewood Retreat, 1889-1923*. Montreal: McGill-Queen's University Press, 1990.

One of the few ventures into the Canadian asylum, *Moments of Unreason* is a social and medical history that places the Homewood Retreat in Guelph, Ontario within an international context. The Homewood Retreat was founded in 1883 as a for-profit asylum in response to middle-class distrust of public institutions. Thus, middle-class expectations and ideals helped shape Homewood and, Warsh argues, the institution came to reflect the patriarchal family in many ways. The careers of its first two medical superintendents, Stephen Lett and Alfred Hobbs, reflected trends in the psychiatric and medical profession. Lett exercised traditional moral management: routine, occupation, diet, and exercise. Hobbs, hired in 1901, was a transitional figure in Canadian psychiatry: a forerunner of scientific psychiatry, he advocated interventionist techniques such as hydrotherapy, electrotherapy, and gynaecological surgery before retiring in 1923. For an account that examines psychiatry in Saskatchewan, see Harley D. Dickinson, *The Two Psychiatries: The Transformation of Psychiatric Work in Saskatchewan, 1905-1984* (1989).

Zaslow, Morris. *Reading the Rocks: The Story of the Geological Survey of Canada, 1842-1972*. Toronto: Macmillan, 1975.

The Geological Survey of Canada (GSC) was the premier department of science in the country in the nineteenth century and retained an important role for years thereafter. Zaslow points out how the GSC had to chart a line between the practical desires of politicians and miners, and the theoretical needs of scientists. Balancing the need to create sound analytical models of geology and to discover mineral wealth for exploitation required talented directors and, sadly, Zaslow demonstrates there were few. As a result, the GSC often functioned as a tool of politicians and business, rather than an independent scientific organization.

Zeller, Suzanne. *Inventing Canada: Early Victorian Science and the Idea of a Transcontinental Nation.* Toronto: University of Toronto Press, 1987.
Scholarly inquiry into the history of science and especially into the ideational origins of science in Canada have not received much attention. This original and often brilliant book helps to fill that void. Zeller is concerned with the way in which ideas of science informed British North America during the Victorian age. In particular, she argues that the rise of inventory sciences such as geology, terrestrial magnetism, meteorology, and botany helped to reshape attitudes about land and encouraged a vision of a trans-continental nation. This book operates on two important levels: first, it provides significant insight into the emergence and practise of Victorian science; and second, it re-evaluates the political debate surrounding Confederation and injects a previously neglected scientific and intellectual dimension.

Sport History

Howell, Colin D. *Northern Sandlots: A Social History of Maritime Baseball.* Toronto: University of Toronto Press, 1995.
This history of Maritime baseball from its origins in the nineteenth century to about 1960 is a superior example of the new social and cultural history. Howell's study of this popular pastime explores notions of class, ethnicity, gender, race, and region; in his view, baseball was a "contested" site in which rivalries between these limited identities abounded. Middle-class reformers in the pre-World War I era sought to appropriate the sport for purposes of social regeneration and moral reform; at the same time, industrial capitalism brought about a new relationship between work time and leisure time that sparked interest in baseball, and participation in the

sport often reflected class, ethnic, religious, and community identities. By 1914, baseball was clearly seen as a masculine sport, a game to be played with "ginger," and there was little room for female participants. Instead, women were essentially spectators, reinforcing a traditional stereotype of women as consumers, not producers. In the interwar period, baseball reinforced regional identity and acted like a "politically inspired Maritime Rights movement." Following World War II, community-based baseball suffered at the hand of an increasingly powerful and diverse post-industrial consumer society.

Kidd, Bruce. *The Struggle for Canadian Sport.* Toronto: University of Toronto Press, 1996.
Kidd examines organizations such as The Amateur Athlete's Union, the Women's Amateur Athletic Federation, the Workers' Sport Association, and the National Hockey League and traces the transformation from amateurism to professional, capitalist-dominated sports ventures. In the case of hockey, Kidd argues that it was the construction of Maple Leaf Gardens and CBC Radio's broadcasting of NHL games that led to the commercialization of the sport.

Lenskyj, Helen. *Out of Bounds: Women, Sport and Sexuality.* Toronto: The Women's Press, 1986.
Out of Bounds explores women in sport in Canada and, more briefly, the United States in the century after 1880. The initial chapters examine the relationship between sport, femininity, and sexuality by investigating restrictions on female sporting participation; thereafter, Lenskyj examines broader questions of male control and how the evolving concept of heterosexuality legitimized constraints on women in sports.

Metcalfe, Alan. *Canada Learns to Play: The Emergence of Organized Sport, 1807-1914.* Toronto: McClelland and Stewart. 1987.
The rampant flag-waving and obscene gushing by CBC commentators over Donovan Bailey's performances at Atlanta and Toronto illustrate the importance of "sport" to Canadians. This is precisely Metcalfe's point: that sport has been enormously important to Canadian society, but has rarely received any serious attention by scholars. Metcalfe examines a broad range of organized sports in the century prior to World War I and integrates his study into larger historical themes. Organized sport was dominated by white middle-class men, emerged principally in Toronto and Montreal, was influenced by both Britain and the United States, and

became more common as leisure time increased. Metcalfe has little to say about the role of women, immigrants, or Native people.

Mott, Morris, ed. *Sports in Canada: Historical Readings.* Toronto: Copp Clark, 1989.
Sport, S. F. Wise argues in an article reprinted in this volume, has been a constant feature of life in Canada. This collection represents the maturation of the discipline of sport history over the past two decades and presents some important articles around the broad chronological parameters of colonial society, the Victorian transition toward standardized equipment, rules, and organized sport, and various aspects of the twentieth-century experience. Mott includes an extensive bibliography of articles and monographs relating to the history of sport in Canada and abroad.

Media and Communication

Babe, Robert E. *Telecommunications in Canada: Technology, Industry, and Government.* Toronto: University of Toronto Press, 1990.
Babe emphasises the corporate responsibility for the social transformation produced by the telecommunications revolution in Canada. This book examines five themes: the mythology of telecommunications, the technology and ramifications of the telegraph and telephone, state regulation of communications, broadcasting, and new technologies. Babe argues that the monopolies that dominate Canada's telecommunications industry are avoidable and that state regulation has been ineffective. He also gives credit to the telecommunications corporations for their financial success. Despite these conclusions regarding regulation and corporate management, the strength of Babe's analysis is his work on the ramifications of telecommunications technology.

Jones, D. B. *Movies and Memoranda: An Interpretive History of the National Film Board of Canada.* Ottawa: Deneau, 1982.
Formed prior to World War II as a counter measure to the American domination of the feature film industry in Canada, the National Film Board (NFB) has evolved into one of the finest producers of documentary short films in the world. It has also become an important instrument of regional development in the Canadian media industry. *Movies and Memoranda* is a sympathetic and nationalistic account of the NFB that lacks critical analysis and evidence of detailed research.

Rutherford, Paul. *When Television Was Young: Primetime Canada, 1952-1967*. Toronto: University of Toronto Press, 1990.
Marshall McLuhan asked the provocative question: What happens to society when a new medium of communications enters the picture? Rutherford provides a survey of television in Canada, roughly during its black and white era, and delves into the effects of television upon society, including a critique of McLuhan's ideas to the question that he had posited. Highly readable despite over 500 pages of text and a healthy selection of charts and tables, this volume also includes a series of focus studies that examine individual programs on specific days such as *The Wayne and Shuster Hour*, *Front Page Challenge*, and *This Hour Has Seven Days*. Rutherford also includes a thorough discussion of the early development of the Canadian Broadcasting Corporation and its rival, Canadian Television. For a more specific study, see Mary Jane Miller's *Turn Up the Contrast: CBC Television Drama Since 1952* (1987). For studies of Canada's most famous communications theorist, see Philip Marchand, *Marshall McLuhan: The Medium and the Messenger* (1989); and W. Terrence Gordon, *Marshall McLuhan: Escape into Understanding/A Biography* (1997).

_____. *A Victorian Authority: The Daily Press in Late Nineteenth-Century Canada*. Toronto: University of Toronto Press, 1982.
Rutherford charts the growth of the daily press, Canada's first mass medium, in the thirty years following Confederation. Like many works in Canadian history, his general theme is one of nation-building and the approach to modernity. Thus, he provides analysis of the gospels of progress, order, harmony, and nation-hood that nineteenth-century journalists preached. As well, Rutherford discusses the nature and rise of the daily press, the metropolitan influence that Toronto and Montreal papers had on their hinterland, and how the press emphatically strove to assume a position of social and moral authority, largely from an urban, middle-class perspective. For a broader study of the media, see Paul Rutherford, *The Making of the Canadian Media* (1978). Victorian Canada's most famous editor, George Brown, is dealt with in J. M. S. Careless, *Brown of the Globe* (2 vols., 1959, 1963).

Vipond, Mary. *Listening In: The First Decade of Canadian Broadcasting, 1922-32*. Montreal: McGill-Queen's University Press, 1992.
Based upon research in government archival records and private papers, this theoretically sophisticated analysis demonstrates that federal civil

servants and Canadian consumer desires shaped radio broadcasting in Canada prior to the passage of the Radio Broadcasting Act in 1932. Canadians began listening in to American radio broadcasts in 1922 and government responded to the public demand for American radio by carefully controlling the power and frequencies of local Canadian efforts to enter the market. As a result, private broadcasters in Canada lagged behind their American counterparts and Canadian nationalists complained about American domination. The stage was thus set for both public control and public ownership of Canadian radio broadcasting.

_____. *The Mass Media in Canada.* Toronto: Lorimer, 1989; rev. ed., 1992.

During the 1988 Free Trade Agreement debates in Canada, few issues were as controversial as the clauses designed to protect Canadian culture from American mass media corporations. Mary Vipond tackles this issue in her ground-breaking survey of the mass media in Canada. She surveys the instruments of the media in Canada from newspapers and magazines to movies, radio, and television, and concludes that Canadian culture is threatened by corporate concentration and commercialisation within the media industry. Vipond argues Canadian attitudes toward the mass media are grounded in two nationalist mythologies. First, Canadians believe that east-west communication linkages are the foundation for the Canadian nation-state. Second, Canadians share an ethic of "liberal developmentalism" and free enterprise with Americans. The mass media in Canada reflects this tension. It is a primarily Canadian-owned and government regulated system that broadcasts American-made products to Canadians. While the government strives to maintain a nationalist media presence, it also allows the media to broadcast American messages to a willing public audience. Based primarily upon published material, this thoroughly referenced book is an indispensable reference resource.

Working Class and Labour History

In an often-quoted article in the *Canadian Historical Review* (1965), Stanley Mealing argued that the writing of Canadian history did "not suggest that Canadian historians have so far made the concept [of social class] a very important part of their working equipment." Four years later in the same journal, Walter Young made an even more damning statement: "few historians are interested in labour history in Canada," he wrote in his review of Gad Horowitz's *Canadian Labour in Politics* (1968) "because they suspect that it is dull, convoluted, and badly pockmarked with initials." Fortunately, since the comments of Mealing and Young, labour and, in particular, working-class history has enjoyed increased scholarly attention and has been the focus of much vibrant and innovative work. Traditionally, labour history in Canada has largely emphasised the study of labour unions, union leaders, and strikes. However, inspired by international scholarship and the turbulent climate of the 1960s, a second generation of historians such as Bryan Palmer, Craig Heron, and Greg Kealey turned their attention to issues of class conflict, the work process, and working-class culture. This second generation of scholars — termed the "new labour history" in the United States — has produced much innovative work and has recently sought to develop affinities with historians of women and ethnicity. Although they pursue much different objectives and utilise more diverse methodologies than Kealey and Palmer, works such as Joy Parr's *The Gender of Breadwinners* (1990) and Ruth Frager's *Sweatshop Strife* (1992), for example, have powerfully illustrated the intersection of class, gender, and ethnicity. More recently, a third generation of labour historians has emerged and has returned to the traditional subject of unions and bureaucracy, but from decidedly neo-Marxist theoretical perspectives.

General Works

Abella, Irving and David Millar, eds. *The Canadian Worker in the Twentieth Century*. Toronto: Oxford University Press, 1978.
A companion volume to Michael Cross' *The Workingman in the Nineteenth Century* (1974), this anthology of documents covers the first

four decades of the twentieth century. This collection focuses on the growth of immigration, industrialization, and urbanization; as a corollary to these developments selections focus upon "the advent of social democracy, national minimum standards of welfare, and the organization of workers in mechanized industry."

Argue, Robert, Charlene Gannagé and D.W. Livingstone, eds. *Working People and Hard Times: Canadian Perspectives.* Toronto: Garamond Press, 1987.
Containing a selection of papers presented at the Fifth Conference on Workers and Their Communities held at the Ontario Institute for Studies in Education in 1984, this collection explores diverse themes meant to be of interest to both popular and academic audiences. The focus is on contemporary issues, and significant attention is paid to those workers most exploited in Canadian society, including immigrant women and women of colour.

Bercuson, David J. and David Bright, eds. *Canadian Labour History: Selected Readings.* Toronto: Copp Clark, 1987; 2nd ed., 1994.
This collection differs significantly from the collected readings edited by Kealey and Warrian (1976) or MacDowell and Radforth (1992). Bercuson and Bright have assembled articles that express radically different conclusions along selected themes. Thus Daniel Drache's overview of Canadian workers that argues that fragmented markets prevented the evolution of a working-class consciousness is countered by Bryan Palmer's critique and assertion to the contrary; likewise, the variant positions of Greg Kealey and David Bercuson on the 1919 strikes are presented, along with David Bright's excellent analysis of the so-called "sympathy" strike in Calgary. Such an approach — which draws from the camps of both the first and second generations of labour history — ensures that students will have access to approaches that emphasises working-class culture, gender, and ethnicity, as well as traditional themes involving unions, strikes, and politics. This work contains a superb bibliography of relevant articles and monographs.

Cherwinski, W. J. C. and G. S. Kealey, eds. *Lectures in Canadian Working-Class History.* Toronto: Committee on Canadian Labour History, 1985.
Originally part of a lecture series, this collection of essays is designed for the general reader. Containing articles by some of Canada's most erudite

historians, this volume has historiographic and regional surveys, more
specific studies of organizations and issues, and two essays specifically
devoted to working women. Though eclectic in composition, this work is
an excellent introduction to working-class history in Canada.

Confédération des syndicats nationaux and Centrale de l'enseignement du
    Québec. *The History of the Labour Movement in Quebec.* trans.
    Arnold Bennett. Montreal: Black Rose Books, 1979; rev. ed., 1988.
The sole general history of the labour movement in Quebec available in
English, this popularly written work (over 15,000 copies have been sold)
provides a chronological account of labour over the past two centuries.
This work emphasises developments since World War II and concentrates
on unions, strikes, and labour legislation; the revised edition pays greater
attention to the condition of the working class, and to the specific
condition of working women.

Craven, Paul, ed. *Labouring Lives: Work and Workers in Nineteenth-*
    Century Ontario. Toronto: University of Toronto Press, 1995.
Working-class historians have traditionally focused upon craft and factory
workers, principally in major urban centres and during the last third of the
nineteenth and early twentieth centuries. Most people in nineteenth-
century Ontario, however, lived on farms and in small rural communities.
Informed by recent currents in the new social history, this collection of
essays explores the experience of working people in some previously
neglected areas: farm labour, housework, lumbering, and institutions such
as the church, law, and family, as well as industrial labour in factories and
on the railway. Despite a diversity of approaches, this collection examines
common themes such as class formation, the nature and meaning of work,
labour relations, and questions of labour supply, recruitment, and
retention.

Cross, Michael S., ed. *The Workingman in the Nineteenth Century.*
    Toronto: Oxford University Press, 1974.
In response to the paucity of primary material that has been published
dealing with the life of the worker, Michael Cross has edited this
collection hoping to elucidate the more ordinary and common existence.
Selections are organized around themes such as farm and frontier, work,
working-class life, social institutions, and organizing the worker. Notable
by its absence is extended reference to issues such as gender, ethnicity, or
religion. In addition, this work shares many sources with the older

tradition of labour history, with frequent use made of Royal Commission
reports, Session Papers, and newspapers.

Cross, Michael and Gregory S. Kealey, eds. *Economy and Society during
  the French Regime, to 1759*. Toronto: McClelland and Stewart, 1983
  _____, eds. *Pre-Industrial Canada, 1760-1849*. Toronto: McClelland
  and Stewart, 1982; rpt.: 1984.
  _____, eds. *The Age of Industry, 1849-1896*. Toronto: McClelland
  and Stewart, 1982.
  _____, eds. *The Consolidation of Capitalism, 1896-1929*. Toronto:
  McClelland and Stewart, 1983.
  _____, eds. *Modern Canada, 1930-1980s*. Toronto: McClelland and
  Stewart, 1984; rpt.: 1985.
Reflecting the commitment to social history that was inaugurate in the
1970s (what Ramsay Cook called the "golden age of historical writing"),
these five volumes reprint many of the most significant articles that reflect
this orientation. While a variety of approaches and interpretations are
offered, the principal orientation is toward the themes of changing
economic forms (hence the periodization of the volumes), the interaction
of classes and groups, workers and working-class culture, and women.
While articles pursue diverse themes, these volumes serve as useful
supplements to working class history.

Frank, David and Gregory S. Kealey, eds. *Labour and Working-Class
  History in Atlantic Canada: A Reader*. St. John's: Institute of Social
  and Economic Research, Memorial University, 1995.
While there was relatively little interest in the history of work in Atlantic
Canada prior to the 1970s, subsequent years have seen much scholarly
work. This reader brings together previously published material around
the themes of pre-industrial work; women, children, and other workers in
the industrial revolution; labour wars; and the rights of labour. There is
a brief introduction to each section, and suggested readings.

Heron, Craig. *The Canadian Labour Movement: A Short History*.
  Toronto: James Lorimer, 1989; 2nd ed., 1996.
A brief account of organized labour and its relationship to provincial and
federal politics, *The Canadian Labour Movement* concentrates on the
construction and dismantling of labour legislation since 1945. Though
Heron discusses the working-class struggle epitomized in the Knights of
Labour, the 1919 strikes, and the Depression strikes, he concludes that

World War II was crucial in establishing large-scale unions, labour codes, and collective bargaining principles. Under pressure from neo-conservative governments in the 1980s, however, many of these measures have been abandoned. Reflecting current research, Heron seeks to incorporate gender and ethnicity into his survey.

Kealey, Gregory S. *Workers and Canadian History*. Montreal: McGill-Queen's University Press, 1995.
A collection of previously published articles, *Workers and Canadian History* illustrates the intellectual interests and development of one of Canada's most prolific and important historians over the past several decades. Responding to the exclusionary nature of military, constitutional, and political history, and to the more recent emergence of post-structuralist thought, Kealey affirms the validity of approaching history through a methodology that emphasises historical materialism. These essays sometimes occupy broad themes: Kealey examines the historiography and intellectual debates surrounding working-class and labour studies over the past two decades. On other occasions, important articles dealing with specific phenomenon are reprinted, including, most notably, Kealey's response to David Bercuson's *Confrontation at Winnipeg* (1974).

Kealey, Gregory S. and Peter Warrian, eds. *Essays in Canadian Working Class History*. Toronto: McClelland and Stewart, 1976.
Urged on by the political debate of the 1960s and the re-emergence of Marxism among many North American intellectuals, this volume redefines "labour history" as "working-class history." Instead of studying workers solely within the confines of trade unions, radical politics, and strikes, the contributors to this ground-breaking volume examine the concept of class both as a vertical (or economic) relationship and as a horizontal (or cultural) relationship. The creation of a class consciousness and the relationship between the classes therefore occupies a central focus in this work. Moreover, the authors suggest a new periodization of Canadian history marked by economic development; thus essays concentrate upon the period between 1850 and 1925, a time in which Canada was transformed from a pre-industrial to an industrial society.

MacDowell, L. S. and I. Radforth. *Canadian Working Class History: Selected Readings*. Toronto: Canadian Scholars' Press, 1992.
Reflecting the increased attention in working-class people, this collection

is marked by a number of diverse themes and methodologies, though all the authors are dedicated to explicating the working-class life. Organized chronologically from the French regime to the 1980s, these articles touch on all regions of the country except for the North. More recent articles by Frager and Iacovetta also introduce the intersection of class, ethnicity, and gender, an approach that is increasingly being explored by Canadian historians.

Morton, Desmond, with Terry Copp. *Working People: An Illustrated History of the Canadian Labour Movement*. Ottawa: Deneau Publishers, 1980; rev. ed., 1984.

Specifically rejecting the class analysis of Bryan Palmer, Greg Kealey, and others, *Working People* provides a brief, but well-illustrated, survey of the labour movement in Canada. Largely ignoring the role of native people as workers, and emphasising events since World War I, Morton and Copp concentrate upon traditional themes such as industrial relations, the rise and fall of labour and political organizations, western radicalism, strikes, and the relationship of workers to governments.

Palmer, Bryan D. *Working Class Experience: Rethinking the History of Canadian Labour, 1800-1991*. Toronto: McClelland and Stewart, 1983; 2nd ed., 1992.

Revised significantly from its earlier publication in 1983, this work relies heavily upon recent secondary literature that examines the working class experience in the workplace, the tavern, and the home. Combining a broad narrative with clear interpretation, *Working Class Experience* argues for the fundamental conflict between labour and capital and seeks to reveal working-class responses. In contrast to Morton's *Working People* (1980), this work pays particular attention to the nineteenth century, an era that Palmer obviously considers crucial to the formation of the working class. The second edition more fully examines the concept of gender, though Palmer concludes that it is ultimately subordinate to class interests. This work contains an exhaustive bibliography.

Palmer, Bryan D., ed. *The Character of Class Struggle*. Toronto: McClelland and Stewart, 1986; rpt., 1988.

A collection of eight essays by a number of prominent working-class historians, this work examines aspects of the creation, struggle, and changing nature of the working class in the face of merchant, industrial, monopoly, and advanced capitalism. *The Character of Class Struggle* is divided into three general chronological sections: the first examines the nineteenth-century experience, the second looks at monopoly capitalism from 1900 to 1950, and finally, several authors examine the worker in the post-World War II era, a time when capital reconciled itself to the need to use state power.

Warburton, Rennie and David Coburn, eds. *Workers, Capital, and the State in British Columbia: Selected Papers*. Vancouver: University of British Columbia, 1988.

In "Class and Race in the Social Structure of British Columbia, 1870-1939" (*BC Studies*, 1980), Peter Ward put forth the controversial argument that race, not class, was the chief characteristic of British Columbia's early social structure. *Workers, Capital, and the State* takes issue with such an argument. Rooted in Marxist theory, the essays in this volume analyse British Columbia's economy from its colonial forms to the emergence of the contemporary capitalist state. Rather than simple economic determinism, the contributors aim for a more sophisticated analysis of British Columbia's economy and the resulting class conflict and social tensions. For an older study of British Columbia's labour history, see Paul Phillips, *No Power Greater: A Century of Labour in British Columbia* (1967).

Working Lives Collective. *Working Lives: Vancouver, 1886-1986*. Vancouver: New Star Books, 1985.

Produced largely by nine academics, with short captions by numerous other authors, this well-illustrated volume examines the social history of 100 years of Vancouver's working class. Organized broadly around the themes of "Working, Living, Organizing," *Working Lives* pays particular attention to working-class culture, issues of gender and ethnicity, and conflicts with capital.

Staples Production and Manual Labour

Bowen, Lynn. *Three Dollar Dreams*. Lantzville, BC: Oolichan, 1987.
_____. *Boss Whistle: The Coal Miners of Vancouver Island Remember*. Lantzville, BC: Oolichan, 1982.

These companion volumes examine the coal miners, mining community, and mining industry of Vancouver Island. Both volumes are popular in orientation, with *Three Dollar Dreams* focusing on the last half of the nineteenth century, and *Boss Whistle* on the twentieth. Highly chronological in orientation, the books use an assortment of personalities and events to elucidate mining techniques and conditions, labour difficulties, ethnic and racial issues, and life in mining communities. The focus is solely on Vancouver Island, with little concern for larger working-class issues or the international nature of the coal industry. *Boss Whistle* makes significant use of oral evidence.

Danysk, Cecilia. *Hired Hands: Labour and the Development of Prairie Agriculture, 1880-1930.* Toronto: McClelland and Stewart, 1995.
Danysk makes an important contribution to both labour and agricultural history in this book. Danysk mined the archives on the prairies and government record collections to recount the activities of one of the most important elements of prairie agriculture, wage labourers. Farm labourers were often impoverished homesteaders searching for extra funds but they also included full time hired men and harvest excursionists. Most important, they shared all the skills of their employers yet obtained few of the rewards of farming. Working within a Marxist framework, Danysk argues that the hired hand was transformed during the agrarian settlement era from the farmer in waiting into the marginalised wage labourer.

Fingard, Judith. *Jack in Port: Sailortowns of Eastern Canada.* Toronto: University of Toronto Press, 1982.
This social history of nineteenth-century seafarers examines work-related institutions and customs and how these concerns "fashioned the sailors' experiences on land." Concentrating upon sailors operating out of the ports of Quebec, Saint John, and Halifax, Fingard argues that there were three identifiable generations of sailors: the earliest group worked on small ships and amidst small crews with little differentiation of labour; in the middle decades of the century, the labour market was internationalized (and the potential for collective action decreased), larger ships were introduced, and shipboard conditions deteriorated; and finally, the third-generation sailor was active until the end of the century and, with the advent of the steam ship and professional longshoreman, witnessed the demise of the sailortown. *Jack in Port* traces several general themes such as the transient nature of the sailor, the role of the crimps who supplied seaman and kept boarding houses, the rhythms of work and leisure, sickness and health, rowdiness and punishment, and the often ineffectual role of the state in implementing meaningful reform. Fingard argues that this group of men has received little attention by working-class historians. Sailors were transient, ostracized by middle-class society, away from

ports for months, and racially, linguistically, and ethnically divided. As such, they rarely acted in class-conscious ways. This is a lively and provocative work that deserves a wide readership.

Howell, Colin and Richard Twomey, eds. *Jack Tar in History: Essays in the History of Maritime Life and Labour*. Fredericton: Acadiensis Press, 1991.

A collection of diverse essays, *Jack Tar in History* examines various aspects of male and female seafarers, ranging from the eighteenth to the twentieth centuries, and across much of the North Atlantic world. The volume is dedicated to the study of the working class and workers' social relations, and draws upon recent developments in those fields. For example, in a previously published essay, Peter Linebaugh and Marcus Rediker demonstrate the existence of a pre-industrial working class on the sea. In addition, Julius Scott argues for the greater freedom of black sailors in comparison to landlocked black workers, and Margaret Creighton explores the constructed nature of work at sea.

Macdowell, Laurel Sefton. *"Remember Kirkland Lake": The History and Effects of the Kirkland Lake Gold Miners' Strike, 1941-1942*. Toronto: University of Toronto Press, 1983.

In the aftermath of the recent labour conflict and tragedy at the Giant Mine near Yellowknife, NWT, it is worth considering earlier struggles between miners and capital. The 3,700 members of the International Union of Mine, Mill, and Smelter Workers had little to support their cause and enormous obstacles to overcome; ultimately, their strike resulted in a devastating defeat for the miners. Yet Macdowell argues that the strike had important and far-reaching implications: the labour movement was spurred towards a more radical and political position, particularly in its alliance with the CCF; the strike provided an opportunity for the training of labour leaders and a more vibrant Canadian unionism; and attention was brought to the anti-worker philosophy and policies of the government expressed through both the press and the pulpit.

McCormack, A. Ross. *Reformers, Rebels and Revolutionaries: The Western Canadian Radical Movement, 1899-1919*. Toronto: University of Toronto Press, 1977.

This is an important work, both for its content and for its place within Canadian historiography. McCormack divides the Western Canadian labour movement into three (sometimes too simplistic) tendencies.

"Reformers" tended to be the most moderate; based their critique of capitalism upon Christian ethics, Gladstonian radicalism, and marxism; and perceived the state as a useful instrument of change. Lacking a precise ideology, "rebels" were advocates of militant unions and syndicalism, and felt that powerful unions could affect change through events such as the general strike. The most radical workers were "revolutionaries" who saw capitalism as inherently exploitive and sought the destruction of the wage system. Although revolutionaries received impetus from the discontent that followed World War I, the long-term trends favoured reformers such as J. S. Woodsworth who sought to moderate the harmful nature of industrial capitalism. *Reformers, Rebels and Revolutionaries* also argues that there was a "basic difference of outlook" between eastern and western workers. Westerners, influenced by foreign radical influence, harsh conditions in resource industries, and the transition to industrial capitalism, were more radical in orientation.

Radforth, Ian. *Bush Workers and Bosses: Logging in Northern Ontario, 1900-1980.* Toronto: University of Toronto Press, 1987.
While this work examines a traditional staple industry, it emphasises working-class culture, the labour process, and the interaction between workers and management. The period prior to World War II depended upon transient, often immigrant, male labourers who were paid by the piece and employed in traditional labour-intensive methods of logging. Workers were not passive, and Finnish bush workers led assaults upon poor working conditions and pay; however, Radforth argues that both the nature of the workforce and the nature of work conspired to impede effective collective action. Because of labour shortages brought about by the war, technological innovation proceeded rapidly. While managers sought control through mechanization, workers also embraced new technology for a variety of reasons, including the relief from physical toil that new skills and technology provided. This excellent study is theoretically informed and makes an important contribution to working-class culture and the labour process in this industry.

Sager, Eric W. *The Merchant Marine of Atlantic Canada, 1820-1914.* Montreal: McGill-Queen's University Press, 1989.
Emerging out of research undertaken through Memorial University's Atlantic Canada Shipping Project, Sager's book focuses upon "working men who got wet." Rather than being a static process, the shipping industry changed dramatically from small pre-industrial crafts in the early

nineteenth century to much larger British commercial operations a century later. With this transition, workers' jobs became much more specialized, the fraternalism of the pre-industrial craft was replaced by a more rigid social structure, and the conflict between labour and capital grew enormously. The argument expressed here is clear: the transition to industrial capitalism and its influence on workers' jobs and lives shared much on land and at sea. Also see the various issues of the Proceedings of the Atlantic Canada Shipping Project sponsored by the Maritime History Group out of Memorial University. For a more anecdotal record of life at sea, see Eric W. Sager, *Ships and Memories: Merchant Seafarers in Canada's Age of Steam* (1993).

Way, Peter. *Common Labour: Workers and the Digging of North American Canals, 1780-1860.* New York: Cambridge University Press, 1993.
Recipient of the Frederick Jackson Turner Award in 1994, *Common Labour* examines a large mass of unskilled, transient workers — who Way argues made up the bulk of the work force, but are rarely studied — and the construction of canals in Canada and the United States. While the horrendous nature of their work did not change significantly between 1780 and 1860, the size of canal construction increased enormously. Thus, the relationship of canallers to their bosses moved from a paternalistic model to an anonymous form of near wage slavery. Because the canal-building boom came later to Canada than to the United States, almost all strikes and riots by the 1840s were in Canada. Significantly, state resources were more quickly used in Canada to suppress these disturbances. Way also notes that canal workers — mostly men, but also a few women and children — displayed little sense of craft pride or the traditions associated with urban artisans. Though canallers held little collective power, they did play a part in the transition to industrial capitalism by opening necessary transportation routes.

Crafts, Industry, and Manufacturing

Copp, Terry. *The Anatomy of Poverty.* Toronto: McClelland and Stewart, 1974.
In one of the initial ventures into the new social history, Copp examines the working class of Montreal between 1897 and 1919. Copp argues that although Montreal experienced substantial and sustained growth during this period, the working class — approximately two-thirds of the

population — suffered from "a culture of poverty" marked by inadequate wages, working conditions, housing, and education. Exposed to the *laissez-faire* economy of the day, Montreal was much like other North American cities, though Copp argues its fate was worse than that of Toronto due to location factors, larger family sizes, and an inadequate tax system.

Heron, Craig. *Working in Steel: The Early Years in Canada, 1883-1935.* Toronto: McClelland and Stewart, 1988.
Working in Steel is, as Heron states, "a book about work"; in particular, it focuses upon the social impact of industrial change in Canada's steel industry. The march of industrial progress in this industry was marked by monopoly capitalism, new ideas in management and organization, and technological innovation. Heron disputes claims that technology wrenched power from skilled workers. Instead, Heron argues that workers responded effectively to technological innovations, drawing on old skills and acquiring new ones in contesting the labour process. The formal and informal resistance of workers to corporate and state power was, however, often ineffective, and, by the 1930s, with unemployed workers outside the factory gates, workers were content to stay in the good books of the foreman and were forced to rely on personal strategies for survival.

Heron, Craig and Robert Storey, eds. *On the Job: Confronting the Labour Process in Canada.* Montreal: McGill-Queen's University Press, 1986.
This eclectic and extremely useful collection contains a dozen articles on male and female workers ranging broadly from individuals involved in staples production to the fast food industry. The authors' concern is with the labour process, that is the interaction of technology, market forces, and the worker in shaping the work environment. Building upon, and reacting against, the work of the American historian Harry Braverman who argued in the 1970s that managers sought control over workers through mechanization, the authors of this volume do not see Canadian workers inevitably losing control of the work process before the onslaught of technological advance; rather, in some industries, workers were able to control and fashion the influences of the new technology. In other cases, societal constructs and technology brought about the feminization of certain industries and created "women's" jobs. This book also contains the observations of workers involved in a Ford assembly line and a Toronto Burger King.

Kealey, Gregory S. *Toronto Workers Respond to Industrial Capitalism, 1867-1892*. Toronto: University of Toronto Press, 1980.
Strongly influenced by the work of Herbert Gutman, David Montgomery and E. P. Thompson, Kealey argues that the last decades of the nineteenth century saw the emergence of a working-class conscience in Toronto. The catalyst was, of course, industrial capitalism, and the transition to an industrial workplace brought enormous stresses to the worker. In the face of increasing division of labour, factory discipline, and harsher conditions, Toronto workers in some industries responded by emphasising their political and cultural autonomy on the shop floor, in workers' organizations, and at the ballot box. Toronto workers, for example, exercised a working-class presence in politics and cast their ballots for the party that would support their labour interests. The result was a number of legislative efforts such as the nine hour act and protective tariffs that favoured the working class.

Kealey, Gregory and Bryan Palmer. *Dreaming of What Might Be: The Knights of Labour in Ontario, 1840-1900*. Toronto: New Hogtown Press, 1982; 2ⁿᵈ ed., 1987.
Doug Kennedy's *The Knights of Labor in Canada* (1956) predictably examines the official pronouncements and leadership of this workers' organ which reached its height of popularity and influence in the last decades of the nineteenth century. Though equally sympathetic, the approach of Kealey and Palmer is much different. Serious practitioners of the new labour history, Kealey and Palmer seek to explain "the human forces behind the doctrines, practices, and campaigns of the 1880s and 1890s" and insist that the Knights of Labour were an integral part of the late nineteenth-century industrial order. Although *Dreaming of What Might Be* focuses on the Canadian experience in Southern Ontario (to the exclusion of Quebec and British Columbia), this is a landmark study in how working-class culture emerged in opposition to the middle-class values of acquisitive individualism. Moreover, although there is less emphasis on how women and children were participants in working-class culture, the authors illustrate that the Knights of Labor made significant efforts to organize women workers and argued for equal and fair pay.

McKay, Ian. *The Craft Transformed: An Essay on the Carpenters of Halifax, 1885-1985*. Halifax: Holdfast Press, 1985.
Written to celebrate the centenary of the United Brotherhood of Carpenters and Joiners of America in Halifax, this work focuses on a

relatively narrow topic but makes important and wide-ranging
conclusions. McKay places Halifax carpenters within the context of a
larger body of skilled workers and notes the transitions of carpenters from
a craft-dominated industry to the consolidation of capitalism and finally,
after the mid-1920s, to an industry marked by industrial legality.

Naylor, James. *The New Democracy: Challenging the Social Order in
     Industrial Ontario, 1914-1925*. Toronto: University of Toronto Press,
     1991.
In contrast to those who argue that the 1919 Winnipeg General Strike and
the radical labour organizations of southwestern Alberta and British
Columbia illustrate the radical nature of western workers, *The New
Democracy* maintains that the working-class struggle in Ontario was no
less a challenge to the existing social order. The rise of working-class
discontent emerged in Ontario for many of the same reason it did in the
West: workers' protest took the form of a "new democracy" that
advocated the right to organize unions, fair wages and representation, and
fundamental changes in female and gendered labour. Finally, Naylor
explores the factors that led to the defeat of working-class militancy in the
1920s. This carefully crafted work does much to correct the view that
Ontario's craft unions were a conservative stronghold and were
unaffected by broader working-class concerns.

Palmer, Bryan D. *A Culture in Conflict: Skilled Workers and Industrial
     Capitalism in Hamilton, Ontario, 1860-1914*. Montreal: McGill-
     Queen's University Press, 1979.
Firmly within the tradition of E. P. Thompson and Herbert Gutman, this
rich and important work examines the vibrancy of working-class culture
in early industrial Hamilton. Though unfettered capitalism had triumphed
by World War I, Palmer shows how a working-class culture, through
sports teams, drinking clubs, and workers' societies and institutions,
developed a sense of solidarity which was crucial both in providing
stability to their lives and resistance in their struggle against capital and
government. Though Palmer focuses on skilled workers, he makes clear
that their experience was not disparate from that of other working groups.
This local study has affinities with the broader international tradition of
examining questions of class; not surprisingly, while extensive direct
comparison is avoided, Palmer clearly believes that the experience of
Hamilton's working class had much in common with industrializing
communities in the North Atlantic triangle.

Pentland, H. Clare. *Labour and Capital in Canada, 1650-1860.* Edited
    with an introduction by Paul Phillips. Toronto: James Lorimer, 1981.
This work is a revised version of Pentland's 1960 Ph.D. dissertation and
has been introduced and edited by Paul Phillips. Published following
Pentland's death in 1978, *Labour and Capital in Canada* is wide-ranging
and highly interpretive, and, in its unpublished form, inspired and directed
many graduate students interested in working-class history. Pentland
argues against the tendency — dominant in the era in which his
dissertation was produced — to see Canada's past without regard to class
distinctions; instead, he traces the nature of labour and the labour market
from its pre-industrial forms to what he saw as a nascent industrial
revolution by the middle of the nineteenth century. Phillip's introduction
places Pentland's work within the context of the historiography of the
previous two decades.

Piva, Michael J. *The Condition of the Working Class in Toronto 1900-
    1921.* Ottawa: University of Ottawa Press, 1979.
Terry Copp's *The Anatomy of Poverty* (1974) established the continual
poverty of Montreal workers during the transition to an industrial
capitalist society. Michael Piva tests Copp's analysis against the working
class of Toronto, making use of a significant statistical data base. He
concludes that real wages were lower, labour unions less influential, and
de-skilling more pronounced in 1920 than they had been two decades
earlier. This work does not examine working-class culture in Toronto,
although Piva is clearly sympathetic to such efforts; instead, he seeks to
establish the condition and structure of the work force as a prelude to
further working-class studies.

Reiter, Ester. *Making Fast Food: From the Frying Pan into the Fryer.*
    Montreal: McGill-Queen's University Press, 1991.
Recent attempts to unionize fast food restaurants and bulk retailers have
met with media fanfare and the predictable company resistance. *Making
Fast Food* examines the rise of the fast food industry and culture, and
presents a case study of a Toronto Burger King. The fast food industry
has created an environment that feeds upon interchangeable labour,
especially young, minority, and female workers. The labour process,
therefore, has been deskilled to such an extent, and workers are under
such strict control, that it no longer matters greatly that most employees
are in their first months on the job.

Gender and Ethnicity

Acton, Janice, Penny Goldsmith, and Bonnie Shepard, eds. *Women at Work: Ontario, 1850-1930.* Toronto: Women's Press, 1974.
Written from a Marxist-feminist perspective that seeks to avoid "vulgar economic determinism," this collection is a valuable addition and illustration of the new social history. *Women at Work* analyses the role of gender in various service sectors (including domestics, nursing, teaching, and prostitution), industry, and attempts to organize workers. These essays collectively argue that the industrialization process often exploited women; in nursing and teaching for example, as these jobs were professionalized during this era, women were accorded status, but did not see corresponding increases in wages. When this work was published, it marked a significant departure from earlier studies of women's history that tended to emphasise biography or the suffrage movement.

Armstrong, Hugh and Pat Armstrong. *The Double Ghetto: Canadian Women and Their Segregated Work.* Toronto: McClelland and Stewart, 1987.
While women have increasingly entered wage-labour occupations since 1941, this work argues that "women's work" remains segregated and that this ghettoization is characterized by low pay and few opportunities for advancement. Additionally, while female wage labour is overwhelmingly concentrated in occupations such as sales, service, teaching, and nursing, responsibilities at home have not declined. The authors also provide a theoretical analysis for the continuing division of labour by sex.

Avery, Donald. *Dangerous Foreigners: European Immigrant Workers and Labour Radicalism in Canada, 1896-1932.* Toronto: McClelland and Stewart, 1979.
The arrival of thousands of immigrants between 1896 and the Great Depression — many from Eastern Europe — profoundly affected Canadian society: the "frontier" regions of Northern Ontario and the Prairies were settled, resource extraction flourished, and, Avery argues, in the face of difficult conditions and Anglo-Canadian nativism, many immigrants disproportionately involved themselves in radical labour organizations. Though many immigrants took on arduous and dangerous jobs for low pay, they were virtually shunned by the Canadian government and patronized by Anglo-Canadian organizations. Driven by a world view brought from the old country and reinforced in the new,

these workers turned to organizations such as the Industrial Workers of the World, the One Big Union, and the Communist Party of Canada. In times of economic difficulty the stereotype of the radical immigrant flourished and harassment, internment, and even deportation were practiced. Avery builds upon A. Ross McCormack's *Reformers, Rebels and Revolutionaries* (1977) by establishing ethnicity as a central component of Canadian labour radicalism.

Dunk, Thomas W. *It's a Working Man's Town: Male Working-Class Culture in Northwestern Ontario.* Montreal: McGill-Queen's University Press, 1991.

In the face of claims that class is just one vehicle of analysis, Dunk's examination of 21 white, young, working-class men in Thunder Bay asserts the centrality of the class experience. This working-class culture is expressed through several themes: it helps to explain, for example, the emergence of pejorative stereotypes of native peoples, the reinforcement of a north-south cultural divide in Ontario, and, most vividly portrayed, the importance of a variant of softball called lob-ball. Dunk sees lob-ball as a working-class activity which inverts the dominant values that the men experience through their working lives. Ironically and unwittingly, Dunk illustrates that their commitment to lob-ball is also accompanied by the influences of consumerism and corporatism.

Frager, Ruth. *Sweatshop Strife: Class, Ethnicity and Gender in the Jewish Labour Movement of Toronto, 1900-1939.* Toronto: University of Toronto Press, 1992.

There has been a recent trend by scholars such as Franca Iacovetta and others to examine relationships among ethnicity, gender, and class. Frager's study of Jewish garment workers in Toronto in the first four decades of the twentieth century fits ably into this pattern. In *Sweatshop Strife* ethnicity and class help to explain the adherence of Jewish workers to labour and socialist movements. Yet, because of the multi-ethnic nature of the working-class environment, Jewish labour leaders could not explicitly focus upon Jewish rights. Morever, Frager argues that women were active participants in labour movements, though gender issues were often subordinated to broader working-class goals.

Gannagé, Charlene. *Double Day, Double Burden: Women in the Garment Industry.* Toronto: The Women's Press, 1986.

Using a garment factory in Toronto as a case study, Gannagé argues that women's work at the workplace and at the home is intertwined and interdependent. Men and women do not share the same work experiences: women — who experience discrimination at work and have greater familial responsibilities — are faced with the "double day." This work pays particular attention to the role of ethnicity in the workplace, the environment in which "women's work" occurs, and the failure of unionism to address fairly gender issues.

Lacelle, Claudette. *Urban Domestic Servants in 19th-Century Canada.* Ottawa: Parks Canada, 1987.
This study focuses upon (largely) female domestic servants in Quebec City and Montreal between 1816 and 1820, and in those cities as well as Toronto and Halifax between 1871 and 1875. While this is not a comprehensive discussion of urban servants, Lacelle does argue that in the latter period a greater percentage of domestics were female, work conditions were poorer, and class barriers were more pronounced.

Lowe, Graham S. *Women in the Administrative Revolution: The Feminization of Clerical Work.* Toronto: University of Toronto Press, 1987.
The nineteenth-century office in Canada, Great Britain, and the United States was dominated by male labour. Lowe argues that the transition to low-wage female clerks between 1890 and 1920 was a result of a dramatic expansion in clerical jobs, larger numbers of educated young women, and administrative changes in which the clerk was no longer in training to be a manager, but occupied a place in factory-like office pools. Clerical work thus underwent "feminization" and was increasingly associated with poor wages and conditions, strict supervision, and high turnover rates.

Martin, Michèle. *"Hello Central?" Gender, Technology, and Culture in the Formation of the Telephone Systems.* Montreal: McGill-Queen's University Press, 1991.
Wide ranging in scope, this work examines the development and impact of the telephone on Central Canada from the 1870s to 1920. In particular, Martin focuses on the role of gender in the emergence of telephone operators. She argues that while young men initially were favoured as operators, the pleasant, yet submissive voice associated with young women, their ready availability as workers, and the perception that this position was one of high status for women, resulted in the feminization of this workforce. As consumers, women also influenced the development

of a telephone culture which emphasised sociability, and Canadian Bell
Company officials were ultimately forced to recognize this market.

Parr, Joy. *The Gender of Breadwinners: Women, Men, and Change in
    Two Industrial Towns, 1880-1950*. Toronto: University of Toronto
    Press, 1990.
One of the most significant works in modern Canadian historiography,
The Gender of Breadwinners is a sophisticated, multi-faceted analysis that
considers the role of gender, class, and, to a lesser degree, ethnicity in two
emerging industrial towns. More specifically, Parr examines Penman's
textile plant in Paris, and the Knetchel Furniture Manufacturing Company
in Hanover, both in Ontario. Parr concludes that the predominantly female
working force of Paris's principal employer challenged traditional
ideologies of work and home. Paris became, in effect, a "women's town"
where the importance of women as breadwinners was reflected in their
increased role in both the home and the community, though traditional
roles continued in politics. In Hanover, German-Canadian male artisans
exerted gender and class rights, both in the workplace and in the
community. The union of these rights gave workers enormous clout in
their dealings with their employers; this contrasts with the 1949 Paris
strike which resulted in a bitter defeat for the Penman workers. This
regional study employs a sophisticated methodology which avoids
monocausal explanations and explores the multivalent uses of gender,
class, and ethnicity.

_____. *Labouring Children: British Immigrant Apprentices to
    Canada, 1869-1923*. Montreal: McGill-Queen's University Press,
    1980; 2nd ed., Toronto: University of Toronto Press, 1994.
The relationship between the rise of urban centres and a large, clearly
identifiable pauper class in Britain, and the need for cheap, malleable
labour in Canada was very close indeed. Over 80,000 pauper children
were shipped across the Atlantic to work as labourers and domestic
servants by Dr. Barnardo and other evangelicals. In this "philanthropic
abduction," children were removed from the vices of urban life for the
moral superiority of rural society where, presumably, greater opportunities
for upward mobility awaited them. There was, however, much abuse, and
Parr emphasises the darker side of this movement and discusses
inadequate schools, the socio-psychological impact of separation, and the
exploitation of child workers.

Phillips, Erin and Paul Phillips. *Women at Work: Inequality in the Labour Market*. Toronto: James Lorimer, 1983; 2nd ed., 1993.

This popularly written work seeks to provide a historical and socio-economic perspective to the lower wages and limited job opportunities made available to Canadian women. This historical phenomenon can be explained by both the nature of industrial capitalism and patriarchy. A central point in *Women at Work* concerns the traditional domestic role of women as "providers"; this role is extended into the industrial sphere with the consequence that women became textile and laundry workers, waitresses, nurses, and school teachers. Domestic roles were therefore replicated and reinforced in the market. This work concludes with a pessimistic account of how micro-computer technology will de-grade and de-skill jobs for women in the clerical and service sectors.

Sangster, Joan. *Earning Respect: The Lives of Working Women in Small-Town Ontario, 1920-1960*. Toronto: University of Toronto Press, 1995.

This study concentrates upon women workers in four large Peterborough workplaces between 1920 and 1960. Informed by a well-defined and cogently introduced materialist-feminist perspective, and incorporating large amounts of oral history, this work focuses upon five themes: "the social construction of women's identity as wage workers'; their experiences of occupational segregation and work culture; their accommodation and resistance to wage work; their responses to economic, family, and social crisis; and, finally, the gradual evolution of the female labour force from 'working daughter to working mother.'" This excellent study obviously considers both public and private spheres, emphasises the active nature of women in creating their own work culture, and situates itself within larger theoretical considerations.

Sugiman, Pamela. *Labour's Dilemma: The Gender Politics of Auto Workers in Canada, 1937-1979*. Toronto: University of Toronto Press, 1994.

Auto workers began organizing in Ontario in the 1930s, and by 1945 the United Auto Workers formed Canada's largest industrial union. While traditional interpretations emphasise the influence of women workers hired during World War II, Sugiman argues that it was those hired in the post-war era that were most influential in demanding equality. During the 1950s, as women became more secure in their jobs and gained a greater sense of union citizenship, workers employed a gendered strategy that, for example, drew upon cultured assumptions of femininity in order to improve workplace conditions and wages. In the 1960s and 1970s they drew upon both feminist and union ideology in order to reject their second class status, and to argue for equality in the workplace and society. Important political change, including the 1970 Ontario Human Rights legislation, came about, in part, as a result of their efforts.

White, Julie. *Sisters of Solidarity.* Toronto: Thompson Educational Publishing, 1993.
In contrast to some who are critical of the contribution of unionism to women's issues, *Sisters of Solidarity* argues that unions have increased women's control over the work environment. White places the obstacles to women's unionization in a historical context, analyses the gendered nature of "women's work" in Canada, and explores the experience of women within unions and the benefits that they have accrued by embracing workers' organizations. For an earlier comment, see Julie White, *Women and Unions* (1980). For a collection of essays that examines the relationship between women and unions in both a historical and contemporary context, see Linda Briskin and Lynda Yanz, eds., *Union Sisters: Women in the Labour Movement* (1983).

Labour and Working-Class Organizations

Abella, Irving. *Nationalism, Communism and Canadian Labour: The C.I.O., the Communist Party of Canada and the Canadian Congress of Labour, 1935-1956.* Toronto: University of Toronto Press, 1973.
In a 1975 review Walter Young described *Nationalism, Communism and Canadian Labour* as "the best book on Canadian labour yet published." A superior piece of scholarship, this volume is a prime example of traditional labour history. Abella is entirely unconcerned with the attitudes and actions of ordinary workers: "The average union member, as almost all studies of the labour movement have shown," he writes, "plays an unimportant role in the affairs of his union." Instead, Abella focuses upon labour leaders and the contest between Communist and anti-Communist leaders for control of the Congress of Industrial Organizations (CIO) and the Canadian Congress of Labour (CCL). The campaign to rid Communists from the CCL was "brutal and perhaps unconstitutional," but, by 1952, was ultimately successful. A second struggle also existed, namely for the autonomy of the Canadian labour movement. Ironically, the CIO came to Canada during the mid-1930s — "it was dragged in"

states Abella — just when it appeared Canadians might regain autonomy over their labour movement. Though the creation of the Canadian Labour Congress (CLC) in 1956 did ensure greater Canadian autonomy, most workers were more concerned over job conditions and wages than who controlled their unions. For a consideration of the CLC as a political pressure group, see David Kwavnick, *Organized Labour and Pressure Politics: The Canadian Labour Congress, 1956-1968* (1972).

Babcock, Robert H. *Gompers in Canada: A Study in American Continentalism Before the First World War*. Toronto: University of Toronto Press, 1974.
Babcock, in a significant contribution to labour history, describes the influence and dominance of Samuel Gompers's American Federation of Labor in Canada prior to World War I. Gompers, sometimes described as the founder of the American labour movement, appointed John A. Flett as an AFL organizer north of the border in 1900; by 1902 over 16,000 Canadians were paying AFL dues, mostly in Ontario. Babcock illustrates the willingness of Canadian workers to respond to international capitalism by subscribing to a continental labour movement.

Bercuson, David. *Fools and Wise Men: The Rise and Fall of the One Big Union*. Toronto: McGraw-Hill, 1978.
While the One Big Union (OBU) never reached the heights proclaimed by its moniker, its influence was felt in the Western Canadian labour movement and the formation of radical political organizations. Bercuson's narrative account relates the social history of those who worked in the mining and logging camps where labour radicalism often emerged vividly. It was out of this environment that advocates of the OBU dedicated themselves to a vague socialist philosophy which sought the organization of men and women, skilled and unskilled workers. Faced with the opposition of government, business, and industrial unions, and imbued with an ill-defined, utopian philosophy, the OBU was ultimately a pathetic failure. Save for some mention of the OBU's limited activities elsewhere, Bercuson concentrates on Western Canada. This work, therefore, argues that the labour movement in the West was more radical and extreme than its eastern counterpart, a conclusion that has been much debated by working-class historians. Among numerous other studies, see Jeremy Mouat, "The Genesis of Western Exceptionalism: British Columbia's Hard Rock Miners, 1895-1903," *Canadian Historical Review* (1990).

Forsey, Eugene. *Trade Unions in Canada 1812-1902*. Toronto: University of Toronto Press, 1980.
Long in the making and providing a massive amount of information, *Trade Unions in Canada* is an important study of early Canadian unionism. More a compilation of facts and events than a comprehensive history, the book's emphasis is upon trade unions as organizations, union leaders, strikes, and politics. Forsey makes little effort to examine the lives of union members or union culture, and ignores much of the historiography of the 1970s. Of related interest are H. A. Logan, *Trade Unions in Canada: Their Development and Functioning* (1948); and Charles Lipton, *The Trade Union Movement of Canada, 1827-1959* (1966; 4ᵗʰ ed., 1978).

Leier, Mark. *Red Flags and Red Tape: The Making of a Labour Bureaucracy*. Toronto: University of Toronto Press, 1995.
In a nuanced and theoretically informed work, Leier attempts to provide insight into Werner Sombart's 1906 query: Why is there no socialism in North America? Using the Vancouver Trades and Labour Council (VTLC) as a case study, Leier examines the interplay between bureaucracy, class, and ideology from 1889 to 1910 in rising to Sombart's challenge. Leier notes that approaches to bureaucracy are often polarized: some on the left argue that if "the working class is ever to rise up, all that is to be done is to replace the labour bureaucrats with a revolutionary cadre"; others, in contrast, see the revolutionary spirit of workers thwarted by the actions of union officials. Leier takes a middle ground and undertakes three tasks: first, a theoretical discussion of labour bureaucracy; second, an investigation of the early history of the VTLC; and finally, an examination of the ideology and personnel of early leaders of the VTCL.

_____. *Where the Fraser River Flows: The Industrial Workers of the World in British Columbia*. Vancouver: New Star Books, 1990.
Arguing against interpretations that have seen the IWW as doomed to defeat, Leier maintains that they presented a "plausible and powerful alternative to capitalism and state socialism." Well-researched, *Where the Fraser River Flows* argues that the assaults of capitalism on workers' skills, job control, and conditions spurred a syndicalism that advocated direct and widespread economic action and the organization of all workers. While the revolutionary spirit of the wobblies had diminished by the 1920s, this study emphasises their importance in British Columbia.

Palmer, Bryan D. *Solidarity: The Rise and Fall of an Opposition in British Columbia.* Vancouver: New Star Books, 1987.

The Solidarity movement emerged from a coalition of unions, social activists, and political organizations in response to the legislative agenda of Premier Bill Bennett and the Social Credit government in 1983. In the summer of that year, Bennett proposed legislation that would weaken union rights, reduce public services, and centralize power in the Cabinet; large protests resulted over the next four months before a compromise position (or defeat according to Palmer) was reached. Palmer places the solidarity movement within the context of historical national and international currents, and ultimately concludes that the movement did not reach its goals because of leadership failures.

Schwantes, Carlos. *Radical Heritage: Labor, Socialism, and Reform in Washington and British Columbia, 1885-1917.* Seattle: University of Washington Press, 1979.

A rare comparative history, this work examines the radical heritage in the Pacific Northwest in the three decades prior to 1917, a period of rapid and significant change. In many ways the regions paralleled one another, particularly in the growth of industrial capitalism and in the response of workers — through both organized and unorganized efforts — to confront this changing environment. In other cases, the differences were profound: unionism was more class conscious in British Columbia and more directed to trying to affect political change, sometimes through radical and socialist parties. The American commitment to individualism meant that capitalism triumphed over collective solutions such as socialism. This work presents a more mature synthesis of American events than Canadian.

Steedman, Mercedes, Peter Suschnigg, and Dieter K. Buse, eds. *Hard Lessons: The Mine Mill Union in the Canadian Labour Movement.* Toronto: Dundurn Press, 1995.

In 1993 a conference was held in Sudbury to celebrate the centenary of the International Union of Mine, Mill and Smelter workers which began in 1893 as the Western Federation of Miners; this volume is the result of that event. Combining academic, popular, and oral history accounts, this collection examines themes such as change and continuity in unions and labour laws, health and safety, technology, and the role of gender in the union movement. In 1993 the Mine Mill membership voted to merge with the Canadian Auto Workers Union.

Sufrin, Eileen. *The Eaton Drive: The Campaign to Organize Canada's Largest Department Store, 1948-52.* Toronto: Fitzhenry and Whiteside, 1982.

In post-World War II Canada, Eaton's was one of the country's largest employers with 30,000 employees, one half of whom worked in Toronto. Eileen Tallman Sufrin, a union organizer in the 1940s, has written a blow by blow and highly personal account of the ultimately unsuccessful drive to organize Eaton's employees between 1948 and 1952. According to Sufrin, in the face of Eaton's propaganda and obstructionism, and due to now outdated labour legislation, employees rejected unionization.

Zerker, Sally F. *The Rise and Fall of the Toronto Typographical Union 1832-1972: A Case Study of Foreign Domination.* Toronto: University of Toronto Press, 1982.

This institutional history examines an important labour organization, particularly in its nineteenth-century form. Although Toronto printers initially experienced some success in managing technology, they were still forced to join the International Typographical Union (ITU) in 1866 in order to protect workers' rights. Zerker argues, however, that joining the ITU had few long-term benefits, and the international union exhibited little flexibility or appreciation of the Toronto Typographical Union's (TTU) particular concerns. This was graphically illustrated in 1964 when the ITU rejected a last minute strike settlement favoured by the TTU and union jobs were lost in the Toronto printing industry.

The State and Confrontation

Abella, Irving, ed. *On Strike: Six Key Labour Struggles in Canada, 1919-1949.* Toronto: James, Lewis & Samuel, 1974.

Seeking to introduce labour history into the mainstream of Canadian historiography, the essays in this collection examine the Winnipeg General Strike, the Estevan coal miners' strike of 1931, the Stratford furniture strike of 1933, the Oshawa General Motors strike of 1937, the Windsor Ford strike of 1945, and the Asbestos strike of 1949. There are, unfortunately, no essays dealing with strikes in Atlantic Canada or British Columbia. For a broader study of unrest that emphasises labour history rather than workers, see Stuart Jamieson, *Times of Trouble: Labour Unrest and Industrial Conflict in Canada, 1900-66* (1968). For a more thorough study of the Windsor strike, see Herb Colling, *Ninety-Nine Days: The Ford Strike in Windsor, 1945* (1995).

Bercuson, David. *Confrontation at Winnipeg: Labour, Industrial Relations and the General Strike*. Montreal: McGill-Queen's University Press, 1974; rev. ed., 1990.

D. C. Masters' classic work, *The Winnipeg General Strike* (1950), emphasised the political and ideological origins of the strike. Utilizing a much broader range of sources, David Bercuson expands on Masters' thesis by arguing that labour-capital tensions emerged out of the rapid expansion in immigration and urbanization that so marked "boom" towns like Winnipeg in the first decades of the twentieth century. The pressures of these demographic changes combined with poor wages and working conditions, unemployment, inflation, and heavy-handed tactics by management to result in Canada's most celebrated strike in 1919. Striking workers, with some rare exceptions, did not seek the violent overthrow of the existing order; rather, they sought the amelioration of the poor conditions that plagued their lives. Bercuson maintains that the Winnipeg General Strike was an example of Western exceptionalism and radicalism; this argument has been challenged by individuals such as Greg Kealey in an article reprinted in *Workers and Canadian History* (1995). The final chapter in the revised version contains a useful summary of the various challenges to *Confrontation at Winnipeg* and Bercuson's defense of his interpretation. For briefer accounts, see David Bercuson and Kenneth McNaught, *The Winnipeg Strike: 1919* (1974), and J. M. Bumsted, *The Winnipeg Strike of 1919: An Illustrated History* (1994).

Craven, Paul. *An Impartial Umpire: Industrial Relations and the Canadian State, 1900-1911*. Toronto: University of Toronto Press, 1980.

This important study of industrial relations in the first decade of the twentieth century emphasises the personality of W. L. Mackenzie King. As Canada's first Deputy Minister of Labour and, after he entered politics, Minister of Labour, King was instrumental in implementing important legislation such as the Conciliation Act of 1900 and, especially, the Industrial Disputes Investigation Act (IDIA) of 1907, which became the basis for Canadian industrial relations policy. Dense and sophisticated in its analysis, *An Impartial Umpire* argues that dissociating themselves from the *laissez-faire* orthodoxy of an earlier generation, new political economists such as King both accepted the legitimacy of trade unions and endorsed a positive and active role for the state. State apparatus thus acted as an "impartial umpire" in the resolution of labour disputes. This work provides important insights to the intellectual formation of King, and

examines the effectiveness of Canada's industrial policy through a series
of labour disputes.

Dumas, Evelyn. *The Bitter Thirties in Québec.* trans. Arnold Bennett.
    Montreal: Black Rose, 1975.
Originally published in French in 1970, this volume provides a narrative
history — largely based on oral evidence — of a series of 12 strikes in
Quebec in the 1930s and 1940s. Thus, Dumas attempts "to learn from the
very lips of the principal actors" about how these strikes influenced
working-class lives. For an account of Quebec's most famous strike
following World War II, see Pierre Trudeau, *The Asbestos Strike* (1956)

Hoar, Victor, ed. *The On to Ottawa Trek.* Toronto: Copp Clark, 1970.
The decade-long depression of the 1930s was punctuated by the attempted
march to Ottawa by some 1,800 unemployed men, and its suppression on
1 July 1935 in Regina by RCMP and government forces. Hoar has
collected a series of documents relating to workers and working
conditions in the 1930s, the trek to Ottawa, and the Regina Riot. For a
personal memoir of the Trek, see Ronald Liversedge, *Recollections of the
On to Ottawa Trek* (1973). This volume, edited by Victor Hoar, also
contains a large selection of primary documents relating to the Relief
Camp Workers' Strike and the Ottawa Trek.

Penner, Norman. *Winnipeg 1919: The Strikers' own History of the
    Winnipeg General Strike.* Toronto: James, Lewis & Samuel, 1973.
Arguing for an account more sympathetic to the strikers' cause than that
of D. C. Masters's *The Winnipeg General Strike* (1950), Penner has
edited and introduced this volume of primary sources. The three bodies
of collected material include the Defence Committee's history of the
strike (1919), the address of Peter Heenan to the House of Commons
(1926), and excerpts from W. A. Pritchard's address to the jury (1920).
Penner provides an introduction to the workers' perspective on the strike;
this work also contains an important collection of photographs.

Russell, Bob. *Back to Work? Labour, State and Industrial Relations in
    Canada.* Scarborough, ON: Nelson Canada, 1990.
Sometimes placing the Canadian experience along side that of the United
States, Russell examines the history of industrial relations from the 1847
Masters and Servants Act to contemporary Canada. *Back to Work?*
maintains that the Canadian state has often acted in a coercive manner in

Masters and Servants Act to contemporary Canada. *Back to Work?* maintains that the Canadian state has often acted in a coercive manner in restricting the rights of labour, particularly after World War II. This work is based upon extensive primary research and attempts to place almost 150 years of labour-state relations in a historical context.

Waiser, Bill. *Park Prisoners: The Untold Story of Western Canada's National Parks, 1915-1946.* Saskatoon: Fifth House Publishers, 1995. The Banff-Jasper highway is arguably one of the most spectacular transportation routes in the world; it has, regrettably, tragic and unfortunate origins. *Park Prisoners* examines the use of forced labour in Western Canadian national parks during and between the two world wars. Waiser includes discussions on "pauper immigrants," relief workers and transients during the Depression, conscientious objectors, Japanese Canadians, and German POWs, all of whom provided poorly paid labour for various make-work projects. This work is well-researched and illustrated, but unfortunately does not provide a thorough analysis of the coercive use of state power that led to such abuses.

Women's and Family History

The genres of women's and family history has been among the most productive and innovative areas in Canadian scholarship over the past decade. Prior to the emergence of limited identities scholarship, Canadian historiography had emphasised white, male political figures with few references to women at all. Those histories that sought to consider women tended to focus upon female worthies or, in the case of Catherine Cleverdon's classic *The Women Suffrage Movement in Canada* (1950), the achievement of female suffrage. The second wave of feminism emerging out of the 1960s challenged the private and public worlds of Canadians, and helped — along with the new social history — to transform the writing of women's history. Increasingly, the focus shifted from individuals and elites to include larger groups of individuals and the more common experience. Correspondingly, approaches shifted away from the hagiographic toward more theoretically sophisticated works. Thus, the writing of women's history has shared much with other areas of Canadian historiography. Women's history has, however, made several unique contributions to Canadian scholarship: for example, fundamental questions about the use of evidence and methodologies have been asked; the traditional periodization that focuses around political events has been challenged; gender has come to be seen as a social construct as much as a biological one; and research into sexuality and the family has largely emerged out of this discipline.

General Works

Bristow, Peggy, Dionne Brand, Linda Carty, Afua P. Cooper, Sylvia Hamilton, and Adrienne Shadd. *"We're Rooted Here and They Can't Pull Us Up": Essays in African Canadian Women's History*. Toronto: University of Toronto Press, 1994.
The six essays collected here seek to refute two notions: that black people — and, more specifically, black women — arrived only recently, and, second, that Canada has a non-racist heritage. This volume presents essays on three centuries of African Canadian settlement in Nova Scotia, fleeing female slaves and the underground railroad, the experience of black

women in mid-nineteenth century Kent County and early twentieth century Ontario, the life of teacher and abolitionist Mary Bibb, and a critique of state power which sought to exploit black, female labour.

Burnett, Jean, ed. *Looking into My Sister's Eyes: An Exploration in Women's History*. Toronto: Multicultural History Society of Ontario, 1986.
Emerging out of a 1985 conference held at the University of Toronto, this volume was an early venture into a previously neglected field of women's history. The 13 papers in *Looking into My Sister's Eyes* focus upon ethnic women's history in Ontario; more specifically, this volume contains essays on British, Italian, Finnish, Jewish, Polish, Greek, Mennonite, Ukrainian, Macedonian, Armenian, and Chinese women, with particular emphasis upon the first four decades of the twentieth century. Although this volume is eclectic in nature, it does consider issues of family, identity preservation, work, and class.

Cook, Ramsay, and Wendy Mitchinson, eds. *The Proper Sphere: Women's Place in Canadian Society*. Toronto: Oxford University Press, 1976.
A collection of documents from the mid-nineteenth to mid-twentieth centuries, *The Proper Sphere* draws from a variety of sources that present opinions for and against women's rights in politics, law, education, and suffrage; as well, several selections argue for women as the moral bastions of home and country.

Griffiths, N. E. S. *Penelope's Web: Some Perceptions of Women in European and Canadian Society*. Toronto: Oxford University Press, 1976.
Originally a series of television lectures, *Penelope's Web* is wide-ranging over time and geography, and an extremely provocative work. Griffiths argues that modern sexism emerged in Europe at the end of the seventeenth century with changing demographics — longer lives, population growth, and the rise of towns — and the onset of industrialization. In Canada, women and men managed as relatively equal partners in rural and frontier societies; with industrialization and urbanization, sexist stereotypes grew in strength.

Iacovetta, F. and M. Valverde, eds. *Gender Conflicts: New Essays in Women's History*. Toronto: University of Toronto Press, 1992.

A collection of essays by a number of prominent feminist scholars, *New Essays* explores the complexities of gender in politics, law, religion and social reform, ethnicity, consumerism, and heterosexual conflict.

Light, Beth and Alison Prentice, eds. *Pioneer and Gentlewomen of British North America, 1713-1867*. Toronto: New Hogtown Press, 1980.
Light, Beth and Joy Parr, eds. *Canadian Women on the Move, 1867-1920*. Toronto: New Hogtown Press and the Ontario Institute for Studies in Education, 1983.
Light, Beth and R. Pierson, eds. *No Easy Road: Women in Canada, 1920s-1960s*. Toronto: New Hogtown Press, 1990.

In response to Simone de Beauvoir's observation in 1949 that women "have no past, no history," these companion volumes are an effort to make available "records of the past as the women of Canada experienced it." These works mine a huge variety of material: letters; diaries; apprenticeship indentures; court, school, church, and government records; songs; advertisements; drawings and photographs; travelers' accounts; and newspaper stories are some of the principal sources. This series also pursues several themes: the passage of women from childhood to old age; the tension between domestic and public life; and the juxtaposition of women's needs and concerns with the demands of the economy, government, church, advertisers, and others.

Parr, Joy and Mark Rosenfeld, eds. *Gender and History in Canada*. Mississauga, ON: Copp Clark, 1996.

The essays in this collection are obviously informed by the concept of gender; that is, that being male or female is not simply biological, but is socially constructed and reconstituted. Essays range chronologically from New France to contemporary Canada, and examine themes such as race, nationalism, sexuality, work and leisure, popular culture, and family among both men and women, including both heterosexual and homosexual individuals. Joy Parr's introductory essay provides an excellent survey of the writing of gender history in Canada.

Prentice, Allison, Paula Bourne, Gail Cuthbert Brandt, Beth Light, Wendy Mitchinson, and Naomi Black. *Canadian Women: A History*. Toronto: Harcourt Brace Jovanovich, 1988; 2nd ed., 1996.
_____, ed. *Canadian Women: A Reader*. Toronto: Harcourt Brace Jovanovich, 1996.

A ground breaking study when it first appeared, *Canadian Women* spans from the experience of early contact First Nations women to contemporary Canada. This survey identifies three major transition periods: the transition from pre-industrial society to industrial; World War I and the achievement of two goals of the early women's movement, suffrage and prohibition; and World War II and the massive entry of women into the labour force. Within each of four chronological sections, the authors explore the nature of women's work and material culture, family life, public culture, and politics. The appendix contains a healthy representation of relevant tables and figures, and there is an excellent bibliography. An effective complement to the survey, *Canadian Women: A Reader* recognizes similar transitions, and reproduces both traditional and innovative, new material.

Strong-Boag, Veronica. *The New Day Recalled: Lives of Girls and Women in English Canada.* Markham, ON: Penguin Books, 1988.
A recipient of the prestigious Macdonald Prize, *The New Day Recalled* begins with the question: what happened to Canadian women after the vote was won? Utilizing a life-cycle approach that considers childhood, youth, marriage, work, and growing old, Strong-Boag examines the experience of middle-class, urban women in English-Canada between the wars. In the post-World War I era, expectations of a "New Day" for women proved to be folly; instead — although more women worked for wages, continued their education, sued for divorce, and began to participate in the political process — their lives had an essential continuity to previous pre-suffrage generations. For example, marriage and homemaking remained the idealized goal and predominant occupation, and female networks continued to be crucial in workplaces, organizations, and institutions of all kinds, including within the political sphere.

Strong-Boag, Veronica and Anita Clair Fellman, eds. *Rethinking Canada: The Promise of Women's History.* Toronto: Copp Clark, 1986; 3rd ed., Toronto: Oxford University Press, 1997.
The various editions of this collection illustrate the maturation and currents of Canadian women's history. More attention is given to women who do not belong to either of Canada's two "founding" nations, and monocausal explanations are avoided; instead, attention is paid to how the identities of ethnicity, class, sexuality, (dis)ability, and others interact with that of gender. This collection is designed to be useful in three types of classes: introductions to Canadian history, Canadian studies, and Canadian women's history. The editors provide a short introduction to each selection in order to situate it within some historical context.

Trofimenkoff, Susan Mann and Alison Prentice, eds. *The Neglected Majority: Essays in Canadian Women's History.* 2 vols. Toronto: McClelland and Stewart, 1977, 1985.

These two volumes are useful, but eclectic, introductory collections. The first was intended to meet the political and scholarly challenges of the 1970s, and sought to incorporate women into academic and non-academic discourse; the second illustrates the increasing sophistication of this area of study and a greater commitment to interdisciplinary approaches and feminist scholarship.

Regional Studies

Anderson, Karen. *Chain Her by One Foot: The Subjugation of Women in Seventeenth-Century New France.* New York: Routledge, 1991.

Drawing upon feminist theory, a Foucaultian analysis of power relations, and the *Jesuit Relations*, Anderson argues that Jesuits realized the power and status that Huron and Montagnais women held in pre-contact societies, and quickly sought to restore them to their "natural" position: one of subjugation. Although the Huron — toward whom Anderson directs the bulk of her argument — had gendered divisions of labour prior to contact, *Chain Her by One Foot* maintains that women held the privileged position; contact resulted in the adoption of a Christian perspective of the sexes and an aggressive assault on the position and status of women.

Cavanaugh, Catherine A. and Randi R. Warne, eds. *Standing on New Ground: Women in Alberta.* Edmonton: University of Alberta Press, 1993.

A recent and eclectic collection of academic work, *Standing on New Ground* explores aspects of women in Alberta from early female missionaries to the present. The emphasis is upon the formal and informal roles that women played within public institutions, most of which were dominated by men.

The Clio Collective. *Quebec Women: A History.* Trans. Roger Gannon and Rosalind Gill. Toronto: The Women's Press, 1987.

A pioneering effort, this work — along with Prentice *et al.*, *Canadian Women* (1986; 2nd ed. 1996) — is reflective of the dramatic growth of secondary literature on women's history since the 1970s. This work is, however, somewhat uneven: there is little discussion of Native women, and over half the volume deals with the twentieth century. *Quebec Women* challenges the periodization of traditional texts of French Canada and provides excellent treatments of domestic life, work, education, and the contemporary women's movement.

Creese, Gillian and Veronica Strong-Boag, eds. *British Columbia Reconsidered: Essays on Women.* Vancouver: Press Gang Publishers, 1992.

Latham, Barbara and Cathy Kess, eds. *In Her Own Right: Selected Essays on Women's History in British Columbia.* Victoria: Camosun College, 1980.

Historians have not always incorporated gender history into regional perspectives. Frustrated at the lack of attention paid to women in the writing of British Columbia's history, Latham and Kess compiled a collection that contains no contributions by academic historians. Instead, interested researchers, students, and political activists have examined aspects of women's history in the province, largely focussing upon personalities, women's organizations, politics, and unions. *British Columbia Reconsidered* reflects the increased attention that academics have given to women's history. The 21 essays in this volume are divided into sections on pioneering, politics, domestic life, culture, work, and poverty; in contrast to *In Her Own Right*, there is greater attention paid to issues involving race and rural women. There is also a useful bibliography.

De Brou, David and Aileen Moffatt, eds. *"Other" Voices: Historical Essays on Saskatchewan Women.* Regina: Canadian Plains Research Centre, University of Regina, 1995.

The first collection of essays on Saskatchewan women's history, *"Other" Voices* endorses a polyphonic approach in order to examine the various interactions between gender and race, ethnicity, class, religion, and language. In addition, the essays in this volume seek to give voice to "other" women beyond those of the social, economic, and political elite.

Fowler, Marion. *The Embroidered Tent: Five Gentlewomen in Early Canada.* Toronto: Anansi, 1982.

This work presents brief biographical sketches of five English gentlewomen who immigrated to Upper Canada and Ontario in the eighteenth and nineteenth centuries. Each of the women — Elizabeth Simcoe, Susanna Moodie, Catharine Parr Traill, Anna Jameson, and Lady Dufferin — was literate and published or left behind manuscripts, some of which, in the case of works by Moodie and Traill, remain common on undergraduate reading lists. Fowler's emphasis is upon the conflict between the values of the mother country and the realities of early Canada.

Guildford, Janet and Suzanne Morton, eds. *Separate Spheres: Women's Worlds in the 19th-Century Maritimes*. Fredericton: Acadiensis Press, 1994.

In the preface to *A Not Unreasonable Claim* (1979), Linda Kealey regretfully acknowledged that historical research relating to women in Atlantic Canada was largely inchoate and few references to that region were made. *Separate Spheres* offers a useful corrective. The essays collected here examine a variety of Maritime women —African-Nova Scotian women, female immigrants, teachers, writers, and preachers, as well as those who joined in civic parades or aggressively defended their rights — in regard to the ideology of "separate spheres." This collection explores the ambiguity and influence of such an ideology: it assigned women to the private sphere and oppressed all regardless of class, age, or race; simultaneously, separate spheres ideology was also used "to negotiate power in the home and to make claims in public based upon a respectability rooted in domesticity."

Hopkins, Monica. *Letters from a Lady Rancher*. Edited and introduced by Shelagh Jameson. Calgary: Glenbow Museum, 1981.

Jackel, Susan, ed. *A Red Flannel Shirt and Liberty: British Emigrant Gentlewomen in the Canadian West, 1880-1914*. Vancouver: University of British Columbia Press, 1982.

Morton, W. L. with Vera Fast, eds. *God's Galloping Girl: The Diaries of Monica Storrs*. Vancouver: University of British Columbia Press, 1979.

Silverman, Eliane. *The Last Best West: Women on the Alberta Frontier*. Montreal: McGill-Queen's University Press, 1984.

The "frontier" of the Canadian West has too often been defined solely in masculine terms. These collections of primary documents relating to women's experiences in the Canadian prairies during the re-settlement era help to correct that perception. The editors provide commentary and annotations throughout the books, and introductory essays are useful starting points for research on women during this period of prairie history.

Kealey, Linda, ed. *Pursuing Equality: Historical Perspectives on Women in Newfoundland and Labrador*. St. John's: Institute of Social and Economic Research, Memorial University, 1993.

Concentrating upon the political and legal history of women in the nineteenth and twentieth centuries, this collection aims to understand how women's lives were shaped by the social structures that surrounded them. Underlying the close relationship between public and private lives, essays examine women's suffrage, law and legal reforms, and the modern women's movement. This volume concludes with lengthy and useful appendices relating to law, politics, and contemporary feminism.

Kinnear, Mary, ed. *First Days, Fighting Days: Women in Manitoba History.* Regina: Canadian Plains Research Centre, University of Regina, 1987.
An eclectic collection of nine essays, this volume examines topics such as child rearing practices of a Methodist missionary family with a Cree nurse, prairie press women and suffrage activism, and urban workers; it also has a useful essay on the uses of artifactual evidence for historians.

Lévesque, Andrée. *Making and Breaking the Rules: Women in Quebec, 1919-1939.* Trans. Yvonne M. Klein. Toronto: McClelland and Stewart, 1994.
While female suffrage was achieved federally and in English Canada in the years during and immediately following World War I, women in Quebec did not get the provincial vote until 1940. During the interwar period, Quebec was a strongly patriarchal society, and Lévesque discusses the social and sexual standards by which women were expected to abide and, in particular, examines those who challenged the norm, particularly in areas of sexuality or reproduction. These "deviants" rejected idealized notions of womanhood and motherhood through pregnancy outside of marriage, abortion, or prostitution. Despite not fitting societal ideals, Lévesque argues that such behavior was tolerated by authorities more than repressed, although repression depended upon how great a threat the "deviant" behavior was seen to be to the familial and social order.

Parr, Joy, ed. *A Diversity of Women: Ontario, 1945-1980.* Toronto: University of Toronto Press, 1995.
An interdisciplinary collection of ten essays, this work examines changing ideas about women in post-World War II Ontario. The authors seek to understand how beliefs about women were formed in the 35 years after the war, with regard to both what others expected and how women came to see their own predicaments. This collection reflects some of the diversity of women's experience: for example, Nora Cebotarev examines rural women,

Franca Iacovetta the "new Canadian" who experienced discrimination on
the basis of both gender and race, and Marlene Brant Castellano and
Janice Hill introduce four women whose work has been to reclaim
knowledge traditionally entrusted to Native women.

Potter-MacKinnon, Janice. *While the Women Only Wept: Loyalist Refugee*
  Women in Eastern Ontario. Montreal: McGill-Queen's University
  Press, 1993.

The Loyalist myth still resonates deeply among Anglo-Canadians and has
been the subject of much academic study. *While the Women Only Wept* is
the foremost study of the sizable number of Loyalists who were women.
Potter-MacKinnon examines the hardship Loyalist women endured during
the revolution: they were forced to look after family, farms, and
businesses, and face Patriot Committees during the absence of husbands
and older sons. During the conflict and after, loyalism was constructed as
a masculine concept, and — in contrast to the experience of patriot women
— the role of women was de-emphasised and ignored. While this study
focuses upon women who ended up near present-day Kingston, Potter-
MacKinnon notes similarities with those Loyalists who ended up in Nova
Scotia and New Brunswick. *While the Women Only Wept* should be read
alongside the work of David Mills and Jane Errington. For a recent
exploration of gendered identities in Upper Canada, see Cecilia Morgan,
Public Men and Virtuous Women: The Gendered Languages of Religion
and Politics in Upper Canada, 1791-1850 (1996).

Religion, Moral and Social Reform

Brouwer, Ruth Compton. *New Women for God: Canadian Presbyterian*
  Women and Indian Missions, 1876-1914. Toronto: University of
  Toronto Press, 1990.

Foreign missions were an important element of Canadian national and
imperialist identity during the Victorian and Edwardian eras. In her study,
Brouwer examines the dual role of women and church denomination in
this field of interest. Women's roles emerged from the dual notion that
they had a special affinity for religious and moral responsibilities and a
particular interest in social services and public health. Once in the mission
field in India, women found their role challenging and rewarding, though
they often experienced failure in terms of evangelism and religious
conversion. These women discovered that internal church politics,
focussed upon gender, were as difficult a trial as serving in the mission

itself. The paradox of "opportunity and constraint" was a common problem for women during this era, and Brouwer's book adds significantly to knowledge of gender relations in Canada. Also see Rosemary Gagan, *A Sensitive Independence: Canadian Methodist Women Missionaries in Canada and the Orient, 1881-1925* (1992).

Cook, Sharon Anne. *"Through Sunshine and Shadow": The Woman's Christian Temperance Union, Evangelicalism, and Reform in Ontario, 1874-1930*. Montreal: McGill-Queen's University Press, 1995.
The Woman's Christian Temperance Union (WCTU) was one of the largest and most productive evangelical temperance organizations in nineteenth-century Ontario. Cook argues for the regional distinctiveness of the Ontario WCTU — as opposed to its national American and Canadian varieties — and maintains that the organization developed an "evangelical feminism" that promoted a personal and public activism that sought to defend the family and middle-class values. Further, Cook argues that in the 1920s a conservative and more limiting evangelicalism supplanted the ideology of "evangelical feminism," and the movement consequently lost much of its momentum and influence.

Danylewycz, Marta. *Taking the Veil: An Alternative to Marriage, Motherhood, and Spinsterhood in Quebec, 1840-1920*. Toronto: McClelland and Stewart, 1987.
This rewarding work integrates French-Canadian scholarship regarding the Roman Catholic church with the burgeoning literature on women's lives and experiences. Danylewycz provides a compelling examination of the choices made by French-Canadian women during the late nineteenth century and the effects of these choices upon French-Canadian society. Life within the church was both sequestered and challenging. Women could, and did, influence the communities within which they worked. Danylewycz thus demonstrates how the nuns achieved status and influence within the confines of a patriarchal church structure. Using social historical techniques of demography and class analysis, she also carefully constructs a human portrait of the nuns. This work argues that life in the religious orders offered certain rewards to women and, contrary to some models, becoming a nun should not be considered a surrogate marriage.

Griffiths, Naomi E. S. *The Splendid Vision: Centennial History of the National Council of Women of Canada, 1893-1993*. Ottawa: Carleton University Press, 1993.

Commissioned by the National Council of Women of Canada (NCWC), *The Splendid Vision* is a readable survey of the organizational structure, aims and activities, and personalities of this middle-class, volunteer association. More sympathetic to the NCWC than Strong-Boag's *The Parliament of Women* (1976), Griffiths evaluates the council's successes and failures in advocating for women's rights, improvements in the workplace, and various reform efforts.

Hallett, M. and M. Davis. *Firing the Heather: The Life and Times of Nellie McClung.* Saskatoon: Fifth House, 1993.
A chronological and readable account of McClung's life, *Firing the Heather* provides a sympathetic interpretation of McClung's adult years, particularly her life as a wife and mother, her efforts at political and moral reform, her involvement with the United Church and the CBC, and her career as a writer. This work also presents a mature critique of McClung's fictional writings and insights into her middle-class, Anglo-Canadian Christian liberalism.

Howard, Irene. *The Struggle for Social Justice in British Columbia: Helena Gutteridge, the Unknown Reformer.* Vancouver: University of British Columbia Press, 1992.
Helena Gutteridge was the first woman to be elected to the Vancouver city council in 1937, and an active advocate for the rights of women and workers before ending her working career as a cannery worker in the 1940s. *The Struggle for Social Justice* is a public — rather than private — biography, and Howard insightfully discusses the international currents that shaped Gutteridge's reform efforts, her many reform and union activities, her political involvement with the CCF and in civic politics, and her interest in the post-World War II peace movement.

Kealey, Linda, ed. *A Not Unreasonable Claim: Women and Reform in Canada, 1880s-1920s.* Toronto: The Women's Press, 1979.
The decades surrounding the onset of the twentieth century witnessed a tremendous growth in women's organizations, most of which were run by middle-class women and devoted to a wide range of political and social reforms. The essays in this collection examine a variety of reform efforts, and many suggest that the ideology of "maternal feminism" — that the special role of women as mothers gave them the duty and right to participate in the public sphere — was influential in shaping the reform movement.

Muir, Elizabeth Gillan. *Petticoats in the Pulpit: The Story of Early Nineteenth-Century Methodist Women Preachers in Upper Canada.* Toronto: The United Church Publishing House, 1991.
The story of early Methodist preachers has largely focused on individuals such as William Case, partially because of the popularization of the male itinerant missionary by the nineteenth-century historian John Carroll. Muir chronicles the lives and careers of female Methodist preachers — and, in particular, Barbara Heck — in the early nineteenth century. Muir argues, however, that by the mid- and late-nineteenth century women had largely stopped preaching and been confined to other forms of ministry. This was so because of the increasing conservatism that permeated Canadian Methodism, beginning with the union with British Wesleyans in 1833. In contrast, Muir notes the more progressive stance of American Methodists where women moved toward ordination in the late nineteenth century.

Muir, Elizabeth Gillan and Marilyn Färdig Whiteley, eds. *Changing Roles of Women Within the Christian Church in Canada.* Toronto: University of Toronto Press, 1995.
Emerging out of a conference held at the Centre for the Study of Religion in Canada at Emmanuel College, Toronto, *Changing Roles of Women* — the contents of which have been extensively reviewed by fellow contributors to the volume — provides a useful, but eclectic, introduction to a too frequently neglected topic. The essays explore Catholic and Protestant traditions from the nineteenth century to the post-World War II era, and seek to examine the ways in which the Christian church both limited women's roles and made opportunities for them. This work has an extensive bibliography of published and unpublished work.

Strange, Carolyn. *Toronto's Girl Problem: The Perils and Pleasures of the City, 1880-1930.* Toronto: University of Toronto Press, 1995.
This excellent study explores the changing nature of culture, demographics, and work between 1880 and 1930 in Toronto, and its implications for young women in particular. During this period young women increasingly left behind domestic service for work in the industrial and clerical sectors. These young wage earners — with more time for leisure and fewer domestic responsibilities than previous generations — were seen as potential threats to urban order. With attention to class and ethnicity, Strange explores the images constructed of these young women, reform-minded attempts to control adolescent sexuality, and resistance to these attempts by some individuals.

Strong-Boag, Veronica. *The Parliament of Women: The National Council of Women of Canada, 1893-1929.* Ottawa: National Museum of Man, 1976.
One of the earliest Ph.D. dissertations in Canadian women's history, Strong-Boag's *The Parliament of Women* examines the National Council of Women of Canada (NCWC) from its genesis in 1893 to its decline in the late 1920s. The NCWC was dominated by middle-class, reform-minded, urban women dedicated to solving the challenges and problems of industrialization and urbanization, as well as advocating women's issues such as suffrage. The NCWC endorsed the ideology of separate spheres, and women were urged to embrace their role as public mother in responding to the needs of society. While the NCWC achieved some success during World War I, in the decade following the war the organization suffered from internal tensions, imprecise goals, and declining membership and influence.

Warne, R. *Literature as Pulpit: The Christian Social Activism of Nellie L. McClung.* Waterloo: Wilfrid Laurier University Press, 1993.
Recent informal polls surrounding celebrations of Alberta women indicate that most Canadians (and Albertans) cannot name the "Famous Five" — Nellie McClung, Emily Murphy, Irene Parlby, Henrietta Muir Edwards, and Louise McKinney — who succeeded in 1929 in securing a court decision that women were indeed "persons" in matters of rights and privileges. Although McClung, along with Murphy, are arguably the best known of the five, Warne argues that insufficient attention has been paid to "Our Nell," particularly in the area of her Christian social activism. Focusing upon her most prominent work, *In Times Like These*, and her four novels, Warne argues that McClung's activism — her commitment to female suffrage, temperance, pacifism, and the ordination of women, for example — emerged out of, and was reinforced by, her religious convictions. Social transformation of society, therefore, was to be accompanied by spiritual renewal. Still popular and delightfully ironic is McClung's *In Times Like These* (1915; rpt., 1972), edited by Veronica Strong-Boag.

Politics and Law

Bacchi, C. *Liberation Deferred? The Ideas of the English-Canadian Suffragists, 1877-1918.* Toronto: University of Toronto Press, 1983.
Liberation Deferred? argues that the suffragette movement was composed

of two distinct groups: the first, a smaller body of radicals who campaigned for the vote as one step toward sexual equality; the second, and larger, group of reformers who wanted to obtain the vote in order to preserve the family, home, and the moral purity of society. Although there was some similarity in background between the two groups, and they often co-existed, ultimately the more conservative elements came to dominate. In contrast to Catherine Cleverdon's *The Woman Suffrage Movement* (1950), which cast the suffragette movement as liberal and progressive, Bacchi argues that it was a class-based social reform movement rather than a revolution.

Backhouse, Constance. *Petticoats and Prejudices: Women and the Law in Nineteenth-Century Canada.* Toronto: The Women's Press, 1991.
Canadian legal history has, until recently, made few efforts to analyse the relationship between gender and law. Backhouse argues that the nineteenth-century legal system was a prime example of a formal patriarchal institution. Carefully placing the Canadian legal system in historical context, Backhouse primarily examines nineteenth-century law and how it relates to women in issues of marriage, family, and sexuality, although she also includes a chapter on labour legislation. While women were under the rule of a patriarchal institution, and often subjected to a double standard on the basis of gender, Backhouse also notes the influence of class and ethnicity on how "justice" was dispensed.

Bashevkin, Sylvia B. *Toeing the Line: Women and Party Politics in English Canada.* Toronto: Oxford University Press, 1985; 2nd ed., 1993.
Arguing that contemporary Canadian political parties are organized upon a gender-based division of labour, Bashevkin finds that women are under-represented in positions of power and influence; they are, in effect, "toeing the line" rather than formulating policy and legislation. Bashevkin argues that the political history of women in English Canada from suffrage to the contemporary feminist movement has been marked by a tension between a desire for political independence and conventional partisanship. *Toeing the Line* provides an analysis of women in contemporary politics and the impact of affirmative action on political participation, and sets the Canadian experience in a comparative context.

Brodie, J. *Women and Politics in Canada.* Toronto: McGraw-Hill Ryerson, 1985.

This slim volume explores the experiences of over 300 women who were candidates for municipal, provincial, or federal office between 1945 and 1975. Brodie has surveyed female candidates from British Columbia to Atlantic Canada, although fewer Quebec women are represented. Among other conclusions, Brodie finds that gender was a significant obstacle in the recruitment and election of women candidates, that women were more likely to be elected at the municipal level, that minority parties were more likely to field female candidates than majority parties, and that women were too often relegated to "lost-cause" seats.

Carbert, Louise I. *Agrarian Feminism: The Politics of Ontario Farm Women.* Toronto: University of Toronto Press, 1995.
Seymour Lipset's *Agrarian Socialism* (1950) weakly sought to prove that socialism could emerge from farmers and male-dominated farm organizations rather than solely from industrial workers. Carbert, in contrast, examines the feminist content in farm women's organizations and argues that women's opinions about politics and feminism are closely related to their role in agricultural production. There are two principal parts to this work: a review of farm women's organizations in English Canada and, more substantively, a contemporary survey of political opinions among Ontario farm women.

Chunn, Dorothy. *From Punishment to Doing Good: Family Courts and Socialized Justice in Ontario, 1880-1940.* Toronto: University of Toronto Press, 1992.
An excellent examination of a little studied topic, *From Punishment to Doing Good* analyses the emergence of family courts within the context of an increasingly urban society and the establishment of the welfare state. Although reformers often had ambiguous or even contradictory goals, Chunn argues that the movement from a *laissez-faire* political economy toward a welfare state was accompanied by the creation of the informal justice of family courts. Women were active in shaping the courts to their own benefit, although the courts also acted to reinforce middle-class, domestic ideals.

Crowley, T. *Agnes Macphail and the Politics of Equality.* Toronto: James Lorimer, 1990.
Agnes Macphail was the first woman elected to Parliament, in 1921, and an early supporter of the CCF. This lively biography provides insight into Macphail's personality, presents some aspects of her personal and public

life, and explores the democratic socialist and feminist issues to which she devoted much of her career. In particular, Crowley argues that Macphail's feminist beliefs have been neglected, and provides an instructive account of the nature of the early feminist movement in Canada. For a more popular account that makes extensive use of Macphail's own speeches and writings, see Doris Pennington, *Agnes Macphail: Reformer* (1989).

Dubinsky, Karen. *Improper Advances: Rape and Heterosexual Conflict in Ontario, 1880-1929*. Chicago: University of Chicago Press, 1993.
A ground breaking work into the history of sexuality in Canada, *Improper Advances* examines — in contrast to the Victorian fear of the evils of urban life — sexual violence against women in 25 counties in small-town and rural Ontario. Dubinsky's concern is largely with working-class women rather than middle-class reformers, and she explores the impact of gender, class, ethnicity, marital status, and locale in understanding sexual violence. As would be expected, married, upper-class, Anglo-Canadian men were rarely convicted of any sexual crime. Women were not, however, passive victims; instead, Dubinsky argues that women were active in fighting sexual violence, either through physically fighting back or through the more formal venue of the courts.

Kealey, Linda and Joan Sangster, eds. *Beyond the Vote: Canadian Women and Politics*. Toronto: University of Toronto Press, 1989.
This collection of 13 essays concentrates on the period between the suffrage era and the rise of contemporary feminism. The aim of this work is to illustrate that, despite popular perceptions, women made "vibrant and varied" political contributions after winning the vote. Essays introduce readers to feminist interpretations of women in politics and to their involvement in socialist and communist parties, non-traditional political groups such as the peace movements, and farm and ethnic organizations. Particular attention is paid to women on the left, and this work is sensitive to the intersection of class, culture, and gender.

Knowles, Valerie. *First Person: A Biography of Cairine Wilson, Canada's First Woman Senator*. Toronto: Dundurn Press, 1988.
After the courts decided that women were indeed "persons" in 1929, Mackenzie King chose his friend Cairine Wilson as Canada's first female senator. Though not an aggressive suffragist like Nellie McClung or Emily Murphy, Wilson became known for her work relating to social reform, and as an advocate of the rights of refugees.

Kome, P. *Women of Influence: Canadian Women and Politics*. Toronto: Doubleday, 1985.
In an ironic "great man" tradition, Kome examines a number of women involved in politics and the political process in the six decades following the suffrage movement. While Kome provides little analysis and context, there is a useful appendix of women who served in Parliament and in provincial legislatures. For a similar work that concentrates on the century prior to World War II, see Isabel Bassett, *The Parlour Rebellion: Profiles in the Struggle for Women's Rights* (1975); or Jean Bannerman, *Leading Ladies: Canada, 1639-1967* (1977), which examines leading female politicians, doctors, lawyers, and educators.

Mander, C. *Emily Murphy: Rebel*. Toronto: Simon & Pierre, 1985.
Murphy was the first female magistrate in the British Empire and a principal figure in the 1929 Persons Case. *Rebel* is a brief, popular, and largely uncritical narrative of Murphy's life and career. Emily Murphy still awaits an academic biography.

Newton, Janice. *The Feminist Challenge to the Canadian Left, 1900-1918*. Montreal: McGill-Queen's University Press, 1995.
This work presents some of the women drawn to the political left in the early socialist movement; individuals such as Mary Cotton Wisdom, Ruth Lestor, Bertha Merrill Burns, Sophie Mushkat, and others were attracted to socialist movements in an effort to transform both the public and private spheres. Socialist women ultimately failed to transform the Canadian left because of domestic and maternal duties, and, significantly, because of the opposition of male comrades who were often as sexist as their counterparts in other political parties. Newton argues that in the 1920s — with suffrage won in English Canada — the left no longer felt compelled to champion women's issues and organized feminism suffered as a result.

Rooke, P. and R. Schnell. *No Bleeding Heart: Charlotte Whitton, A Feminist on the Right*. Vancouver: University of British Columbia, 1987.
Charlotte Whitton was an integral member of the Canadian Welfare Council, an outspoken advocate of gender equality, and, when she became mayor of Ottawa in 1951, the first female mayor of a Canadian city. This biography traces Whitton's career, presents insight into her complex personality, and provides a useful corrective to the historiography that often concentrates upon women of the left.

Sangster, Joan. *Dreams of Equality: Women on the Canadian Left, 1920-1950*. Toronto: McClelland and Stewart, 1989.
The political left has traditionally been seen as a promoter of women's issues. Sangster discusses the role of women in the Cooperative Commonwealth Federation (CCF) — the predecessor of the NDP — and the Communist Party of Canada (CPC) from the 1920s to the aftermath of World War II. Beginning with the establishment of the CPC in 1921 and the CCF in 1933, women had "dreams of equality"; however, women continually faced obstacles at home, in the workplace, and, Sangster argues, within both political parties. While both parties actively recruited women, gender issues were never a priority. *Dreams of Equality* includes brief biographies of a number of women who were active in both parties.

Work

Cohen, Marjorie Griffin. *Women's Work, Markets, and Economic Development in Nineteenth-Century Ontario*. Toronto: University of Toronto Press, 1988.
Economists and historians have traditionally emphasised the role of staple production in Canada's emerging economy. Such an approach tends to focus on the importance and role of men in the exploitation, transportation, and sale of such resources. Cohen serves to correct this view of Canadian history. While *Women's Work* recognizes the importance of staples production in the first part of the nineteenth century, Cohen argues that increasingly women entered the market economy — as producers and sellers of dairy produce, vegetables, and textiles, and later as paid workers — as the century progressed. The pattern that emerged in Ontario was, therefore, much different from that in England, where industrialization intensified gendered divisions of labour.

Errington, Elizabeth Jane. *Wives and Mothers, Schoolmistresses and Scullery Maids: Working Women in Upper Canada, 1790-1840*. Montreal: McGill-Queen's University Press, 1995.
Because women did not vote, take part in politics, build canals or work regularly on the shop floor, or engage in other forms of "productive" work, Errington notes that they have, until recently, been largely written out of histories of Upper Canada. Utilizing a definition of work that takes into account both paid and unpaid labour, as well as the expectation, purpose, place, and conditions of work, Errington examines work as a wife and mother, domestic labour in both the farm/artisan household and that of the

"bighouse" of more affluent members of society, and the sometimes intersecting lives of those who ran small businesses. This is a seminal work, marred — as the author admits — only by the cursory attention given to the impact that race, ethnicity, and religion had on working women.

Kinnear, Mary. *In Subordination: Professional Women, 1870-1970.*
Montreal: McGill-Queen's University Press, 1995.
In the century prior to 1970 somewhere between 10 and 20 percent of women in paid positions were in occupations defined as "professional." Kinnear examines women in five professions — university teachers, physicians, lawyers, nurses, and school teachers — in Manitoba over this period. In these professions women faced three principal obstacles: unequal pay with men (although only in teaching was there an explicitly differential pay scale for women), lack of control in the workplace, and the belief that marriage and the professions were not compatible. While women professionals were often in subordination to men, they also were insubordinate in the face of discrimination: for example, in the midst of the Depression, when the Winnipeg school board wished to decrease women teachers' salaries without a corresponding decrease of men's, women formed their own teachers' association, an organization that lasted until 1966. *In Subordination* also includes useful and lengthy appendices. For a treatment of the professions that emphasises men, see R. D. Gidney and W. P. J. Millar, *Professional Gentlemen: The Professions in Nineteenth-Century Ontario* (1994).

Latham, Barbara K. and Roberta J. Pazdro, eds. *Not Just Pin Money: Selected Essays on the History of Women's Work in British Columbia.*
Victoria: Camosun College, 1984.
The volume emerged out of the Women's History in British Columbia Conference held at Camosun College in 1984. It reflects the eclectic nature of conferences: essays range from the journalistic to the academic, from the "great women" tradition to material feminist and women-centred approaches. The common theme is women's work, in both its paid and unpaid forms; several essays examine the interaction between women's work and issues of ethnicity and class.

Luxton, Meg. *More than a Labour of Love: Three Generations of Women's Work in the Home.* Toronto: Women's Press, 1980.
This work examines three generations of domestic work in Flin Flon,

Manitoba, from the 1920s to the 1970s. Flin Flon is, in many ways, a frontier and "masculine" town, and there were few opportunities for women to obtain paid employment outside of the home. Luxton notes the changes in domestic work over these three generations of women and argues for the economic importance of unpaid, domestic work.

Pierson, Ruth Roach. *"They're Still Women After All": The Second World War and Canadian Womanhood.* Toronto: McClelland and Stewart, 1986.
Traditional interpretations have emphasised the opportunities in work and status that World War II provided women. In contrast, Pierson argues that the war provided little real opportunity for women to advance in influence. This examination of government attitudes and actions notes that government job training programs between 1937 and 1947 emphasised domestic work and banned women from occupations such as logging or mining. Only with the mobilization of men in 1941 did the government encourage women — single women first, then married women without children — to move into "men's" jobs. Women who entered the military were paid less than male counterparts, were not protected from venereal disease as effectively, and tended to occupy traditional female jobs.

Tippett, Maria. *Emily Carr.* Toronto: Oxford University Press, 1979.
A comprehensive and well-researched work, this volume provides enormous insight into one of Canada's greatest painters. Tippett provides a careful account of Carr's early life in Victoria; her close, but troubled, relationship with her father; her years of study in San Francisco, England, and France; and the intellectual and cultural forces that shaped Carr's life and her development as an artist. Although the focus is upon Carr as artist, Tippett also draws upon Carr's literary efforts and a wide range of unpublished material. Among numerous other studies, see Doris Shadbolt, *The Art of Emily Carr* (1979) for an excellent analysis of Carr's development as an artist.

Contemporary Women's Movement

Adamson, Nancy, Linda Briskin, and Margaret McPhail. *Feminist Organizing for Change: The Contemporary Women's Movement in Canada.* Toronto: Oxford University Press, 1988.
An excellent survey text, *Feminist Organizing for Change* provides a history of the first and second waves of the Canadian feminist movement,

examines contemporary issues from a socialist-feminist perspective, and provides an account of the reasons why contemporary feminists have failed to transform society in fundamental structural ways. The authors also discuss prescriptions for future change. For an eclectic anthology that examines topics such as Native, immigrant, and pioneer women, as well as assorted subjects involving family, law, medicine, and the media, see Sandra Burt, Lorraine Code, and Linsay Dorney, eds., *Changing Patterns: Women in Canada* (1988; 2nd ed., 1993).

Backhouse, C. and D. Flaherty, eds. *Challenging Times: The Women's Movement in Canada and the United States.* Montreal: McGill-Queen's University Press, 1992.
Resulting from a conference held at the University of Western Ontario in 1989, this collection is especially valuable in its exploration of the formative influences of the women's movement in Canada and the United States, and, in particular, feminists in Quebec. In addition, there are essays on women's studies projects, race, violence, economic issues, and reproductive rights.

Brodie, Janine, Shelley A. M. Gavigan, and Jane Jenson. *The Politics of Abortion.* Toronto: Oxford University Press, 1992.
Emerging out of a conference devoted to *Morgentaler v. The Queen* (1988) held at Harvard University in 1988, this volume focuses upon the historical and changing nature of the abortion debate. *The Politics of Abortion* has three essential parts: Jenson provides some historical context to the debate from the 1960s onward, particularly in light of the contemporary women's movement; Brodie examines some parliamentary debates on abortion and the introduction of Bill C-43, a Mulroney government compromise that was defeated in the Senate in 1991; and Gavigan provides an analysis of the legal dimension of this issue.

Kinnear, Mary. *Margaret McWilliams: An Interwar Feminist.* Montreal: McGill-Queen's University Press, 1991.
Margaret Stovel was born in 1875, became the first woman to graduate in political economy from the University of Toronto, had careers as a journalist, author, and teacher, and eventually became a four-term alderman for Winnipeg. Kinnear investigates the intellectual and religious motivations of McWilliams — who married Roland McWilliams, who became lieutenant-governor of Manitoba in 1940 — and explores the gradual development of her feminist beliefs.

Vickers, Jill, Pauline Rankin, and Christine Appelle. *Politics as if Women Mattered: A Political Analysis of the National Action Committee on the Status of Women.* Toronto: University of Toronto Press, 1993.
Established in 1971 on the heels of a Royal Commission, the National Action Committee of the Status of Women (NAC) has become a significant voice for women's issues. This theoretically sophisticated book describes the origins and evolution of NAC, its internal politics, and its place within the political and cultural milieu.

Childhood and Family History

Arnup, Katherine. *Education for Motherhood: Advice for Mothers in Twentieth-Century Canada.* Toronto: University of Toronto Press, 1994.
This useful work examines the prescriptive literature available to mothers (not parents) by the government, medical profession, and mass media in the first six decades of the twentieth century. Beginning with the concern over child mortality in the years of the century, Arnup demonstrates the increasing influence of the medical community over the mother's role, with seemingly little resistance from the latter. Significant change in the child-rearing advice occurred over this period: early theories of "habit training" were replaced by the post-World War II child-centreed philosophy of Dr. Benjamin Spock that emphasised the psychological well-being of the young. Finally, Arnup attempts to illustrate the influence that prescriptive literature had on mothers' daily lives.

Arnup, Katherine, Andrée Lévesque, and Ruth Roach Pierson, with the assistance of Margaret Brennan, eds. *Delivering Motherhood: Maternal Ideologies and Practices in the 19th and 20th Centuries.* London: Routledge, 1990.
An important contribution to women's history and the social history of medicine, *Delivering Motherhood* contains 14 articles that examine concepts of motherhood, largely focusing upon childbirth. Jane Lewis provides an excellent historiographic essay of the international literature on childbirth; subsequent articles range regionally from British Columbia to Newfoundland, and examine topics such as the medicalization of childbirth, midwifery, birth control and abortion, single mothers, and the role of conservative beliefs and male agendas in shaping the ideology and practices of motherhood.

Bradbury, Bettina. *Working Families: Age, Gender and Daily Survival in Industrializing Montreal*. Toronto: McClelland and Stewart, 1993.
Integrating ethnicity, gender, class, and age into the relatively recent study of Canadian families, this brilliant work examines two working-class wards in late nineteenth-century Montreal. Dedicating to explicating how "working class men and women fed, clothed and sheltered themselves," Bradbury employs a gendered approach to ideas of labour and home. Utilizing a empirical and materialist methodology, this work examines the "family economy" as a means of providing sustenance and support for working families; such a term, however, does not imply equality between family members, and within each family unit gender and generational expectations and legal rights existed, often amidst great conflict.

Bradbury, Bettina, ed. *Canadian Family History: Selected Readings*. Toronto: Copp Clark, 1992.
Composed of 17 essays ranging chronologically from initial contact to the 1980s, this volume concentrates on the themes of marriage and family formation, work of family members, and links between families and the economy, the legal system, and the state. Bradbury has chosen articles that examine Native and fur trade families, urban and rural environments, and cover most periods of the family life cycle.

Campbell, D. and D. Neice. *Ties That Bind: Structure and Marriage in Nova Scotia*. Port Credit, ON: The Scribblers' Press, 1979.
Using data from 3,000 marriage licenses, *Ties That Bind* examines marriage patterns of Nova Scotians between 1947 and 1966. The authors discuss a variety of themes, including age of marriage, ethnicity, religion, occupational categories, and gender patterns.

Comacchio, C. *"Nations are Built of Babies": Saving Ontario's Mothers and Children, 1900-1940*. Montreal: McGill-Queen's University Press, 1993.
Using Ontario as a case study, Comacchio examines the changing nature of child and mother care in the face of the development of industrial capitalism. Prior to World War I such care was most often undertaken by private, mostly female, reform-minded efforts; thereafter, the state and a male-dominated medical profession assumed more influential roles.

Luxton, Meg and Harriet Rosenberg. *Through the Kitchen Window: The Politics of Home and Family*. Toronto: Garamond Press, 1986.

This work seeks to shatter several myths about women in the home: that a women's place is in the home, that women at home do not work, that the home is a "haven in a heartless" world, and that women have considerable power and influence in the home. The separately written articles examine homemakers in Flin Flon, wives of union leaders, and provide a feminist analysis of the work environment of the home.

McKenna, Katherine M. J. *A Life of Propriety: Anne Murray Powell and Her Family, 1755-1849.* Montreal: McGill-Queen's University Press, 1994.
Katherine McKenna argues that a feminist biography must pursue different questions than its traditional counterparts. *A Life of Propriety* presents a linear narrative of Anne Murray Powell's childhood in England, early years in Boston, marriage to William Powell, and subsequent travels to England and in the North American colonies, before finally settling in York, Upper Canada. In addition, McKenna explores more innovative questions: in particular, she examines the gender roles and identities which William, Anne, and their child inhabited, and explores the Powells' marriage and Anne's relationship to her male and female children.

Morton, Suzanne. *Ideal Surroundings: Domestic Life in a Working-Class Suburb in the 1920s.* Toronto: University of Toronto Press, 1995.
Following the Halifax explosion in 1917, the working-class community of Richmond Heights — a name selected by residents in the 1920s — was rebuilt, a pioneering effort in the history of Canadian urban planning. Using a wide variety of primary sources and informed by feminist theory, Morton examines the interaction of class, gender, and age in this newly constructed community, with emphasis upon the home and family rather than the workplace. Organized along a reversed life cycle that begins with the elderly and ends with single young woman, *Ideal Surroundings* explores the social environment of Richmond Heights, the construction of gender ideals among both young and old, notions of respectability and commercial culture, and the working-class family economy.

Parr, Joy, ed. *Childhood and Family in Canadian History.* Toronto: McClelland and Stewart, 1982.
Recognizing that childhood and family are historical, as well as biological, constructs, this collection is an early and important contribution. Collectively, the authors examine childhood and family with as broad a compass as possible: the private sphere is not separate from the public,

and political, social, and economic realities are entwined with children's lives and their experience in families. Specific articles include such topics as eighteenth-century New France, the fur trade era, urban and rural society in the nineteenth and early twentieth centuries, and "progressive" child-care workers in the interwar period.

Rooke, Patricia and R. L. Schnell, eds. *Studies in Childhood History: A Canadian Perspective.* Calgary: Detselig Enterprises Limited, 1982.
A collection of eight essays, this volume has two principal sections: the first presents more theoretical perspectives on utilitarianism, the pragmatic and progressive ideas of John Dewey, and the American psychologists Homer Lane and J. B. Watson, all influences emerging from beyond Canada; the second comprises a series of case studies.

Smandych, Russell, Gordon Dodds, and Alvin Esau, eds. *Dimensions of Childhood: Essays on the History of Children and Youth in Canada.* Winnipeg: Legal Research Institute, University of Manitoba, 1991.
The result of a conference held at the University of Manitoba, these essays illustrate some recent themes in the writing of the history of childhood in Canada. Monocausal explanations are rejected, children are seen as active participants in shaping society, and increased attention is given to children as economic assets, physical and sexual abuse, non-delinquent children, feminist approaches, and children outside Ontario.

Sutherland, Neil. *Children in English-Canadian Society.* Toronto: University of Toronto Press, 1976.
An important contribution to Canadian history, *Children in English-Canadian Society* is the first work dedicated to understanding the rise of a child-welfare movement during the industrialization of Canada. During this period of social change and upheaval, the role of childhood became an important issue for social reformers. Sutherland provides a crisp and entertaining study of the efforts of reformers to change the role of schools, to provide public health programs, and to encourage the state to take responsibility for child welfare. His book contains analyses of such diverse topics as kindergarten, domestic science, pasteurization of milk, and factory legislation.

Ward, W. Peter. *Birth Weight and Economic Growth: Women's Living Standards in the Industrializing West.* Chicago: University of Chicago Press, 1993.

Relying on data for Edinburgh (1847-1920), Vienna (1865-1930), Dublin (1869-1930), Boston (1872-1900), and Montreal (1851-1904), Ward presents a series of case studies which analyse the relationship between a mother's economic well-being and the birth weight of her children. Significantly, Ward finds that the children of white working women in Montreal and Boston had higher mean birth weights than their counterparts in Europe, and were less affected by adverse economic swings.

_____. *Courtship, Love, and Marriage in Nineteenth-Century English Canada.* Montreal: McGill-Queen's University Press, 1990.
In a pioneering but controversial contribution, Ward explores the public and private worlds of romance and marriage in eastern English Canada between 1780 and 1914. Ward argues that during this period courtship underwent a transformation from an activity in which the church, family, and society all had considerable influence to one, by the latter part of the nineteenth century, in which individuals had considerably more autonomy.

Ethnic and Immigration History

Because of the emphasis placed upon multiculturalism in Canada, Canadian historians have written a number of excellent works in the field of ethnic history. These works have focused primarily upon the immigrant community or the reception the immigrants received from the Anglo-Protestant host community. The two different perspectives have led to an interesting dynamic. Those studies focusing upon the immigrant groups often emphasise the agency of immigrants and their ability to preserve and foster their ethnic identity. Those studies focusing upon the reception given to immigrants have critically identified a high level of racism and nativism in Canada and explored the persecution and assimilation pressures brought to bare upon the immigrants. Few scholars have resolved the inconsistency of a society persecuting ethnic minorities yet fostering the maintenance of ethnic identities.

General Works

Avery, Donald. *Reluctant Host: Canadian Responses to Immigrant Workers, 1896-1994.* Toronto: McClelland and Stewart, 1995.
This survey of Canadian immigration policy is divided into two parts. Part one examines the period to 1956 when Europeans dominated the immigration stream. Part two covers the period since 1956 as Caribbean, Asian, and African immigrants entered Canada in greater numbers. Avery argues that Canadian immigration policy reflects Canadian attitudes towards race, class, and economic self-interest. He notes, moreover, that the immigration policy has been shaped by pressure group politics from capitalists and employers, labour groups, and ethnic communities.

Burnet, Jean R. and Howard Palmer. *Coming Canadians: An Introduction to Canada's Peoples.* Toronto: McClelland and Stewart, 1988.
The general editors of the Generations Series, Burnet and Palmer, offer this synthesis of ethnic history and the ethnic experience in Canada as a general introduction to the series. Following two useful introductory essays, the book contains broad thematic chapters blending ethnic history into both national and regional historiography. The book covers the

themes of economy, family, education, religion, politics, organizations, and the media. Throughout, Burnet and Palmer emphasise two themes: the creation of a pluralist society, and the unique individual experiences of different ethnic groups.

Broadfoot, Barry. *The Immigrant Years: From Europe to Canada, 1945-1967.* Vancouver: Douglas and McIntyre, 1986.
Based upon interviews conducted by Broadfoot and lacking references, *The Immigrant Years* is limited for research purposes. Broadfoot's introductions do contextualize the stories somewhat, and the book is a useful introduction to the powerful emotions produced by the migration experience.

Dirks, Gerald E. *Canada's Refugee Policy: Indifference or Opportunism?* Montreal: McGill-Queen's University Press, 1978.
Gerald Dirks writes an extremely detailed and scholarly account of Canadian policy toward refugees between 1930 and 1970. Dirks argues that Canadian policy toward refugees has always been guided by popular racist and nativist sentiment, bureaucratic pettiness, and economic self-interest. Canada, for example, responded to nativism and anti-Semitism in the 1930s, by blocking the entry of German Jews. Similarly, Canada refused to sign the United Nations 1951 convention on refugees until 1969 over fears Canada would have a moral obligation to accept refugees. Political squabbles between the various government departments prevented Canada from formulating an effective response toward displaced persons following World War II. Only after the Suez and Hungarian Crisis of 1956, as Canada sought to establish an international reputation for humanitarian aid, did the Canadian government develop a more accepting policy toward refugees.

Hawkins, Freda. *Critical Years in Immigration: Canada and Australia Compared.* Montreal: McGill-Queen's University Press, 1989.
Freda Hawkins looks at recent immigration policies in Canada and Australia and discusses the parallel transition that has led both countries to abandon racist immigration strategies. She argues that the desire to remain British (hence white) in both Canada and Australia produced the racist immigration policies of the early twentieth century. Under the guidance of sensitive and talented bureaucrats after 1970, however, both countries adopted more inclusive immigration policies. The study is well documented although its analytical framework is weak.

Knowles, Valerie. *Strangers at Our Gates: Canadian Immigration Policy, 1540-1990*. Toronto: Dundurn Press, 1992.
This popular history of Canadian immigration by journalist Valerie Knowles catalogues over four centuries of Canadian immigration policy. Containing some useful references and void of major factual errors, *Strangers at Our Gates* is a useful introduction to the topic for the novice reader.

O'Gallagher, Marianna. *Grosse Ile: Gateway to Canada, 1832-1937*. Quebec: Carraig Books, 1984.
An eclectic narrative about the quarantine station on an island in the St. Lawrence, the book provides a sympathetic account of the immigrant experience — particularly the Irish immigrant experience — at Grosse Ile and joins this account with an administrative history of the facility.

Palmer, Howard and Tamara Palmer, eds. *People of Alberta: Portraits of Cultural Diversity*. Saskatoon: Western Producer Prairie Books, 1985.
Between 1885 and 1921, immigrants streamed into Alberta and a new society was created. In this collection of essays, the writers bring life to the various ethnic groups that exist in Alberta. The essays vary from surveys of the plethora of scholarly work on certain ethnic communities to the pioneering examinations of some less frequently considered ethnic communities.

Troper, Harold Martin. *Only Farmers Need Apply: Official Canadian Government Encouragement of Immigration from the United States, 1896-1911*. Toronto: Griffin House, 1972.
The classic study of the immigration policy during the Laurier years, *Only Farmers Need Apply* is recommended reading for students interested in western Canadian settlement and Canadian immigration policy generally. Troper investigates the policy initiatives of Clifford Sifton and Frank Oliver, western Canadian politicians in charge of immigration during this period, and argues that their emphasis upon attracting prairie farmers and discouraging other immigrants was discriminatory and racist. Troper's work has been challenged from two different perspectives. D. J. Hall's two volume biography *Clifford Sifton* (1981,1985) offers a more sympathetic approach to Sifton's initiatives; and in a series of articles — the most important of which is printed in R. D. Francis and H. Palmer, eds., *The Prairie West* (1992) — economist Ken Norrie suggests that the policy initiatives had little effect upon the immigration boom of the

period. For an anecdotal study of immigration, see Pierre Berton, *The Promised Land: Settling the West, 1896-1914* (1984).

Tulchinsky, Gerald. *Immigration in Canada: Historical Perspectives.* Toronto: Copp Clark, 1994.
This collection of essays explores several main themes: government policy regarding immigration from the colonial period onward; the practical considerations and prejudices of government policy; patterns of racial and religious exclusion; the response of immigrants to their own experience; and notions of gender and class and the immigrant experience. There is a good select bibliography.

Whitaker, Reg. *Double Standard: The Secret History of Canadian Immigration.* Toronto: Lester & Orpen Dennys, 1987.
Utilizing previously unavailable government sources, Whitaker examines post-World War II immigration policy. He argues that Cold War hysteria and concern for security — principally expressed through the RCMP and government officials — helped frame discriminatory immigration practices. In the immediate post-war era, for example, efforts were made to limit numbers from Eastern Europe because of the fear of Communist infiltrators; ironically, Nazi sympathizers who came to Canada were not viewed with the same suspicion.

Nativism, Racism, and Anti-Semitism

Abella, Irving and Harold Troper. *None Is Too Many: Canada and the Jews of Europe, 1933-1948.* Toronto: Lester & Orpen Dennys, 1982.
This thoroughly researched book describes one of the numerous racist policy decisions which can be found in Canadian history. Abella and Troper examine Canada's failure to accept Jewish refugees fleeing Hitler's Germany. The authors note the general Canadian attitudes of nativism during this period, but they carefully discuss the indifference and, more important, the active hostility toward Jews in the highest ranks of Canadian government officials. Anti-Semitism rather than any generalized anti-immigration sentiment, they conclude, prevented Jews from coming to Canada.

Bassler, Gerhard P. *Sanctuary Denied: Refugees from the Third Reich and Newfoundland Immigration Policy, 1906-1949.* St. John's: Institute for Social and Economic Research, Memorial University, 1992.

Although Newfoundland included refugees as an acceptable category of immigrant in 1906, fewer than 25 refugees were admitted to Newfoundland prior to its entry into Canada in 1949. Working with a vast array of archival sources, Bassler argues that Newfoundlanders, a relatively isolated, homogenous ethnic community ruled by a small merchant clique, turned their backs on all non-British immigration. "Come-from-aways" were undesirable and feared intruders, and Newfoundland's immigration record reflected this attitude. Newfoundland, consequently, turned its back on Jewish refugees from Hitler's Germany.

Davies, Alan, ed. *Anti-Semitism in Canada: History and Interpretation.* Waterloo: Wilfrid Laurier University Press, 1992.
This good collection of articles examines the roots of anti-Semitism in Canada. The authors are from a number of academic disciplines, and their work demonstrates that anti-Semitism emerged from inter-group conflict, although there is some recognition that anti-Semitism is simply irrational and exists even in the absence of Jews.

Delisle, Esther. *The Traitor and the Jew: Anti-Semitism and the Delirium of Extreme Right-Wing Nationalism in French Canada from 1929-1939.* Toronto: Robert Davies Publishing, 1993.
Abbé Lionel Groulx, who died in 1967, is still seen as one of the intellectual forerunners of the sovereigntist movement. Enormously controversial, *The Traitor and the Jew* argues that Groulx's writings in journals, newspapers, and histories, displayed a strident anti-semitism. As a historian — or rather, as Delisle argues, as a myth-maker — Groulx argues that the majority of francophones descended in an unadulterated line from original French colonists. Delisle argues that Groulx interwove a racial cosmogony with biblical overtones in order to illustrate that French Canada was indeed the chosen race. Further, she argues that Groulx actively propagated the notion that any deviation from the purity of the race, either in the form of the Traitor or the Jew, was to be condemned. This work has been criticised for its use of source material and its controversial conclusions; extraordinarily rare for a former Ph.D. dissertation, this volume has spent time on several best-seller lists.

Hillmer, Norman, Bohdan Kordan, and Lubomyr Luciuk, eds. *On Guard for Thee: War, Ethnicity and the Canadian State, 1939-1945.* Ottawa: Committee for the History of the Second World War, 1988.

The crucible of war inflamed Canadian nativist and racist popular attitudes and influenced Canadian policy toward ethnic minorities. The ten essays and three commentaries in this volume cover the spectrum of ethnic groups and their relationship with the Canadian government: Robert Bothwell examines refugee atomic scientists, Bruno Ramirez looks at Italian-Canadians, Donald Avery deals with attitudes toward European refugees generally, and — in a controversial essay — J. L. Granatstein and Greg Johnson argue that the treatment of Japanese-Canadians during the war was justified in the context of the wartime hysteria and the government's inability to properly assess the Japanese threat in the Pacific.

McKague, Ormond, ed. *Racism in Canada.* Saskatoon: Fifth House, 1991.
The eighteen previously published essays in this anthology are collected in five sections, only one of which is historical. The sections deal with personal experiences, historical investigation of particular racist responses, structural racism, oppression in combination, and a glance at the future. The book is most useful as an introduction to the current racial problems in Canada, but historians will find useful the essays by Bruce Sheppard on Black migration to the Canadian prairies, and Gillian Creese on Chinese-Canadian agency in response to west coast racism.

Roberts, Barbara. *Whence They Came: Deportation from Canada, 1900-1935.* Ottawa: University of Ottawa Press, 1988.
Roberts argues Canada used deportation, or at least the threat of deportation, to save the state from assuming responsibility for the unemployed, the poor, and the disabled, and to control the activities of socially and politically undesirable groups in Canada. In other words, the Canadian government used deportation to maintain social and economic control. Drawing upon extensive archival records, Roberts points to several examples where evidence was fabricated and legal principles flouted in the deportation process.

Robin, Martin. *Shades of Right: Nativist and Fascist Politics in Canada, 1920-1940.* Toronto: University of Toronto Press, 1992.
Political scientist Martin Robin debunks Canadian mythologies regarding a tolerant, multicultural society in this thorough study of racism in Canada between the two world wars. Robin argues that the narrow Catholic nationalism of Quebec, the cultural imperialism of English Canada, and

economic fears of the public inspired and shaped numerous fascist and racist organizations in Canada. Many of these groups entered and prospered in the political sphere and others influenced the policies of the King and Bennett governments. This book provides useful context for more specific studies such as Irving Abella and Harold Troper, *None Is Too Many* (1982), and Lita-Rose Betcherman, *The Swastika and the Maple Leaf: Fascist Movements in Canada in the Thirties* (1975).

Satzewich, Vic. *Racism and the Incorporation of Foreign Labour: Farm Labour Migration to Canada since 1945*. London: Routledge, Chapman & Hall, 1991.

Sociologist Vic Satzewich examines Canada's policies toward migrant labour in the labour intensive fruit and vegetable farms of southern Ontario. He argues that racism guided Canadian policy toward the use of immigrant labour. British and other European immigrants displaced by World War II were brought to Canada to work on the farms but allowed to move into other occupational fields. Non-european immigrants, especially American and Caribbean Black labourers, entered as indentured servants and were required to leave following the completion of their labour. Using documents from the Canadian immigration department, Satzewich concludes Canadian immigration policy was framed along racist lines.

Swyripa, Frances and John Herd Thompson, eds. *Loyalties in Conflict: Ukrainians in Canada During the Great War*. Edmonton: Canadian Institute of Ukrainian Studies, 1983.

A large number of historians have examined the treatment of Japanese-Canadians during World War II, but surprisingly little attention has been given to other ethnic groups classified as enemy aliens. This collection, focusing on the Ukrainian-Canadians, offers some insight into the World War I period. Essays discuss the Canada's treatment of Ukrainian-Canadians during the war (some were interned as enemy aliens), and the general nativist attitudes of anglo-Canadians during the war.

The Asian Experience

Adachi, Ken. *The Enemy That Never Was: Canada and the Japanese Canadians*. Toronto: McClelland and Stewart, 1976.

Adachi argues that the evacuation of Japanese-Canadians in 1942 was the culmination of a series of racist responses from white British Columbians.

Adachi draws a distinction between the *Issei* — the first generation — and the *Nissei* — second generation — regarding their response to Canadian policies and their efforts to accept and adapt to the Canadian community. Although the Canadian government is blamed for accommodating the racist policies of British Columbians, Adachi also found problems in the *Nissei* willingness to tolerate racist policies.

Anderson, Kay. *Vancouver's Chinatown: Racial Discourse in Canada, 1875-1980*. Montreal: McGill-Queen's University Press, 1991.
This work argues that Vancouver's Chinatown was not primarily a creation by Chinese immigrants, but was constructed in both real and imagined terms by the dominant Anglo-Canadian society. Drawing upon the theoretical work of Gramsci, Foucault, and Edward Said, *Vancouver's Chinatown* argues that the Chinese were created as the Other, an outsider who was literally and figuratively excluded from the boundaries of the dominant culture. This process helped to create and reinforce the identity and self-image of the Anglo-Canadian community, and also served to legitimize racist attitudes and actions. Anderson also examines racial discourse for over a century and notes how perceptions of Chinatown changed from that of a "celestial cesspool" to that of an "ethnic neighbourhood" with the advent and greater acceptance of official multiculturalism in the 1960s. Even after a century, the argument goes, Chinatown is still regarded as distinct and defined from without, even though it is now presented in more benign terms. *Vancouver's Chinatown* is an influential work but has been criticised for the lack of agency it accords Chinese-Canadians.

Buchignani, Norman and Doreen Indra, with Ram Srivastava. *Continuous Journey: A Social History of South Asians in Canada*. Toronto: McClelland and Stewart, 1985.
A volume in the "Generations: A History of Canada's Peoples" series, *Continuous Journey* is the best overview of the experiences of South Asians such as the Sikh, Pakistani, and Thai people. It presents the information in an approachable framework, and readers will become aware of both the agency of the immigrant communities as they try to protect their cultural heritage and the nativist responses in Canada.

Chadney, James G. *The Sikhs of Vancouver*. New York: AMS Press, 1984.
Anthropologist James Chadney presents a record of his field work in

Vancouver during 1972 and 1973, and concludes that "resource competition" is the primary variable creating and maintaining ethnic identity amongst Vancouver Sikhs. Chadney discusses the Sikh role in the lumber industry and real estate but provides little evidence to substantiate his findings.

Dawson, J. Brian. *Moon Cakes in Gold Mountain: From China to the Canadian Plains.* Calgary: Detselig, 1991.
Chinese labourers were amongst the first immigrants to the Canadian prairies during the agrarian settlement era and continue to be an important constituency of the prairie population today. Brian Dawson provides a strong factual catalogue of their experiences in Alberta based upon numerous interviews and archival sources. Although interpretation is not the strength of this book, it does contribute to some interesting historical debates about the nature of Chinese immigration. Dawson, for example, argues that early Chinese immigrants to the prairies were "sojourners" rather than settlers. He also suggests that the lack of communication between the Chinese community and other elements of the society led to mutual suspicion and misunderstanding.

Jensen, Joan M. *Passage from India: Asian Immigrants in North America.* New Haven, CT: Yale University Press, 1988.
Joan Jensen's study is one of the useful works on Asian immigration that transcends the United States-Canadian boundary and explores the immigrant experience in a North American context. She focuses on the racist and nativist attitudes of west coast society. Resentment and fear of economic competition amongst west coast workers, she argues, resulted in relatively similar responses in both the United States and Canada. The exclusionary policies implemented after the 1907 race riots, for example, required significant cooperation between Canadian, American, and British authorities. Jensen also demonstrates that growing Indian nationalism and the perceived threat this nationalism posed to the British Empire made it easier for Canadian and American officials to respond to popular racist pressure.

Johnston, Hugh. *The Voyage of the Komagata Maru: The Sikh Challenge to Canada's Colour Bar.* Toronto: Oxford University Press, 1979; rpt., Vancouver: University of British Columbia Press, 1989.
Based upon archival research in Canada and India, Johnston has written the most thorough account available of the Komagata Maru incident. In

1914 almost 400 Sikhs, who also happened to be British citizens, left India aboard the Komagata Maru for British Columbia; they were met with hostility and resistence, and, unable to disembark, remained in the Vancouver harbour for more than two months before finally returning to India. In India the failed immigrants were set upon by troops and 18 were killed. Johnston effectively illustrates the widespread opposition to Indian immigration, the political and legal environment that allowed discriminatory laws and actions, and links the Canadian and Indian phases of the trip.

Li, Peter S. *Chinese in Canada*. Toronto: Oxford University Press, 1988. Sociologist Peter Li argues that the Chinese in Canada, plagued by continued racism, are still foreigners. He argues that the Chinese Canadian community is defined by alienation. Li's work, based primarily on secondary sources, adds little new insight to the field.

Roy, Patricia E. *A White Man's Province: British Columbian Politicians and Chinese and Japanese Immigrants, 1858-1914*. Vancouver: University of British Columbia Press, 1989.
This survey of Chinese and Japanese immigration from the Fraser River gold rush to World War I argues that while Chinese workers were initially extended a measure of tolerance in the 1850s, this shifted to outright hostility as labour shortages were replaced by economic competition. Labour and capital were, therefore, divided over Asian immigration, and some of the strongest agitation for anti-Asian legislation emerged from unions and workers. While Roy emphasises economic factors more so than Peter Ward, she does note that racial intolerance is more complex than simple economics: the Chinese custom of sojourning and racial stereotypes over public health and morality all contributed, for example, to anti-Asian legislation and sordid events such as the 1907 Vancouver riot.

Roy, Patricia E., J. L. Granatstein, Masako Iinio, and Hiroko Takamura. *Mutual Hostages: Canadians and Japanese During the Second World War*. Toronto: University of Toronto Press, 1990.
A collaborative effort by Canadian and Japanese historians, this book aims to present a balanced approach to this difficult topic. The authors stress Canada's limited knowledge about Japanese Canadians and the role of public opinion during the war in an effort to explain the government's willingness to relocate Japanese Canadians. Although they acknowledge

the role of racism in the evacuation, the authors tend to absolve the government of racist motives. For a contrary view, see the response by Reg Whitaker in the *Canadian Historical Review* (1991).

Sunahara, Ann Gomer. *The Politics of Racism: The Uprooting of Japanese Canadians During the Second World War.* Toronto: Lorimer, 1981.

Ann Sunahara passionately argues that the internment of Japanese Canadians during World War II was the direct result of British Columbian racism. Fears of Japanese-Canadian aggression during World War II were unfounded, as all of the information available to the Canadian government concluded. The war was merely a catalyst for action amongst British Columbian racists. The federal government, moreover, used the war as an excuse to solve what it perceived as the Japanese "problem."

Takata, Toyo. *Nikkei Legacy: the Story of Japanese Canadians From Settlement to Today.* Toronto: NC Press, 1983.

A popular illustrated history of Japanese-Canadians, this book emphasises the growth of the community, its struggle for acceptance prior to World War II, and the devastating experiences of the internment camps. *Nikkei Legacy* contains little information on the growth and successes of the Japanese Canadian community since 1950.

Thompson, Richard H. *Toronto's Chinatown: The Changing Social Organization of an Ethnic Community.* New York: AMS Press, 1989.

Most studies of Asian immigration to Canada focus on the response of the Canadian majority. In this book, Richard Thompson instead examines the effect of immigration on the Chinese community in Toronto, concluding that increased class conflict occurred. In four useful chapters he reviews the changing nature of Canadian immigration policy and the immigrants who were permitted to enter the country. While the first wave of immigrants consisted primarily of male labourers, the liberalization of Canadian immigration policies in 1947 and 1967 and subsequent arrival of Hong Kong Chinese immigrants led to an increase in the number of women and children, and to increased variation in occupational status, class, and background within the Chinese-Canadian community in Toronto. Thompson then examines the social and economic dynamics within the newly heterogenous community as different elites competed for power and authority.

Ward, W. Peter. *White Canada Forever: Popular Attitudes and Public Policy Toward Orientals in British Columbia*. Montreal: McGill-Queen's University Press, 1978; 2nd ed., 1991.
The nativism directed toward Asian immigrants to British Columbia has been well documented. This study of anti-Oriental attitudes — with a tangential chapter that explores the Komagata Maru incident in 1914 — examines such attitudes over almost a century. Ward downplays arguments that emphasise that economic strains were central to the emergence of racist attitudes. Instead, drawing upon the theoretical work of Neil Smelzer and H. Hoetink, Ward maintains that in a pluralistic or segmented society, there exists inherent racial tension. The emphasis, therefore, is on psychological tensions as the principal factor in creating racial animosity. "The main objection to the Chinese," Ward quotes a west coast senator as saying, "is that they are not of our race and cannot become a part of ourselves." Ward provides a clearly written overview of the dominant society's anti-Asian stereotypes, and of some of the racist legislation and actions that resulted.

The East European Experience

Balan, Jars. *Salt and Braided Bread: Ukrainian Life in Canada*. Toronto: Oxford University Press, 1984.
A lucid, illustrated, and analytical history of the Ukrainian Canadian community based primarily upon secondary literature, *Salt and Braided Bread* is an excellent introduction for students unfamiliar with the topic. After a good historical overview of the Ukrainian immigration experience, Balan breaks his analysis into chapters on the distinctive regional experiences of Ukrainian Canadians.

Danys, Milda. *Lithuanian Immigration to Canada After the Second World War*. Toronto: Multicultural History Society of Ontario, 1986.
Based on government files and interviews, this book is a useful contribution to the literature on post-1945 immigration and specifically Canadian attitudes toward displaced persons. Danys concludes that Canadian immigration policy after the Second World War was neither altruistic nor humanitarian. She demonstrates that Canada's buoyant economy and a continued shortage of low-skilled labour underlay the government's willingness to accept the refugees. Lithuanian migrants, eager to leave the displaced persons camps of Europe, often hid skills and education from the Canadian officials in order to gain acceptance. The

Lithuanians completed their indentures and then incorporated themselves into the mainstream fabric of Canadian society, often resuming earlier career directions.

Friesen, John W. and Michael Veregin. *The Community Doukhobors: A People in Transition.* Ottawa: Borealis, 1989.
This book, along with works such as George Woodcock and Ivan Avakumovic, *The Doukhobors* (1977) and Carl Tracie, *"Toil and Peaceful Life"* (1996), provides an enlightening study of acculturation within one of Canada's most distinctive ethnic communities. The Doukhobors, a pacifist and communal Russian people, fled persecution in Europe to build a free community in Canada. Based upon archival evidence and extensive interviews, Friesen and Veregin provide readers with considerable insights into Doukhobor values and beliefs before looking at two specific Doukhobor settlements in southern Alberta. The authors then analyse Doukhobor efforts to protect their culture from assimilation and to adapt their culture to mainstream prairie society.

Janzen, William. *Limits on Liberty: The Experience of Mennonite, Hutterite, and Doukhobor Communities in Canada.* Toronto: University of Toronto Press, 1990.
All three of these groups fled religious persecution and came to Canada with assurances that their religious beliefs would be respected. All three groups incorporated aspects of communal land holding arrangements, pacifism, and autonomous education systems into their religious culture. Despite the Canadian government's assurances, however, these aspects of their culture came under increasing attack following their immigration to Canada. In this thoroughly researched book, Janzen analyses the changing attitudes of the Canadian government, the limits placed upon each group's cultural autonomy, and the responses of different Mennonite, Hutterite, and Doukhobor communities to the changing policies.

Jeletzky, T. F., ed. *Russian Canadians, Their Past and Present.* Ottawa: Borealis, 1983.
One of the few sources for information on Russians in Canada, outside of the material on the Doukhobors, this collection is an attempt to provide readers with an overview of the Russian immigrant experience. The papers were compiled specifically for publication and thus present a relatively unified examination.

Loewen, Roy. *Family, Church, and Market: A Mennonite Community in the Old and New Worlds*. Toronto: University of Toronto Press, 1993.
Royden Loewen is interested in the relationship between settlement, markets, and culture. His case study examines the Kleine Gemeinde, a small Mennonite group with settlements in Russia, Canada, and the United States. Using statistical, archival, and anecdotal evidence, Loewen constructs a detailed portrait of rural and Mennonite life with a sensitivity for both the family and women. Loewen not only offers readers sophisticated analysis of Mennonite faith and its emphasis upon the family but also explores Mennonite adaptations to environmental conditions and their responses to commercialization of agriculture. He argues that the cultural backdrop of Mennonite life, faith and family, explains the Mennonite experience in Canada, the United States, and Russia. For a three volume survey of the Mennonite Experience see Frank Epp's two volumes, *Mennonites in Canada, 1786-1920: The History of a Separate People* (1974), and *Mennonites in Canada, 1920-40: A People's Struggle for Survival* (1982); and T. D. Regehr, *Mennonites in Canada, 1939-1970: A People Transformed* (1996).

Luciuk, Lubomyr and Stella Hryniuk, eds. *Canada's Ukrainians: Negotiating an Identity*. Toronto: University of Toronto Press, 1991.
Published in celebration of the one hundredth anniversary of the arrival of Ukrainians in Canada, *Canada's Ukrainians* examines themes such as immigration and settlement, community and religion, and the state. Many of the articles are revisionist in nature, and any researcher interested in Ukrainian-Canadians will find this collection invaluable.

Luciuk, L. Y. and B. S. Kordan. *Creating a Landscape: A Geography of Ukrainians in Canada*. Toronto: University of Toronto Press, 1989.
An excellent historical atlas, *Creating a Landscape* is a useful reference source and educational aid for students examining the Ukrainian-Canadian experience. The atlas is divided into five categories: the homeland, immigration and settlement, cultural characteristics, organizational life, and the historical experience. Each sequence of maps is accompanied by a useful textual analysis.

Lupul, Manoly, ed. *A Heritage in Transition: Essays in the History of Ukrainians in Canada*. Toronto: McClelland and Stewart, 1982.
This collection is an overview of the political, cultural, economic, and social history of Canada's Ukrainians. Many of the essays remain useful

sources for research in the field, but students would be wise to look at Lubomyr Luciuk and Stella Hryniuk, *Canada's Ukrainians* (1991), for a more up-to-date overview of Ukrainian-Canadian history.

Patrias, Carmela. *Patriots and Proletarians: Politicizing Hungarian Immigrants in Interwar Canada.* Montreal: McGill-Queen's University Press, 1994.

Patrias examines the experiences and politics of over 30,000 Hungarian immigrants who came to Canada during the interwar period. These immigrants largely divided themselves into two ideological groups: conservative, pro-Hungarian "patriots," and more radical, pro-communist "proletarians." Patrias analyses how ideology influenced politics, group consciousness, and the immigrant experience.

Petryshyn, Jaroslav. *Peasants in the Promised Land: Canada and the Ukrainians, 1891-1914.* Toronto: Lorimer, 1985.

Few periods of Canadian immigration history have been as thoroughly investigated as the era from 1896 to 1914, and Jaroslav Petryshyn's book is a welcome addition to this literature. Looking at the Canadian government immigration policy, nativism, and cultural response of immigrants through the lens of Ukrainian migration, Petryshyn brings fresh insights to the topic. Petryshyn notes that Canadian immigration policy was primarily grounded in the economic needs of the country — accepting primarily agriculturalists prior to 1905, and industrial labourers thereafter. Ukrainian immigrants to Canada reflected these trends. Petryshyn also notes that Ukrainian efforts to preserve their cultural heritage awakened similar interests in other immigrant groups and help explain the multicultural perspectives of prairie society.

Subtelny, Orest. *Ukrainians in North America: An Illustrated History.* Toronto: University of Toronto Press, 1991.

Containing an excellent array of photographs and based upon memoirs and archival sources, this work is a useful introduction to the topic of Ukrainian immigration. Subtelny identifies three waves of Ukrainian immigrants — pre-World War I, inter-war, and post-World War II — and describes the Ukrainian experience as one of cultural, spiritual, and political diversity. Subtelny also examines the different experience of Ukrainian immigrants in Canada and the United States and explains why Ukrainian-Canadians have been more successful in preserving and protecting their ethnic identity.

Sutherland, Anthony X. *The Canadian Slovak League: A History, 1932-1982*. Toronto: Canadian Slovak League, 1984.

A thoroughly researched, congratulatory essay on an institution devoted to preserving Canadian Slovak ethnic heritage, this book will assist readers interested in ethnic group agency and cultural preservation in Canada. Sutherland demonstrates quite clearly how political changes in Europe, specifically the role of Slovak nationalism in Czechoslovakia, help to define the Canadian institution and its goals.

Swyripa, Frances. *Wedded to the Cause: Ukrainian-Canadian Women and Ethnic Identity, 1891-1991*. Toronto: University of Toronto Press, 1993.

Swyripa explores the construction of Ukrainian-Canadian identity and specifically the role of women in this process. Swyripa argues that two elite groups shaped and constructed identity. Ukrainian nationalists emphasised language, religion, and maintenance of traditional customs. Ukrainian socialists emphasised class struggle and labour activism. The challenges faced by Ukrainians in Ukraine therefore helped shape the construction of a Ukrainian-Canadian identity. This identity, Swyripa, notes, had regional, political, and ideological variations. She argues that Ukrainian-Canadian women not only fostered and maintained their ethnic identity, but also negotiated their gender roles within the identity. They were Ukrainian-Canadians first, women second. The construction of ethnic identity therefore had significant implications for Ukrainian-Canadian women. Thoroughly researched and documented, *Wedded to the Cause* is an important book for students interested in ethnicity or identity construction.

Tracie, Carl. *"Toil and Peaceful Life": Doukhobor Village Settlement in Saskatchewan, 1899-1918*. Regina: Canadian Plains Research Centre, 1996.

The Doukhobors came to Canada amidst the great agricultural settlement boom on the Canadian prairies. They established 57 agricultural villages in three reserved blocks in northern Saskatchewan. Faced with intimidation from local farmers and an increasingly unsympathetic federal government, they soon abandoned their communal villages and reserved lands. Tracie, a historical geographer, delves into the cultural landscape of the Doukhobor experiment in Saskatchewan. He analyses site location, the pattern of agriculture, and the conflict between the Doukhobors, the government, and local farmers which eventually disrupted the community.

Woodcock, George and Ivan Avakumovic. *The Doukhobors*. 2nd ed. Toronto: McClelland & Stewart, 1977.
Originally published by Oxford University Press in 1968, this updated study traces the history of the Doukhobors from eighteenth-century Russia to contemporary Canada. The authors pay attention to issues such as the immigration process, Doukhobor leaders, conflicts between community and state, distinctions between more orthodox members and the more zealot and violent Sons of Freedom, and pressures toward assimilation.

The Irish and Scottish Experience

Akenson, Donald Harmon. *Small Differences: Irish Catholics and Irish Protestants, 1815-1922: An Interpretational Perspective*. Montreal: McGill-Queen's University Press, 1988.
_____. *Being Had: Historians Evidence and the Irish in North America*. Port Credit, ON: P. D. Meany, 1985.
In these two books, Akenson makes his powerful revisionist argument that the Irish identity supersedes Catholic and Protestants divisions in North America. Akenson argues historians of the Irish experience in North America have misused the evidence and fostered interpretations more suited to their own ideological outlooks. Together these books are a controversial and critical attack on the historical profession.

_____. *The Irish in Ontario: A Study in Rural History*. Montreal: McGill-Queen's University Press, 1984.
Akenson's book is one of the classic texts in Canadian rural history. Akenson establishes the Irish as the most important ethnic community in Canada and demonstrates that, contrary to the pattern identified in the United States, the Irish in Canada were predominantly successful farmers and rural artisans. Focussing his attention on Leeds and Landsdowne Townships at the eastern end of Lake Ontario, Akenson discusses Irish attitudes and behaviours through a micro analysis of their rural lifestyle. He analyses the patterns established prior to large scale Irish migration and discusses the changes that emerged as the Irish occupied the district. Using census data, local government records, local association records, and church records among other sources, Akenson demonstrates that both Irish Protestants and Catholics were predominantly rural, equally successful in economic terms, and politically significant.

Bumsted, J. M. *The People's Clearance: Highland Emigration to British North America.* Edinburgh: Edinburgh University Press, 1982.

Scottish Highlanders migrated to the Maritimes and Upper Canada in large numbers in the late eighteenth and early nineteenth century. Many historians associate this large migration wave with the policy of Clearance in Scotland; Bumsted argues, however, that prior to 1815, the migration to Canada was the people's choice rather than a programme forced upon them by Clearance.

Elliot, Bruce S. *Irish Migrants in the Canadas: A New Approach.* Montreal: McGill-Queen's University Press, 1988.

Elliot follows the migration experiences of 775 Protestant families who left southern Ireland for Canada between 1815 and 1855. His study provides critical information into the push and pull factors of rural migration from pre-famine Ireland and on the kinship and family connections that defined the immigrant experience in Canada. Elliot concludes that emigration from Ireland and internal migration in Canada were both carefully conceived economic strategies designed to improve the family's condition of life. Like most works on the Irish experience in Canada, Elliot concludes that these strategies were generally successful.

Handcock, W. Gordon. *Soe Longe As There Comes Noe Women: Origins of English Settlement in Newfoundland.* St. John's: Breakwater Press, 1989.

This book, ostensibly about the English settlers in Newfoundland, is also a general history of Newfoundland settlement and community formation in the eighteenth and early nineteenth centuries. Handcock examines the migratory fishery and its resistance to settlement, the development of the resident fishery, the origins of the outposts and St. John's merchant community, and the effects of economic transitions on Newfoundlanders. Along the way, the reader is treated to a sophisticated analysis of English migration patterns and their role in Newfoundland's development.

Houston, Cecil J. and William J. Smyth. *Irish Emigration and Canadian Settlement: Patterns, Links, and Letters.* Toronto: University of Toronto Press, 1990.

A collaborative effort by Canadian and Irish based historical geographers, *Irish Emigration and Canadian Settlement* is essential reading. In the pre-Confederation era, the Irish composed the single largest ethnic group in Canada — larger than the English or Scots — and shaped the policy decisions made during that era. This book is divided into three sections. The first section examines the emigration from Ireland and discussing in great detail the push and pull factors which motivated the Irish migrants. The second section deals with their settlement in Canada and pays particular attention to the spatial and occupational patterns of the community. Finally, the third section presents letters home from the Irish in Canada. What emerges is a portrait of diversity, of a community marked by differentiation rather than cohesiveness, and a community that remained proudly Irish.

_____. *The Sash Canada Wore: A Historical Geography of the Orange Order in Canada.* Toronto: University of Toronto Press, 1980.
The Orange Order was a powerful institution in nineteenth-century Canada. In this volume, Houston and Smyth isolate the Orange Order from the larger patterns of Canadian history to provide detailed information on the location of Orange Lodges and the size and composition of their membership. Also see Scott W. See, *Riots in New Brunswick: Orange Nativism and Social Violence in the 1840s* (1993).

MacKay, Donald. *Flight from Famine: The Coming of the Irish to Canada.* Toronto: McClelland and Stewart, 1990.
_____. *Scotland Farewell: The People of Hector.* Toronto: McGraw Holt Rinehart, 1980.
These popular and poorly documented histories of Irish and Scottish migration prior to 1850 are basic introductions. Although the books fail to investigate scholarly questions regarding ethnic identity and the immigrant experience, they are well written and well supplied with lively anecdotes.

McLean, Marianne. *The People of Glengarry: Highlanders in Transition, 1745-1820.* Montreal: McGill-Queen's University Press, 1991.
In this detailed demographic analysis of one Upper Canadian county, McLean argues that the Highlanders who came to Glengarry County were cleared in Scotland. With few opportunities to get land in Scotland they migrated to Canada and were attracted to Glengarry because early Loyalists of Highland heritage had settled in the area. In Glengarry, they built strong kinship networks and continued their clan-based social organization. They thus integrated easily into the emerging British North American society and became Scottish-Canadians. McLean demonstrates that kinship, land inheritance, and community crossed the Atlantic.

Norton, Wayne. *Help Us to a Better Life: Crofter Colonies in the Prairie West*. Regina: Canadian Plains Research Centre, 1994.
This narrative book about Scottish settlement on the northern prairies is a useful addition to the literature on the Scots and prairie settlement. Under the auspices of the Imperial Colonization Board, Scottish settlers came to Saskatchewan and Manitoba between 1896 and 1906 settling in designated enclaves. Norton demonstrates that the colonization schemes were, on the whole, unsuccessful and the enclaves soon reflected the multicultural landscape of rural Saskatchewan and Manitoba.

Power, Thomas P., ed. *The Irish in Atlantic Canada, 1780-1900*. Fredericton: New Ireland Press, 1991.
Toner, Peter M., ed. *New Ireland Remembered: Historical Essays on the Irish in New Brunswick*. Fredericton: New Ireland Press, 1988.
Irish migration to the Atlantic region in the early nineteenth century changed the characteristics of the local society dramatically. These two excellent collections provide an overview of the Irish experience in the Atlantic region.

Other Ethnic Communities

Brown, Michael. *Jew or Juif? Jews, French Canadians, and Anglo-Canadians, 1759-1914*. Philadelphia: Jewish Publication, 1987.
Based upon Brown's doctoral dissertation, this thoroughly researched book places Canadian Jews within the dynamic of Anglo-French relations in Canada. Brown argues that anti-Semitism often increased during periods of French-English conflict.

Clairmont, Donald H. J. and Dennis W. Magill. *Africville: the Life and Death of a Canadian Black Community*. Rev. ed. Toronto: Canadian Scholars' Press, 1987.
African-Canadians in Nova Scotia have a particularly strong attachment to the place once called Africville. Established before 1850 by refugees from American slavery, Africville was a community plagued by poverty. It became a dumping ground for Halifax garbage and one of Canada's most problematic slums; in 1967 a residential relocation began as the area underwent urban redevelopment. Residents were moved from the area to new low cost housing projects in metropolitan Halifax under the guise of liberal-welfare rhetoric. This book, originally published in 1974, is a history of Africville and a study of the relocation. Readers interested in

Nova Scotian African-Canadians in general should consult Brigdal Pachai, *Beneath the Clouds of the Promised Land: The Survival of Nova Scotia's Blacks*, 2 vols. (1987, 1990).

Ganzevoort, Herman. *A Bittersweet Land: The Dutch Experience in Canada, 1890-1980*. Toronto: McClelland and Stewart, 1988.
A book in the Generations Series, Ganzevoort investigates the experience of a group he calls "the invisible ethnic." Although Dutch immigrants maintained a distinctive identity in Canada primarily through the Christian Reformed Church, they quickly identified themselves with the Anglo-Protestant host community and their children became indistinguishable from the larger Canadian majority. By the end of his study, Ganzevoort leads readers to the conclusion that the Dutch in Canada no longer exist; they are simply Canadian.

Godfrey, Sheldon J. and Judith C. Godfrey. *Search Out the Land: The Jews and the Growth of Equality in British Colonial America, 1740-1867*. Montreal: McGill-Queen's University Press, 1995.
Traditional interpretations of British North America have — if they paid any attention to Jewish people at all — emphasised either "the absence of early Jewish roots in Canada or the issue of anti-semitism." These themes, the authors argue, "are not justified by further examination of the facts." This well-researched volume — the bibliography is a crucial starting point for researchers contemplating further work on Jews in British North America — argues that Jews formed a significantly larger percentage of the English-speaking population in eighteenth- and early nineteenth-century Canada than has previously been acknowledged.

Grenke, Arthur. *The German Community in Winnipeg, 1872-1919*. New York: AMS Press, 1991.
One of the very few studies of German-Canadians, *The German Community in Winnipeg* explores many of the difficult problems that have led most historians to ignore this ethnic group. Grenke discovered that many German migrants to Canada originated in Austria-Hungary or Russia and had incorporated linkages to non-German communities in their places of origin. They did not share religious or cultural ties and existed primarily as a linguistic community. Hence even defining the community itself is problematic for the historian. In Canada, furthermore, the German community was marked by a high degree of transience and thus social organizations were difficult to maintain. The crisis of World War I and

the closure of German social clubs and the German-language newspapers thus caused a significant crisis in the German community.

Hornby, Jim. *Black Islanders: Prince Edward Island's Black Community*. Charlottetown: Institute of Island Studies, 1991.
This short book looks at the history of African-Canadians in Prince Edward Island from their arrival in the 1870s as slaves owned by Loyalists to their disappearance as a community in the 1900s. The author argues that their arrival in bondage influenced the attitudes of white Islanders toward the newly arrived settlers long after slavery had disappeared. For a popular study of British Columbian African-Canadians, see Crawford Killian, *Go Do Great Things* (1978).

Iacovetta, Franca. *Such Hardworking People: Italian Immigrants in Post-War Toronto*. Montreal: McGill-Queen's University Press, 1992.
Extending and enhancing the work of John Zucchi, Franca Iacovetta looks at the large wave of Italian immigration to Toronto following World War II. She examines old world background, migration, work, family, community, organizations, politics, and the reaction of the host society. Throughout the book she demonstrates a sensitivity to both gender and class-based analysis. She concludes that the Italians slowly integrated into Canadian society and that post-war immigration to Toronto was strikingly similar to the pre-war experience.

Kahn, Alison. *Listen While I Tell You: A Story of the Jews of St. John's Newfoundland*. St. John's: ISER, 1987.
Eastern European Jews came to Newfoundland at the beginning of the twentieth century. Small in numbers, they established a pragmatic community but maintained a deep attachment to their faith. Alison Kahn sketches the efforts by these Jews to preserve their faith and provide for their children in a community which lacked "institutional completeness."

Lapointe, Richard and Lucille Tessier. *Francophones of Saskatchewan: A History*. Regina: Campion College, 1988.
This work is an illustrated narrative of the French-Canadian experience in Saskatchewan. They note that the attitudes of the community have transformed over time from optimism that a new Quebec could be created in the west to *la survivance* and campaigns to protect education rights to fears for their future in the economic chaos of the depression to a new *fransaskois* identity as an element of French-Canadian identity.

Lehmann, Heinze. *The German Canadians, 1750-1927: Immigration, Settlement, and Culture.* Trans. Gerhard Bessler. St. John's: Jesperson Press, 1986.

Although Lehmann's essays are sixty years old, they remain one of the few monograph sources on German-Canadians. His detailed gathering of information about German-Canadians is an invaluable source for modern historians. His writings, however, reflect the concerns of Nazi Germany for expatriate Germans. Lehmann feared that German ethnic identity in Canada would disappear in the face of North American liberal-individualism.

Leonoff, Cyril Edel. *The Jewish Farmers of Western Canada.* Vancouver: The Jewish Historical Society, 1984.

A reprint of articles previously published in *Western States Jewish History*, this book is the only manuscript that examines the small Jewish farm community on the Canadian prairies. Leonoff focuses upon three distinctive colonization schemes and the communities that developed. He effectively demonstrates that contrary to popular belief, Jewish people did settle as farmers on the prairies and did contribute to the development of prairie society. Readers might also consult Leonoff, *Pioneers, Pedlars, and Prayer Shawls* (1978) for a similar study of Jews in British Columbia and Yukon.

Lindstrom-Best, Varpu. *Defiant Sisters: A Social History of Finnish Immigrant Women in Canada.* Toronto: Multicultural History Society of Ontario, 1988.

In this valuable book, Lindstrom-Best integrates ethnicity with a study of gender and work. She focuses attention upon the everyday lives of Finnish women, their marriages, child rearing and homemaking tasks, and their pursuit of wages in the unrelenting work associated with domestic employment and camp life. These Finnish women, she argues, were not satisfied with their lives and constantly sought to improve their living condition. Finnish women, she notes, brought a tradition of labour organization and political activism to Canada. Although ignored by the male leadership of the Finnish labour movement, Lindstrom-Best discovered these women shared the radicalism of Finnish men, and were, in fact, defiant sisters.

Loken, Gulbrand. *From Fjord to Frontier: A History of the Norwegians in Canada.* Toronto: McClelland and Stewart, 1980.

A narrative history of Norwegians in Canada, this book is typical of many of the ethnic biographies in the Generations Series published with the assistance of the Canadian government. It is a useful starting point for research and contains good references.

Potestio, John and A. Pucci, eds. *The Italian Immigrant Experience.*
    Thunder Bay: Canadian Italian Historical Association, 1988.
This collection of eight essays presented at a 1980 conference is intended to shed light on the Italo-Canadian experience, and includes contributions by Robert Harney, John Zucchi, Franc Sturino and Bruno Ramirez. The topics covered included push and pull factors resulting in Italian immigration, agency within the immigrant community to circumvent Canadian immigration policies, and the behaviour of Italian immigrants in Canada.

Ramirez, Bruno. *On the Move: French-Canadian and Italian Migrants in the North Atlantic Economy, 1860-1914.* Toronto: McClelland and Stewart, 1991.
The international transfer of people and labour has been of central importance to Canada's colonial and national history. Ramirez focuses upon two interconnected case studies, the upper Southern Apennines in Italy, and Berthier County in Quebec and explores the migratory patterns of these two societies. Peasants in the Apennines were exploited by the local bourgeoisie, the *galantuomoni*, and many men (primarily) migrated to Quebec to take wage labour jobs in railroad construction or mining, and settle in places such as Montreal. Such migration was opposed by the local elites in the Apennines, for it increased the price of peasant labour; others supported it, for some wages earned in North America returned to Italy and helped expand the national economy, as well as permitting some peasants to purchase their own plot of land. The nature of the peasant-*galantuomini* relationship thus changed enormously in the decades prior to World War I. Ramirez's analysis of Berthier County argues against the stereotype of rural Quebec as a static society, resistant to economic change. After 1860 the commercialization of Quebec agriculture sent many francophone families to the New England textile mills, a trend that slowed only with changing American labour laws in the early twentieth century. Thus, for very different reasons and involving very different groups of people, *On the Move* argues that Quebec was both a source and a destination for rural migration in the last decades of the nineteenth century.

Rasporich, Anthony W. *For a Better Life: A History of Croatians in Canada*. Toronto: McClelland and Stewart, 1982.
One of the best narrative histories in the Generations Series, this book is an ethnic biography of Croatian-Canadians. It studies Croatian migration through the lens of immigration studies examining both push and pull factors in Croatian migration. Rasporich also identifies the reactions of the host community and explores the phenomenon of post-World War II immigration to Canada generally.

Speisman, Stephen A. *The Jews of Toronto: A History to 1937*. Toronto: McClelland and Stewart, 1987.
Speisman examines the Jewish experience in Toronto from 1830 to 1937. He argues that the Toronto Jews were a heterogenous community plagued by internal conflicts. Although early Jewish settlers in Toronto came from British and German backgrounds, the immigration of a significant East European Jewish population led to changes and conflict. Indeed, he notes that the Toronto Jewish identity emerged in the efforts to manage these internal conflicts. Particularly important were the efforts at acculturation amongst East European Jews and the retreat from orthodox practice this entailed.

Walker, James St. G. *The Black Loyalists: The Search for a Promised Land in Nova Scotia and Sierra Leone, 1783-1870*. New York: Africana Publishing and Dalhousie University Press, 1976; 2nd. ed., Toronto: University of Toronto Press, 1992.
An outstanding book, thoroughly researched and referenced, and recently reprinted, *The Black Loyalists* remains the definitive study of this often forgotten group. Walker traces the Black Loyalists as they made an effort to settle in Nova Scotia, confronted racism and discrimination, and then left to take on a new experience as Nova Scotians in Sierra Leone. Walker argues that the people constructed a distinctive Loyalist identity in this process. This book has significant implications for the study of both African-Canadians and Loyalists in Canada. For a general survey of African-Canadians, readers could consult Walker's *A History of Blacks in Canada: A Study Guide for Teachers and Students* (1980).

Winks, Robin W. *The Blacks in Canada*. New Haven CT: Yale University Press, 1971; rpt. Montreal: McGill-Queen's University Press, 1997.
This work explores the African-Canadian experience from the early

seventeenth century to the 1960s, and pursues four main goals: to reveal something of the nature of prejudice in Canada; to examine how Canadian attitudes toward immigration and ethnic identity differ from those in the USA; to place African-Canadians in the context of Canada's national history; and, finally, due to the heavy migration of African-Canadians from the USA, to explore Canadian-American cultural relations.

Zucchi, John E. *Italians in Toronto: Development of a National Identity, 1875-1935*. Montreal: McGill-Queen's University Press, 1988.
Thoroughly researched and referenced, *Italians in Toronto* is one of the best examinations of an ethnic group in Canadian history writing. Zucchi argues that distinctive Italian identities such as Sicilian and Calabrian slowly merged into a greater Italian-Canadian identity between 1875 and 1935. The catalysts for this new constructed identity, Zucchi notes, were the emergence of Italian nationalism in Italy during the Mussolini era and the immigrants' adjustment to a new urban community. The workplace, church, and community organizations in Toronto blurred the regional distinctiveness of Italian-Canadians. The emerging identity was confirmed in the 1920s when Italy sent consuls to North America to arouse favourable sentiment for Mussolini's fascist nationalism. A more detailed demographic analysis can be found in Zucchi, *The Italian Immigrants of the St. John's Ward* (1981); for a study on Italians in Montreal, see Bruno Ramirez and Michael Del Balso, *The Italians of Montreal: From Sojourning to Settlement* (1980).

Regional and Urban History

Regional history is one of the oldest genres of Canadian history. Walter Sage identified five geographical and historical regions — British Columbia, the Prairies, Ontario, Quebec, and the Atlantic — in a paper in the *Report of the Canadian Historical Association* (1937) and to this list should be added the North. Moreover, W. L. Morton (the Prairies), Margaret Ormsby (British Columbia), and W. S. MacNutt (the Atlantic) wrote wonderful textbooks on regional themes in the period prior to 1970. Regional history is also linked to the staples, laurentian, and metropolitan interpretations of Canadian history. Historians writing in these traditions often focused upon the political and economic expressions of the hinterland, and identified it as regionalism. Regional history, however, should not be confused with the study of regionalism. It is also one of the limited identities fields of Canadian history and scholars have recently made a significant effort to discover the distinctive qualities of a particular region rather than merely focusing upon events such as regional protest. Still few writers use region as a theoretical or analytical device; instead, it is more common for scholars to examine themes and subjects within a regional context. For this reason, we have integrated urban history, another field that examines multiple themes within an areal construct.

General Works

Bercuson, David J. *Canada and the Burden of Unity.* Toronto: Macmillan, 1977.
This collection of eight angry articles by prairie and maritime historians reflects the extraordinary regionalism in Canada during the 1970s. These essays catalogue the failure of the federal Canadian government to redress regional economic disparities, and the regional grievances that followed. The angry tone of this collection led Ramsay Cook to renounce regional history in "The Burden of Regionalism," *Acadiensis* (1983).

Brodie, Janine. *The Political Economy of Canadian Regionalism.* Toronto: Harcourt Brace Jovanovich, 1990.
Brodie tries to move away from a geographical determinist approach, toward regions and aims to build a case for functional regions and

regionalism based upon political economy. First, Brodie outlines her neo-Marxist approach to regionalism in Canada and, in the process, provides one of the best theoretical overviews of regionalism available in Canadian scholarship. She argues that Canadian regionalism emerged because of uneven economic development, the nature of Canada's capitalist business class, and the political structure of Canada. Second, Brodie outlines how Canadian national policies have provoked regional responses, and the role of provincial governments as voices of regional discontentment.

Careless, J. M. S. *Frontier and Metropolis: Regions, Cities, and Identities in Canada Before 1914.* Toronto: University of Toronto Press, 1989.
J. M. S. Careless's article, "Frontierism, Metropolitanism, and Canadian History" in the *Canadian Historical Review* (1954) established metropolitanism as one of the dominant themes in Canadian historiography. Metropolitanism challenged the frontier theory of development, sought to reconcile centralist and regional approaches, and recognized that "a chain, almost a feudal chain of vassalage, wherein one city may stand tributary to a bigger centre and yet be the metropolis of a sizable region of its own." Metropolitanism was, therefore, reciprocal: cities and hinterlands influenced one another, and even larger cities such as Toronto and Montreal were in a hierarchical relationship to London and New York. For a wider-ranging collection of Careless's essays, see *Careless at Work: Selected Canadian Historical Studies* (1990).

Elkins, David J. and Richard Simeon. *Small Worlds: Provinces and Parties in Canadian Political Life.* Toronto: Methuen, 1980.
Many writers find the roots of Canadian regionalism in the federal political system. In this collection of essays and addresses, Elkins and Simeon discuss the role of provincial governments and political parties in fostering Canadian regionalism.

Matthews, Ralph. *The Creation of Regional Dependency.* Toronto: University of Toronto Press, 1983.
Matthews uses world systems analysis, its emphasis on centre and periphery, and the inherent underdevelopment of hinterland regions, in order to explain Canadian regionalism. He argues that Canada's political and economic structure fostered uneven economic development and regional dependency. His analysis is focused upon Newfoundland and the Maritimes and is not easily adapted to the western Canadian regional situation. His work is often undervalued by western Canadian historians.

McCann, L. D., ed. *Heartland and Hinterland: A Geography of Canada.*
    Scarborough, ON: Prentice-Hall, 1984; rev. ed., 1987.
This text extends regional geography "beyond the bounds of descriptive analysis" and provides a sophisticated application of metropolitanism and world-systems analysis to Canada's past. To accomplish his goals, McCann brings together work by the leading regional geographers in Canada. The text begins with two excellent theoretical pieces that identify both the strengths and weaknesses of the analytical framework. They are followed by essays discussing the emergence of an industrial heartland in the St. Lawrence River basin and the challenges faced by this system in the modern era. The third, and largest, section examines each hinterland region and attempts to explain the current economic and political climate of those regions.

British Columbia

Barman, Jean. *The West Beyond the West: A History of British Columbia.*
    Toronto: University of Toronto Press, 1991; rev. ed., 1996.
In *British Columbia: A History* (1958), Margaret Ormsby reflected the historical sensibilities of her day: her work was primarily concerned with politics and the male myth-makers of Canada's Pacific province. Barman's synthesis is much different in approach and content. Reflecting her own research interests in education and social history, *The West Beyond the West* strives to incorporate aboriginal groups, women, and ethnic minorities into the narrative. For example, Barman devotes an entire chapter to Native peoples from the gold rush to 1945; this era, particularly after the turn of the century, has only recently been an area of study. To the great relief of those beyond the lower mainland, this readable text also demonstrates regional sensitivity toward the political and cultural archipelago that is British Columbia. Although British Columbia has been well served by recent texts, Ormsby's work is still worth consulting for its political narrative. For sheer enjoyment and careful attention to myth, see George Bowering, *Bowering's BC: A Swashbuckling History* (1996); for another excellent popular study, see George Woodcock, *British Columbia: A History of a Province* (1990).

Johnston, Hugh J. M., ed. *The Pacific Province: A History of British Columbia.* Vancouver: Douglas & McIntyre, 1996.
In contrast to Jean Barman's general history of British Columbia, *The Pacific Province* is the combined effort of a dozen scholars who not only

contribute chapters in their own area of expertise, but have also commented on those of others. This general survey consists of thematic chapters — Douglas Cole contributes an excellent essay on B. C. culture, for example — organized along chronological lines. Native peoples are not ignored following the end of the fur trade, and this volume integrates much of the recent literature dealing with the province.

Robin, Martin. *The Rush for Spoils: The Company Province, 1871-1933.* Toronto: McClelland and Stewart, 1972.
_____. *Pillars of Profit: The Company Province, 1934-1972.* Toronto: McClelland and Stewart, 1973.
These works constitute a political-economic history of British Columbia from its entry into Confederation to the end of the political dynasty of W. A. C. Bennett. Sometimes criticised for errors of fact, both volumes argue that British Columbia was predominantly a company province; that is, the alliance between large corporations and government dominated the political and economic environment of the province. Out of this informal alliance emerged a polarized society, and Robin clearly sympathizes with the radical responses that accompanied unfettered capitalism.

Roy, Patricia E. *A History of British Columbia: Selected Readings.* Toronto: Copp Clark, 1989.
A collection of previously-published articles, this volume examines themes involving Native peoples, the gold rush, government, natural resources, education, class, race, and the province's relationship to the federal government. There is a brief bibliography.

Thorner, Thomas, ed. *Sa T'se: Historical Perspectives on Northern British Columbia.* Prince Rupert, BC: New Caledonia Press, 1989.
A series of previously-published essays on northern British Columbia, this collection focuses upon Native societies, economic and political developments, and relationships between the northern part of the province and the lower mainland.

Ward, W. Peter and Robert A. J. McDonald, eds. *British Columbia: Historical Readings.* Vancouver: Douglas & McIntyre, 1981.
The essays collected here examine four areas of historical enquiry: Native-European relations, racial tensions, labour militancy and radicalism, and economic development. In addition, Allan Smith's introductory article still provides a useful, although dated, interpretation of the writing of British

Columbia's history over the past century. For a volume that contains selections ranging from H. H. Bancroft in the 1880s to contemporary articles, see J. Friesen and H. K. Ralston, *Historical Essays on British Columbia* (1980).

The Prairies

Allen, Richard, ed. *A Region of the Mind: Interpreting the Western Canadian Plains.* Regina: Canadian Plains Research Centre, 1973.
This collection of essays is a useful introduction to the issues that scholars engaged in the 1970s. The articles review earlier interpretations, offer specific case studies, and suggest new interpretive models. Although most of the essays are dated, three deserve special mention: W. L. Morton provides a clear summary of his interpretive framework in "A Century of Plains and Parkland," John Bennett looks at prairie residents' adaptation to the environment in "Adaptive Strategy and Processes," and Eli Mandel analyses prairie fiction writing in "Images of Prairie Man."

Archer, John H. *Saskatchewan: A History.* Saskatoon: Western Producer Prairie Books, 1980.
Commissioned by the Saskatchewan Archives Board to commemorate the seventy-fifth anniversary of the province, this book is a narrative history of the "wheat province." Although Archer begins the book with the land and aboriginal people, he focuses primarily upon the traditional themes of political and economic development. Thus, Archer successfully catalogues the major political developments from 1870 to 1980 but gives only cursory coverage to the fur trade. Native peoples, ethnic minorities, women, farmers, and labourers appear in the work only when their activities enter the political sphere.

Bercuson, David J., ed. *Western Perspectives 1.* Toronto: Holt Rinehart Winston, 1974.
Bercuson, D. and P. Buckner, eds. *Eastern and Western Perspectives: Papers from the Joint Atlantic Canada/Western Canadian Studies Conference.* Toronto: University of Toronto Press, 1981.
Gagan, David, ed. *Prairie Perspectives.* Toronto: Holt Rinehart, 1970.
Francis, D. and H. Ganzevoort, eds. *The Dirty Thirties in Prairie Canada.* Vancouver: Tantalus Research, 1980.
Klassen, Henry C., ed. *The Canadian West: Social Change and Economic Development.* Calgary: University of Calgary, 1977.

Palmer, Howard, ed. *The Settlement of the Canadian West*. Calgary: University of Calgary Press, 1984.

Palmer, Howard, ed. *The New Provinces: Alberta and Saskatchewan, 1905-1980*. Vancouver: Tantalus, 1980.

Rasporich, A. W., ed. *The Making of the Modern West: Western Canada Since 1945*. Calgary: University of Calgary Press, 1984.

Rasporich, A. W. and Henry Klassen, eds. *Prairie Perspective 2*. Toronto: Holt Rinehart Winston, 1973.

Trofimenkoff, Susan Mann, ed. *The Twenties in Western Canada*. Ottawa: National Museums of Canada, 1972.

The published proceedings of the discontinued Western Canada Studies Conference — and in one case the combined proceedings of the Atlantic and Western Canadian Studies Conference — these volumes, like most conference proceedings, contain both outstanding and less useful articles. The conferences brought together scholars interested in literature, folk culture, politics, social structure, geography, and history, and the published papers reflect these diverse interests. Many of the conferences were focussed upon specific themes, and the collected essays thus represent useful starting points for students interested in these topics.

Breen, David. *The Canadian Prairie West and the Ranching Frontier, 1874-1924*. Toronto: University of Toronto Press, 1982.

The first substantive study of Canada's ranching frontier, Breen's book remains the best work in this field. Breen argues that the Canadian ranching frontier bore little resemblance to the one emerging in the United States; instead, Canada organized ranching in a fashion similar to agrarian settlement through a system of long-term leases. As a result, the ranching community remained a hinterland to Montreal's metropolitan system rather than a self-sufficient frontier. The ranching community, furthermore, was predominantly British and sought to maintain a stratified, class-based society.

Coates, Ken and Fred McGuiness. *Manitoba: The People and the Province*. Edmonton: Hurtig, 1987.

When W. L. Morton wrote *Manitoba: A History* (1957) he argued that the province had a distinctive character often ignored by national historians. Although Coates and McGuiness continue the tradition of Manitoba's distinctiveness, their approach is largely popular. *The People and the Province* is a well-written narrative which focuses upon social and political history from 1870 to the present, is not burdened or blessed with reference notes, and is well-illustrated. Interspersed amongst the text are vignettes shaped around popular Manitoba personalities, organizations, and events. Native peoples, who are so prominent in other works by Coates, are little dealt with, particularly after the turn of the century.

Conway, John. *The West: The History of a Region in Confederation.* Toronto: James Lorimer, 1983.

As the title suggests, this book examines the place of the four western provinces in the Canadian nation. In this left-nationalist interpretation, Conway argues that the political and economic relationships created and shaped by the National Policy are the foundation for western dissatisfaction and regional protest. The failure of western politicians to win concessions from the federal government produced waves of protest, including the Métis resistance of 1869 and 1885, the 1919 Winnipeg General Strike, the Progressive, CCF and Social Credit parties; and federal-provincial confrontations over resource management in the 1970s.

Dick, Lyle. *Farmers "Making Good": the Development of Abernethy and District, Saskatchewan, 1880-1920.* Ottawa: National Historic Parks and Sites, 1989.

Dick's work — together with works such as David Jones's *Empire of Dust* (1987), Royden Loewen's *Family, Church, and Market* (1994), and Paul Voisey's *Vulcan* (1988) — provides an excellent overview of the multi-faceted agricultural settlement process on the Canadian prairies. Dick examines the district around the homestead of W. R. Motherwell, an important Saskatchewan farm leader and politician. Although the book is based upon an important member of the social and economic elite of Saskatchewan farm society, Dick makes it clear that settlement and farming included both winners and losers. Based upon a sophisticated statistical data base and narrative sources, the book examines three essential themes: the economy of homesteading and farming, the social structure of farm life, and the emergence of agrarian ideologies especially the notion of progress.

Foster, John E., ed. *The Developing West: Essays on Canadian History in Honour of Lewis H. Thomas.* Edmonton: University of Alberta Press, 1983.

Lewis H. Thomas was an important figure in Western Canadian history serving as Provincial Archivist in Saskatchewan and teaching at the University of Saskatchewan (Regina) and the University of Alberta. Many of his prominent students and colleagues contribute essays to this *festschriften*.

Friesen, Gerald. *River Road: Essays on Manitoba and Prairie History.*
    Winnipeg: University of Manitoba Press, 1996.
A collection of seventeen essays written by Gerald Friesen since the publication *The Canadian Prairies* (1984), *River Road* is a snapshot of the present directions in prairie history. Friesen divides the book into sections on Language and Culture, Dominant and Alternative Cultures, and Towards a New Synthesis. The essays, some of them previously published and others given as presentations at conferences and symposiums, reflect Friesen's interest in Native, Métis, labour, ethnic, post-modernist, and comparative history. The more intriguing essays make comparisons between Canada and Australia or Argentina, ask questions about the prairies and Constitutional debates in Canada, and re-examine the historiographical debates within the field of prairie history.

_____. *The Canadian Prairies.* Toronto: University of Toronto Press,
    1984.
The Canadian Prairies is as much an interpretive analysis of prairie history as a genuine textbook. This work is crafted around the themes of environment, multicultural heritage, hinterland economic development, and political protest. This approach helps Friesen unify, for the first time, the fur trade era and the modern settlement society in his portrayal of the region's past. Friesen's work provides ample and sympathetic coverage to aboriginal peoples, workers, and immigrants. Unfortunately, women outside of the suffrage and progressive movements are not dealt with adequately, and significant trends in post-World War II society receive cursory treatment. Friesen's text is thoroughly referenced, and students will find the notes a useful source for seminal work in the field.

Gibbins, Roger. *Prairie Politics and Society: Regionalism in Decline.*
    Toronto: Butterworth, 1980.
Political scientist Roger Gibbons argues that prairie regionalism was fostered by a relatively homogenous economic structure based upon the rural-based agricultural economy. In the period after 1950, urbanization and industrialization of the prairie provinces led to a reduction in regionalism. Writing just before the National Energy Policy Crisis, the rise of the Western Canada Concept party, and the emergence of the first organized Western Canadian separatist movement, it is clear that Gibbins

obviously underestimated the continued importance of prairie regional alienation. Gibbins's book, however, forces readers to come to grips with the new urban-based prairie society and provides a refreshing new interpretation of prairie development.

Jones, David C. *Empire of Dust: Settling and Abandoning the Prairie Dry Belt*. Edmonton: University of Alberta Press, 1987.
Jones looks at the failure of agricultural settlement in the region known as the Palliser's Triangle. In this thoroughly referenced book, Jones notes how experts and promoters created mythologies about the district that lured settlers into the region. The science of agriculture, however, could not adapt to the arid conditions of Palliser's Triangle and by 1926 many of the district's farmers had abandoned their farms in despair.

Jones, David C. and Ian MacPherson, eds. *Building Beyond the Homestead: Rural History on the Prairies*. Calgary: University of Calgary Press, 1985.
A collection of papers from a 1984 conference on rural history at the University of Victoria, *Building Beyond the Homestead* is a useful introduction to prairie rural history. Essays examine themes such as banking, education, women, farm hands, and scientific agriculture. Like most collections of essays, this book lacks a coherent thesis, but individually many of the papers make valuable contributions.

McGowan, Don C. *The Green and Growing Years: Swift Current, 1907-1914*. Victoria: Cactus, 1983.
_____. *Grassland Settlers: The Swift Current Region during the Era of the Ranching Frontier*. Regina: Canadian Plains Research Centre, 1975.
These two volumes — and, in particular *Grassland Settlers* — provide a useful analysis of the settlement experience in the drylands. McGowan focuses upon the town builders and the small-scale merchants in Swift Current, and how they respond to the aspirations, successes, and failures of the surrounding hinterland community. McGowan also integrates regional and national events, and demonstrates how these forces influenced the patterns of local development.

McKillop, A. B. *Contexts of Canada's Past: Selected Essays of W. L. Morton*. Toronto: Macmillan, 1980.
W. L. Morton was western Canada's premier and most influential

Regional and Urban History 293

historian. The essays reprinted in this volume provide a general overview of Morton's development as a historian and reflect the diversity of his historical interests. Of particular interest to readers will be Morton's seminal essay "The Bias of Prairie Politics," that challenged Canadian historians to break from the traditions of the laurentian thesis.

Melnyk, George, ed. *From Riel to Reform: A History of Protest in Western Canada*. Saskatoon: Fifth House, 1992.
A large collection of previously published articles, Melnyk selects articles that examine not only the political protests, but also those protests emerging from the Métis and prairie mythology.

Palmer, Howard, with Tamara Palmer. *Alberta: A New History*. Edmonton: Hurtig, 1990.
This book is best described as a cultural history of Alberta firmly within the tradition of limited identities scholarship. *Alberta: A New History* does not ignore the traditional themes of prairie history such as resource extraction, agriculture, and regional protest, but unlike treatments in comparable texts on Saskatchewan, Manitoba, and Ontario, political history is minimized. Both Palmers' research interests lie in ethnic history, and this aspect of Alberta history is emphasised. Alberta is described as an immigrant and multicultural community often besieged by a male Anglo-Saxon dominant culture. There is an excellent bibliography of important secondary literature.

Taylor, Jeffery. *Fashioning Farmers: Ideology, Agricultural Knowledge and the Manitoba Farm Movement, 1890-1925*. Regina: Canadian Plains Research Centre, 1994.
Taylor uses post-modernist and feminist theory to examine the politics of the Manitoba farm movement in the period to 1925. He argues that a tradition of radical agrarian protest was submerged by a pro-capitalist business philosophy during this period. This ideological transformation, Taylor argues, occurred because of the powerful role of Manitoba Agricultural College as the instrument through which knowledge was communicated to farmers.

Thompson, John Herd. *The Harvests of War: The Prairie West, 1914-1918*. Toronto: McClelland and Stewart, 1978.
One of the most influential works on the Canadian West, *The Harvests of War* is a study of prairie culture under the stress of wartime conditions.

Thompson uses a thematic approach in his study examining issues such as the ideology of war, the wheat economy, ethnic relations, the social reform movement, the conscription crisis, and the Union government. The war Thompson argues, changed the prairies by exaggerating certain pre-war characteristics and limiting others. Post-war prairie culture, he concludes, was considerably different from that which preceded the conflict.

Voisey, Paul. *Vulcan: The Making of a Prairie Community*. Toronto: University of Toronto Press, 1988.
A wonderful analysis of a southern Alberta district from the arrival of the homesteaders until the crisis of the Great Depression, *Vulcan* is mandatory reading for those interested in prairie agriculture, community formation, leisure activities, and prairie identity. Voisey argues that historians must be aware of the complex interaction of tradition, environment, frontier, and metropolis if they hope to understand prairie community formation. He then skilfully weaves statistical information drawn from the census with a narrative drawn from diaries, newspapers, and the archival record to demonstrate his point. Voisey's examines the economics of prairie agriculture, merchant trade, and speculation, and the social aspects of sport, leisure, school, and church.

Upper Canada and Ontario

Bothwell, Robert. *A Short History of Ontario*. Edmonton: Hurtig, 1986.
It is ironic that Canada's largest and arguably most prosperous province has historically been poorly served by regional surveys. It is this void which Bothwell seeks to fill. *A Short History of Ontario* provides a brief summary of the economic and political developments of the province over the past two centuries. This work is traditional in focus: emphasis is placed upon staples development and the rise of modern industry, provincial-federal relationships, and the few men who governed the affairs of the province. Bothwell is less successful, however, in trying to explain the experience of women in Ontario's history, the place of Native peoples following settlement, or the life of the working-class individual. Designed for the general reader, this work does relate "the common experience of the province," but only within clearly delineated parameters.

Gagan, David. *Hopeful Travellers: Families, Land, and Social Change in mid-Victorian Peel County, Canada West*. Toronto: University of Toronto Press, 1981.

Utilizing manuscript census returns, detailed statistical analysis, and the writings of numerous settlers, Gagan analyses the social and economic strategies of rural families and the influence of external market forces on patterns of rural life in Peel County. In the thirty year period between 1840 and 1870, Peel County was transformed from a pioneer rural region to a modern, commercial agricultural district. The period was marked by mobility, farm expansion and consolidation, the emergence of local elites, and a marked change in the role of the family in the farm economy. Property ownership, he argues, was the single most important variable for determining social standing and economic success.

Hall, Roger, William Westfall, and Laurel Sefton Macdowell, eds. *Patterns of the Past: Interpreting Ontario's History.* Toronto: Dundurn Press, 1988.
This collection celebrates the centenary of the founding of the Ontario Historical Society and contains an eclectic mix of sixteen previously unpublished essays. The essays reflect much of the research that has emerged out of limited identities scholarship.

Johnson, J. K. and Bruce G. Wilson, eds. *Historical Essays on Upper Canada: New Perspectives.* Ottawa: Carleton University Press, 1991.
The original edition of *Historical Essays on Upper Canada* (1975) claimed "to cover economic, political, intellectual, social, cultural, and other topics." This volume covers similar ground but reflects the more sophisticated theoretical approaches of recent historians and increased attention to women, workers, ethnicity, and law. There is an extensive bibliography. Among numerous other collections, see David Keane and Colin Read, ed., *Old Ontario: Essays in Honour of J. M. S. Careless* (1990); F. H. Armstrong, H. A. Stevenson, and J. D. Wilson, eds., *Aspects of Nineteenth-Century Ontario: Essays Presented to James J. Talman* (1974); and Donald Swainson, ed., *Oliver Mowat's Ontario* (1972).

Piva, Michael, ed. *A History of Ontario: Selected Readings.* Toronto: Copp Clark, 1988.
Reflecting diverse methodologies and interests, this volume provides an introduction to some of the main streams of Ontario's history. *A History of Ontario* examines themes such as settlement and agriculture, the transition to urbanization and industrial capitalism, education and reform movements, resource development, gender, ethnicity, and politics. There is a useful bibliography.

White, Randall. *Ontario, 1610-1985*. Toronto: Dundurn Press, 1985.
Commissioned by the Ontario Heritage Foundation Local History Series, this work places Ontario in its regional context. The approach is popular and largely occurs along political and economic lines; like Robert Bothwell's *A Short History of Ontario* (1986), White's work pays attention to the role of staples production and an interventionist state in the development of the Ontario economy. Similarly, Native peoples largely disappear in the nineteenth century, and little attention is paid to the particular roles of women. In contrast to Bothwell's work, White emphasises the historical geography of the settlement process. Also see Joseph Schull, *Ontario Since 1867* (1978).

New France and Quebec

Behiels, Michael D., ed. *Quebec Since 1945: Selected Readings*. Toronto: Copp Clark, 1987.
A useful collection of articles relating to contemporary Quebec, this volume is organized into seven sections: Duplessis and his critics, the Quiet Revolution, organized labour, federal-provincial relations, language bills, the rise of the Parti Québécois, and prospects for Quebec nationalism. Very different interpretations and conclusions are presented, and a useful annotated bibliography is included.

Dechêne, Louise. *Habitants and Merchants in Seventeenth-Century Montreal*. Trans. Liana Vardi. Montreal: McGill-Queen's University Press, 1992.
Translated and revised almost twenty years after it was first published, *Habitants and Merchants* explores socio-economic structures and activities in a colonial society over two generations. This book is one of the most important local studies in Quebec history. Informed by Annales historiography, Dechêne adopts a structural approach that makes significant use of statistical evidence, especially notarial records. Dechêne explores the nature of the emerging capitalist economy and argues that there was little integration between agricultural production and the market economy of the fur trade. Montreal's social history was influenced heavily by economic structures; capitalism, Dechêne argues categorically, was the prime factor in social and cultural change. Montreal was not isolated from the larger world, since it developed like colonial societies elsewhere. Dechêne offers a valuable corrective to studies that emphasise only the fur trade economy of New France.

Eccles, W. J. *The Canadian Frontier, 1534-1760.* New York: Holt
   Rinehart Winston, 1969.
This study examines New France as a frontier, particularly in its
commercial, religious, settlement, and military aspects. Whereas Francis
Parkman saw Louis, Count de Frontenac as a hero, Eccles emphasises the
role of the merchant in the growth of New France, with little real analysis
into the role played by Native peoples. Eccles has written numerous other
studies including, *Canada Under Louis XIV, 1669-1701* (1964), and
Essays on New France (1987).

Greer, Allan. *Peasant, Lord and Merchant: Rural Society in Three
   Quebec Parishes, 1740-1840.* Toronto: University of Toronto Press,
   1985.
An impressive study that challenges the interpretation of rural Quebec put
forth by individuals such as Fernand Ouellet, R. Cole Harris, and W. J.
Eccles, *Peasant, Lord and Merchant* examines the rural parishes of Sorel,
St. Ours, and St. Denis in the century prior to 1840. Greer finds little
evidence of Ouellet's long-term agricultural crisis; instead, he concludes
that while wheat crops did fail some years — in 1806 or in the 1830s, for
example — "there is no evidence of any dramatic or decisive change
deserving the term 'crisis.'" Further, Greer argues that a feudal socio-
economic structure characterized rural Quebec, and that feudal obligations
upon peasants were more onerous than has previously been recognized. He
also concludes that as merchant capitalism intruded in the eighteenth
century it did not substantially change the peasant economy. Indeed, Greer
argues that merchant ventures largely fit into the existing socio-economic
structure, and merely created new lines of dependency through debt.
Because the feudal order was left intact, he argues, "the establishment of
a full-blown capitalist society was strangled in the cradle."

Hamilton, Roberta. *Feudal Society and Colonization: The Historiography
   of New France.* Gananoque, ON: Langdale Press, 1988.
In this important historiographical essay, Roberta Hamilton suggests that
historians of New France, influenced by the debate over the Conquest and
the economy of nineteenth-century Quebec, have asked the wrong
questions. She argues that New France was both colonial and feudal in the
era prior to Conquest. Working from a neo-Marxist perspective and
making extensive use of the secondary literature, Hamilton argues that
capitalism made few inroads into New France prior to the Conquest and
that, in reality, the feudal system became more entrenched in the early

eighteenth century. At Conquest, she notes, New France resembled Old France. To understand New France, she argues, historians should be less concerned with the bourgeoisie and pay more attention to the seigneurial system, habitant agriculture, the metropolis, and the church.

Linteau, Paul-André, René Durocher, and Jean-Claude Robert. *Quebec: A History, 1867-1929*. Toronto: James Lorimer, 1983.
Linteau, Paul-André, René Durocher, Jean-Claude Robert, and François Ricard. *Quebec Since 1930*. Trans. Robert Chodes and Ellen Garmaise. Toronto: James Lorimer, 1991.
This two-volume synthesis of Quebec from Confederation onward is a massive and important scholarly contribution. These volumes broadly focus upon socio-economic, demographic, cultural, and political developments. The authors argue that Quebec's transition to industrial capitalism was much like that of other areas (particularly Ontario's), and its development was, therefore, "normal." There is relatively little attention paid to the role of the church within Quebec society.

Little, John Irvine. *Crofters and Habitants: Settler Society, Economy, and Culture in a Quebec Township, 1848-1881*. Montreal: McGill-Queen's University Press, 1991.
In this excellent rural history, John Little examines the Scottish and French Canadian settlers in Winslow Township. Based upon extensive statistical evidence, the book examines the subjects of settlement, demography and family, economy, and cultural retention. The local economy, Little notes, depended upon agricultural production for home consumption and seasonal employment in the forest industry. Little also discovered far less mobility amongst settlers in Winslow Township than the patterns noted in other local studies. Furthermore, he argues the marginal nature of the local economy and the relatively slow process of incorporating the family economy into the industrial capitalist milieu provided for stronger cultural retention. As a result, Little concludes two relatively stable, independent, but exclusive communities emerged. For another local study providing valuable insight into rural Quebec, see François Noël, *The Christie Seigneuries: Estate Management and Settlement in the Upper Richelieu Valley, 1760-1854* (1992).

_____. *Nationalism, Capitalism, and Colonization in Nineteenth-century Quebec: The Upper St. Francis District*. Montreal: McGill-Queen's University Press, 1989.

In this local study, John Little examines the process of colonization and settlement in the marginal lands within Quebec. Most early interpretations of the colonization movement conclude that it was a conservative, clerical-based response to urban migration and industrial capitalism. Little argues that the colonization schemes, in reality, reflected a search for new economic opportunities. He examines the promotional efforts of the church, state, and capital interests and discovers that colonization was a flawed response by the "petit-bourgeois to the rise of industrial capitalism." The colonization schemes, however, were doomed to failure because none of the promoters recognized the need to establish a small producer-based agri-forest economic system, and instead promoted subsistence farming and seasonal employment in the forest industry.

Miquelon, Dale. *The First Canada: to 1791*. Toronto: McGraw-Hill Ryerson, 1994.
A slim volume by a leading authority, *First Canada* provides an introduction to New France and offers an interpretation of the concept of the *ancien régime* in the eighteenth century. Miquelon explores this concept in terms of linkages; that is, the relationship of persons to persons, most often across great differences in social status and authority. Some values inherent in the *ancien régime* became common in the First Canada; others did not travel so well. Miquelon also takes issue with many "Montreal School" nationalists who maintain that pre-Conquest New France was a forward-looking and progressive society.

_____. *New France, 1701-1744: "A Supplement to Europe."* Toronto: McClelland and Stewart, 1987.
One of the best volumes in the Centenary Series, this work explores the expansion and colonization of New France. As the title suggests, Miquelon place New France within an imperial framework, particularly in his discussions of political and economic considerations. Some attention is paid, however, to societal linkages between France and its colony, and Miquelon explores the connections of family, tradition, and patronage.

Miquelon, Dale, ed. *Society and Conquest: The Debate on the Bourgeoisie and Social Change in French Canada, 1700-1850*. Vancouver: Copp Clark, 1977.
In this important book Dale Miquelon introduces readers to the historiography of New France, Quebec, and the role of the Conquest. In his introduction, Miquelon explains the differences in interpretation

between the Montreal and Laval schools of Quebec history, but also notes that both seek to explain the apparent inferior economic condition of Quebec in the nineteenth century. He selects excerpts from the work of Maurice Séguin, Michel Brunet, and Guy Frégault (the Montreal school) that illustrate that the Conquest effectively decapitated Quebec society by eliminating the French Canadian bourgeoisie. He contrasts their work with selections from the work of Jean Hamelin and Fernand Ouellet (the Laval School) that emphasise the noblesse (non-capitalist) social mentalité of French Canadians and the resulting structural weaknesses in the economy of New France and later Quebec. While the Montreal school sees the Conquest as a disaster, the Laval school considers it insignificant.

Ouellet, Fernand. *Economy, Class and Nation in Quebec: Interpretive Essays*. Translated and edited by Jacques A. Barbier. Toronto: Copp Clark, 1991.
Fernand Ouellet is, without doubt, one of Canada and Quebec's most important historians. These essays — previously published in French — run chronologically from New France to contemporary Quebec and are united by their critique and ultimate rejection of nationalistic tendencies in the writing of Quebec's history. The initial section contains essays which examine the *ancien régime* in New France and in the century after the Conquest, with particular attention to the origins, character, and function of the nobility. The second section examines the relationship between agriculture, other economic ventures, and seasonal labour, particularly as it relates to the movement of the Québécois to the countryside. Third, *Economy, Class and Nation* includes several historiographic essays examining social issues in terms of class, gender, and ethnicity. Ouellet concludes with a brief interpretation of the impact of the Quiet Revolution.

_____. *Lower Canada, 1791-1840: Social Change and Nationalism*.
Trans. Patricia Claxton. Toronto: McClelland and Stewart, 1980.
This enormously important volume in the Centenary series — originally published as *Le Bas-Canada, 1791-1840* in 1976 — utilizes a vast amount of quantitative data to argue that the emergence of French-Canadian nationalism in the early nineteenth century was largely a product of socio-economic crises, rather than the oppressive hand of British rule. Ouellet examines the nature of the agricultural crisis, demography, politics in Lower Canada, and the Rebellions of 1837-1838. Also see Ouellet's seminal *Economic and Social History of Quebec, 1760-1850* (1966).

Trofimenkoff, Susan Mann. *The Dream of Nation: A Social and Intellectual History of Quebec.* Toronto: Macmillan of Canada, 1982.
A superb synthesis of the history of Quebec, this work focuses upon French-speaking Quebecois "since they have always been the source of greatest puzzlement to English Canada." While not ignoring political or military events, the focus is on intellectual and social themes such as the role of the church, ultramontanism, expressions of nationalism, and the impact of urban and industrial development. In addition, more than previous surveys, Trofimenkoff integrates women and the rise of feminism into her synthesis; less attention is given to French-speaking Canadians and their relationship to Native people. For an older and less useful survey of the political and intellectual history of Quebec, see Mason Wade, *The French Canadians, 1760-1967* (2 vols.; rev. ed. 1968).

Trudel, Marcel. *The Beginnings of New France, 1524-1663.* Trans. Patricia Claxton. Toronto: McClelland and Stewart, 1973.
A condensation of three previous works, this volume in the Centenary Series examines the French fact in the so-called New World. Trudel identifies three major periods: until 1603 the first phase was marked principally by a series of fruitless efforts; second, from 1604 to 1627 relatively weak efforts were made to develop the fur trade; finally, although the third era often resembled is predecessor, the years prior to 1663 saw a system of land distribution and social structures transplanted from France. Other volumes in this series dealing with New France include W. J. Eccles, *Canada Under Louis XIV, 1669-1701* (1964), Dale Miquelon, *New France, 1701-1744* (1987), and G. F. G. Stanley, *New France, 1744-1760* (1968).

Young, Brian and John Dickinson. *A Short History of Quebec: A Socio-Economic Perspective.* Toronto: Copp Clark, 1988.
While an important school of Quebec historiography has emphasised the province's ideological traditions, Young and Dickinson concentrate on a socio-economic perspective. While such an approach does not ignore ideological implications, the concentration is clearly upon socio-economic developments and transitions, and their relationship to issues of region, class, gender, and ethnicity. Such an emphasis leads to, for example, the subordination of the political act of Confederation to the transition to industrial capitalism between 1815 and 1886. Young and Dickinson argue that such a transition was so fundamental that insights into this period can not be divorced from it. Correspondingly, the role of the Catholic church

is downplayed, although the significance of growing secularization in modern Quebec is acknowledged.

Atlantic Canada

Arsenault, Georges. *The Island Acadians, 1720-1980.* Charlottetown: Ragweed Press, 1989.
Arsenault has spent much of his career studying the Acadian population of Prince Edward Island, publishing most of his work in French. This effective narrative examines the cultural and linguistic survival of the Acadian population. The Acadians were largely expelled during the Seven Years War, but many returned as tenants and struggled to restore their distinctive cultural identity.

Brym, Robert J. and R. James Scouman, eds. *Underdevelopment and Social Movements in Atlantic Canada.* Toronto: New Hogtown Press, 1979.
This collection of ten previously published essays reflects Marxist and metropolitan interpretations of Atlantic Canada and examine topics such as the fishermen's unions, the inshore fishery, farm cooperatives, colonial exploitation, the myth of political conservatism in Atlantic Canada, and neo-nationalism in Newfoundland. While the theme of capitalist exploitation links the essays, overall cohesiveness is lacking.

Buckner, Phillip A. and John G. Reid, eds. *The Atlantic Region to Confederation: A History.* Toronto: University of Toronto Press, 1994.
Forbes, E. R. and D. A. Muise, eds. *The Atlantic Provinces in Confederation.* Toronto: University of Toronto Press, 1993.
One of the most significant collaborative ventures in modern Canadian historiography, these volumes seek to do for Atlantic Canada what Gerald Friesen's *The Canadian Prairies* (1984) did for the West. The last attempt at a maritime synthesis, W. S. MacNutt's *The Atlantic Provinces: The Emergence of Colonial Society, 1712-1857* (1965), is limited in scope, overly concerned with colonial and political affairs, and entirely dismissive of the colony of Newfoundland. *The Atlantic Provinces in Confederation* and *The Atlantic Region* — with over two dozen prominent contributors — reflect much of the dynamic work of the past several decades. The contributions have been divided chronologically, with more emphasis on the nineteenth and twentieth centuries, and a single thematic chapter on Newfoundland in the second volume. Within a broad

constitutional and political framework, significant attention is given to aboriginal peoples, gender, class, and ethnic minority groups. Thus, for example, Stephen A. Davies and Ralph Pastore begin the first volume by emphasizing that Native society was dynamic in nature and that the original inhabitants were active participants in the economic systems which followed contact; while less prominent in the second volume, the lives of Native people find expression right up to John Reid's contribution on the 1970s. Throughout these excellent volumes, regional stereotypes about the "hidebound conservatism of Maritimers" and the region's economic and cultural lethargy are dispelled.

Bumsted, J. M. *Land, Settlement, and Politics on Eighteenth-Century Prince Edward Island.* Montreal: McGill-Queen's University Press, 1987.
Prince Edward Island was divided into 67 proprietary land grants in 1767, given by lottery to "suitable" applicants. The land system was intended to create a colonial elite and ensure settlement at minimal cost to the Crown. The division between tenant farmer and absentee proprietor would be the focal point for political debate in P. E. I. for the next century. Most historical accounts castigate the proprietors, but Bumsted argues that during the initial stages of development the proprietors rarely recouped their investments. Political campaigns against the proprietors, he notes, were usually orchestrated by others interested in obtaining the proprietary title. Sadly, Bumsted's analysis is limited to the eighteenth century, and the period around the Confederation era, when debates regarding the absentee landlords reached their peak, still awaits adequate treatment.

Conrad, Margaret, ed. *Making Adjustments: Change and Continuity in Planter Nova Scotia, 1759-1800.* Fredericton: Acadiensis Press, 1991.
This collection of 18 essays on New England settlers in Nova Scotia. The collection is broken into five thematic sections: Contexts, Diversities, Case Studies, Explorations, and Future Directions. The essays are uneven in quality, scope, and theoretical rigidity, but *Making Adjustments* is still a good introduction to the literature and the scholars active in this field.

Daigle, Jean, ed. *The Acadians of the Maritimes: Thematic Studies.* Moncton: Centre d'étude acadiennes, 1982.
The English edition of the 1980 collection, *The Acadians of the Maritimes* is an introductory survey of Acadian history from settlement to the 1970s. Daigle's introductory essay provides a synthesis of Acadian history, and

is followed by a series of essays that examine settlement, economy, education, and folklore.

Forbes, Ernest R. *Challenging the Regional Stereotype: Essays on the 20*th *Century Maritimes.* Fredericton: Acadiensis Press, 1989.
This book contains eleven essays by Ernest Forbes outlining his perspectives on Maritime history. Forbes emphasises dual themes of the role of government and economic policy in regional development. Forbes deconstructs the mythology of a conservative Maritime regional population unable and unwilling to adapt to the modern industrial capitalist world. Instead, he argues that Maritimers have made significant efforts to accommodate the new industrial capitalist economy, but have always failed to receive favourable government assistance at key moments in the process.

_____. *Maritime Rights: The Maritime Rights Movement, 1919-1927, a Study in Canadian Regionalism.* Montreal: McGill-Queen's University Press, 1979.
Traditionally, Canadian historians have emphasised protest parties of the West and have, therefore, contributed to the mythology of the conservative, staid nature of the Atlantic region. Forbes challenges this myth. He argues that post-World War I discontent emerged initially among farmer and labour organizations over poor economic conditions, changes in freight rates, and the well-founded belief that Ottawa favoured central Canadian companies over the interests of the Maritime region. In the 1925 federal election, a coalition of labour organizations, farmers, business, and politicians helped to contribute to King's initial defeat and to the King-Byng constitutional crisis that followed. This discontent died out, however, by the late 1920s with improved economic conditions and small concessions such as those recommended by the Duncan Royal Commission.

Griffiths, Naomi. *The Contexts of Acadic History, 1686-1784.* Montreal: McGill-Queen's University Press, 1992.
_____. *The Acadians: The Creation of a People.* Toronto; McGraw-Hill Ryerson, 1973.
In these two books, Naomi Griffiths provides succinct and critical analysis of the structure of Acadian society. She argues that geography, environment, community, and family produced an independent and distinctive community along the Bay of Fundy. This community was

challenged constantly by the metropolitan desires of Britain and France, and, as a result of their independence, the Acadians were eventually expelled from their lands.

Hornsby, Stephen J. *Nineteenth Century Cape Breton: A Historical Geography*. Montreal: McGill-Queen's University Press, 1992.
The study of Atlantic Canada has produced some superb examples of historical geography. Hornsby explores the socio-economic development and immigration patterns of Cape Breton through the course of the nineteenth century. During this period, Cape Breton developed from a region of small fishing outposts to one that numbered almost 90,000 and boasted a much more diversified economy. Cape Breton's reliance upon the staples of fish and coal, and the deficient nature of its agricultural sector, however, did not provide the economy with viable potential for economic growth.

Mackinnon, Neil. *The Unfriendly Soil: The Loyalist Experience in Nova Scotia, 1783-1791*. Montreal: McGill-Queen's University Press, 1986.
Thousands of loyalists migrated to Nova Scotia after 1781 and attempted to establish new communities in the colony. Most failed to achieve their goals, and by 1791 a massive out-migration occurred as loyalists returned to the United States. This book analyses this brief and tumultuous period of Nova Scotia history. Unlike many books on the loyalists, *The Unfriendly Soil* does not dwell upon the long-term significance of loyalist ideology upon Canada, but instead focuses upon the turmoil and chaos which characterised the refugee experience. For a more general and popular study, see Lesley Choyce, *Nova Scotia: Shaped by the Sea* (1997).

Morrison, James H. and James Moreira, eds. *Tempered by Rum: Rum in the History of the Maritime Provinces*. Porters Lake, NS: Pottersfield Press, 1988.
Trade with the West Indies, particularly the rum trade, is an important aspect of Maritime history. These papers from a 1986 conference — which examine both economic and social aspects of the trade — are divided into sections on the manufacture and consumption of rum, prohibition and smuggling of rum, and the logistics of the rum trade.

Rawlyk, George. *Nova Scotia's Massachusetts: A Study of Massachusetts-Nova Scotia Relations, 1630-1784*. Montreal: McGill-Queen's University Press, 1973.

Rawlyk surveys the relationship between Massachusetts and Nova Scotia and revises several of the conclusions reached by J. B. Brebner's pioneering books *New England's Outpost* (1927) and *The Neutral Yankees of Nova Scotia* (1937). He concludes that Massachusetts's interest in Nova Scotia emerged from economic considerations and a desire to limit French colonial expansion in North America. Massachusetts required good relations with the Acadians in order to maintain access to the cod fishery and to sustain the developing trade relationships, but feared the increase of French colonial power in the region. As a result, Massachusetts conducted a series of sporadic military forays into the region.

Reid, John G. *Six Crucial Decades: Times of Change in the History of the Maritimes.* Halifax: Nimbus Publishing, 1987.
A series of lectures delivered at St. Mary's University, this book is aimed at both academic readers and the general public. Reid emphasises the changes which have occurred in the Maritimes and examines six crucial decades to illustrate his thesis: the 1600s and the founding of Acadia, the 1750s and the exile of the Acadians, the 1780s and the arrival of the Loyalists; the 1860s and Confederation, the 1880s and industrialization, and the 1920s and the Maritime Rights Movement.

_____. *Acadia, Maine and New Scotland: Marginal Colonies in the Seventeenth Century.* Toronto: University of Toronto Press, 1981.
A leading historians of Maritime regionalism, John Reid successfully demonstrates that the particular regional circumstances of this region led the European metropolitan powers to fail in their efforts to incorporate these colonies into the mercantilist economic system. Instead, he concludes that aboriginal peoples and Massachusetts merchants were a far more important influence upon the European settlements in this region.

Sharpe, Errol. *A People's History of Prince Edward Island.* Toronto: Steel Rail Publishing, 1976.
A narrative history of P. E. I., written from a subtle Marxist perspective, Errol Sharpe's work is a useful introduction. He argues that P. E. I., a small hinterland in a colonial capitalist economy, was doomed to be exploited rather than developed.

Smitheram, Verner, David Milne, and Satadal Dasgupta, eds. *The Garden Transformed: Prince Edward Island, 1945-1980.* Charlottetown: Ragweed Press, 1982.

Eleven essays from a number of disciplines, this collection reviews the decline of agriculture in Prince Edward Island and the transformation of the local society since World War II. Topics covered include politics, historical consciousness and pastoral mythologies, land use, tourism, education, and urbanization.

Weale, David and Harry Baglole. *The Island and Confederation: The End of an Era*. Summerside, PEI: Williams and Crue, 1973.
Well-illustrated but lacking references, this book is of limited use to researchers. It does, however, clarify certain issues surrounding Prince Edward Island's decision to join Confederation in 1873. The authors divide the book in two sections. The first examines the history and culture of P. E. I. from 1767 to 1873; the second the six years of negotiation for entry following the original Confederation agreements of 1873. Although popular accounts suggest Prince Edward Island resisted Confederation in order to improve the financial aspects of the deal, the authors argue that Islanders resisted Confederation because it feared a loss of autonomy.

Wynn, Graeme. *Timber Colony: A Historical Geography of Early Nineteenth Century New Brunswick*. Toronto: University of Toronto Press, 1981.
This award-winning study is valuable to those interested in the history of New Brunswick and Atlantic Canada generally, as well as forestry, business and environmental history, and state formation. A historical geographer, Wynn places the relationship between people and landscape at the centre of this study. Wynn ably describes how and why people transformed the New Brunswick landscape through the timber industry. In addition, Wynn explores merchant-government relations, the political process, and the emergence of large-scale capitalist enterprises in the timber business.

The North

Berger, Thomas R. *Northern Frontier, Northern Homeland: The Report of the Mackenzie Valley Pipeline Inquiry*. 2 vols. Toronto: James Lorimer, 1977.
Justice Berger spent three years compiling evidence from social scientists, environmental scientists, and aboriginal groups in attempting to assess the impact of constructing an oil pipeline in the Mackenzie River valley. This report surveys the history of the Canadian north and illuminates issues of

importance to aboriginal lands claims, economic development and the environment, and government administration in the north.

Coates, Kenneth. *Canada's Colonies: A History of the Yukon and Northwest Territories*. Toronto: James Lorimer, 1985.
A popular account by one of Canada's premier northern historians, *Canada's Colonies* is the best historical overview of the North. Encompassing at least three distinct regions (Yukon, Western Arctic, and Eastern Arctic) and four distinct cultures (Dene, Métis, Inuit, and White), the north presents a daunting task to anyone trying to write a survey. In contrast to Morris Zaslow, Coates is sympathetic to northern aspirations, while still emphasising the impact of southern Canadian activities. Canada, therefore, treated the region like a colony and acted only when southern benefits were apparent. Although the book lacks references, it contains a good bibliography and remains the best choice as a survey text for courses on northern history.

Coates, Ken S. and William R. Morrison. *The Alaska Highway in World War II: The U. S. Army of Occupation in Canada's Northwest*. Oklahoma City: University of Oklahoma Press, 1992.
Canada had pursued a policy of benign neglect in the Arctic prior to World War II. The entry of 33,000 American soldiers and civilian contractors to upgrade a series of airfields along the Northwest Staging Route, build a highway from Dawson Creek, BC, to Fairbanks, Alaska, and construct the CANOL oil pipeline from Norman Wells to Whitehorse, YT, slowly changed the Canadian attitude. In this book, Coates and Morrison take the emphasis off the Alaska Highway's affect on Canadian government policy, and look instead on how the projects affected the local population including the Native peoples. For a series of excellent essays, see Ken Coates, ed., *The Alaska Highway: Papers of the Fortieth Anniversary Symposium* (1985); and Bob Hesketh, ed., *Three Northwest War Projects* (1995).

_____. *Land of the Midnight Sun: A History of the Yukon*. Edmonton: Hurtig, 1988.
The monolithic image of the Yukon as Klondike is one which Coates and Morrison, the two most prodigious interpreters of the Canadian North, obviously seek to qualify. This synthesis ranges from a brief discussion pre-contact Native peoples to the post-World War II struggle of aboriginal and non-Native inhabitants for recognition from the federal government.

While the sometimes romantic Klondike gold rush is not neglected, aboriginal/non-Native relationships within the larger economic environment are emphasised; indeed, Coates and Morrison argue that until the 1898 orgy for gold, Native people were the dominant partner. While for much of the past century the federal government has treated the Yukon simply as a resource to be exploited, this volume optimistically concludes by suggesting that the dramatic renaissance of Native culture and the gradual devolution of decision-making authority may result in a change in this colonial relationship.

Diubaldo, Richard J. *Stefansson and the Canadian Arctic*. Montreal: McGill-Queen's University Press, 1978.

Vilhjalmur Stefansson was one of Canada's earliest and most controversial experts on the Arctic. He made several expeditions to the region between 1908 and 1920 and mapped several uncharted regions in the archipelago. Later, he became a vocal proponent of northern development. Stefansson's contribution to Canadian exploration and his important role in establishing Canadian sovereignty in the Arctic, however, remains little studied. Diubaldo's study attempts to correct this oversight. Diubaldo argues that Stefansson's expeditions were, on the whole, extremely successful but the explorer failed to play the proper political games within the Geological Survey of Canada (GSC). Opponents in the GSC, therefore, convinced Canadian officials that Stefansson was an extravagant eccentric and his work was disregarded. As a result, Stefansson's exploits were ignored in Canada and the explorer lived his life in virtual exile in the United States. For other studies of ventures to the North, see C. Stuart Houston ed. *Artic Artist: The Journal and Paintings of George Back, Midshipman with Franklin, 1819-1822* (1994); and M. J. Ross, *Polar Pioneers: John Ross and James Clark Ross* (1994).

Francis, Daniel. *Discovery of the North: The Exploration of Canada's Arctic*. Edmonton: Hurtig, 1986.

This account of Arctic exploration by one of Canada's gifted popular historians is an excellent introduction to the topic. Francis is clearly aware of the most recent scholarship in the field and presents it in a provocative and exciting narrative. The book touches upon all the important issues of Arctic exploration, including early efforts by British explorers in the eastern Arctic, Scandinavian expeditions at the turn of the century, and Canada's efforts to preserve Arctic sovereignty.

Morrison, William R. *Showing the Flag: The Mounted Police and Canadian Sovereignty in the North, 1894-1925*. Vancouver: University of British Columbia Press, 1985.

The Royal North West Mounted Police (RNWMP) were sent to the Yukon territory in 1894 not only to protect law and order, but also to maintain a Canadian government presence in the region. This dual role would continue for the next thirty years. Morrison demonstrates that RNWMP activity in the Canadian north focussed primarily upon establishing sovereignty, and, to a lesser degree, law and order; concerns about social welfare rarely entered the equation. Although critical of police attitudes towards Native people and of individual lapses in judgement by a few officers, Morrison's well-researched and documented book endorses a wholesome and heroic image of the RNWMP.

Page, Robert. *Northern Development: The Canadian Dilemma*. Toronto: McClelland and Stewart, 1986.

The proposal to build a pipeline through the Mackenzie River valley in the 1970s provoked outrage amongst Canadian environmentalists; led to a far reaching study of the economic, social, and environmental ramifications of the project; and encouraged natural and social scientists to study the issue of northern development. This book looks at the investigative work by the Mackenzie Valley Pipeline Inquiry. Page skilfully weaves the scientific evidence collected by the inquiry with the broad perspective of northern social and economic development. He is critical of the corporate and political sector, and quietly supportive of Thomas Berger, the inquiry's chair.

Ross, W. Gillies. *Arctic Whalers, Icy Seas*. Toronto: Irwin, 1985

Ross effectively links interpretive commentary with extracts from the log books and reports of whalers in this fine history of an essential Arctic industry. Readers will discover an intriguing analysis of daily life in a whaling crew and the interaction between whalers and the local Inuit population. His earlier book *Whaling and Eskimos* (1976) is also useful.

Zaslow, Morris. *The Opening of the Canadian North, 1870-1914*. Toronto: McClelland and Stewart, 1971.
_____. *The Northward Expansion of Canada, 1914-1967*. Toronto: McClelland and Stewart, 1988.

These two volumes prepared for the Canadian Centenary Series are the most detailed surveys of the history of Canada's north. Zaslow takes a broad view of the northern region and includes information on the boreal forest and Pre-Cambrian shield as well as the Arctic. As the time period covered in these books would suggest, Zaslow focuses his analysis on the metropolitan agents of southern expansion — including fur traders, missionaries, police, scientists, businessmen, and government bureaucrats — rather than on the indigenous population of the region. Zaslow's work has become a standard source, but should be compared with the alternative perspective in Ken Coates, *Canada's Colonies: A History of the Yukon and Northwest Territories* (1985).

Zaslow, Morris, ed. *A Century of Canada's Arctic Islands, 1880-1980.*
    Ottawa: Royal Society of Canada, 1981.
This collection of papers from the 23rd symposium organized by the Royal Society of Canada, is an excellent introduction to the literature and themes of arctic history. The contributors come from both the natural and social sciences, and the themes investigated include reports of scientific investigations, Canadian sovereignty and arctic defence, and Canadian government administration.

Urban History

Acheson, T. W. *Saint John: The Making of a Colonial Urban Community.*
    Toronto: University of Toronto Press, 1985.
In 1815 Saint John was a small, highly-stratified garrison town, burdened or blessed with a powerful social elite. In a brilliant and multi-faceted study, T. W. Acheson examines the transition of Saint John from a town into a city. By 1860, as in many other centres, this urban process was accompanied by growing economic inequality, ethnic diversity, new transportation, financial, social and industrial institutions, and large-scale population movement. By the middle of the nineteenth century, people of Irish descent formed over one half the population. Acheson argues that these immigrants were defined by both ethnicity and religion, and explores their socio-economic integration into the community and, after 1840, the disintegration of the Irish community into Roman Catholic and Protestant factions. In addition, Acheson notes the influence of evangelicalism — principally via the Methodists — which grew from a marginal force in 1820 to a central element by 1850. This movement, he argues, came closest of any philosophy to reflecting the spirit and temper of the age, and "played a critical role in defining the urban community."

Artibise, Alan. *Winnipeg: A Social History of Urban Growth, 1874-1914.*
   Montreal: McGill-Queen's University Press, 1975.
The first forty years of Winnipeg's history saw it grow from a small
hamlet to Canada's third largest city by 1911 and the recipient of the
moniker, the "Chicago of the North." Influenced by the American historian
Sam Bass Warner Jr. and his studies of Boston and Philadelphia, Artibise
has produced a thematic study that examines Winnipeg's rapid
industrialization and building of infrastructure, reform efforts, civic
politics, and especially the role of its elites. In particular, this volume
chronicles the dominance of the business elite and their control of civic
politics: Winnipeg was, Artibise argues, created and informed "by
businessmen for business purposes." There was, therefore, little civic
effort to ensure adequate health and housing, and the city's working-class
and ethnic minorities suffered as a result.

Artibise, Alan, ed. *Town and City: Aspects of Western Canadian Urban
   Development.* Regina: Canadian Plains Research Centre, 1981.
This valuable collection of fifteen papers touches various aspects of
western Canadian urban development, including two important
introductory essays on the prairie and British Columbian urban "systems."
Each essay is thoroughly referenced, and the volume contains an important
statistical abstract. Researchers will discover articles on the development
of townsites, city-building and boosterism, and urban social history.

Artibise, Alan F. *Winnipeg: An Illustrated History.* Toronto: James
   Lorimer, 1977.
Brennan, William J. *Regina: An Illustrated History.* Toronto: James
   Lorimer, 1989.
Careless, J. M. S. *Toronto to 1918: An Illustrated History.* Toronto: James
   Lorimer, 1984.
Foran, Maxwell. *Calgary: An Illustrated History.* Toronto: James
   Lorimer, 1978.
Lemon, James T. *Toronto Since 1918: An Illustrated History.* Toronto:
   James Lorimer, 1985.
Roy, Patricia. *Vancouver: An Illustrated History.* Toronto: James Lorimer,
   1980.
Taylor, John H. *Ottawa: An Illustrated History.* Toronto: James Lorimer,
   1986.
Weaver, John C. *Hamilton: An Illustrated History.* Toronto: James
   Lorimer, 1982.

Together with the Canadian Museum of Civilization, James Lorimer has commissioned "The History of Canadian Cities Series" in order to provide entry into a more comprehensive understanding of Canada's urban past. Although popular in orientation, these volumes are written by respected academics who have focussed upon similar themes: ethnic relationships, regionalism, provincial-municipal interaction, social mobility, labour relations, and urban and economic development. These works are profusely illustrated, provide some statistical material, and contain introductory bibliographies.

Fingard, Judith. *The Dark Side of Life in Victorian Halifax*. Porters Lake, NS: Pottersfield Press, 1989.

This study examines the lives of 91 recidivists such as Mary Ford, who was born to a poverty-stricken family, married into another, and was in and out of jail at least 25 times before dying at age 21. As the example of Mary Ford illustrates, poverty and the creation of an underclass were often hereditary, or the product of poor education or mental illness; gender and race also contributed to vulnerability and black women, for example, were vastly over-represented among Halifax's prostitutes. Moreover, frequent incarceration was not necessarily something to be avoided; Fingard argues that since stone-breaking was not introduced to Rockhead until 1868, many saw prison as a refuge, and it may have even prolonged lifespans. In addition, Fingard notes that the rise and influence of "evangelical millenarianism and Catholic social action combined with new notions of urban order, domestic ideology and industrial discipline" brought increased societal attention to social problems. In an argument that will be disputed by some working-class historians — who also object to Fingard's neglect of the abuses of industrial capitalism in creating an underclass — *The Dark Side of Life* argues that as a result of outside intervention, much of the autonomy of the lower orders was lost.

Goheen, P. G. *Victorian Toronto, 1850 to 1900: Pattern and Process of Growth*. Chicago: University of Chicago, 1970.

This study of Toronto traces its development from a pre-industrial to an industrial city. Utilizing an ecological paradigm informed by the work of Sam Bass Warner Jr. and University of Chicago sociologists, Goheen emphasises the stages of development a city goes through in response to economic and technological change. Goheen acknowledges class, ethnic, and religious differences in pre-industrial Toronto, but argues that there were not necessarily geographical distinctions between them. By 1870,

however, economic change and the introduction of street cars had made
suburbs more possible, and geographical differentiation was more explicit.
Urban historians who emphasise class, however, often challenge Goheen's
conclusion that wealth and status did not result in spatial segregation from
the onset of a city's development. Nevertheless, *Victorian Toronto* still
remains a premier example of the ecological model of urban development
in Canada. Also see Frederick H. Armstron, *A City in the Making:
Progress, People, and Perils in Victorian Toronto* (1988).

Kalman, Harold. *A History of Canadian Architecture.* 2 vols. Toronto:
    Oxford University Press, 1994.
The first major survey of Canadian architecture in almost 30 years, this
work is a significant and important achievement. Ranging chronologically
from New France to post-modernism, Kalman defines architecture, or
"built environment" broadly: that is, just about everything people have
built. Significantly, Kalman sees architecture as both the design and
expression of a culture, and these volumes therefore provide a summary
history of Canada along the theme of humanity's need to provide shelter
and buildings. A rich text is accompanied by over 800 illustrations.

Katz, Michael B. *The People of Hamilton, Canada West: Family and
    Class in a Mid-nineteenth Century City.* Cambridge: Harvard
    University Press, 1975.
This outstanding study is based upon an extensive statistical data base
compiled from the manuscript census returns. Katz examines the period
of transition in Hamilton from merchant-based metropolitan community
to industrial city. He explores the "relationships among occupation,
wealth, transiency, social mobility, ethnicity, property ownership,
residential patterns, and family composition," and effectively illustrates
the class-based stratification that accompanied this transformation. The
city slowly became divided along the lines of occupational status and
wealth. Interestingly, Katz also concludes that Hamilton did not have as
significant racial or ethnic cleavages as comparable American cities
during this period.

Linteau, Paul-Andre. *The Promoter's City: Building the Industrial Town
    of Maisonneuve, 1883-1918.* Toronto: James Lorimer & Company,
    1985.
Between 1883 and 1918 the Montreal suburb of Maisonneuve grew from
a small rural village to a leading industrial centre. Arguing that the

traditional picture painted by Quebec's clerical-nationalist ideology has emphasised "agriculturalism" and "ruralism," Linteau was drawn to the phenomenon of rapid urbanization of towns such as Maisonneuve and numerous others. In the years prior to World War I, the greatest catalyst to urbanization involved attracting industrial capital; thus, tax exemptions, cash grants, and a vigorous advertising campaign were employed. In addition, in the decade prior to the war, civic leaders aimed to construct a model city, complete with large public buildings, boulevards, and an ambitious beautification program. Linteau argues that the majority of these city promoters were French Canadians, and that "land capital" was an important economic foundation for the francophone bourgeoisie.

MacDonald, Norbert. *Distant Neighbours: A Comparative History of Seattle and Vancouver*. Lincoln: University of Nebraska Press, 1988.
MacDonald looks at the similarities and differences in the development of these two Pacific communities. In a chronological study, he compares their early history as frontier towns, the impact of the transcontinental railways, their competition for hinterland production, the effects of war and depression, and the development of municipal politics. MacDonald's study demonstrates that differences between the two cities emerged from their roles as American or Canadian port cities, and the very different national perspectives on the role of entrepreneurs and government. This thoroughly referenced book is a fine comparative study of businessmen and politicians.

McDonald, Robert A. J. *Making Vancouver: Class, Status, and Social Boundaries, 1863-1913*. Vancouver: University of British Columbia Press, 1996.
The half century between the establishment of the first saw mill on Burrard Inlet and the onset of World War I saw the transformation of the small village of Granville into the metropolitan centre of Vancouver, the fourth largest city in Canada. Well-researched and theoretically informed, this is a superb social history of Vancouver during its transition to industrial capitalism. Employing collective biographies of four groups of people — business leaders, social leaders, civic leaders, and labour activists — *Making Vancouver* argues that concepts of status, class, ethnicity, and race were all crucial to the construction of social identities. For an excellent collection of essays along similar themes, see Robert A. J. McDonald and Jean Barman, ed., *Vancouver Past: Essays in Social History* (1986).

Rutherford, Paul, ed. *Saving the Canadian City: the First Phase, 1880-1920. An Anthology of Early Articles on Urban Reform.* Toronto: University of Toronto Press, 1974.
Divided into four sections — public utilities, social issues, town planning, and municipal government — *Saving the Canadian City* presents a collection of essays from (largely) middle-class reformers who were confronted by the problems and challenges of urbanization.

Stelter, Gilbert and Alan Artibise, ed. *The Canadian City: Essays in Urban and Social History.* Ottawa: Carleton University Press, 1984.
The essays in this collection represent the best scholarship in the field in the 1980s. Thoroughly referenced and analytical, *The Canadian City* is divided into sections on urban development to 1850, metropolitanism, the physical environment, urban society, and urban government. For a collection of more current articles, see Gilbert Stelter, ed., *Cities and Urbanization: Canadian Historical Perspectives* (1990).

Wade, Jill. *Houses for All: The Struggle for Social Housing in Vancouver, 1919-50.* Vancouver: University of British Columbia Press, 1994.
Vancouver enjoys an international reputation as one of the world's most livable cities; yet, it has a housing crisis. Wade's study of the social history of housing illustrates that this is not a recent phenomenon: *Houses for All* documents the problems of overcrowding, poor construction, and house shortages, and dissects efforts by governments and individuals to provide some solution to these problems.

External Relations and Military History

Until recently, diplomatic and military history in Canada has focussed primarily upon two themes: first, the nature of Canada's relationship with the British Empire; and second, the nature of Canada's relationship with the United States. Traditional and left-nationalist interpretations have argued that Canada had cast off the shackles of British imperialism only to enter into a dependency relationship with the United States after 1945. They cast blame upon the Liberal governments led by Mackenzie King, Louis St. Laurent, and Lester Pearson. A revisionist perspective emerged in the 1970s. Influenced by the work of American scholars, revisionists did not dispute the colonial nature of Canadian-American relations, but argued that the weakness of Britain following World War II left Canadian politicians with no room to manoeuver. The Liberal governments in Canada, faced with this difficult set of circumstances, had made all efforts to protect Canadian sovereignty. More recently, Canadian historians, influenced by the American post-revisionists, have recently developed a more sophisticated interpretation of external relations. The middle power thesis accepts that Great Power politics dominate the larger world picture and that Canada will always be a partner in the Western alliance. Canada, as a middle power, has to pursue its national security and economic interests within this reality. The issue of Canadian-American relations has lost its dominance in the 1990s as Canadian historians have begun to turn their attention to the Pacific rim and military history. Indeed, a new generation of Canadian military historians appears to be emerging.

Readers should be aware that many Canadian diplomats have been active writing the history of Canadian external affairs; however, only the works of the two best writers, John Holmes and Escott Reid, have been included. The foundation for much of Canadian diplomatic and military history is the work of Colonel C. P. Stacey, James Eayrs, and Donald Creighton, and readers would be wise to consult their works.

General Works

Canada in World Affairs. 14 vols. Ottawa: Canadian Institute of International Affairs. 1967 — .

317

Commissioned by the Canadian Institute of International Affairs, this series of manuscripts is an invaluable source of detailed information on Canadian foreign policy since 1939. Well-researched and thoroughly documented, these volumes cover Canadian external affairs in two year intervals. The most recent volumes published include, Charlotte Girard, *Canada in World Affairs, 1963-65*, and Peter Dobell, *Canada in World Affairs, 1971-73*.

Department of External Affairs and International Trade, Historical Section. *Documents on Canadian External Relations*. 16 vols. Ottawa: Department of External Affairs, 1967 — .

The Department of External Affairs and International Trade contracts prominent scholars to collect, edit, and publish archival documents related to Canadian external relations. Documents related to Canadian external affairs up to 1950 are currently available. The series is organised chronologically and, although early volumes contain documents from several years, the most recent volumes cover only a single year.

Eayrs, James. *In Defence of Canada. I: From Great War to the Great Depression* . Toronto: University of Toronto Press, 1964.

_____. *In Defence of Canada. II: Appeasement and Rearmament.* Toronto: University of Toronto Press, 1965.

_____. *In Defence of Canada. III: Peacemaking and Deterrence.* Toronto: University of Toronto Press, 1972.

_____. *In Defence of Canada. IV: Growing Up Allied.* Toronto: University of Toronto, Press, 1980.

_____. *In Defence of Canada. V: Indochina, The Roots of Complicity.* Toronto: University of Toronto Press, 1983.

This five-volume series provides the foundation for the middle power thesis that dominates historical writing on Canada's diplomatic policies. Each volume covers a period of Canadian diplomatic history focussing on one major event, and generally follow chronological time periods. These volumes were written over a twenty year period and, as might be expected, the author's positions change on some issues and there is significant variation in the quality of scholarship. A general interpretive thread holds *In Defence of Canada* together: a strong nationalist, Eayrs believes that Canada must retain a foreign policy independent from that of the United States, and he dislikes and distrusts those diplomats and politicians who tend to court the American relationship.

Granatstein, J. L., ed. *Towards a New World*. Toronto: Copp Clark, 1992. A companion volume to his *Canadian Foreign Policy* (1993), the articles in *Towards a New World* cover topics in Canadian external relations outside the North Atlantic Triangle and focus on the modern period of internationalism. This collection is useful for courses that focus upon Canada's role in the Commonwealth, the United Nations and peacekeeping, and foreign economic development assistance. This book has a good select bibliography.

_____. *Canadian Foreign Policy: Historical Readings*. Toronto: Copp Clark, 1986; 2nd ed., 1993.
This collection of seminal articles and primary source material is best used as a textbook for courses that focus on Canadian relations with Britain and the USA. The collection includes a good bibliographic essay, and the references in the individual articles are excellent.

Granatstein, J. L. and Norman Hillmer. *Empire to Umpire: Canada and the World to the 1990s*. Toronto: Copp Clark, 1994.
The best overview of Canadian external relations, Granatstein and Hillmer look at Canadian foreign policy from Confederation, with particular emphasis on the twentieth century. More specifically, this book begins in earnest with the Boer War and the creation of the Department of External Affairs in 1909. Faced with a crisis caused by Canada's reliance upon imperial diplomacy, Canadian officials struggled to define its international role outside of the British and American spheres of influence. The authors — as the title suggests — argue that Canada shifted its focus from empire to umpire in international affairs. Analytically sound and extremely readable, *Empire to Umpire* also contains an excellent annotated bibliography.

Holmes, John W. *The Shaping of Peace: Canada and the Search for World Order, 1943-57*. 2 vols. Toronto: University of Toronto Press, 1979, 1982.
Despite the chronology reflected in the title, these two volumes contain a somewhat broader survey of Canadian foreign policy. The first volume begins with the interwar period and ends in 1945; volume two covers the period following the creation of the United Nations through to 1957. Holmes examines issues such as Canada's role in international peacemaking, its role in the Commonwealth, the changing relationship with the United States, and the evolution of the North Atlantic Triangle.

_____. *Canada: A Middle-Aged Power*. Toronto: McClelland and
    Stewart, 1976.
This collection of essays is an excellent rebuttal to traditionalist, left-
nationalist, and isolationist perspectives on Canadian foreign affairs. A
long-time diplomat, John Holmes participated in many of the conferences,
discussions, and back room meetings that shaped Canadian foreign policy
during the post-World War II era, and has become one of the most
perceptive commentators on diplomatic policy. His work — often
pragmatic and sceptical in nature — reflects the emergence of the middle
power thesis.

Milner, Marc, ed. *Canadian Military History: Selected Readings*.
    Toronto: Copp Clark, 1993.
This collection of readings contains older nationalistic contributions and
representations of the "new military history" that explores links between
the military experience and larger society. Organized into chronological
sections, particular attention is paid to actual operations or the
organization of the armed forces for the purpose of fighting. This volume
contains a good select bibliography. Also see, B. D. Hunt and R. G.
Haycock, eds. *Canadian Defence: Perspectives in Policy in the Twentieth
Century* (1993).

Nossal, Kim Richard, ed. *An Acceptance of Paradox: Essays on
    Canadian Diplomacy in Honour of John W. Holmes*. Toronto:
    Canadian Institute of International Affairs, 1982.
This collection of essays by students of John Holmes is useful but lacks
cohesiveness. While essays range widely, Kim Nossal's article on
relations with China in the 1940s, and Donald Story's on Canadian policy
in the 1931 Manchurian Crisis are particularly important.

Stacey, C. P. *Canada and the Age of Conflict, 1867-1921*. Toronto:
    University of Toronto Press, 1979.
_____. *Canada and the Age of Conflict, 1921-1948*. Toronto:
    University of Toronto Press, 1981.
C. P. Stacey's work is a superb overview of the political, military, and
diplomatic foundations of Canada's external affairs policy, and remains
a standard text for students of the subject. These books are the
culmination of Stacey's research into Canada's military and external
affairs policies and are filled with the numerous anecdotes. Two issues are
crucial to understanding Stacey's interpretation. First, although Stacey is

at times critical of British policies, he is quite clearly an Anglophile. Second, despite Stacey's effort to remain objective, he is at times overly critical of Mackenzie King, O. D. Skelton and other officials at external affairs who pursued policy objectives that he considers overly nationalistic and perhaps parochial. He is also critical of their efforts to improve Canadian-American relations.

Diplomats and Policy Development

Bercuson, David. *True Patriot: The Life of Brooke Claxton, 1898-1960.*
    Toronto: University of Toronto Press, 1993.
A traditional biography, *True Patriot* explores the tumultuous life of Brooke Claxton rather than the chaos and values of his times. A member of Canada's small upper class, Claxton fought in World War I, influenced the creation of the Canadian Broadcasting Corporation, served briefly as Prime Minister King's parliamentary secretary and as Minister of National Health and Welfare, before becoming Canada's Minister of National Defence from 1946 to 1954. As Minister of National Defence, he confronted the transition of the military from war to peace, the emergence of the Cold War and the formation of NATO, and the Korean War. This biography provides character and personality to one of Canada's influential diplomatic and military decision makers.

Bothwell, Robert. *Loring Christie: The Failure of Bureaucratic*
    Imperialism. New York: Garamond, 1988.
A member of the Round Table, a small group of men trying to redesign the British Empire, Loring Christie is the best Canadian example of bureaucratic imperialism. He was a leading government bureaucrat, an influential advisor to Robert Borden, and a leading Canadian nationalist-imperialist in the tradition of the individuals examined in Carl Berger's *The Sense of Power* (1970).

Granatstein, J. L. *A Man of Influence: Norman Robertson and Canadian*
    Statecraft, 1929-68. Ottawa: Duneau, 1981.
Norman Robertson served in the Department of External Affairs, primarily as under-secretary but also at various other diplomatic and bureaucratic postings, from 1929 to 1965. His influence, especially during the critical 1941 to 1946 period, was "enormous and continuing." In this biography of one of the leading civil service mandarins, Jack Granatstein ably illustrates the important role of personality in the making of

Canadian foreign policy. Granatstein shows how Robertson's genius for strategy development led to his rapid promotion within External Affairs, but also how his complete inability to organise his work limited his success. Moreover, Robertson worked effectively as under-secretary only under Mackenzie King's government. Despite Robertson's recognized skill and experience, neither Prime Minister St. Laurent or Diefenbaker developed effective working relationships with him and, as a result, his influence waned.

Hilliker, John F. *Canada's Department of External Affairs: The Early Years, 1909-1946*. Montreal: McGill-Queen's University Press, 1990.
Hilliker, John and Donald Barry. *Canada's Department of External Affairs: Coming of Age, 1946-68*. Montreal: McGill-Queen's University Press, 1995.
Hilliker is the head of the historical section in the Department of External Affairs and this two-volume history is the official institutional biography. In volume one, Hilliker traces the Department of External Affairs from its origins on the desk of a single bureaucrat to a small, but highly professional, government department. In volume two, Hilliker and Barry continue to follow External Affairs' development as it became a large and powerful arm of the federal civil service staffed by the "best and the brightest" in Canada.

Holmes, John W. *The Better Part of Valour: Essays on Canadian Diplomacy*. Toronto: McClelland and Stewart, 1970.
This collection of essays by the former Assistant Under-Secretary of State for External Affairs is a splendid introduction to the fundamental ideas that underlay Canadian foreign policy. The collection includes sections on international Organizations, the Commonwealth, the Atlantic community, Canada and the United States, the Pacific area, and the western hemisphere. Holmes provides a useful commentary to each section.

Holmes, John W., ed. *No Other Way: Canada and International Security Institutions*. Toronto: Centre for International Studies, 1987.
In 1984 a "small expert conference" at the Centre for International Studies met to discuss the functioning of the United Nations and North Atlantic Treaty Organisation, and Canada's roles in these international institutions. While not primarily a book about policy makers or policy, the contributors are officials experienced in Canadian diplomacy and their arguments, pragmatic and moderate, provide insights into Canadian policy

making. None stand out more prominently than John Holmes, the leading spokesperson of Canada's diplomatic bureaucracy, and this volume provides a useful introduction to his arguments.

Nossal, Kim Richard. *The Politics of Canadian Foreign Policy.* Scarborough: Prentice-Hall, 1985.
"Who makes the decisions that define Canada's role in world politics and under what conditions are those decisions made?" Kim Nossal's answer is simply that Canadian policy formation is constrained by circumstance as much as by politics or personality. Nossal demonstrates that Canadian policy makers must respond to Canada's geographic proximity to the United States, Canadian economic structure, and its limited military and diplomatic capacity. Under these conditions, public opinion and the political process play a limited role. Nossal argues that only the elections of 1911 and 1963 occurred within a decisive foreign policy framework. Although questions can be raised about Nossal's unwillingness to concede political influences in the policy-making process — it is hard to believe Mackenzie King ignored the political process, for example — readers will find his analysis useful and insightful.

Reid, Escott. *Radical Mandarin: The Memoirs of Escott Reid.* Toronto: University of Toronto Press, 1989.
Unlike so many memoirs, *Radical Mandarin* avoids some of the self-congratulatory rhetoric and demonstrates a willingness and desire to back up his recollections with detailed research. Like John Holmes, Escott Reid is both an academic commentator and a former diplomat. Reid was involved in Canadian policy making in issues such as appeasement, NATO, India and the Commonwealth, and the establishment of the World Bank. He ended his career teaching at York University. His comments on the formulation of policy and the role of politicians in the diplomatic process are fascinating and intriguing.

The North Atlantic Triangle

Bothwell, Robert. *Canada and the United States: The Politics of Partnership.* Toronto: University of Toronto Press, 1992.
A study of Canadian-American political and economic relationships concentrated on the post-World War II era, Bothwell tries to correct the overly negative view of this relationship that has emerged in traditional and left-nationalist interpretations. Bothwell argues that Canadians and

Americans have been able to function creatively and effectively together. He emphasises the duality of the Canadian-American relationship — economic and security interests are always linked — and the ability of Canadian diplomats to use this duality to their advantage. Although Bothwell's work is a useful antidote to the left-nationalist work of Kari Levitt and Wallace Clement, two problems emerge. First, Bothwell covers the period 1763 to 1945 in a single chapter and thus his book is really a study of Canadian-American relations in the Cold War. Second, he ignores culture and the politics of culture. Still, all readers interested in Canadian-American relations will find this short book a useful and thoroughly researched introduction.

Cuff, R. D. and J. L. Granatstein. *American Dollars — Canadian Prosperity: Canadian-American Economic Relations, 1945-1950.* Toronto: Samuel-Stevens Hakkert, 1978.

In the aftermath of World War II, Canadian-American relations were strengthened through military alliances and cross-border economic investments. Canadian historians, both traditional and left-nationalist, argue Canadian sovereignty is thereby threatened, and that Canada has become an economic dependency of the United States. In Donald Creighton's classic account *The Forked Road* (1976), for example, the Liberal government was characterized by its ability to make the wrong choices. In this well-researched work, Cuff and Granatstein re-examine the critical five-year period following the war. They note that both American and Canadian policymakers had to deal with the problems resulting from the economic decline of Britain and Western Europe. Canada faced a further problem as an unfavourable trade balance with the United States threatened to wipe out its U. S. dollar reserves. Cuff and Granatstein argue that Canadian officials skilfully lobbied a friendly American executive for financial and trade concessions, but in return opened Canada to increased American capital investment and made accessible essential and strategically important raw resources. While Canada has no doubt become increasingly dependent upon the United States, this relationship was a circumstance of geo-political realities rather than any pan-North American zeal on the part of the Liberal government.

_____. *Ties that Bind: Canadian-American Relations in Wartime from the Great War to the Cold War.* Toronto: Samuel-Stevens Hakkert, 1975; 2nd ed., 1977.

A collection of previously published and three original essays, this book

examines the issues and agreements that emerged during the critical
periods of the two world wars and the Cold War. The authors argue that
under the circumstances of crisis, Canadians and Americans created
systems and structures to manage their relationship that changed the
relationship in ways neither country foresaw or desired. The economic
agreements of these years linked the two economies and limited Canadian
independence in the long term at the same time as they increased
Canada's ability to act autonomously in the short term. These essays
provide a good introduction to the consensus interpretation that dominated
the study of Canadian-American relations for two decades.

Granatstein, J. L. *How Britain's Weakness Forced Canada into the arms
of the United States*. Toronto University of Toronto Press, 1989.
A short, clear, and provocative enunciation of the middle power thesis of
Canadian foreign affairs, this work should be read by all students
interested in Canadian foreign policy. Granatstein denounces the
traditional interpretation that argues that Canada's growing relationship
with the United States was not the result of an insidious plot by the
Mackenzie King government, but rather the inevitable transformation of
Canadian policy as Britain declined as a world power. While his emphasis
upon structural changes and geopolitical realities provides a valuable
contribution to the study of the North Atlantic Triangle, Canada and the
politicians and diplomats who make Canadian policy are at times made to
appear as non-entities with few choices and little opportunity for
creativity — an interesting conclusion since Granatstein calls these men
the best and the brightest in *The Ottawa Men* (1982).

Granatstein, J. L. and Norman Hillmer. *For Better or Worse: Canada and
the United States to 1990*. Toronto: Copp Clark, 1991.
This textbook examines Canadian-American relations from a liberal
nationalist perspective. Focussing upon economic and political
relationships rather than cultural, the book is an effective enunciation of
what is now called the Granatstein thesis. Canada, the authors argue, was
forced to turn to the United States for economic and military assistance,
and through the skill of its diplomats and foreign affairs bureaucrats has
managed to maintain at least some of its independence in that relationship.

Hillmer, Norman, ed. *Partners Nevertheless: Canadian-American
Relations in the Twentieth Century*. Toronto: Copp Clark, 1989.
A reader on Canadian-American relations, this collection includes both

scholarly articles and a selection of primary documents from both the Canadian and American perspectives. The selections cover the period from the Alaskan Boundary Dispute to free trade. The collection also has a good selected readings section.

Mahant, Eldegard E. and Graeme Mount. *An Introduction to Canadian-American Relations*. Toronto: Methuen, 1984; rev. ed., 1991.
Mahant and Mount's work is a useful narrative of Canadian-American relations. In its second edition, the authors avoid some of the more vitriolic nationalism apparent in the first edition. Summarising the tremendous body of literature available on the subject, the authors conclude that, although imbalanced in favour of the United States, Canadian-American relations have been beneficial to both countries. As in any such synthesis, some issues are covered more successfully than others. Although the authors try to cover a broad spectrum of relations, readers will find a detailed study of the modern economic relationship but will be disappointed by the lack on insight into cross-border cultural issues. This oversight is especially significant since some Canadian scholarship emphasises that Canadian policies toward the United States is ultimately grounded in the need for cultural protection.

McKercher, B. J. C. and Lawrence Aronsen, eds. *The North Atlantic Triangle in a Changing World: Anglo-American-Canadian Relations, 1902-1956*. Toronto: University of Toronto Press, 1996.
A historiographic introduction, seven scholarly essays, and an afterword, this collection examines diplomatic and military relations in the North Atlantic Triangle. The essays by Roger Sarty, Greg C. Kennedy, Gregory A. Johnson and David Lenarcic, B. J. C. McKercher, John A. English, Lawrence Aronsen, and Martin Kitchen provide a chronological account of the changing relationship within the North Atlantic Triangle. These essays demonstrate that while cultural ties and kinship were important elements of Anglo-American-Canadian diplomacy, all three countries primarily pursued their national self-interest. The book contains a good select bibliography.

Moyles, R. G. and Doug Owram. *Imperial Dreams: British Views of Canada, 1880-1914*. Toronto: University of Toronto Press, 1988.
During the height of late nineteenth-century imperialism, Canada occupied a prominent place in the British mind. This work examines nine stereotypical views of Canada — the vanishing "Indian," the wild west,

and the land of economic opportunity, for example — and pursues two main objectives: to provide insightful analyses of these stereotypes, and, second, to provide some of the flavour of the original literature.

Muirhead, B. W. *The Development of Postwar Canadian Trade Policy: The Failure of the Anglo-European Option.* Montreal: McGill-Queen's University Press, 1992.
Another book that examines Canadian-American relations in the critical post-World War II era, Muirhead argues that Canadian policymakers sought to restore the British trade relationship and develop a new multilateral trade system under the auspices of the General Agreement on Tariffs and Trade. Their efforts were thwarted, however, by British emphasis upon the sterling bloc, old imperial visions of the trade relationship, and European protectionism. Faced with an electorate that demanded growth and prosperity, Canadian officials had no alternative but to foster a closer economic relationship with the United States. Muirhead thus challenges left-nationalist interpretations which criticise the Liberal government for fostering the American relationship and selling out Canadian sovereignty in the post-war period.

Stewart, Gordon. *The American Response to Canada since 1776.* East Lansing, MI: Michigan State University Press, 1992.
Gordon Stewart is one of the few scholars to examine Canadian-American relations from an American perspective. He challenges two essential mythologies in Canadian-American studies: that relations between Canada and the United States have not always been cordial; and, second, that the USA has not pursued an imperialist policy toward Canada. Rather, Stewart concludes that the American response to Canada should be understood as an effort to separate Canadian affairs from those of the British Empire so that Canada would function independently in a North American context.

Thompson, John Herd and Stephen Randall. *Canada and the United States: Ambivalent Allies.* Montreal: McGill-Queen's University Press, 1994.
A survey of Canadian-American relations, this text will be quite useful to students and instructors. *Ambivalent Allies* is thoroughly documented and, like the comparable text by J. L. Granatstein and Norman Hillmer, *For Better or Worse* (1991), avoids some of the anti-American polemic that characterizes early works in this field. Written by a Canadian cultural

historian working in the United States and an American foreign policy historian working in Canada, this book covers the broad spectrum of Canadian-American relations including politics, diplomacy, and economic and cultural issues. Indeed, the authors' coverage of cultural issues sets the book apart from other works in the field. The book, furthermore, demonstrates a clear grasp of both Canadian and American perspectives. The Canadian-American relationship is characterized by the differences between the two countries, the authors argue, but Americans underestimate and Canadians exaggerate the differences.

Wigley, Philip. *Canada and the Transition to Commonwealth: British-Canadian Relations, 1917-26.* Cambridge: Cambridge University Press, 1977.
Beginning with the Imperial Conferences at the beginning of the twentieth century, negotiations between the Britain and the dominions during a series of international events — Versailles, the Anglo-Japanese Alliance, the Chanak crisis, and the Lausanne and Locarno Treaties — transformed the British Empire into a Commonwealth. Canadian historians often give Canadian Prime Minister Mackenzie King an important role in this transition. King certainly influenced the shape of the Commonwealth, but Wigley clearly demonstrates that confrontations between the British Foreign Office and Colonial Office were far more significant.

Trade and Commerce

Aronsen, Lawrence Robert. *American National Security and Economic Relations with Canada, 1945-1954.* Westport, CT: Praeger, 1997.
Aronsen argues that economic relations between the United States and Canada in the post-World War II era have been infrequently discussed, particularly by revisionist American scholars. Consequently, he analyses the economic aspects of American national security policy and what benefits Canada stood to gain by integrating its industrial defence and resource production with that of the United States during the King and St. Laurent governments from 1945 to 1954. In contrast to some Canadian nationalist historians like Kari Levitt and Wallace Clement, and to Canadian liberal historians like J. L. Granatstein, Aronsen argues that Canada used its relationship with the United States strategically for its own economic benefit, particularly in areas involving high technology such as aircraft, electronics, and automobiles.

Doern, G. Bruce and Brian W. Tomlin. *Faith and Fear: The Free Trade Story*. Toronto: Stoddart, 1991.

Few issues inspire a more heated political debate in Canada than free trade with the United States. The debate regarding the 1988 Free Trade Agreement, focussing upon sovereignty, nationalism, and social programs, was both spirited and vicious. Doern and Tomlin manage to avoid polemical rhetoric and present an objective political analysis of the negotiations. They argue that the Mulroney government entered into free trade negotiations for political rather than ideological or economic reasons. Because the Canadian government initiated the discussions and had a greater interest in their success, the Canadian negotiators functioned from a position of weakness and managed to win only a minimally acceptable outcome. Canadians, as a result, were divided by the deal and, in the authors' conclusions, the 1988 election did not resolve these divisions. The book concludes with a speculative chapter regarding the possible impact of the deal. This book should be read alongside Michael Hart, *Decision at Midnight* (1994).

Drummond, Ian. *Imperial Economic Policy, 1917-39: Studies in Expansion and Protection*. Toronto: University of Toronto Press, 1974.

One of Canada's leading economic historians, Ian Drummond's work is less a work about Canadian diplomatic policy than a study about the failure of the British imperial economic system. Drummond clearly demonstrates that the various Dominions in the Empire had little incentive or desire to cooperate within a coherent economic system. Imperial economic policy, as a result, simply stumbled from one expedient to the next. Canadian Prime Minister R. B. Bennett's efforts at restoring the imperial trade system at Ottawa in 1932 failed because of the divergent economic interests that had developed. This book casts doubt upon the traditional interpretations that argue that Canada could have used the Empire as an alternative to closer American ties.

Drummond, Ian and Norman Hillmer. *Negotiating Freer Trade: The United Kingdom, the United States, Canada, and the Trade Agreements of 1938*. Waterloo: Wilfrid Laurier University Press, 1989.

In Canada, free trade usually involves discussions of national identity, continentalism, and economic consequences. This book about the 1938 free trade agreements is distinctive in that it avoids these issues. The 1938 free trade agreement, afterall, involved all three partners in the North

Atlantic Triangle, had little impact in the political arena, and had few economic consequences prior to the beginning of World War II. This book instead focusses upon the diplomacy and negotiations that resulted in a free trade agreement. The authors carefully focus on the objectives of the each of the three countries, the role of the negotiators, and the careful efforts made at compromise.

Hart, Michael, with Bill Dymond and Colin Robertson. *Decision at Midnight: Inside the Canada-US Free-Trade Negotiations*. Vancouver: University of British Columbia Press, 1994.

Produced by participants in the process, this book looks at the 1983 to 1988 period of consultation, political lobbying, and finally, face-to-face negotiations that produced the Free Trade Agreement (FTA). It is more than a polemic or recollection, however; instead *Decision at Midnight* is a lucid, well researched, and thoroughly documented account of the negotiations. The authors' ideological perspective is clearly presented in the introduction. Should Canadians "stick with the tried and true or break with the past and start anew?" For the authors the choice was clear: Canada had to pursue a new and courageous trade option. Despite the heated political climate and tough, skilled American negotiators, the authors argue persuasively that Canada won several important concessions in the FTA negotiations, and that the deal was a success. Readers should consult this book in conjunction with G. Bruce Doern and Brian Tomlin, *Faith and Fear* (1991).

Hill, Mary O. *Canada's Salesman to the World: The Department of Trade and Commerce, 1892-1939*. Montreal: McGill-Queen's University Press, 1977.

A lengthy and sometimes turgid administrative history, *Canada's Salesman* traces the Department of Trade and Commerce from its origins as an international marketing agency to its modern role as a marketing, regulatory, and financing agency for Canadian businesses. Important Canadian government agencies such as the Canadian Wheat Board, the National Research Council, and Statistics Canada originated within the Department of Trade and Commerce, and Hill carefully illustrates the bureaucratic and political pressure that led to the expansion of this government department.

Levitt, Kari. *Silent Surrender: the Multinational Corporation in Canada*. Toronto: Macmillan, 1970.

Silent Surrender is a classic and important example of the left-nationalist interpretation of Canadian-American relations. Her chapter titles effectively illustrate her argument: the re-colonization of Canada, the old mercantilism and the new, the rise of the nation state, regression to dependence, who decides?, metropolis and hinterland, and the harvest of lengthening dependence. Kari Levitt argues that American multinational corporations, for years encouraged to invest in Canada by Liberal governments, were successful in appropriating Canadian wealth. Canada, moreover, had effectively slid into a position of cultural, political, and economic dependence on the United States. An economist by training, Kari Levitt's work is built upon traditional Canadian economic themes of the staples thesis and metropolitanism.

Plumbtre, A. F. W. *Three Decades of Decision: Canada and the World Monetary System, 1944-75.* Toronto: McClelland and Stewart, 1977.
Canadian foreign policy after World War II was intricately interwoven with economic issues. Written from a Canadian viewpoint, Plumbtre's book is a study in international trade and finance. He begins with discussions about trade and finance during the World War II which led to the Bretton Woods agreements and concludes with the era of stagflation in the 1970s and the reform of the International Monetary Fund (IMF) in 1976. He argues that the monetary system was created to enhance prosperity through trade, but limited Canada's ability to use monetary policy to promote economic expansion. The IMF succeeded marvellously in the 1950s. The increased importance of European currencies (especially the Deutsch mark) and diminished financial position of the United States, however, damaged the system, and Canadian officials have made several attempts to limit the erosion.

Stairs, Denis and Gilbert Winham. *The Politics of Canada's Economic Relationship with the United States.* Toronto: University of Toronto Press, 1985.
Canada considered the possibility of free trade with the United States in the early 1980s, and appointed the Royal Commission on the Economic Union and the Developmental Prospects for Canada to make enquiries. The Commission called upon historians, economists and political scientists to investigate the probable consequences of a free trade deal. This report is one of the research studies prepared under the Royal Commission's mandate.

Stone, Frank. *Canada, the GATT, and the International Trade System.* 2nd ed. Montreal: Institute for Research on Public Policy, 1992.
In the second edition of this classic work, three new chapters on the trading relationships of the 1980s are added. This book is the best study of Canada's role in the General Agreement on Tariffs and Trade (GATT) and other international trade organisations and treaties. Stone examines the origins, structure, and operations of GATT and the multilateral trade system that emerged following World War II.

Canada at War

Bercuson, David. *Maple Leaf Against the Axis: Canada's Second World War.* Toronto: Stoddart, 1995.
Unlike most Canadian history books on the Second World War, *Maple Leaf Against the Axis* contains little political or diplomatic history. It is, instead, a book about fighting, soldiers, sailors, and airmen, death, and victory. Bercuson examines the structure and preparedness of the Canadian armed services in 1939 and effectively illustrates the growth of the institution and the skills learned in the experience of battle. Relying primarily upon secondary sources, Bercuson effectively discusses every major campaign in which Canadian troops, sailors, and airmen participated. This book will be useful to military historians and the general reader.

_____. *Battalion of Heroes: The Calgary Highlanders in World War II.* Calgary: The Calgary Highlanders Foundation, 1994.
One of the numerous regimental histories produced in Canada — and the only one annotated in this bibliography — Bercuson's book is demonstrative of the high level of quality this genre has achieved. A volunteer unit, the Calgary Highlanders landed in Normandy 6 July 1944. During the conquest of Europe the unit suffered a higher rate of casualties than any regiment in the Canadian Army. Thoroughly referenced and researched, *Battalion of Heroes* provides the reader with insight into the role of individual soldiers, military units, and strategic planning during World War II.

Dancock, Daniel D. *The D-Day Dodgers: The Canadians in Italy, 1943-1945.* Toronto: McClelland and Stewart, 1991.
Dancock examines the Canadian campaign in Italy in this lengthy narrative filled with anecdotes of personal experiences. Readers will

begin to understand the trauma of the street and mountain battles in Italy; at the same time, the politics of coalition warfare and the strategic decisions of field commanders resonate in the background. Based upon secondary sources, the book best serves as an introduction to one aspect of the Canadian military experience in World War II.

_____. *Welcome to Flanders Fields: The First Canadian Battle of the Great War — Ypres, 1915.* Toronto: McClelland and Stewart, 1988.
Based upon a variety of archival and secondary sources, thoroughly referenced, and containing an excellent bibliography, this book argues Canadian soldiers were poorly prepared and poorly led at the beginning of World War I. They embarked for war impatiently seeking glory; they found, instead, mud and blood at Ypres. Dancocks follows the Canadian activities at Ypres and outlines military mistakes, errors in judgment, and even good luck.

Dow, James. *The Arrow.* Toronto: James Lorimer, 1979.
During the 1950s, Canada attempted to design and sell a state-of-the-art military interceptor aircraft. The expensive project was cancelled and the prototypes destroyed by Prime Minister John Diefenbaker in 1959. James Dow examines the political and military decisions that led to the Arrow's planning and eventual destruction in a clear and effective manner. His work, however, is filled with bias. He laments the decision of the Diefenbaker government and is critical of the aircraft's opponents. Readers should consult the relevant pages of Denis Smith's biography of Diefenbaker, *Rogue Tory* (1995) for a more balanced appraisal.

English, John A. *The Canadian Army and the Normandy Campaign: A Study of Failure in the High Command.* New York: Praeger, 1991.
English argues that the Canadian Army in Normandy was ineffective in the field because it was poorly led. He first examines Canada's military from 1918 to 1944, and discovered a military with an entrenched militia tradition and poor operational focus. Under these conditions, officers were poorly selected and trained. English then demonstrates how poor leadership hindered the Canadian military effort in Europe during World War II. Thoroughly researched and referenced, this book is one of the best new works in Canadian military history.

Granatstein, J. L. *The Generals: The Canadian Army's Senior Commanders in the Second World War.* Toronto: Stoddart, 1993.

In sharp contrast to Stephen Harris, *Canadian Brass*, (1988) and John A. English, *The Canadian Army and the Normandy Campaign*, (1991), Granatstein provides a sympathetic portrayal of the sixty-eight World War II Canadian generals. Granatstein argues that insufficient training, low pay, and poor morale characterised the small Canadian army professional army officer class prior to World War II. It was a wonder, he notes, that the Canadian generals had even limited success. Granatstein's emphasis is on the personalities and politics of the Canadian generals; he provides only superficial coverage of strategy and battle tactics.

_____. *Canada's War: The Politics of the Mackenzie King Government, 1939-45*. Toronto: Oxford University Press, 1975.
Granatstein has written a history of Canada's participation in World War II around the personality of Prime Minister William Lyon Mackenzie King. During World War II, decisions regarding Canada's participation overseas and regarding the domestic policies needed to organise and pursue the conflict were made in the Prime Minister's Office. A small cadre of individuals — senior bureaucrats and trusted cabinet colleagues — discussed and implemented Canada's war policies. Granatstein argues that King — his frustrations, rationalisations, political instincts, and sense of national destiny — guided the decision making process. This excellent and balanced treatment is useful to those interested in Canada's role in World War II and Mackenzie King's political philosophy.

Granatstein J. L. and J. M. Hitsman. *Broken Promises: A History of Conscription in Canada*. Toronto: Oxford University Press, 1977.
No issue has divided Canadians like conscription for overseas military service. In both world wars, Canadian prime ministers promised not to conscript men for service. In both cases, they eventually broke their promises and implemented compulsory military service. In addition, in both cases the issue divided Canadians not only along French and English lines, but also along the lines of urban and rural, worker and businessman, and Conservative, Liberal, and socialist. For a study of opposition to war in Canada, see Thomas Socknat, *Witness Against War: Pacifism in Canada, 1900-1945* (1987).

Granatstein, J. L. and Des Morton. *Marching to Armageddon: Canadians and the Great War, 1914-1919*. Toronto: Lester Orpen Dennys, 1989.
_____ . *A Nation Forged in Fire: Canadians and the Second World War*. Toronto: Lester Orpen Dennys, 1989.

A two-volume history of Canadian involvement in world war, these illustrated books are an excellent introduction to both the Canadian activities on the war front and the effect of war at home. Written by two of Canada's senior military historians, these books present an excellent synthesis of the literature.

_____. *Bloody Victory: Canadians and the D-Day Campaign, 1944.* Toronto: Lester & Orpen Dennys, 1984.
Granatstein and Morton provide the best historical examination of the Canadian participation in the 1944 D-Day invasion of Normandy. They divide the book into four chapters on planning, D-Day, Caen, and Falaise, and place an excellent collection of photographs between each chapter. The authors ably demonstrate that Canadians played an important and often overlooked roll in the 1944 campaign, and that the invasion of Europe was a war of attrition that took a severe toll on the soldiers who participated.

Hadley, Michael L. *U-boats Against Canada.* Montreal: McGill-Queen's University Press, 1985.
During World War II, Canada's navy grew to Great Power proportions. Its primary objective, convoy protection, placed the Royal Canadian Navy (RCN) at the forefront of the Battle of the Atlantic and the war against the German U-boats. Surprisingly, this well researched book is the one of the few to address this topic in detail. Captain Hadley successfully introduces the reader to the nature of submarine warfare, the technological limitations of both the U-boats and the RCN ships sent to destroy them, and the dramatic limitations on both participants produced by the North Atlantic climate.

Hadley, Michael L. and Roger Sarty. *Tin-pots and Pirate Ships: Canadian Naval Forces and German Sea Raiders, 1880-1918.* Montreal: McGill-Queen's University Press, 1991.
Tin-pots and Pirate Ships is an excellent examination of the Canada's limited naval forces in the early twentieth century. Canada relied completely upon the Royal Navy for coastal protection in the late nineteenth century. Faced with increasing British pressure for Canada to assist in maritime defence, Canada was forced to address the issue of a navy. Unable to reach a consensus in Parliament, and faced with resistance from the militia, Canada's navy prior to World War I consisted of two old British ships, the *Rainbow* and *Niobe*. Still, Canada did

contribute to World War I naval defence, even if the ships were little more than "tin pots." This book neatly analyses the failure of Canada's naval policy.

Harris, Stephen J. *Canadian Brass: The Making of a Professional Army, 1860-1939.* Toronto: University of Toronto Press, 1988.
Following Confederation, Canadians, like their American counterparts, distrusted professional soldiers. As a result, Canada had a small, highly political, and ill prepared militia force prior to World War I. The experiences in the trenches, however, made it clear to Canada's professional officers that an experienced and trained military force was necessary. In the years prior to World War II, this small force emerged. Stephen Harris argues that the struggle for existence characterized Canada's army experience. Forced to deal with stingy politicians and compete with other, more politically important, government departments, the Canadian officer needed more political than military skills. It seems amazing that a few skilled combat leaders emerged at all. An excellent and well researched book, *Canadian Brass* is a useful addition to the work by James Eayrs, C. P. Stacey, and Desmond Morton.

Miller, Carman. *Painting the Map Red: Canada and the South African War, 1899-1902.* Montreal: McGill-Queen's University Press, 1993.
Imperialism is a topic much discussed in Canadian history, and yet the penultimate crisis of the imperialist era, the South African War is rarely discussed in detail. The only full-length study of the South African war, *Painting the Map Red* corrects this oversight. Miller minutely examines the South African experience, including the decision to enter the war, political debates, the activities of Canadians in the field, and the rise of French Canadian nationalism. Miller argues that while traditional interpretations which emphasise the divisions between French- and English-Canadians regarding the war have merits, English-Canada's response was neither monolithic nor idealistic. Furthermore, he shows how the experiences in South Africa affected the development of the Canadian military. This first-rate book is highly recommended to those interested in military affairs in South Africa or British imperialism.

Milner, Marc. *The U-Boat Hunters: The Royal Canadian Navy and the Offensive Against German Submarines.* Toronto: University of Toronto Press, 1994.
Marc Milner addresses the politics, strategy, and technology of

antisubmarine warfare in this interesting and well researched book. Milner shows how an understaffed, poorly trained, and poorly equipped Royal Canadian Navy (RCN) in 1943 emerged as an important partner in the U-Boat war in the North Atlantic by 1945. His portrayal is sympathetic to the RCN, yet critical when warranted. Students interested in naval history and the Battle of the Atlantic, will find this book approachable and insightful.

Morton, Desmond. *When Your Number's Up: The Canadian Soldier in the First World War*. Toronto: Random House, 1993.
This book provides an outstanding narrative of the experiences of Canadian soldiers in the trenches of France. Morton deals with the circumstances confronting soldiers with passion and sensitivity.

_____. *Silent Battle: Canadian Prisoners of War in Germany, 1914-1918*. Toronto: Lester Publishing, 1992.
Despite a 1931-32 commission of enquiry, Desmond Morton argues that the plight of the 3,842 Canadians who languished in German prisoner-of-war camps during World War I has been forgotten. Drawing upon his formidable knowledge of the secondary literature, government archives, and the records of several prisoners of war preserved in the National Archives of Canada, Morton seeks to correct this oversight. This book is a stunning portrayal of life in a German prisoner-of-war camp and the difficulty the prisoners faced upon returning home after the war.

_____. *A Military History of Canada*. Edmonton: Hurtig, 1985.
A survey text designed for the general reader, *A Military History of Canada* remains the only narrative of Canada's entire military experience. The first chapter covers the *Ancien Regime* and Iroquois warfare, and the last chapter the Cold War. Throughout this work Morton provides a readable and informative account of not only Canada's military engagements in the field, but also of the diplomatic, political, and social contexts of war. Although this book contains no references, it does have a lengthy bibliographic essay.

_____. *Canada and War: A Military and Political History*. Scarborough, ON: Butterworths, 1981.
A historical survey of the Canadian military, *Canada and War* shows how Canada's armed services have been transformed from a volunteer militia into a large, professional, poorly equipped force and the consequent

problems this transformation has produced. Continuing a pattern he began in *Ministers and Generals* (1970), Morton emphasises the political elements of Canada's armed services — everything from procurement to Defence Ministers, the civilianization of operational decision making, and unification — but provides equal treatment for Canada's military efforts abroad. This work is an approachable introduction to Canada's military for general readers, students, and non-specialists.

_____. *The Canadian General: Sir William Otter*. Toronto: Hakkert, 1974.
Chief of the Canada general staff until 1912, William Otter personifies the nineteenth century Canadian militia soldier. He joined Canada's volunteer military in 1859 and participated at Ridgeway in 1866 (the militia's first engagement) and in the 1885 North-West Rebellion before taking command of Canada's contingent in the Boer War and then becoming the highest ranking officer in Canada. This book, however, is more than a simple biography of a career soldier. Morton uses Otter's career to explore the history and development of the Canadian militia.

_____. *Ministers and Generals: Politics and the Canadian Militia, 1868-1904*. Toronto: University of Toronto Press, 1970.
Superbly documented and researched, *Ministers and Generals* marks the ascendency of Desmond Morton as Canada's premier military historian. Morton carefully leads the reader through the transformation of the militia from a tool of political patronage and British imperialism, into a semi-professional army in service of Canadian national goals. The key to this transition, he argues, was the relationship between the British professional generals who commanded the force and the ministers of the militia who exercised parliamentary control. Early politicians, unsure of the militia's purpose, used it as a relatively cheap system of political patronage. The militia, as a result, had virtually no administrative or logistical services and was organized along local rather than national lines. Seeking to create a fighting force which could assist the British imperial army, the generals fought to develop a militia freed from political machinations. The emergence of Canadian nationalism, the development of Canadian officers, and the reduction of political patronage in the militia solved this conflict. In 1904, Dr. Frederick Borden, the minister of the militia, dismissed the Earl of Dundonald as general officer and created a Canadian general staff. The Canadian parliament finally took control of its armed services.

Morton, Desmond and W. A. B. Douglas, eds. *Canada as a Military Power. Revue Internationale d'Histoire Militaire*, No.51. Ottawa: Commission Canadienne d'Histoire Militaire, 1982.

Morton and Douglas have put together a collection of essays which link the military experience with Canada's foreign policy objectives. The collection includes two introductory overviews and follows with a series of essays related to specific issues of concern to Canadian military history. The collection includes articles by Stephen Harris on the formation of the Canadian Corps during World War I, Ruth Roach Pierson on women and mobilization in World War II, and Lawrence Aronsen on Canadian-American industrial cooperation. While readers interested in an overview of Canada's military policies will be disappointed, those searching for insight on a particular topic would be wise to consult this collection.

Preston, Richard A. *The Defence of the Undefended Border: Planning for War in North America, 1867-1939*. Montreal: McGill-Queen's University Press, 1977.

Both the British and Americans believed that a war between them, fought in North America, was a remote possibility. Both navies recognized this problem and concentrated their efforts in other directions. Yet both armies developed contingency plans for a North American war. Richard Preston examines these plans and concludes that they existed primarily because both armies sought suitable opponents for institutional and training requirements. Ironically, in Canada, this institutional contingency plan would be the basic plan for military action by the Canadian army prior to World War II. Preston's work is a suitable companion for the pioneering work by James Eayrs in volume one of *The Defence of Canada*.

Stacey, C. P. *Arms, Men and Government: The War Policies of Canada, 1939-1945*. Ottawa: Information Canada, 1970.

Sponsored by the Department of Defence, *Arms, Men and Government* is a systematic examination of Canada's military decision making in World War II. Like other work by Stacey, it is critical of the Mackenzie King government, calling Canada's war policies uncoordinated and politically orchestrated. His work, however, shows his sophisticated understanding of Canada's problematic role in the war. Always considered a junior partner in the Allied cause, Canadian politicians, diplomats, and military commanders found themselves on the periphery of war planning on both the battle front and the domestic front. Moreover,

Stacey recognizes that the Mackenzie King government's consideration of the political ramifications of war policies was appropriate and necessary. Readers should also consult J. L. Granatstein, *Canada's War* (1975).

Steele, Ian K. *Warpaths: Invasions of North America.* New York: Oxford University Press, 1994.

Ian K. Steele, a military and imperial historian, continues the path-breaking work he started in *Guerillas and Grenadiers: The Struggle for Canada, 1689-1760* (1969) in this provocative book. Steele examines the interaction and conflict between Europeans — Dutch, Spanish, French, and English — and between Europeans and Indian peoples in North America. As in his earlier work, Steele continues to respect the military abilities of European regular soldiers and adds a new-found respect for Native warriors as well. Indeed, Steele notes that pathogens and technology were the two elements of war that defeated Native communities in North America. Steele's knowledge of the technology of warfare is one of the strengths of this book. Steele also draws heavily on imperial motivations in analysing North American war. Colonies, Steele argues, originated with different purposes, and their interaction with other colonies and the aboriginal population often reflected this orientation. With about half of the book focused upon the Seven Years' War, any students interested in the Conquest and the end of the French presence in Canada will find this book important.

Vance, Jonathan. *Objects of Concern: Canadian Prisoners of War Through the Twentieth Century.* Vancouver: University of British Columbia Press, 1994.

In *Silent Battle: Canadian Prisoners of War in Germany, 1914-1919* (1992), Desmond Morton rightly points out that early histories of the Canadian Expeditionary Force during World War I neglected Canadian POWs. Vance argues that although the image of the "forgotten men" has been used so often as to become a cliche, it is not entirely accurate. In a well-researched and well-argued work, Vance examines the experience of Canadian POWs in the nineteenth and, in particular, the twentieth centuries. Vance discusses the varied experience of POWs; attempts by the government to prepare men for capture and to reintegrate them into society following release; substantial efforts by government, military, private organizations, and individuals to feed and clothe captives; and the development of international law regarding prisoners of war.

The Cold War and Internationalism

Bercuson, David. *Canada and the Birth of Israel: A Study in Canadian Foreign Policy.* Toronto: University of Toronto Press, 1985.
David Bercuson demonstrates that Canadian diplomats formulated policy regarding the formation of Israel following a careful appraisal of the impact the issue had on relations between Britain and the United States. Neither Zionist, Arabic, nor Canadian public opinion influenced the decision making process. Rather than follow the lead of either British or American diplomats, Canadian officials followed their own instincts and predilections during the crisis, and as a result, Canada's policy toward Israel often appeared spasmodic. Still, Bercuson concludes Canada played an important role in the process by consistently supporting the creation of Israel and helping to reconcile the British towards this goal. Balancing Canada's interests between those of the United States and Great Britain continued to be a theme in Canadian foreign policy in the Cold War era, and Bercuson's book is an important contribution to our understanding of this issue.

Black, J. L. and Norman Hillmer, eds. *Nearly Neighbours: Canada and the Soviet Union from Cold War to Détente and Beyond.* Kingston,ON: R. P. Frye, 1989.
The articles in this collection represent the best efforts of Canadian scholars to deal with Canada's role in the Cold War. Canada, it is clear, shared the Americans' fear and distaste for the USSR. Still, Canada attempted to maintain relations and influence Soviet domestic policy, especially in the face of domestic pressure from Ukrainian-Canadians.

Bothwell, Robert and J. L. Granatstein. *Pirouette: The External Affairs Policy of Pierre Trudeau.* Toronto: 1990.
From 1945 to 1968, Canadian foreign policy was founded in friendly relations with the United States — especially in trade and defence — support for NATO, and condemnation of the Soviet Union. In the first two years of his term as prime minister, Pierre Trudeau transformed Canada's foreign policy: he recognized Communist China, warmed relations with the USSR, cut back on Canadian contributions to NATO, and pursued the "third option" in trade policy — improved trade with Europe and Asia — because he feared Canada relied too heavily upon the American market. By the mid-1970s, however, Trudeau was moving in a new direction. He emphasised peacekeeping, foreign aid and the non-

white Commonwealth, and even purchased military equipment to maintain the country's commitment to NATO. By the mid-1980s, Canada again shifted foreign policy under Trudeau as relations between the prime minister and President Reagan deteriorated. By 1984, Trudeau was on an unsuccessful peace mission in the style of Lester Pearson. Bothwell and Granatstein call this continuous shifting of foreign policy priorities a "pirouette" and argue that Trudeau lacked sustained interest in foreign policy and defence issues.

Bothwell, Robert and J. L. Granatstein, eds. *The Gouzenko Transcripts: Evidence Presented to the Kellock-Taschereau Royal Commission of 1946.* Ottawa: Deneau, 1982.
The most celebrated spy scandal in Canadian history, the Gouzenko affair of 1945-46 resulted in a five-month investigation by a Canadian Royal Commission and in eleven criminal and espionage convictions. Although the Report was made public in July 1946, the transcripts of testimony and the evidence collected by the Commission remained secret. Finally in 1981, the Canadian government released the 6,000 pages of testimony, which are the basis for this book. The usefulness of these transcripts is limited, however, because the evidence upon which the interrogations took place is missing and the editors were unwilling to provide significant annotations and explanation for the material presented. As a result, someone familiar with Canadian political, scientific, industrial, diplomatic, and military history will make connections with the transcripts. The general reader and the uninitiated will be lost.

Creighton, Donald. *The Forked Road: Canada, 1939-1957.* Toronto: McClelland and Stewart, 1976.
This book is part of the Canadian Centenary Series and is not truly a book in diplomatic or military history. It is in the field of diplomatic history, however, where its influence has been most significant. Highly polemic, this book is the classic attack on the post-war Liberal government and its growing American connections. Creighton argues that Canada had always used British and imperial connections to avoid being absorbed by the United States. Prime Minister Mackenzie King, Creighton strenuously argues, chose to develop the American relationship instead, and as a result, Canada's sovereignty was (and is) threatened. Ironically, Creighton's work provides the foundation for left-nationalist, anti-American scholarship opposing American investment in Canada, and also acts as a foil for the work of J. L. Granatstein and Robert Bothwell.

English, John and Norman Hillmer, eds. *Making a Difference? Canada's Foreign Policy in a Changing World Order*. Toronto: Lester, 1992.
The proceedings of a conference of foreign policy practitioners, journalists and academics, this collection of essays looks at the impact of Canadian diplomacy on the modern world order. The essays cover not only traditional topics such as Canadian-American relations, Britain and the Commonwealth, the United Nations, and NATO, but also topics such as the Pacific Rim, la Francophonie, disarmament, and peacekeeping. Together the essays conclude Canada has made a difference.

Evans, Paul M. and Michael B. Frolic, eds. *Reluctant Adversaries: Canada and the People's Republic of China, 1949-70*. Toronto: University of Toronto Press, 1991.
This collection of eleven essays examines the problems surrounding the recognition and development of relations with Communist China. The essays cover all aspects of this question from Canadian missionary activity to the influence of American attitudes to the attitudes of policy makers to the Trudeau initiative. This book reflects the growing interest in Canada's international relations in the Pacific and is an important contribution to the field.

Granatstein, J. L. and David J. Bercuson. *War and Peacekeeping: From South Africa to the Gulf War — Canada's Limited Wars*. Toronto: Key Porter, 1991.
This book examines Canadian participation in international conflicts outside of the two world wars. What becomes clear is that Canada has been involved in virtually every major international conflict as either a participant or a peacekeeper.

Granatstein, J. L. and Douglas Lavender. *Shadows of War, Faces of Peace: Canada's Peacekeepers*. Toronto: Key Porter, 1992.
According to Granatstein and Lavender, Canadians were at first uncertain about the role of peacekeeper and their involvement in Suez in 1956. The awarding of the Nobel Prize to Lester Pearson, and the international recognition Canada received, however, convinced Canadians that the role of helpful fixer was indeed a good one. Peacekeeping, the authors demonstrate, has never been truly successful, merely delaying conflicts, and is an expensive commitment, Canadians, nevertheless, have developed a powerful mythology about peacekeeping and it remains an essential element of Canadian foreign policy.

Haydon, Peter T. *The 1962 Cuban Missile Crisis*. Toronto: Canadian
Institute of Strategic Studies, 1993.
Haydon, a former officer in the Canadian navy, provides a detailed
critique of Canadian activity during the Cuban Missile Crisis. Haydon
argues that Diefenbaker failed to fulfil Canada's commitments to the
United States under the NORAD agreements. He is laudatory toward
Canadian military officers who disobeyed the prime minister by placing
Canadian troops and ships on alert as requested by the president of the
United States.

Jockel, Joseph. *No Boundaries Upstairs: Canada, the United States and
    the Origins of North American Air Defence, 1945-58*. Vancouver:
    University of British Columbia Press, 1987.
In this short and thoroughly researched book, Joseph Jockel analyses the
negotiations which led to the signing of the North American Air Defence
(NORAD) treaty between Canada and the United States. Jockel notes that
the American and Canadian air forces agreed that a strategic military
alliance was necessary, but that the negotiation of such a deal had to take
Canadian diplomatic sensibilities into account. By 1954, however, the
Eisenhower administration had concluded that the Distant Early Warning
system and an integrated air defence were necessary to American national
security. Canada, faced with the prospect of independent American
actions, reluctantly agreed to coordinate the effort through NORAD.

Langdon, Frank. *The Politics of Canadian-Japanese Economic Relations,
    1952-1983*. Vancouver: University of British Columbia Press, 1983.
In one of the few books to address Canadian trade and economic policy
which does not deal with the North Atlantic Triangle, Frank Langdon
argues that Canadian economic self-interest, Cold War concerns, and the
Canadian-American trade relationship have guided Canadian economic
policies towards Japan. These relations have for the most part been
cordial. In the first years, Canada supplied Japan with raw materials,
restricted Japanese fishing in Canadian waters, and provided limited
access to Canadian markets for Japanese manufactured goods. Japanese
investment in forestry and mining was encouraged, and important trade
links between western Canada, especially British Columbia, and Japan
were forged. After 1968, Canadian policy changed. Canada sought access
to Japanese markets for Canadian manufactured goods and made efforts
to use Japan as a balance to the increased Canadian reliance upon the
American market. This book is thoroughly documented.

Legault, Albert and Michel Fortmann. *Diplomacy of Hope: Canada and Disarmament, 1945-1988*. Montreal: McGill-Queen's University Press, 1992.

Originally published in French in 1989, this is a well-researched and well-documented account of Canada's disarmament policies and diplomacy. The authors note that each effort at destroying or containing armaments, weapons, or defence systems was ultimately surpassed by a new, more dangerous weapon system. The authors weave Canada's dependence upon the United States, the role of science and technology, and Canada's efforts to establish a middle power constituency into the text. Students and scholars enquiring into the negotiations surrounding a particular disarmament issue will find this book a highly useful and enlightening resource.

Levant, Victor. *Quiet Complicity: Canadian Involvement in the Vietnam War*. Toronto: Between the Lines, 1986.

This left-nationalist interpretation of Canadian involvement in Vietnam accuses Canada of assisting the American activities in the region. Levant is extremely critical of Canadian diplomats on the International Control Commission and the role they played in transmitting American demands and perspectives to the North Vietnamese government. Levant argues that Canada's Cold War opposition to Communism interfered with the country's ability to play a neutral role in Vietnam.

Levitt, Joseph. *Pearson and Canada's Role in Nuclear Disarmament and Arms Control Negotiations 1945-57*. Montreal: McGill-Queen's University Press, 1993.

In this post-revisionist book about the early efforts to control the use of the atomic bomb, Levitt disputes the middle power interpretation of Canadian diplomatic history. Rather than seek a middle ground, Levitt concludes that on issues of Cold War security Canada placed itself on the side of the Western Alliance and pursued its national security interests. Canada, because of the role it played in the Manhattan Project, was the only lesser power to participate in nuclear arms control talks. Although Canada could have used its privileged position to represent non-nuclear powers in the discussions, Levitt argues Lester Pearson chose instead to support the efforts of the United States to retain nuclear hegemony in the Western Alliance. Readers interested in Canadian foreign policy, arms control, and the Cold War will find Levitt's book thoroughly researched and decidedly anti-American.

Lyon, Peyton V. and Tareq Ismael, eds. *Canada and the Third World.* Toronto: Macmillan, 1976.

A collection of nine essays on Canada's involvement with the third world, this book is a good summary and overview of Canada's involvement in issues outside the North Atlantic Triangle and Cold War confrontation. An introduction examines Canada's role as an international peacekeeper and distributor of foreign aid. Seven essays are devoted to specific regional areas of the third world: South Asia, Anglophone Africa, Francophone Africa, Latin America, the Carribean, the Middle East, and Southeast Asia. The final essay addresses Canada's international development policy.

Mackenzie, David. *Canada and International Civil Aviation, 1932-1948.* Toronto: University of Toronto Press, 1989.

Few case studies of Canadian participation in making international agreements exist. David Mackenzie's book is a useful correction. Examining the rise of the international network of airlines and the creation of the International Civil Aviation Organization, Mackenzie argues Canadian diplomats played a critical role by mediating between British and American positions. They also defended Canadian self-interest by effectively using Canada's critical geographic location along the direct route from London to New York. Mackenzie's book is another example of how Canadian diplomats used the North Atlantic Triangle to assert Canadian independence.

Nash, Knowlton. *Kennedy and Diefenbaker: Fear and Loathing Across the Undefended Border.* Toronto: McClelland and Stewart, 1990.

Knowlton Nash, for years the anchor of CBC national news, was a correspondent in Washington during the Kennedy administration. He witnessed first hand the stormy relationship that developed between the president and Canada's Prime Minister John Diefenbaker. Nash admits to sympathizing with Kennedy and his criticism of Diefenbaker is harsh. His account of Canadian-American relations in this era is, nevertheless, balanced. Especially of interest to readers will be Nash's description of the Cuban Missile Crisis. He blames Diefenbaker for the breakdown in Canadian-American relations which followed this event.

Nossal, Kim Richard. *Rain Dancing: Sanctions in Canadian and Australian Foreign Policy.* Toronto: University of Toronto Press, 1994.

While a great power tends to use sanctions as a weapon of national security, Kim Nossal argues that middle powers impose sanctions for different reasons. Looking at several case studies from recent Canadian and Australian diplomacy, he argues that punitive calculus, coalition and domestic politics, and the personal attitudes of leaders and diplomats are far more important factors. Moreover, he concludes, they are largely ceremonial. He describes this process as rain dancing: an act which accomplishes little but makes the participant feel like something is being done about an important problem.

Reid, Escott. *On Duty: A Canadian at the Making of the United Nations, 1945-6*. Toronto: McClelland and Stewart, 1983.
Drawing upon his years of experience in the Canadian foreign affairs department, Escott Reid became one of the most insightful commentators and critics of Canadian foreign policy. In this recollection of the creation of the United States, Reid sheds interesting light on Canada's effort to find a middle power role in the new organisation. He blames other members of the Canadian team (notably Hume Wrong and Charles Ritchie), the obstinance and arrogance of the superpowers, and emerging East-West tensions for the failure of Canada's vision.

_____. *Time of Fear and Hope: The Making of the North Atlantic Treaty, 1947-1949*. Toronto: McClelland and Stewart, 1977.
A carefully crafted book by a participant in the negotiations, *Time of Fear and Hope* is essential reading for those interested in the creation of NATO. In a useful corrective to those who believe Canada moved into the American orbit following World War II, Reid makes it clear that Canadian diplomats considered the Americans their most important ally, but that they still considered Europe of tremendous political and economic importance during this period. Moreover, Reid effectively demonstrates that Canada's continued North Atlantic Triangle mindset often made it difficult for Canadian bureaucrats to consider or understand other areas of world importance. Reid's book is a useful addition to the literature on post-World War II Canadian foreign policy and should be considered with James Eayrs, *In Defence of Canada, IV* (1980), and Denis Smith, *Diplomacy of Fear* (1987) for a study of NATO.

Rochlin, James. *Discovering the Americas: The Evolution of Canadian Foreign Policy Towards Latin America*. Vancouver: University of British Columbia Press, 1994.

The Canadian "discovery" of Latin America is relatively recent. While Canada had significant economic relations with Latin America in the early twentieth century, attempts to foster a greater political presence were thwarted by complicated ties to Great Britain and the United States. Rochlin traces Canada's relationship with Latin America in the early twentieth century, the enormous impact of World War II on the global position of Canada and Latin America, the reorientation of Canadian foreign policy under Pierre Trudeau, and the establishment of a more intense economic relationship under the Mulroney government.

Ross, Douglas A. *In the Interests of Peace: Canadian and Vietnam War,*
    1954-73. Toronto: University of Toronto Press, 1984.
This thoroughly researched and referenced book — in comparison to Victor Levant's *Quiet Complicity* (1986) — is a balanced account of Canadian activity in Vietnam. Ross argues that Canada reluctantly agreed to participate on the International Control Commission (ICC) (along with India and Poland) and then found itself forced to defend western and American interests in the face of partisanship from Poland and anti-Americanism from India. As the western member of the ICC, Canada acted in the interests of peace, transmitting the American position to the North Vietnamese and attempting to explain the American resolve to the Communist government. Canada, meanwhile, also transmitted similar information about the North Vietnamese to the United States.

Schultz, John and Kimitada Miwa, eds. *Canada and Japan in the*
    Twentieth Century. Toronto: University of Toronto Press, 1991.
Fifteen articles (most original) by Japanese and Canadian scholars (mostly historians), this collection is a valuable introduction to a subject which has long been ignored by Canadian diplomatic historians. The articles each address particular topics of interest such as the treatment of Japanese-Canadian immigrants, the changing nature of Canadian-Japanese relations in the 1930s, the suicide of Canadian diplomat E. H. Norman, the dispatch of Canadian troops to Hong Kong in 1941, and the nature of Canadian-Japanese-American trade relations. Together the articles suggest that during the twentieth century, Canadian-Japanese relations have changed from a concern about diplomacy and the treatment of Japanese immigrants in Canada to military and trade concerns. The collection also makes it clear that the relationship is unequal. Canada is the supplier of raw resources and the purchaser of Japanese manufactured goods and technology. Because of its topic matter and the impressive level

of research, this is an invaluable book for students of Canadian external relations.

Smith, Denis. *Diplomacy of Fear: Canada and the Cold War, 1941-1948.*
    Toronto: University of Toronto Press, 1988.
Historical work on Canada's Cold War experience is often parochial in its focus, ignoring the realities of superpower rivalries, and seemingly ignorant of the American literature on this subject. *Diplomacy of Fear* is a significant correction to this historiographical problem. Denis Smith writes within a post-revisionist framework and situates Canada's Cold War experience within the larger framework of Soviet-American rivalry; as well, he provides a useful reminder that the Cold War was not simply an American phenomenon. Smith concludes that fear, originating in the inability of western diplomats to understand the Soviet Union, influenced Canada's decision to participate in a collective security system.

Stairs, Denis. *The Diplomacy of Constraint: Canada, the Korean War, and the United States.* Toronto: University of Toronto Press, 1974.
Relying primarily upon published documents and extensive interviews, Stairs has produced the only book-length study of Canada's involvement in Korea. In the era following World War II, Canada could no longer exist in isolation in its "fire proof house" and had to take on international commitments through the United Nations. Although Canada shared with the United States a distrust and fear of the Soviet Union, its leaders feared an Asian conflict would lead to a larger war in Europe. Stairs argues Canada participated in the Korean conflict in order to constrain aggressive and irresponsible American policies in the region. Stairs' book remains important, but readers should be aware that an article by Robert Prince in the *Journal of Canadian Studies* (winter 1992-3) questions his argument.

Swainson, Neil A. *Conflict over the Columbia: The Canadian Background to an Historic Treaty.* Montreal: McGill-Queen's University Press, 1979.
The resources of the Columbia River have been (and continue to be) contested ground between Canada and the United States. Swainson explores the events, actions, and circumstances of the Columbia River Treaty, one of the most important international agreements Canada has negotiated. Swainson considers this treaty, signed and ratified between 1961 and 1964, as a study in the policy formation process involving both national and provincial governments.

Author Index

Abel, Kerry, 8, 28, 53
Abella, Irving, 8, 9, 204, 224, 228, 261, 264
Acheson, T. W., 8, 311
Acton, Janice, 219
Adachi, Ken, 264
Adamson, Nancy, 251
Ainley, Marianne Gosztonyi, 189
Airhart, Phyllis D., 168
Aitken, H. G. J., 119
Ajzenstat, Janet, 66
Akenson, Donald, 8, 274
Albert, Jim, 79
Alexander, David, 149, 150
Allen, Richard, 168, 288
Anderson, Karen, 236
Anderson, Kay, 265
Appelle, Christine, 253
Archer, John H., 288
Argue, Robert, 205
Armour, Leslie, 161
Armstrong, Christopher, 97, 120, 132
Armstrong, F. H., 295, 314
Armstrong, Hugh, 219
Armstrong, Pat, 219
Armstrong, Robert, 145
Arnup, Katherine, 253
Aronsen, Lawrence, 326, 328
Arrison, Sonia, 92
Arsenault, Georges, 302
Artibise, Alan, 312, 316
Asch, Michael, 54

Audet, Louis-Philippe, 189
Avakumovic, Ivan, 69, 79, 270, 274
Avery, Donald, 1, 219, 258
Axelrod, Paul, 181, 187
Axtell, James, 33
Axworthy, Thomas S., 70
Azoulay, Dan, 99

Babcock, Robert H., 225
Babe, Robert E., 201
Bacchi, C., 244
Backhouse, Constance, 245, 252
Baggaley, Carman, 153
Baglole, Harry, 307
Balan, Jars, 269
Balcom, B. A., 150
Ball, Norman R., 133, 154, 189, 197
Bannerman, Jean, 248
Banting, Keith G., 79
Barman, Jean, 54, 181, 286, 315
Barry, Donald, 322
Bashevkin, Sylvia B., 245
Baskerville, Peter, 8, 114, 120, 133
Bassler, Gerhard P., 261
Bassett, Isabel, 248
Beal, Bob, 49
Beal, Carl, 26
Bebbington, David W., 175
Beck, J. Murray, 109, 110
Behiels, Michael, 101, 296
Bell, David, 176

Careless, J. M. S., xiv, 4, 12, 98, 152, 202, 285, 312
Carrigan, Owen, 83
Carroll, William K., 115
Carter, Sarah A., 55, 58
Carty, Linda, 232
Carty, R. K., 88
Cavanaugh, Catherine A., 236
Chadney, James G., 265
Chaikin, Ira, 56
Cherwinski, W. J. C., 205
Choyce, Lesley, 305
Christian, William, 162
Christie, Nancy, 81, 169
Chunn, Dorothy, 246
Churchryk, Patricia, 59
Clairmont, Donald H. J., 277
Clarke, Brian P., 170
Clark-Jones, Melissa, 155
Clarkson, Stephen, 70
Clement, Wallace, 116, 134
Cleverdon, Catherine, 232
Clifford, N. Keith, 170
Coates, Kenneth S., 23, 56, 289, 308, 311
Coburn, David, 210
Code, Lorraine, 252
Cohen, Marjorie Griffin, 249
Cole, Douglas, 35, 56
Coleman, William, 102
Colling, Herb, 228
Comacchio, C., 254
Comeau, Pauline, 24
Conrad, Margaret, 4, 110, 303
Conway, John, 290
Cook, Peter, 135
Cook, Ramsay, xiv, 4, 64, 71, 102, 170, 233
Cook, Sharon Anne, 241
Cooper, Afua P., 232

Cooper, Barry, 36
Copp, Terry, 209, 214, 218
Corbet, Elise A., 141
Cornellier, Manon, 71
Cox, Bruce Alden, 24
Crane, David, 155
Craven, Paul, 206, 229, 231
Creese, Gillian, 237
Creighton, Donald, 5, 62, 68, 149, 324, 342
Crerar, Duff, 171
Cross, Michael, 204, 206, 207
Crowe, Keith J., 24
Crowley, Terry, 12, 246
Cruikshank, Julie, 29
Cruikshank, Ken, 155
Cruise, David, 121
Crunican, Paul, 90
Cuff, R. D., 324

Dacks, Gurston, 112
Daigle, Jean, 303
Dancock, Daniel D., 332, 333
Danylewycz, Marta, 241
Danys, Milda, 269
Danysk, Cecilia, 211
Darling, Howard J., 122
Darroch, Gordon, 146
Dasgupta, Satadal, 306
Davies, Alan, 262
Davis, M., 242
Dawson, J. Brian, 266
Dawson, R. MacGregor, 71
De Brou, David, 237
Dechêne, Louise, 296
Deering, Cheryl, 59
Delâge, Denys, 36
Del Balso, Michael, 283
Delisle, Esther, 262
DeMont, John, 135

Subject Index

Aberhart, W., 75, 90-91, 93-96, 178
abortion, 194-95, 239, 252-53
Acadians, 302, 303, 304-5
Action libérale nationale, 103
African-Canadians, 205, 212, 232-33, 238, 258, 263, 277-79, 282-83, 313
Africville, 277-78
agriculture, 13, 131; and Native peoples, 55; in Ontario, 147-48; in Quebec, 117, 147; in the West, 131, 141, 211, 289-90, 292-94
air transportation, 159, 346
Alaska Highway, 113, 308
Alaskan Boundary Dispute, 74, 326
Alberta, 15, 58, 61, 90-91, 94-7, 121, 123, 129-30, 236, 238, 260, 293
alcohol, 180, 305
Alline, Henry, 176-77
Anglican church, 47, 171-72, 180
Anglo-Canadian Relations. See British Empire-Commonwealth
Annales, 13, 296
anti-Semitism, 259, 261-64, 277-78
archaeology, 35, 193
architecture, 314
Arctic, 24, 54, 57, 113, 193-94,

307-311; and whaling, 310
See Yukon and Northwest Territories
armed forces, 16, 104, 320, 332-40
Atlantic Canada, 14, 109-12, 122, 149-53, 164, 176, 177, 179, 191, 207, 211-14, 277, 284, 302-307
atomic energy, 154-55
Australia, 259

baby-boomers, 166
Baldwin, Robert, 98-99
banking, 118, 133, 136, 142-45, 159
Banting, Frederick, 190-91
Baptist church, 176-77, 182, 185-88
Beauharnois Scandal, 158
Bennett, R. B., 69, 73-75, 77, 264, 329
Bennett, W. A. C., 89, 287
Beothuk, 31
Big Bear, 29
Blackfoot, 29-32
Blacks. See African-Canadians
Blakeney, Allan, 92
Bloc Québécois, 71
Boer War, 319, 336
Borden, Robert Laird, 69-70, 321
Bouchard, Lucien, 71
Bourassa, Henri, 104-8

365

sport, 16, 199-201
staples thesis, xiii, 12, 114-17,
    114-20, 249, 284
steel industry, 138, 159; and
    workers, 215
Stefansson, Vilhjalmur, 309
Strachan, John, 180, 185
strikes, 95, 207-8, 212-14, 227-
    30
suburbs, 314
Sulté, Benjamin, 13, 46

tar sands, 123, 129
tariffs, 118, 155
teachers. *See* education
telecommunications, 140, 201-3,
    221
television, 202-3
Thompson, Sir John, 78
Tlingit, 29
Toronto, 20, 82, 170, 178, 183,
    185, 200, 215-16, 218, 220-
    21, 228, 243, 268, 279, 282-
    83, 285, 312-14
tourism, 163
treaties with Native peoples, 55,
    58, 60, 85
Trudeau, Pierre Elliot, 61, 69-
    70, 101, 105, 122, 341-42
Tsmishian, 34, 42, 47

Ukrainian-Canadians, 264, 269,
    271-73, 341
unemployment, 82, 135
Union Nationale, 101-3, 108
United Church of Canada, 100,
    168, 170, 173, 177, 242
United Nations, 319-20, 347
United States of America. *See*
    Canadian-American relations

universities, 64, 165-67, 181-89,
    193, 250
Upper Canada. *See* Ontario
utilities, 120-21, 123-24, 128

Vancouver, 210, 226, 265-66,
    312-13, 315
Vancouver Trades and Labour
    Council, 226
Vietnam War, 345, 348

War of 1812, 32, 163,
welfare, 63, 79-83, 115, 169-70,
    246, 248
West Indies, 305
whaling, 130, 310
Whitney, Sir James, 98
Winnipeg, 252, 278, 312
Winnipeg General Strike (1919),
    205, 208, 217, 229, 230, 290
women, 12, 59, 63, 83, 164, 181,
    186-89, 191, 195-96, 200,
    205, 207, 209, 216, 273, 280;
    and politics, 97, 234-35, 239,
    241-42, 244-49; and work,
    205-6, 219-24, 249-51. *See* fur
    trade
Women's Christian Temperance
    Union (WCTU), 178, 241
Woodsworth, J. S., 75, 168, 178,
    213
working-class culture, 12, 19,
    191, 204-11, 212-18, 220-24
World War I, 72, 80, 85, 134,
    168, 171, 181, 186, 191, 244,
    264, 289-90, 318, 333, 335,
    338-39
World War II, 80, 186, 231, 251,
    262-63, 267-68, 318, 332-35,
    338-39

About the Authors

Brian Gobbett is a Ph. D. candidate at the University of Alberta. His research interests lie primarily in nineteenth-century Canadian intellectual and cultural history.

Robert Irwin obtained his Ph. D. in history at the University of Alberta in 1995. His research focuses on western Canada. He is interested in agricultural, environmental, regional, and native history.